THE TRANSMISSION OF KNOWLEDGE IN MEDIEVAL CAIRO

Princeton Studies on the Near East

THE TRANSMISSION OF KNOWLEDGE IN MEDIEVAL CAIRO

A SOCIAL HISTORY OF ISLAMIC EDUCATION

Jonathan Berkey

PRINCETON UNIVERSITY PRESS

PRINCETON, NEW JERSEY

PUBLISHED BY PRINCETON UNIVERSITY PRESS, 41 WILLIAM STREET,
PRINCETON, NEW JERSEY 08540
IN THE UNITED KINGDOM: PRINCETON UNIVERSITY PRESS, OXFORD

LIBRARY OF CONGRESS CATALOGING-IN-PUBLICATION DATA

BERKEY, JONATHAN PORTER.
THE TRANSMISSION OF KNOWLEDGE IN MEDIEVAL CAIRO : A SOCIAL
HISTORY OF ISLAMIC EDUCATION / JONATHAN BERKEY.
P. CM.—(PRINCETON STUDIES ON THE NEAR EAST)
INCLUDES BIBLIOGRAPHICAL REFERENCES (P.) AND INDEX.
ISBN 0-691-03191-6
1. ISLAMIC RELIGIOUS EDUCATION—EGYPT—CAIRO—HISTORY. 2. EGYPT—
INTELLECTUAL LIFE. 3. CAIRO (EGYPT)—INTELLECTUAL LIFE.
I. TITLE. II. SERIES.

BP64.E32C353 1992 297′.7—DC20 91-21262 CIP

THIS BOOK HAS BEEN COMPOSED IN LINOTRON CALEDONIA

PRINCETON UNIVERSITY PRESS BOOKS ARE PRINTED
ON ACID-FREE PAPER, AND MEET THE GUIDELINES FOR
PERMANENCE AND DURABILITY OF THE COMMITTEE ON
PRODUCTION GUIDELINES FOR BOOK LONGEVITY
OF THE COUNCIL ON LIBRARY RESOURCES

PRINTED IN THE UNITED STATES OF AMERICA

1 3 5 7 9 10 8 6 4 2

To My Parents

CONTENTS

Acknowledgments ix

Note on Transliteration, Names, and Dates xi

ONE
Introduction 3

TWO
Instruction 21

THREE
Institutions 44

FOUR
Professors and Patrons: Careers in the Academic World 95

FIVE
Religious Education and the Military Elite 128

SIX
Women and Education 161

SEVEN
Beyond the Elite: Education and Urban Society 182

Bibliography 219

Index 229

ACKNOWLEDGMENTS

AL-ZARNŪJĪ, the author of a treatise on education that will figure prominently in this book, advised his readers that "in the study of science one does not acquire learning nor profit from it unless one holds in esteem knowledge and those who possess it. One must also glorify and venerate the teacher." This book began as a dissertation at Princeton University, and during my time as a student there I had the fortune to study with a number of truly venerable teachers and scholars. It was in a seminar of A. L. Udovitch's that I first experimented with Mamluk history, and it was under his direction that this project first took shape. His interest in a dynamic mixture of social and cultural history has proved a source of great excitement, and has always helped me to see the broader implications of my own work. I cannot imagine having undertaken a project such as this without the skills and tools necessary for research in Islamic history that I acquired in a seminar with Bernard Lewis. Since then, Professor Lewis has consistently shared with me his vast knowledge of the historical legacy of the Middle East, and has patiently read through several successive drafts of this work, repeatedly saving me from a host of errors. Peter Brown has, from my first days at Princeton, provided inspiration for how exciting history can be; he has also read the entire manuscript, and brought to bear on it his extraordinary historical insight. I owe a special word of thanks to William Jordan, who kindly agreed to cross the Mediterranean (figuratively, of course) to read and comment upon my work, but who also, as much as anyone else, shaped my identity as a historian. I hope he will not flinch from that burden. Altogether, these teachers form a "chain of authority" that my medieval subjects would, I think, appreciate.

At various stages of its incubation, this book also benefited from critical readings by a number of other colleagues and friends, in particular Remie Constable, Jonathan Katz, Amy Singer, and Lucette Valensi. Christopher Taylor read every word of the book, most of them several times over; as a fellow Mamlukist, but also as a close friend and intellectual companion, his comments were especially valuable. At different points, Norman Itzkowitz, Gary Leiser, Shaun Marmon, Carl Petry, and Paula Sanders offered much needed advice and encouragement. Portions of the book were presented at a writers' colloquium in Princeton University's Department of History; a seminar at the American Research Center in Egypt in the summer of 1987; a Princeton University/École des Hautes Études colloquium on the transmission of religious knowledge in March 1989; and the annual meeting of the American Research Center in Egypt in April 1989 in Philadelphia. I am grateful to the participants of each for their helpful comments. A shorter version of Chapter Six appeared in a volume on gender issues in Middle Eastern history edited by Nikki Keddie and Beth Baron; my thanks to Yale University Press for permission to reprint. I am also grateful to Margaret Case of the Princeton University Press for her constant support and encouragement, and to the Press's two anonymous outside readers for helping me to avoid several embarrassing pitfalls. For any into which I stumbled, despite the help of all these individuals, named and unnamed, I am of course responsible.

I received financial support for this project from a number of different institutions over the years, including the Princeton University Department of History, the Fulbright-I.I.E. research program, and the American Research Center in Egypt. Several individuals made my stay in Cairo for the purpose of research considerably more productive. I am especially grateful to Mme. Sawsan ʿAbd al-Ghānī at the National Archives; Dr. Husām al-Dīn King at the Wizārat al-Awqāf; Dr. Saʿīd al-Banhāwī at the National Library; Dr. Aymān Fuʾād Sayyid at the Maʿhad Iḥyāʾ al-Makhṭūṭāt al-ʿArabiyya; Dr. Robert Betts and the staff at the American Research Center; and Dr. Ann Radwan and her colleagues at the office of the Fulbright Commission. Dr. Muḥammad M. Amīn of Cairo University patiently helped me to decipher the medieval deeds of endowment on which much of this study is based; and Dr. Elizabeth Sartain of the American University in Cairo graciously shared with me her extensive knowledge of and unmatched sensitivity to the textual legacy of the Mamluk period.

On a more personal note, I want to thank, first of all, my parents. They are responsible in so many practical and spiritual ways for nurturing my interests in history and in the Middle East that it is necessarily to them that I dedicate the book. My wife, Vivien, has been so deeply involved in the writing of this book (in more ways, perhaps, than she would acknowledge) that it is difficult for me to conceive of it without her. But I prefer not to think of her relationship to my work, or mine to hers, in terms of debts and obligations. It would be better to say, simply, that we live and work as one.

NOTE ON TRANSLITERATION, NAMES, AND DATES

IN GENERAL, I have followed the system of transliteration of Arabic names and words used by the *Encyclopedia of Islam*, with a few minor but common variations: for example, "q" for "ḳ" and "j" for "dj." For certain Arabic words and personal and place names that are commonly found in English texts or dictionaries, I have preferred to use the less technical form: for example, Quran, not Qur'ān; muezzin, not mu'adhdhin; ulama, not 'ulamā'; Cairo, not al-Qāhira. I have also frequently indicated the plural of Arbaic nouns simply by adding an "s," rather than giving the correct Arabic form (e.g., madrasas, rather than madāris). For the sake of convenience, dates are generally given according to the Western calendar. When an Islamic date is given for any reason, it is identified by the conventional abbreviation A.H.

THE TRANSMISSION OF KNOWLEDGE IN MEDIEVAL CAIRO

I

INTRODUCTION

"SEEK knowledge, even as far away as China." So goes a famous injunction of the Prophet Muḥammad to the men and women of the Islamic community. Relatively few would actually travel to what was, for medieval Muslims, quite literally the ends of the earth, but the "journey in search of knowledge" became almost a trope of the biographies of merchants and princes as well as religious scholars. Whether or not the attribution of the tradition to the Prophet is genuine, it accurately reflects a principle generally held in the Islamic world, and which formed a common theme of medieval literature: namely, that the pursuit of knowledge (*ʿilm*), and specifically religious knowledge, is an activity always worthy of approbation and encouragement.[1] Treatises praising knowledge and its acquisition repeated didactic anecdotes aimed at fostering a proper sense of values among those who would be students. One said of al-Shāfiʿī, the eponymous founder of one of the four principal rites of Sunni law, that he paid no attention to the advances of a slave-girl purchased for him by his students, much to her dismay. Frustrated after vainly waiting for him throughout the night, she returned to the trader who had sold her, complaining that he had bound her to a "crazy man." The scholar, unfazed, responded simply and sincerely that "the crazy man is he who knows the value of knowledge, and who then squanders it, or hesitates so that it passes him by."[2]

Islam's high estimation of the value of knowledge translated naturally into broad-based social and cultural support for education. All Muslims are encouraged to acquire at least a functional familiarity with those texts—in particular the revealed Quran and the traditions (*ḥadith*) that embody sayings, commands, and stories handed down from the Prophet Muḥammad and his companions—that form the basis of Islam as a religion and as an all-embracing way of life. This does not mean that every Muslim will or should become a scholar of the religious and legal sci-

[1] The tradition is cited in Shams al-Dīn Muḥammad al-Sakhāwī, *al-Maqāṣid al-ḥasana fī bayān kathīr min al-aḥādīth al-mushtahara ʿalā ʾl-alsina* (Cairo, 1956), 63. For general remarks on the importance of knowledge in the Islamic tradition, see Franz Rosenthal, *Knowledge Triumphant* (Leiden, 1970).

[2] Abū ʾl-Hilāl al-Ḥasan al-ʿAskarī, *al-Ḥathth ʿalā ṭalab al-ʿilm waʾl-ijtihād*, Hamidiye (Istanbul), Ms. 1464/3 [= Maʿhad Iḥyāʾ al-Makhṭūṭāt al-ʿArabiyya, Ms. "Taṣawwuf" No. 124], fol. 15r.

ences, or that all need be versed in the intricacies of the *sharīʿa*, the Islamic law that is far more than a "holy law." On the other hand, according to a late twelfth- or early thirteenth-century treatise, "it is necessary for the Muslim to strive for as much knowledge as he may have need in his station, whatever that is." Every believer must know, for example, what God requires of the faithful in terms of prayer, fasting, paying the alms tax, or performing the pilgrimage. Merchants must know enough of the law to avoid commercial practices abhorrent to it. The principles and precepts of the law of Islam, as derived from the Quran, ḥadith, and the consensus of the community, represent the revelation of God's will in its widest possible sense. And since knowledge of God's will is the surest means to avoid the sins of avarice, arrogance, profligacy, and more, "learning is prescribed for all of us."[3]

Muslim sensibilities, at least as refracted through the writings of the educated elite themselves, placed scholars of the religious and legal sciences at the pinnacle of society and at the vanguard of the forces it marshalled to defend itself against enemies and to bring order and meaning to its members. Aḥmad Amīn, the twentieth-century Egyptian scholar and writer, described in his autobiography the difficulties he had in marrying, despite his good appearance, respectable pedigree, and comfortable income: the turban he wore, which indicated to all his religious education and orientation, acted as a social impediment, discouraging prospective brides and their families.[4] In earlier centuries, such prejudices did not predominate, despite the contempt and ridicule apparent in popular tales about inept schoolteachers, such as those found in *The Thousand and One Nights*. True scholars, on the contrary, were revered, and the sons and daughters of a prominent jurist or professor made suitable spouses for the children of the political and military elite. A late medieval treatise on education approvingly quoted the ḥadīth that "nothing is more powerful than knowledge. Kings are the rulers of the people, but scholars [*al-ʿulamāʾ*] are the rulers of kings."[5] This represented no vague claim that the pen was mightier than the sword. The scholars of the religious sciences, especially jurisprudence and the Prophetic traditions, were guardians of an organic body of knowledge the transmission of which largely shaped Muslim culture, and which in itself defined the legitimacy of kings. Another tradition proclaimed that "one scholar [*faqīh*] is more powerful against the Devil than a thousand worshippers."[6]

[3] Burhān al-Dīn al-Zarnūjī, *Taʿlīm al-mutaʿallim, ṭarīq al-taʿallum* (Cairo, 1977), 9, 11, trans. G. E. von Grunebaum and Theodora M. Abel, *Instruction of the Student, the Method of Learning* (New York, 1947), 21, 22.

[4] Aḥmad Amīn, *My Life*, trans. Issa J. Boullata (Leiden, 1978), 121.

[5] Al-ʿAskarī, *al-Ḥathth ʿalā ṭalab al-ʿilm*, fol. 6r-v.

[6] Specifically, a scholar of jurisprudence; the ḥadīth reads *faqīh wāḥid ashadd ʿalā*

It was *knowledge* that moved mountains, and the powers of this world, whether human or diabolical, could not overcome it.

The point of a tradition extolling the power of learning, as opposed to that of acts of piety and ritual, was not to belittle worship and prayer, the outward manifestations of piety and submission to God by individuals and the community. That knowledge which Muslim society treasured above all else and transmitted from one generation to the next was not a disembodied collection of principles unrelated to the exigencies of daily life. On the contrary, knowledge that mattered was to a large extent knowledge of the guidelines by which men and women should live, and thus learning itself impelled Muslims to act according to the principles it proclaimed.[7] But the traditions that sing the praises of learning and of scholars do suggest the extraordinary emphasis that Muslim religion and civilization placed upon knowledge, specifically religious knowledge, and the power inherent in the process and object of instruction. Traditions that ascribe to the Prophet statements such as "the superiority of the learned man [*al-ʿālim*] over the worshipper [*al-ʿābid*] is like my superiority over the least of you" may reflect in part the self-interest of the scholars who collected, edited, and commented upon the ḥadīth and who, in some cases, admittedly fabricated them.[8] On the other hand, they also reflect the community's judgment that, in a very real sense, learning *is* worship, that the study and transmission of the revealed word of God and the sayings of His prophet, and of the system of law to which the revelation pointed, are the fundamental service God demands of His creatures.

Its emphasis on knowledge and learning, perhaps more than any other feature, sets Islam squarely within the Near Eastern monotheistic tradition, and in particular links it to Judaism, whose own preoccupation with study, with teaching, and with the book is well-known. Contemporaries may have been aware of the broader tradition: a late medieval Muslim treatise described "what appears in praise of knowledge in the word of God as He handed it down in the Torah, the Gospel, and the Quran."[9] Indeed, the education of Jews in the medieval Near East, as reflected in the records of the Cairo Geniza, parallels that of Muslims in its curricular

---

'l-shayṭān min alf ʿābid, as cited in Muḥammad b. ʿAbd al-Raḥmān al-ʿUthmānī, *Iḍāḥ al-taʿrīf bi-baʿḍ faḍāʾil al-ʿilm al-sharīf*, Princeton University Library, Yahuda Ms. No. 4293, fol. 4v. Cf. Rosenthal, *Knowledge*, 247–48.

[7] See Ira Lapidus' insightful discussion of ʿilm as a component of *adab*, "Knowledge, Virtue, Action: The Classical Muslim Conception of *Adab* and the Nature of Religious Fulfillment in Islam," in *Moral Conduct and Authority*, ed. Barbara Daly Metcalf (Berkeley, 1984), esp. 39.

[8] This particular tradition is found in Muḥammad b. ʿĪsā al-Tirmidhī, *Sunan*, "Kitāb al-ʿIlm," No. 19; cf. ʿAbd Allāh b. ʿAbd al-Raḥmān al-Dārimī, *Sunan*, "Kitāb al-ʿIlm," No. 32.

[9] Al-ʿUthmānī, *Iḍāḥ al-taʿrīf*, fol. 3r.

emphasis on law, its pedagogy and institutions, and even in the language and metaphors that the surviving documents use to characterize the world of learning: the "wandering scholar" is as much a trope of Jewish history and legend as it is of the Muslim historical and biographical record.[10] Islam's emphasis on learning and scholarship may also serve to distinguish Islam from medieval European civilization. A fourteenth-century Muslim writer could routinely assert the spiritual power of the scholar against that of one thousand worshippers. How many contemporary Europeans would have made the same claim?

The Madrasa

From the beginning, then, Islam was a religion of the book and of learning, a society that esteemed knowledge and education above almost every other human activity. It was several centuries, however, before Muslim societies developed a network of institutions specifically devoted to religious knowledge and its propagation. In the medieval Muslim societies of the Near East, the institution of education par excellence was the *madrasa*, a noun of place derived directly from a verb meaning "to study" and related etymologically to the Hebrew *midrāsh*, used in medieval Egypt to refer to a variety of institutions devoted to traditional Jewish learning.[11] The madrasa has received considerable attention from historians in recent years, and their research provides us with a composite picture of the character of that institution.[12]

Islam, like Judaism, is very much a religion of the law, and scholars

[10] S. D. Goitein, *A Mediterranean Society: The Jewish Communities of the Arab World as Portrayed in the Documents of the Cairo Geniza* (Berkeley, 1971), 2:201–02 and passim.

[11] Goitein, *Mediterranean Society*, 2:199.

[12] The most important work is that of George Makdisi, published in a number of articles and in *The Rise of Colleges* (Edinburgh, 1981), which traces the rise of the madrasa from its origins in Nishapur and the Islamic East through its phenomenal spread in Iraq and Syria in the eleventh and twelfth centuries. Note especially his "Review of Previous Scholarship," ibid., 292–311. See also Dominique Sourdel, "Réflexions sur la diffusion de la madrasa en orient du xie au xiiie siècle," *Revue des études islamiques* 44 (1976), 165–84, and Janine Sourdel-Thomine, "Locaux d'enseignements et madrasas dans l'islam médiéval," ibid., 185–97. Gary Leiser studied the madrasa in Egypt during the Ayyubid period in "The Restoration of Sunnism in Egypt: Madrasas and Mudarrisūn, 495–647/1101–1249," dissertation, University of Pennsylvania (1976); see also his article "The *Madrasa* and the Islamization of the Middle East: The Case of Egypt," *Journal of the American Research Center in Egypt* 22 (1985), 29–47. A. L. Tibawi challenged several aspects of Makdisi's early conclusions in "Origin and Character of *al-Madrasah*," *Bulletin of the School of Oriental and African Studies* 25 (1962), 225–38, an article to which we will have occasion to return. But Makdisi's work remains the locus classicus for the institutional history of medieval Islamic education. For a full bibliography of previous work on the madrasa, see *Encyclopedia of Islam*, 2nd edition, s.v. "Madrasa," by J. Pedersen and George Makdisi.

have identified the madrasa as necessarily, if not exclusively, an institution for instruction in Islamic jurisprudence (*fiqh*). The model developed by George Makdisi and others presents an institution specifically devoted to the study of Islamic jurisprudence according to one or more of the four "orthodox" rites of law in Sunni Islam, the Shāfiʿī, Ḥanafī, Mālikī, or Ḥanbalī. Other subjects elemental to a religious education, such as Quranic exegesis (*tafsīr*), ḥadīth, or the linguistic sciences might also form part of the madrasa's curriculum, but only as ancillaries to the study of law.[13] Certainly the curriculum offered in the madrasa concentrated on the traditional religious and legal sciences, to the exclusion of the so-called "foreign" rational sciences inherited from the Hellenistic world. Education in the madrasa, while traditional, was nonetheless of a "higher" character, focusing on the textbooks and commentaries written and compiled by Islamic scholars over the centuries, the students having acquired a preliminary grounding in the Quran and the Arabic language either in a primary school or from family members. These madrasas provided endowed professorships and student stipends in one or more of the religious and legal sciences, and, often, accommodations for both instructor and instructed.

Much of the previous scholarly literature has focused on the origins of the madrasa and its growth in Central Asia, Iraq, and Syria, and can only be briefly summarized here.[14] Originally, of course, most instruction in the Islamic religious and legal sciences took place not in institutions formally devoted to education, but in mosques, where religious scholars would sit in teaching circles (*ḥalqa*, *majlis*) with their students. The systematization of Islamic law in the eighth and ninth centuries and the gradual coalescence of the various rites resulted in the need for more prolonged and intensive study than had formerly been the pattern. Beginning in Iraq and the eastern provinces of the Muslim empire in the tenth century, hostelries (*khāns*) began to be established next to mosques prominent for the teaching that went on inside them. These khāns served as convenient accommodations for students and teachers who came to Baghdad and elsewhere from other cities or outlying areas, allowing them the opportunity to concentrate more intensively on their academic subjects.

The process that saw the growth of "mosque-khān complexes" culminated in the tenth and eleventh centuries in the establishment of madrasas. Islamic governments themselves never assumed financial respon-

[13] See *Encyclopedia of Islam*, 2nd edition, s.v. "Madrasa"; Makdisi, *Colleges*; cf. Leiser, "Restoration," 410. On the emphasis on law and legal matters in medieval Jewish education in the Near East, see Goitein, *Mediterranean Society*, 2:205–10.

[14] Except where cited, most of the following material on the origin and spread of the madrasa is drawn from Makdisi, *Colleges*, esp. 9–34.

sibility for the inculcation of the religious sciences; rather, these new institutions were established and endowed as a pious act by wealthy individuals, usually but not exclusively members of the ruling political elite. Devoted by the terms of the legal documents establishing their endowments (*waqf*, pl. *awqāf*) principally to the study and transmission of Islamic law and the other religious sciences, the madrasas provided the physical structure for instruction and income to support professors (*mudarris*, pl. *mudarrisūn*) and students. The first madrasas were probably constructed in Khurāsān, but it was the Saljūq *wazīr* (minister) Niẓām al-Mulk (d. 1092) who popularized the institution in the central provinces of the Islamic empire, specifically in Iraq. His famous madrasa, the Niẓāmiyya in Baghdad, became the model for those established in Syria by the twelfth-century Muslim princes Nūr al-Dīn ibn Zangī and Salāḥ al-Dīn ibn Ayyūb (Saladin) and their successors.

Even if the madrasa was not always and explicitly a device of Sunni governments in their struggle against Shiʿi sectarianism, as a previous generation of scholars thought, it was nonetheless associated in a more general way with the assertion in the high Middle Ages of a self-consciously traditionalist and, in the wake of the Crusades, militant Sunni Muslim identity. The new institution proved to be extremely popular in those lands in which Sunni Islam re-established its preeminence following the decline and collapse of the Shiʿi governments that had dominated the Islamic East during the tenth and eleventh centuries. By the death of Saladin in 1193, there were already thirty madrasas in Damascus; between the end of the twelfth century and the Mongol invasions in the mid-thirteenth, sixty new madrasas were established in the Syrian capital.[15] In Egypt, no doubt because of the lingering presence of the Fatimid regime, which followed the Ismāʿīlī branch of Shiʿism, the madrasa was a relative latecomer. Egypt's first madrasa may have been established as early as 1097, and several founded by Sunni ministers to the late Fatimid caliphs were already functioning in Alexandria by the time Saladin abolished the Shiʿi caliphate and established his Ayyubid dynasty.[16] Saladin did establish the first madrasa in the Egyptian capital itself, or, more precisely, in the neighboring city of al-Fusṭāṭ, in 1170. Under his patronage, and that of his successors and other individuals, at least thirty-two madrasas for instruction in Islamic jurisprudence and related subjects were founded in the urban metropolis of Cairo/al-Fusṭāṭ by the time of the Mamluk coup against the last Egyptian Ayyubid.[17]

[15] Sourdel, "Diffusion," 175.

[16] Leiser, "Restoration," 114–19, 131–51, 151–52ff; cf. Muḥammad M. Amīn, *al-Awqāf wa'l-ḥayāt al-ijtimāʿiyya fī miṣr* (Cairo, 1980), 234.

[17] On the institution of the madrasa in Ayyubid Egypt, see Leiser, "Restoration," passim, and "The *Madrasa*," passim.

Thus, by the middle of the thirteenth century the madrasa had established itself as the primary forum for religious education throughout the Islamic Middle East, and in particular in the Egyptian and Syrian provinces of the Mamluk empire. The institution, like higher education itself, was a largely urban phenomenon. The principal cities of Syria—Damascus, Aleppo, Jerusalem, and others—were home to numerous madrasas and to many of the most reputable scholars of the later Middle Ages, and consequently attracted students from other Muslim countries as well as from the Syrian hinterland. In Egypt, the port city of Alexandria boasted a number of these schools, as did several of the smaller towns of the Nile Delta and the southern provinces.[18] But it was Cairo, more than any other city of the later Middle Ages, that developed a reputation as a vital center of traditional Muslim learning. With the devastation of Baghdad by the Mongols in 1258 and the destructive, albeit temporary invasions suffered successively by Syria from the mid-thirteenth century on, Cairo became a haven for scholars and other refugees. But another, more important factor contributed to the city's standing as the principal seat of Muslim scholarship and instruction. Under the aegis and through the munificence of the Mamluk military elite that ruled much of the Near East in the later Middle Ages, the Egyptian capital became the cultural hub of the central Islamic world.

The Mamluk Regime, 1250–1517

In 1250, following the defeat of the Sixth Crusade led by Louis IX of France and the death of the last effective sultan of Saladin's dynasty, al-Malik al-Ṣāliḥ Najm al-Dīn Ayyūb, the government of Egypt passed into the hands of a warrior caste of slave origins, the Mamluks (literally, "those who are owned," "slaves"). This is not the place for a detailed review of Mamluk history; a growing literature on the subject now includes several works of a general nature in addition to more focused studies.[19] But a brief review of the structure of the sultanate and the character

[18] On the madrasas of Syria, see Ira Lapidus, *Muslim Cities in the Later Middle Ages* (Cambridge, Mass., 1967), and ʿAbd al-Qādir b. Muḥammad al-Nuʿaymī, *al-Dāris fi tārīkh al-madāris* (Damascus, 1948). Jean-Claude Garcin's seminal study, *Un centre musulman de la Haute-Égypte médiévale: Qūṣ* (Cairo, 1976), collates much of the information available on the madrasas of southern Egypt; it may be supplemented with the fourteenth-century biographical dictionary by Kamāl al-Dīn Jaʿfar al-Udfūwī, *al-Ṭāliʿ al-saʿīd, al-jāmiʿ asmāʾ nujabāʾ al-ṣaʿīd* (Cairo, 1966).

[19] At least two surveys are now available in English that cover all or a part of the Mamluk period: P. M. Holt, *The Age of the Crusades: The Near East from the Eleventh Century to 1517* (London, 1986); and Robert Irwin, *The Middle East in the Middle Ages* (London, 1986). More useful to the social historian is Lapidus, *Muslim Cities*, esp. (as an introduction to Mamluk urban history) 9–43. For more detailed studies, see the various articles and

of its ruling elite will provide background essential to understanding the social history of Islamic education in the Mamluk capital.

The phenomenon of a slave army was not new to the Near East. For several centuries, regimes in various corners of the Islamic world had relied upon a soldiery drawn from slaves purchased and trained specifically for a military purpose.[20] With the coup of the Mamluks of the sultan al-Malik al-Ṣāliḥ against his son and successor, however, a band of those soldiers actually seized the reins of state. From 1250 until the Ottoman conquest of Cairo in 1517, the Mamluk military elite held a monopoly on the institutions and mechanisms of government in Egypt and, for most of that time, in Syria and the Ḥijāz as well. Historians usually divide the Mamluk period, somewhat arbitrarily, into two unequal halves. During the "Turkish" period (1250–1382), the corps of Mamluks was drawn principally from among Kipchak Turks. The following century and a half is referred to as the "Circassian" period, because of the predominance of Circassians among the Mamluk elite.[21]

Whatever their precise ethnic roots, these Mamluks were by origin neither Arab nor Muslim. Imported at a young age from, primarily, the Caucasus and the Eurasian steppe, they were converted to the Muslim religion, taught Arabic, and trained as warriors to defend the lands of Islam. Upon the conclusion of their training they were freed, and entered the service of the government, or of particular Mamluks within it, in a variety of military and political capacities. From their number were drawn the sultan, who wielded central authority, and the amirs (military officers) of varying ranks who held the chief positions of government.

Superimposed upon the structure of Mamluk government was a more ancient political institution. From the middle of the eighth century, the Sunni world had been ruled, at least in theory, by caliphs of the ʿAbbasid family, based in Iraq. Of course, effective political power had long since passed to local regimes, but the ʿAbbasid caliphs remained as figureheads of Sunni unity and legitimacy. Following the Mongol destruction of Baghdad in 1258, refugees claiming to be members of the caliphal family settled in Cairo and were recognized by the Mamluks as the authentic caliphs. But real power remained in the hands of the Mamluks, and specifically in those of the sultan and the leading amirs. Politics under the

---

monographs by David Ayalon, which remain the most important works on the period and on the Mamluks as a social and political group.

[20] A growing body of literature surrounds the institution of the slave army; see Daniel Pipes, *Slave Soldiers and Islam* (New Haven, 1981).

[21] The Turkish period is also sometimes called the "Baḥrī" period, and the Circassian period the "Burjī." The Arab historians, however, refer to the former period as *dawlat al-turk*, and the latter as *dawlat al-jarkas*. See *Encyclopedia of Islam*, 2nd edition, s.v. "al-Baḥriyya" and "al-Burdjiyya" (both by David Ayalon).

Mamluks was rarely a stable game, however, and the political history of the regime, in its early decades as well as at its end, was punctuated by frequent coups and continual competition and maneuvering among the amirs.

In large part this instability resulted from what was perhaps the most astonishing characteristic of the Mamluk system. The Mamluks, as a ruling elite, reproduced themselves—not biologically, through the establishment of family dynasties, but by the constant importation of fresh young male slaves. As individuals, of course, the Mamluks married, often into the local academic and religious elites, a fact of some importance for the history of educational institutions. But the sons of Mamluk sultans and amirs were, in general, systematically excluded from succeeding to their fathers' offices and political prerogatives, and within a generation or two had largely blended into the local population. Even the new sultan was not usually drawn from among the sons of the former ruler, but from among the leading amirs.[22] Both the sultans and the amirs were therefore responsible for the supply of fresh Mamluks each generation. These new recruits were selected, trained, and ultimately freed by their Mamluk masters, to whom they developed a deep attachment. Their masters in turn depended upon the reliability and martial skill of their own Mamluks in the incessant jockeying for political power.

If one of the political consequences of the rejection of the dynastic principle was instability, a result of the continual importation of new Mamluks was to perpetuate a cultural and social divide between rulers and ruled. At the very heart of their domains, the Mamluks formed a breed apart. The formal conversion of young Mamluks to Islam may have been more sincere in some cases than in others, but many Mamluks routinely indulged in what were blatantly non-Islamic practices. For most, some dialect of Turkish remained the principal language of communication, although some grew more accomplished in the Arabic language of the native Egyptians than others. Trained in the martial arts and monopolizing the business of the defense of the realm, the Mamluks found themselves, by training, inclination, and occupation, distinct from those they governed.

With the Mamluk military caste both sworn to defend the Islamic realm and in some ways profoundly alienated from it, the social and cul-

[22] There were, of course, exceptions—exceptions that at times predominate so much as to seem almost the rule. From time to time, especially at the beginning of the Mamluk period, the son of a sultan would succeed to his father's throne. Often, however, this was only a prelude to a subsequent coup by one or more powerful amirs. The first half of the Mamluk period was dominated by the rule of al-Manṣūr Qalāwūn (d. 1290) and his sons and grandsons, but of the latter only two managed to establish effective, if not permanent rule: al-Nāṣir Muḥammad (d. 1340) and, for a short time, al-Ashraf Shaʿbān (d. 1376).

tural gap separating the Mamluks from the indigenous population over whom they ruled understandably produced a certain social tension. The ambivalent character of this relationship between rulers and ruled is not, perhaps, historically unusual. What is remarkable, and requires explanation, is that the Mamluks took as keen an interest as they did in religious matters and Islamic education. Chapter Five will explore the complex ties that bound the Mamluks to both the institutions and the process of learning. For the present, it is enough to take note of a concatenation of factors that left the transmission of religious knowledge in some ways dependent on the voluntary donations of members of the ruling military elite: the absence of anything resembling a corporate ecclesiastical organization capable of owning, supporting, and perpetuating an institutional structure; the general failure of the state itself to systematically support religious institutions, or, more precisely, the lack of any notion that supporting them was its responsibility; the long tradition of individual charity in Islam; and the vast wealth amassed by the military and political elites. All of these factors combined to cast the burden of supporting the religious and educational infrastructure on individual Mamluks. Both the first and last effective sultans, al-Muʿizz Aybak (d. 1257) and al-Ashraf Qānṣūh al-Ghawrī (d. 1517), established institutions of higher learning in Cairo, as did virtually all important Mamluk rulers, as well as many amirs who did not themselves reach the sultanate. The Mamluks were thus largely responsible for at least the physical and financial infrastructure of Islamic education in the Egyptian capital.

Higher Religious Education in Mamluk Cairo

The purpose of this study is to investigate the people, processes, and institutions involved in higher religious education in Cairo from the middle of the thirteenth to the beginning of the sixteenth centuries. By higher religious education, we mean instruction in and the transmission of those texts that preserved and presented the principles and "knowledge" that Muslims, as individuals or as a group, needed in order to live a fully Muslim life. Given the fundamental importance of the law in Islam, much of that education focused on the science of jurisprudence, and legal studies formed an important component of the curriculum of most Islamic schools. But other subjects were included, and indeed the boundaries between them and jurisprudence, and especially that between ḥadīth and the law, were by no means distinct. The science of jurisprudence had originally grown out of that of ḥadīth, and although it formed a distinct field of intellectual endeavor at least from the time of al-Shāfiʿī (d. 820), it was never wholly independent of the study of the Prophetic traditions, which formed its most important base. The methodologies of learning and instruction in the two fields were not identical, but they were similar in many respects, and shared many of the same values and presuppositions. Many works of legal scholarship consisted principally of quotations from the traditions, and, as we shall see, classes in "jurisprudence" in the schools of Cairo might dwell largely on those same traditions. Together, ḥadīth and jurisprudence formed the core of the *ʿulūm naqliyya*, the "traditional or transmitted sciences," which ultimately traced their authority to the Prophet himself, as opposed to the *ʿulūm ʿaqliyya*, the "rational sciences," which derived from the learning of classical civilization. The rational sciences—such as philosophy, logic, and mathematics—had little part in the curriculum of the schools of higher religious education in Mamluk Cairo, except, for example, in so far as a student encountered logic as an ancillary to his study of the law. But our principal interest is less with the subjects studied than with the broader social world of learning; it lies less in the object of knowledge and in the contents of the books of law, ḥadīth, and similar subjects than in the social context in which those texts were transmitted.

Given the central position of knowledge and learning in Islam, it is not surprising that education and the educated elite have figured prominently in many of the most important works on the social and cultural history of Islamic societies. From earlier research, we know much about the supreme value that Islamic societies have traditionally attached to knowledge, specifically religious knowledge, and its transmission. Recent work, especially the monumental studies by George Makdisi, has directed our attention to the content and form of higher legal education, the early development of the institutions that supported learning and instruction, and the legal framework in which such institutions were established.

The educated elite, perhaps more than any other segment of the population, has received the systematic attention of medievalists. Pathbreaking studies by Ira Lapidus, Richard Bulliet, Roy Mottahedeh, and Carl Petry have illuminated the significant if difficult-to-define role of the ulama (*ʿulamāʾ*) in the social and political life of Islamic cities in different times and places.[23] Their work has given rise to a distinct subfield within the broader range of medieval Islamic history, identified only half-facetiously as "ulamalogy," and many of their conclusions set the stage for this study of education and learning. Still, it is not always easy to define the ulama. On the one hand, the ulama—as those involved in the transmission of religious knowledge—possessed a self-conscious identity that

[23] Lapidus, *Muslim Cities;* Richard Bulliet, *The Patricians of Nishapur: A Study in Medieval Islamic Social History* (Cambridge, Mass., 1972); Roy Mottahedeh, *Loyalty and Leadership in an Early Islamic Society* (Princeton, 1980); Carl Petry, *The Civilian Elite of Cairo in the Later Middle Ages* (Princeton, 1981).

marked them as a distinctive group, and in Mamluk Cairo that identity was as sharply defined as in any other medieval Islamic society. On the other hand, the ulama never constituted an exclusive group, and the same emphasis on knowledge and its transmission that imparted significance to the educated elite also ensured its capacity to absorb, in some limited but meaningful way, large elements of the population from widely different walks of life.[24] Judges and professors were ulama, but so were the members of social, occupational, and cultural groups who might not rely primarily on education or legal activities for a livelihood. This tension was perhaps never so pronounced as in Mamluk Cairo, and will lie at the center of the present study.

The field of medieval Islamic history occasionally suffers from a tendency to treat developments in different Islamic societies as fundamentally comparable and interchangeable, although not in any rigorous comparative sense. Consequently, despite the importance to all Islamic societies of knowledge and learning, the scholarly literature still is short of comprehensive and *circumstantial* social and cultural histories of Islamic education and the transmission of knowledge in the Middle Ages, although two model studies have recently shed much light on the role of traditional education in the modern world.[25] What this study proposes to do is to fill a part of that gap: to offer an interpretation of the social and cultural consequences of Islam's regard for knowledge, and of the construction both of educational institutions and of a diverse community of learning and knowledge, within the parameters of a specific historical and social setting.

For a variety of reasons, Mamluk Cairo offers a unique laboratory for analyzing traditional Muslim education in particular, concrete historical circumstances, allowing the testing of general hypotheses against particular situations. One reason—the extraordinary intellectual vitality of the city and the factors that produced it—was discussed above. That vitality has in turn left a rich historical and literary legacy, as the extensive collections of manuscripts written during the Mamluk period that survive in both European and Near Eastern libraries attest. Multivolume contemporary chronicles and biographical dictionaries, most written by members of the academic and intellectual elite and, in the case of the biographical dictionaries, largely concerned with the education and careers of academics, allow the social historian to reproduce the world of Muslim

[24] Cf. the remarks of Mottahedeh in *Loyalty*, 140–44.

[25] Dale Eickelman, *Knowledge and Power in Morocco: The Education of a Twentieth-Century Notable* (Princeton, 1985); Roy Mottahedeh, *The Mantle of the Prophet* (New York, 1985).

scholarship in the later Middle Ages in finer detail than for any other premodern period.[26]

The study of education in medieval Cairo, in particular, is enriched by the survival of a number of *waqfiyyas*, the deeds of endowment by which individuals established particular academic and religious institutions and that governed the internal constitutional arrangements of the schools.[27] No school was established in a vacuum. Their construction and endowment was certainly left to individuals, usually Mamluks but occasionally other wealthy individuals. Benefactors, however, structured their schools with reference to others already functioning. The deeds of endowment for several madrasas dating from the Mamluk period make explicit reference to practices in other institutions, or stipulate that their stipendiaries follow practices "usual" in other Cairene madrasas. Such references suggest that the terms which structured the activities of particular schools reflected more than the gratuitous whims of individual benefactors. They bespeak a consciousness of a certain commonality of purpose.

But the Islamic law of endowment as it affected institutions of learning allowed considerable leeway to the founder of a school, a point that George Makdisi has brought forcefully to our attention.[28] Not surprisingly, therefore, the nature and structure of institutions created and endowed to support Islamic education in Mamluk Cairo followed no set pattern. The variety of men and women—sultans and amirs, scholars and bureaucrats, the wives and daughters of the same—who undertook the construction of schools of higher religious and legal education guaranteed that those schools would not be uniform. On the most obvious level, for example, religious institutions might be established by individuals of widely differing financial means. Consequently, as we shall see, the schools that were established varied considerably in physical size, in the preference that they allotted to one particular rite, in their commitment to Sufi devotions as well as rigorous academic work, and above all in the value of their endowments (and the income they generated) and the quality of the education they offered.

These endowment deeds offer the historian insight into the arrangement and ordering of educational institutions. In so far as similar endow-

[26] The systematic use to which these sources can be put is clearly demonstrated in Petry's study, *Civilian Elite*. An indispensable guide to Mamluk-period sources is Donald Little, *An Introduction to Mamlūk Historiography* (Wiesbaden, 1970); for a less technical introduction, see the bibliographical survey in Holt, *Age of the Crusades*, 207–16.

[27] Ulrich Haarmann, "Mamlūk Endowment Deeds as a Source for the History of Education in Late Medieval Egypt," *al-Abḥāth* 28 (1980), 31–47; see also the seminal study of the social history of the endowments by Amīn, *al-Awqāf*, esp. 232–61. The lack of such documents from earlier periods of Islamic history comprised one of the principal obstacles to Makdisi's research; see his remarks in *Colleges*, 35.

[28] See *Colleges*, 35–74.

ment deeds do not, apparently, survive in substantial numbers for any other Muslim society before that of the Mamluks in Egypt, this insight is unique. A caveat about institutions, however, is in order. The madrasa undoubtedly played a role of exceptional importance in the study and transmission of Islamic law and the religious sciences, and institutions known as madrasas will lie at the heart of this investigation of higher religious and legal education in Cairo in the later Middle Ages. But an attempt simply to write the history of a particular institution—the "madrasa"—in late medieval Cairo would be fruitless and misleading. In the first place, as others have noted, the Muslim historians and chroniclers applied Arabic architectural terminology very loosely to particular buildings, so that a common, universal definition of the madrasa is, perhaps, impossible to identify.[29] Secondly, as will become clear, higher education was by no means limited to institutions known as madrasas. Instruction in jurisprudence and its related subjects took place in a variety of institutions, many called madrasas, but others not, and the very definition of a madrasa became somewhat murky over the later Middle Ages. As the surviving endowment deeds themselves attest, institutions were called madrasas, mosques (*masjid*, or *jāmiʿ*, "congregational mosque"), or *khānqāhs* (Sufi convents), but the actual activities that took place within them, as described and outlined in the deeds, were often indistinguishable. Moreover, much transpired inside of madrasas that had little direct connection to a rigorous education in the Islamic sciences. Accordingly, we will henceforth refer to institutions partially or completely devoted to higher religious and legal education generically as "schools." This poses the risk of a certain confusion, since the term school can also correspond to the *madhāhib* (sing. *madhhab*), the rites or "schools" of Sunni law. But a deeper confusion would arise were we to refer to all the schools of Mamluk Cairo as madrasas or, as that Arabic word is often translated, "colleges," since many centers of instruction were decidedly *not* madrasas, at least in the terms that medieval Muslims themselves used to describe them. The terms madrasa, khānqāh, masjid, and jāmiʿ will be applied for identification purposes only to *particular* institutions that were commonly called by one name or another.

Indeed, it is important to remember that the institutions themselves played no actual role in Islamic education. The schools existed as buildings and endowments, but Islamic law allowed no corporate identity to any particular institution, and no formal degree system was ever established.[30] As long ago as 1962, A. L. Tibawi pointed out that, the growth

[29] See especially the cogent remarks of R. Hillenbrand in *Encyclopedia of Islam*, 2nd edition, s.v. "Madrasa—Pt. III: Architecture," 1140.

[30] Makdisi, *Colleges*, passim.

of endowed institutions devoted specifically to instruction in the law notwithstanding, Islamic education remained fundamentally and persistently an informal affair. He urged that we not "systematize and formalize educational institutions," and that we recognize that they were "guided by an elastic custom rather than by a rigid theory."[31] Tibawi based his judgments primarily on examples from the early history of the madrasa and other educational institutions in Iraq, Syria, and the Islamic East. Yet centuries after the flourishing of madrasas in Egypt and the Levant, his remarks should remind us to look beyond the institutional structure of higher education to the informal world of personal instructional relationships that guided the transmission of Muslim knowledge. To the social historian, of course, such a warning, far from being restrictive, is fraught with promise.

Consider, for example, the apparent anomaly of several institutions dating from the end of the Mamluk period that were specifically known by contemporaries as madrasas, yet which made no provisions at all for classes in any one of the religious sciences. The madrasa established in 1515 by the Mamluk amir al-Sayfī Baybars, a relative of Sultan Qānṣūh al-Ghawrī, supported an *imām* (prayer leader), a shaykh for Sufis, Quran readers, and a host of other minor religious functionaries—but no teachers or students. Provisions for the madrasa of Sultan al-Ghawrī himself, also established in the early sixteenth century, are in essence the same. The terms of the institution's endowment deed suggest that it hired an imām, a preacher (*khaṭīb*) to deliver the Friday sermon, Quran readers, and muezzins (*mu'adhdhins*) to issue the call to prayer, but no one specifically committed to instruction. In this case, however, the fact that the endowment deed provided for a khānqāh complex directly across the street indicates that the choice of the term madrasa to describe the institution was deliberate.[32]

The fact that madrasas such as those of al-Sayfī Baybars and Sultan al-Ghawrī provided for no lessons—that is, that no salaries were allotted to particular teachers and no stipends for students were provided—did not necessarily mean that the institutions would not be, primarily, places of instruction. The madrasa of al-Ghawrī, for instance, must have functioned as a center of education, for only students and scholars would have benefited from the books of exegesis, ḥadīth, jurisprudence, *uṣūl al-fiqh* and *uṣūl al-dīn* ("foundations of jurisprudence" and "foundations of reli-

[31] Tibawi, "Origin," 230–31.

[32] *Waqfiyyat* al-Sayfī Baybars, Dār al-Wathā'iq No. 313; *Waqfiyyat* Qānṣūh al-Ghawrī, Wizārat al-Awqāf o.s. No. 882; cf. that of Qānī Bāy Qarā, Wizārat al-Awqāf o.s. No. 1019. Doris Behrens-Abouseif, "Change in Function and Form of Mamluk Religious Institutions," *Annales islamologiques* 21 (1985), 73–93, esp. 88–93, discusses these and several other institutions.

gion"), logic, and linguistic sciences that comprised its substantial library, a library that, incidentally, was to be open only on "the days of classes" (*ayyām al-durūs*).[33] Yet why should institutions such as those founded by al-Sayfī Baybars or Sultan al-Ghawrī, clearly labeled madrasas by their deeds of endowment, explicitly provide for no students or teachers among the myriad of men they employed? Why provide stipends, in some cases by no means negligible, for prayer leaders, muezzins, Friday preachers, Sufis and their shaykh, and any number of Quran and ḥadīth readers, not to mention numerous support staff, but none for professors or their students?

The root of the answer may lie in Tibawi's observation that, for all the establishment of endowed and structured institutions of learning, Islamic education remained fundamentally informal, flexible, and tied to persons rather than institutions. It should be kept in mind that the biographical dictionaries of the Mamluk period abound with references to men—and, to a lesser extent, women—who taught one subject or another, but do not always tell us specifically where their classes took place. Similarly, they are rich in information about an individual's teachers, but almost never mention the particular schools in which he studied. The biographers' decision to include certain details from their subjects' academic careers and ignore others reflects their own understanding of the terms by which an education should be evaluated. Contemporaries, in other words, considered the venue of instruction and education to be of secondary importance: what was critical was the character and knowledge of the individuals with whom one had studied. Teaching circles continued to meet in institutions such as those of al-Sayfī Baybars or al-Ghawrī, students gathered there around professors to hear lectures and discuss points of law, even though no professorial chairs or student stipends were provided, because what was ultimately of prime importance was not a stipend, but a relationship with a prominent scholar.

The deteriorating economic circumstances of the late fifteenth century may have encouraged the establishment of madrasas making no formal instructional appointments. Ira Lapidus, examining the Syrian provinces in particular, pointed to a decline in the establishment of charitable endowments over the last century of Mamluk rule, a development linked to the increasing impoverishment of the Near Eastern economy brought on by a more or less constant decline in population, the Mamluks' brutal exploitation of official and unofficial sources of revenue, and, later, shifts in the patterns of Mediterranean commerce. Evidence to be presented below will suggest that, at least with regard to institutions of learning in Cairo, there was in fact little or no decline in the absolute number of new

[33] *Waqfiyyat* Qānṣūh al-Ghawrī, Wizārat al-Awqāf o.s. No. 882, p. 188.

institutions established.[34] Schools established after the middle of the fifteenth century did, however, often economize by dispensing altogether with monthly payments to students and teachers.

Poverty demands choices: which corners are to be cut? The evolving norms of piety and worship in the later Middle Ages, as we shall see, placed premiums on certain forms of religious expression: mystics performing Sufi rituals, the continuous public recitation of the Quran, and localized delivery of the Friday sermon, all of which had become, by the end of the fifteenth century, standard and necessary features of educational institutions. Financial limitations may have spurred an evolution in the conception of the role of wealthy individuals who wished to establish and endow a school. No longer was it their responsibility to provide guaranteed incomes for teachers and students; rather, they were to ensure, in addition to a suitable physical structure and an administrative staff necessary to support it, the performance of essential devotions and corporate worship.

The fact was that the provision of stipends to teachers and students could, if necessary, be eliminated without in fact threatening the transmission of knowledge. The founders of madrasas even in the early years of Mamluk rule had recognized that fact. Consider, for example, the following provision from the deed (dated 1359) that established the madrasa of Sultan Ḥasan:

> If the endowment's income should fall below the [level of the] expenditures stipulated above, the *nāẓir* [the supervisor or controller of the endowment] should first expend what is required for furnishing the buildings and for lighting them, and for the expenses and administration of the *sāqiya* [water wheel], and for the provision of water to the buildings. . . .

Only after the basic physical needs of the institution were satisfied was the controller to disburse salaries to the stipendiaries. But even more significantly, in the event that income fell so precipitously that the school could not afford to pay its beneficiaries even half their stipulated stipend, the controller of the institution was to:

> Begin by paying the preacher and the prayer leaders and the muezzins, then the *bawwābs* [gatekeepers] and the *farrāshūn* [cleaners] and the service staff, then the Quran readers and the orphans [for the primary school] and their teachers and their teachers' assistants, and the servants [of the founder's tomb] and the servant of the water fountain and the *rashshāshūn* [those who were to sprinkle water in the street outside the madrasa, to keep down the dust], and one to supervise the building's roof and the reader of the Quran and the administrators. [They are to be paid] one-half their salaries,

[34] Compare Lapidus, *Muslim Cities*, 37, with Amīn, *al-Awqāf*, passim.

> as stipulated above. Then, the controller should pay the students [of jurisprudence] living in the buildings, and the professors [*mudarrisūn*] and their assistants [*muʿīdūn*] and the teachers [*mutaṣaddirūn*] and half the students of ḥadīth and half the students of exegesis, and the ḥadīth reciter [*qāriʾ al-ḥadīth*], and the *shaykh al-mīʿād* and his readers, and the *mādiḥ*; then [he should spend what he receives] on the rest of the stipulated expenditures.[35]

The founder, in other words, placed a lower priority on the salaries of teachers and students than on those of prayer leaders, preachers, and even some of the service staff. Founders made sure of the *essential*: the creation of a suitable environment for the inculcation of the Islamic religious sciences, an environment conceived in both physical and spiritual terms. The actual educational process could safely be left to itself.

What all this highlights is the persistent informality of Islamic higher education, the activity of a pool of educators and students much larger than the number hired by the institutions established to support that education. Professors might or might not be appointed to teaching posts and receive salaries, but instruction would go on in any case. This study, therefore, will go beyond the institutional framework of education, and will begin by examining the informal system of instruction and the personal relationships on which it was based. Such an approach is liberating for the historian. It frees us from models developed perhaps in the shadow of Western patterns, and based too squarely on institutions and formal structures, and allows us to perceive the process by which Islamic knowledge was transmitted from one generation to the next in all of its social complexity. Islamic education took place in a vibrant world of fluid categories in which social, cultural, and institutional barriers dissolved or at least became indistinct. What will emerge is less a formal system than a dynamic network, loose but comprehensive in its inclusion of various disparate social groups, and extraordinarily effective, not just in transmitting knowledge, but also in forging a common Muslim cultural identity.

[35] *Waqfiyyat* al-Nāṣir Ḥasan, Dār al-Wathāʾiq No. 365, pp. 473–75.

II

INSTRUCTION

MEDIEVAL MUSLIM SCHOLARS, like intellectuals in any time and place, cannot be faulted for their humility. In this Jalāl al-Dīn al-Suyūṭī, a prominent Egyptian teacher and jurist of the late fifteenth century, differed little from his peers, although perhaps his claims were somewhat more controversial. In his autobiography, al-Suyūṭī set forth his own very generous reckoning of his achievements in different fields of intellectual endeavor. At the bottom of his list, along with medicine, al-Suyūṭī mentioned the science of the variant versions of reading and reciting the Quran (*qirā'āt*). This subject, al-Suyūṭī confessed, he did not presume to teach, because in it he had had no teacher. The problem was not that he was unlearned—on the contrary, he wrote a book on the subject—but that he would be unable to transmit his knowledge on the authority of any recognized shaykh.[1]

The personal connection—the educational model relying not simply on close study of a text, but on intensive, personal interaction with a shaykh—has always been central to Islamic education, not simply in Mamluk Egypt. The famous historian Ibn Khaldūn, himself a Maghribī, described in his *Muqaddimah* how, after an intellectually barren period under the Almohad dynasty, rigorous "scientific" learning returned to northwest Africa during the course of the thirteenth century. The triumph of learning there arose not through the reception of unknown or forgotten texts, but through the personal efforts of individual scholars who traveled to the Muslim East, studied there with prominent professors and their pupils, and returned to the Maghrib to pass on the traditions to their own students.[2] Where traditional Islamic education has survived into the modern period, this personal model has remained more or less intact. Muslim education in early twentieth-century Morocco was built around a vibrant, personal system for the transmission of knowledge remarkably similar to the medieval model, in which the intimate relation-

[1] Jalāl al-Dīn al-Suyūṭī, *al-Taḥadduth bi-ni'mat allāh*, ed. Elizabeth M. Sartain (Cambridge, 1975), 204. Cf. Sartain's companion volume, *Jalāl al-dīn al-Suyūṭī: Biography and Background*, 62. Sartain's biographical study of al-Suyūṭī is certainly the most comprehensive and penetrating of any single scholar of the Mamluk period.

[2] Ibn Khaldūn, *The Muqaddimah*, trans. Franz Rosenthal (New York, 1958), 2:427–29.

ships established between students and teachers proved determinative in shaping a student's later career.[3]

Islamic higher education, in late medieval Egypt as in other periods, rested entirely on the character of the relationship a student maintained with his teachers, and not on the reputation of any institution. Cities such as Cairo and Kairouan in North Africa might acquire reputations as centers of learning and scholarship, but nothing like a degree system formally attached to particular institutions of learning was ever established. The choice of a professor, and even of a text to be studied, had always been a highly personal matter, and the spread of institutions devoted specifically to education between the twelfth and the fifteenth centuries did little to change that. On the contrary, the inner dynamic of Islamic educational traditions, which had their origins in the earliest decades of the accumulation and transmission of Muslim learning, triumphed over the temporary attempt to channel instruction into particular institutions. The establishment and endowment of schools and mosques that provided financial support to teachers and students did have profound impact on the educated elite and on social relations within that group, as we shall see in subsequent chapters. But the critical factor that a successful student considered was always the character, intellectual quality, and reputation of his instructor. Treatises on education, both those written during the Mamluk period and those of an earlier era that circulated widely in the later Middle Ages, repeated over and over the qualities to be looked for in a teacher. "Regarding the choice of a teacher," claimed a tract widely popular in the Mamluk period, "it is important to select the most learned, the most pious and the most advanced in years."[4] Other writers on education laid out similar guidelines.[5] The choice was so important that a student arriving in a new city or country was urged to take as long as two months in choosing the proper teacher.[6] The early fourteenth-century scholar and jurist Badr al-Dīn Ibn Jamāʿa, too, recognized in his treatise on education that "it is important that the student look ahead [*yuqaddimu 'l-naẓar*] and ask God to indicate to him from whom he

[3] Dale Eickelmann, "The Art of Memory: Islamic Education and Its Social Reproduction," *Comparative Studies in Society and History* 20 (1978), esp. 496ff.

[4] Burhān al-Dīn al-Zarnūjī, *Taʿlīm al-mutaʿallim, ṭarīq al-taʿallum* (Cairo, 1977), 17–18, trans. G. E. von Grunebaum and Theodora M. Abel, *Instruction of the Student, the Method of Learning* (New York, 1947), 28–29.

[5] Naṣīr al-Dīn Ṭūsī, *Risāla fī faḍl al-ʿilm wa-ādāb al-mutaʿallim*, Dār al-Kutub al-Miṣriyya Ms. 19113b, fol. 17r; Muḥammad b. ʿAbd al-Raḥmān al-ʿUthmānī, *Īḍāḥ al-taʿrīf bi-baʿḍ faḍāʾil al-ʿilm al-sharīf*, Princeton University Library, Yahuda Ms. 4293, fol. 72r.

[6] Ṭūsī, *Risāla*, fol. 17r.

should study," a choice to be made on the basis of the shaykh's learning, age, and character.[7]

The importance of the personal, as opposed to the institutional, connection is immediately apparent in the principal sources on the educated elite of the Mamluk period. The biographical dictionaries of medieval scholars, written by their contemporaries, tell us little about *where* important medieval Muslims studied—aside from an occasional remark that an individual studied a collection of ḥadīth or some other text at a particular madrasa, the dictionaries are virtually silent regarding the schools in which a young pupil received his training. Their silence, however, speaks volumes. It was not that information about an individual's education was unavailable. On the contrary, historians and biographers routinely supplied long lists of a scholar's teachers, a sort of curriculum vitae in which the critical element consisted of the names of those on whose authority one transmitted the texts of Muslim learning. In a fairly typical passage, the historian Shams al-Dīn Muḥammad al-Sakhāwī included in his biography of the Cairene jurist ʿAlam al-Dīn Ṣāliḥ al-Bulqīnī (d. 1464) the names of more than a dozen of his teachers and shaykhs, but no information at all about where ʿAlam al-Dīn had been educated.[8] The message is clear: one's teachers mattered, but venue did not.

An education was judged not on *loci* but on *personae.* Students built their careers on the reputations of their teachers.[9] Naturally, to have studied in some capacity with an especially prominent scholar was an honor eagerly sought after. A biographer, for example, might write of an outstanding jurist such as the Shāfiʿī Walī 'l-Dīn Aḥmad Ibn al-ʿIrāqī (d. 1423) that "the number of his students and those who studied with him increased until there were few outstanding students of any rite who had not studied with him."[10] A student would seek out the most reputable and distinguished teachers he could, in part, of course, because doing so increased his chances of actually learning something. But respected shaykhs imparted to their pupils more than mere knowledge; they also imparted authority, an authority over texts and over a body of learning

[7] Badr al-Dīn Muḥammad Ibn Jamāʿa, *Tadhkirat al-sāmiʿ wa'l-mutakallim fī adab al-ʿālim wa'l-mutaʿallim* (Hyderabad, A.H. 1353), 85.

[8] Shams al-Dīn Muḥammad al-Sakhāwī, *al-Ḍaw' al-lāmiʿ li-ahl al-qarn al-tāsiʿ* (Cairo, 1934), 3:312–14.

[9] Cf. A. S. Tritton, *Materials on Muslim Education in the Middle Ages* (London, 1957), 32.

[10] Al-Sakhāwī, *al-Ḍaw'*, 1:342. Other prominent scholars merited similar accolades, including Ibn Ḥajar al-ʿAsqalānī and Shams al-Dīn Muḥammad al-Basāṭī; see ibid., 2:39, and Jamāl al-Dīn Yūsuf Ibn Taghrī Birdī, *al-Nujūm al-zāhira fī mulūk miṣr wa'l-qāhira* (Cairo, 1929–72), 15:466.

that was intensely personal, and that could be transmitted only through some form of direct personal contact.

The world of traditional Muslim learning retained the notion, developed in the early Islamic period, that personal instruction with a shaykh, and in particular the oral transmission of a text, was superior to private study. Even the various words used to describe the process of education and transmission reflect this bias. Much of the content of Muslim learning was encapsulated in written texts—large compendia or small collections of ḥadīth, scholarly treatises, textbooks, and abridgments. A student did not, however, simply read a book to himself, and in this way acquire knowledge. The operative verbs stress the personal and oral nature of study and instruction. An author published his book not so much through writing and transcription as through dictation (*imlā'*), which he might give either from a written copy or from memory. By the same token, a pupil would not simply read a text silently to himself; rather, he "heard from" (*samiʿa min*) some individual a particular text, that is, he heard the text read or recited from memory by its author, or by one who had himself previously studied the work with another shaykh. Alternatively he might himself "read to" (*qara'a ʿalā*) a teacher, out loud, his own transcription of the text. The preference for personal instruction as opposed to private reading and study, and the belief that only oral transmission is truly legitimate, lies deeply embedded in the Islamic educational system. In places where traditional education has survived into the modern world, this bias has survived even the introduction of printed texts.[11]

To be sure, written texts played an important role in education, and the immense number of manuscripts that survive from, say, the fifteenth century, testify to the important role of the book in a highly literate academic world that remained vibrant throughout the Middle Ages.[12] Ibn Jamāʿa found it necessary to reprove students who used their books as pillows, as fans, or to squash bedbugs, but most viewed them as an indispensable intellectual resource.[13] Schools and mosques in Mamluk Cairo frequently housed large collections of books available for use by the institution's teachers and students, or by visiting scholars. These libraries

[11] Probably the best general discussion of the character of the transmission of Muslim learning is that to be found in Johannes Pedersen, *The Arabic Book*, trans. Geoffrey French (Princeton, 1984), 20–36. George Makdisi also discusses these matters in detail in *The Rise of Colleges* (Edinburgh, 1981), 140–46. See also Tritton, *Materials*, passim, and *Encyclopedia of Islam*, 2nd edition, s.v. "Idjāza." On the survival of this system into the twentieth century, see Eickelman, "Art of Memory," 501.

[12] Cf. the remarks of Franz Rosenthal, *The Technique and Approach of Muslim Scholarship*, in *Analecta Orientalia*, vol. 24 (Rome, 1947), 6–7.

[13] Ibn Jamāʿa, *Tadhkirat al-sāmiʿ*, 172.

attracted copyists, sometimes from great distances: al-Suyūṭī proudly recounted the tale of one Syrian student who wrote "with a good hand" who spent a year in his cell at the Shaykhūniyya *khānqāh* in Cairo, copying more than thirty of the scholar's books, and who later returned to copy twenty more.[14] Ibn Jamāʿa urged students to purchase the texts that they needed whenever possible, but books were expensive, and most were probably forced to undertake the arduous task of transcribing their own copies. The process of writing could help to reinforce that which was learned through the mediation of the shaykh, and through memorization, and to that extent was approved. "The student should always have with him an inkwell, so as to be able to write down what useful things (*fawā'id*) he hears," in the words of one treatise.[15] "What is memorized, flies away," went an aphorism of the famous Naṣīr al-Dīn Ṭūsī; "what is written down, remains."[16] Copying books and writing down notes, however, even those taken at a teacher's dictation, meant little if their content was not fully understood. Ibn Jamāʿa went to some lengths to point out that acquiring books, even large numbers of them, did not itself promote knowledge and understanding. Medieval educators, like their modern counterparts, although perhaps with greater success, urged their students to seize every opportunity to read: he who kept no book in his sleeve, it was said, could have little wisdom in his heart.[17]

But the idea that only individuals could impart true knowledge and grant authority carried over into the very texts transmitted from one generation of scholars to the next. Intellectual activity in the civilizations on both sides of the Mediterranean during the Middle Ages—during what Franz Rosenthal has accurately called the "manuscript age"—consisted largely of replicating, and commenting upon, the literary productions of previous generations. Muslim scholars, however, and especially those in the fields of jurisprudence and tradition, carefully cited authorities for the traditions, verses, or anecdotes they repeated. Long excerpts from earlier works were directly incorporated into new literary productions, a process well illustrated by the prolific author al-Sakhāwī, whose immense biographical dictionary *al-Ḍaw' al-lāmiʿ*, in addition to preserving his own recollections of individual subjects, also simply replicates passages from *Inbā' al-ghumr*, a biographical work by his teacher Ibn Ḥajar al-ʿAsqalānī, as well as information from other late Mamluk historians. The need to rely on some individual or group of individuals for authority im-

[14] Al-Suyūṭī, *al-Taḥadduth*, 156.

[15] Al-ʿUthmānī, *Īḍāḥ*, fol. 67r; cf. Ibn Jamāʿā, *Tadhkirat al-sāmiʿ*, 123–24, 165; al-Zarnūjī, *Taʿlīm*, 51, von Grunebaum and Abel, *Instruction*, 62.

[16] Ṭūsī, *Risāla*, fol. 21v.

[17] Ibn Jamāʿa, *Tadhkirat al-sāmiʿ*, 164–67; al-Zarnūjī, *Taʿlīm*, 55, von Grunebaum and Abel, *Instruction*, 66.

plies a generally conservative attitude toward knowledge and learning, an attitude that found expression in the aphorism, "a good teacher hands on what he has been taught, neither more nor less."[18]

Despite such precautions, the overall attitude toward writing and the physical, written book as a means of transmitting knowledge remained ambivalent. Private reading and note-taking did not in any way obviate the student's obligation to check his reading of a text against that of his shaykh. True knowledge derives only from a learned person, insisted Ibn Jamāʿa, and not from books; those who attempted to rest their education only on the written word were guilty of "one of the most scandalous of acts."[19] Learning requires that one "read with a shaykh [who is] a guide to the correct path, upright, and sincere, and not to proceed independently, [relying on] one's self and one's intelligence."[20] The same, of course, had to be strictly applied to the teachers one chose.

> One should not study with another who himself studied only from books, without having read [them] to a learned shaykh. Taking knowledge from books [alone] leads to spelling errors [*taṣḥīf*] and mistakes [*ghalaṭ*] and mispronunciation [*taḥrīf*]. Whoever does not take his learning [*ʿilm*] from the mouths of men is like he who learns courage without ever facing battle.[21]

Ibn Jamāʿa, who wrote an extended treatise as a guide to education, warned students not to seek their instruction from those "who have studied the hidden meaning of pages [*buṭūn al-awrāq*] but who are not known to keep the company [*ṣuḥba*] of well-versed shaykhs."[22] Ibn Khaldūn reported that some overly eager students felt impelled to study the jurisprudence of the Ẓāhirīs, a school of law (*madhhab*) that had become "extinct" before he wrote in the late fourteenth century, and whose doctrines survived "only in books, which have eternal life." By doing so, however, the great historian suggested that they exposed themselves to the charge of illicit innovation, "as they accept knowledge from books for which no key is provided by scholars."[23] When the Sufis of Andalusia became embroiled in a dispute in the fourteenth century over whether or not one could rely solely on books as guides to a proper and complete mystical experience, to the exclusion of Sufi spiritual masters, it was

[18] Tritton, *Materials*, 50; cf. 66.

[19] *Min aḍarr al-mafāsid*; Ibn Jamāʿa, *Tadhkirat al-sāmiʿ*, 123.

[20] According to Zakarīyā al-Anṣārī, in his short treatise *al-Luʾluʾ al-naẓīm fī rawm al-taʿallum waʾl-taʿlīm* (Cairo, A.H. 1319), 6.

[21] Al-ʿUthmānī, *Īḍāḥ*, fol. 65r. For *taṣḥīf*, the manuscript has *taṣḥīḥ*; a marginal gloss comments, certainly correctly, "perhaps it should be *taṣḥīf*." The text also has *ghilaẓ*, coarseness, for which I have preferred to read *ghalaṭ*.

[22] Ibn Jamāʿa, *Tadhkirat al-sāmiʿ*, 87.

[23] Ibn Khaldūn, *Muqaddimah*, 3:5–6.

pointedly recognized by some that they were *not* questioning the necessity of having a *teaching* master.[24]

Of course, a student could not study at all times under the direct supervision of a shaykh, but certain features of traditional Islamic instruction and study techniques implied the continued presence of the teacher's authority. After classes, and after the departure of their teachers, students were encouraged to study together, to drill each other in their lessons (*mudhākara*), and, when alone, an individual student should "drill himself."[25] But even the act of reading to oneself was not usually a silent one, consisting rather of audibly pronouncing the words of a text. A student should raise his voice in his studies, according to a treatise entitled "The Encouragement to the Search for Knowledge," so that he hears himself read, for "what the ear hears becomes firmly established in the heart," and also because reading out loud keeps the student more attentive.[26] Reading or studying was sometimes described as being accompanied by a "mumbling" or "buzzing" (*hamhama*).[27]

A comparative experience may suggest the significance of this. During the manuscript age, silent reading was the exception rather than the rule in Europe as well. There, at least in the early Middle Ages, because of manuscript traditions in which words were routinely run together, comprehension of the written word required the actual pronunciation of the words of the text. The spread of silent reading had to await certain developments in the art of writing—in particular the use of a cursive script, the clear separation of words in texts, and the use of punctuation. Once established, however, silent, and therefore private reading may have contributed to the development and diffusion of heretical and heterodox teachings.[28] Despite its lack of written vowels, certain peculiarities of Arabic orthography—such as the initial, medial, and final forms for each letter—meant that students *could* read silently and privately, that the

[24] See Muhsin Mahdi, "The Book and the Master as Poles of Cultural Change in Islam," in *Islam and Cultural Change in the Middle Ages*, ed. Speros Vryonis, Jr. (Wiesbaden, 1975), 3–15.

[25] Ibn Jamā'a, *Tadhkirat al-sāmi'*, 142–45. On the importance of a student's peers in the process of traditional education in a modern setting, see Dale Eickelman, *Knowledge and Power in Morocco: The Education of a Twentieth-Century Notable* (Princeton, 1985), 98–100.

[26] Abū 'l-Hilāl al-Ḥasan al-'Askarī, *al-Ḥathth 'alā ṭalab al-'ilm*, Hamidiye (Istanbul), Ms. 1464/3 [= Ma'had Iḥyā' al-Makhṭūṭāt al-'Arabiyya, Ms. "Taṣawwuf" 124], fol. 12v–13r.

[27] Al-'Askarī, *al-Ḥathth*, fol. 11r, 12v–13r. Al-'Askarī here used the word *dars*, which normally means "class," but from the context, as well as from passages elsewhere in his text, it is clear that the term signified "studies," or even "reading," rather than a formal class.

[28] Paul Saenger, "Silent Reading: Its Impact on Late Medieval Script and Society," *Viator* 13 (1982), 367–414.

audible pronunciation of each word was not absolutely essential to conveying at least the obvious meaning of the written word. But nonetheless the system clearly *preferred* reading aloud and the oral transmission of texts, and thereby sought the exact and undeviating replication of the knowledge transmitted through any given book. The practice of audibly pronouncing the words of a book as one read, even as one read to oneself, may have served indirectly to reinforce the authority of a student's shaykh, since, ultimately, a student's reading of a text had to be checked against that of his teacher, and therefore also the authority of the religious tradition for which the shaykh was only the most recent link in a long chain.

More immediately, however, the practice of reading out loud also aided in the process of memorization. Memorization of course played a critical role in the process of mastering virtually any of the Islamic sciences, as it did also in Jewish religious instruction.[29] A young boy would begin his education by committing the Quran to memory, often by the age of seven or eight. The primary schools (*maktab, kuttāb*) frequently annexed to the various institutions of higher learning in medieval Cairo commonly made provisions for supporting the education of various numbers of boys until they reached the age of puberty; once they had moved into adolescence they were to be replaced, "unless they had only a little of the Quran left to memorize."[30] A student continued his religious education by learning by heart a compendium or introductory work (*mukhtaṣar*) in the several fields of knowledge—jurisprudence and its foundations, for example, or grammar—before going on to study and analyze the texts and subjects in greater detail.[31] To assist young students in the process of memorization, popular instructional texts were often set to verse. Such transpositions were extraordinarily common, to judge from the frequency with which Ḥājjī Khalīfa mentions them in his seventeenth-century encyclopedia of Muslim learning. These versifications aided students in the memorization process, and incidentally served to preserve the memory of the otherwise forgettable scholars who usually wrote them. Ibn Muẓaffar, for example, an obscure figure of the late fifteenth century who studied with prominent teachers but who found employment only as a notary, a copyist, and possibly as a deputy qāḍī, nonetheless left his mark on the world of education by versifying a number of important pedagogical works, including a compendium of Shāfiʿī law and a short treatise on the science of ḥadīth.[32]

[29] S. D. Goitein, *A Mediterranean Society: The Jewish Communities of the Arab World as Portrayed in the Documents of the Cairo Geniza* (Berkeley, 1971), 2:174–75, 209.

[30] *Waqfiyyat* Sūdūn, Dār al-Wathā'iq No. 58, ll. 298–305.

[31] Abū Zakarīyā Muḥyī al-Dīn al-Nawawī, *al-Majmūʿ* (Cairo, n.d.), 1:38. On the role of memory generally, see Makdisi, *Colleges*, 99ff.

[32] Al-Sakhāwī, *al-Ḍaw'*, 4:285–86.

The science of traditions placed special emphasis on memory, and the most proficient traditionists were known as "those who have memorized traditions" (*ḥuffāẓ*, sing. *ḥāfiẓ*), but the other religious subjects relied upon memory as well. Biographical dictionaries from the Mamluk as well as earlier periods are replete with entries extolling the praises of scholars with prodigious feats of memorization to their credit. Some of these men were blessed with near-photographic memories, such as the jurist and professor of Mālikī law Ibn Ukht Bahrām (d. 1440), who astounded his peers with his ability to memorize an entire page of text after only two or three readings. More often, however, students and scholars memorized their texts through a rigorous training that stressed the role of memory and through sheer force of will; learning by heart four or five hundred manuscript lines per day was considered a noteworthy achievement.[33] To assist the faint of heart, treatises on education listed those things which aided the memory (including honey, the use of toothpicks, and eating twenty-one raisins per day) as well as foods (such as coriander, eggplant, and bitter apples) that made one forgetful.[34] The emphasis on memorization was not unique to Islamic education, but linked it to broader patterns of traditional and religious instruction in Near Eastern societies. The transmission of Jewish learning, for example, also relied heavily on memory, and this pedagogical similarity did not escape the notice of contemporaries. The fifteenth-century Muslim historian al-Maqrīzī, shortly before his own death, commemorated the passing in 1441 of a Jewish physician and scholar and, in language similar to that used to describe Muslims, mourned the fact that "he left not his equal in memorizing the Torah and the books of the Prophets among the Jews of Egypt."[35] Nor did memorization play a role only in religious and legal subjects: the mosque of Ibn Ṭūlūn hired a professor of medicine who, like his colleagues in the traditional sciences, required his students "to memorize what he selected from among [the books of] medicine."[36] These common patterns ran deep, and where traditional Islamic education has survived in the modern world, memorization of the Quran and other texts remains one if its central features.[37]

But memorization, too, like reading, was an interactive process that drew the student firmly under the authority of his shaykh. It involved, in the first place, a habit of repetition to ensure that that which was memorized was retained. The student should repeat each day that which he

[33] Al-Sakhāwī, *al-Ḍaw'*, 2:78–79, 4:171–72; ʿAbd al-Qādir b. Muḥammad al-Nuʿaymī, *al-Dāris fī tārīkh al-madāris* (Damascus, 1948), 1:245.

[34] Ṭūsī, *Risāla*, fol. 22v–23r; al-ʿAskarī, *al-Ḥathth*, fol. 10v.

[35] Taqī 'l-Dīn Aḥmad al-Maqrīzī, *Kitāb al-sulūk li-maʿrifat duwal al-mulūk* (Cairo, 1934–73), 4:1236.

[36] *Waqfiyyat* Lājīn, Dār al-Wathā'iq No. 17, ll. 359–65.

[37] Eickelman, "Art of Memory," 490.

had learned on previous days, five times if necessary, gradually reducing the number of repetitions until the text was fixed firmly in his mind. Silently reviewing his lessons would not suffice, however; it was "essential not to become accustomed to repeating silently since it is necessary that learning and repetition be carried on with vigor and zeal."[38] And so memorizing, like reading, became a noisy, oral project in which the student repeated his lessons aloud, and thereby submitted his studies to the supervision of his teacher. He should periodically repeat the texts that he has memorized to his shaykh for correction or approval, and the shaykh should himself require his students to repeat the texts in his presence. Academic authorities agreed that attempting to memorize a text on one's own was, like unsupervised reading, a dangerous and scandalous act.[39]

The generally conservative Muslim attitude toward knowledge and learning, which could only have been reinforced by the emphasis on memory, should in no way be taken as an indication that scholarship was sterile and static. Commentators agreed that memorization alone was insufficient: to put his learning to *use*, a student must understand as well as memorize. "Memorizing two words is better than hearing two pages, but understanding two words is better than memorizing two pages"—an aphorism perhaps more elegant in Arabic, but that even in translation powerfully conveys a point.[40] Serious educators maintained a distinction between *riwāya*, the capacity simply to memorize and transmit, and *dirāya*, the ability to use critically the materials memorized and apply them to particular academic and legal problems. Muslim scholars produced vigorous critiques of both ancient and contemporary writers, and academic exchange, at least at the higher levels of the study of jurisprudence, often revolved around the organized disputation (*munāẓara*, *jadal*) of controversial questions.[41] This distinction between the means by which ḥadīth and the basic texts of law were transmitted and the more rigorous and dialectical instruction at the advanced stages of jurisprudence is an important one, and should be borne in mind; it will have consequences for the participation of certain groups, such as women, in the transmission of religious knowledge. But for our present purposes, the important point is that here, too, as in simple reading and memori-

[38] Al-Zarnūjī, *Taʿlīm*, 42, von Grunebaum and Abel, *Instruction*, 53–54 (I have altered somewhat von Grunebaum and Abel's translation); cf. al-ʿUthmānī, *Īḍāḥ*, fol. 36r.

[39] Ibn Jamāʿa, *Tadhkirat al-sāmiʿ*, 54, 113–15, 121–23; al-Nawawī, *al-Majmūʿ*, 1:38; al-ʿUthmānī, *Īḍāḥ*, fol. 68r.

[40] Ṭūṣī, *Risāla*, fol. 19r.

[41] Rosenthal, *Technique*, 41–53, esp. 48–53; Makdisi, *Colleges*, 105–52. On the vitality and critical character of traditional education in twentieth-century Morocco, see Eickelman, *Knowledge and Power*, 33.

zation, the supervisory role of a shaykh was paramount. In a famous passage in which he likened scientific learning to a "craft" (*ṣināʿa*), Ibn Khaldūn acknowledged the importance of engaging actively in discussion and disputation, rather than relying solely on memory. But, as in any craft, such learning required instruction, and therefore also "a tradition [*sanad*] of famous teachers."[42]

Since individual teachers played the decisive role in the shaping of a student's academic identity, the transmission of knowledge was regulated, not by any formal system of institutional degrees, but by the license (*ijāza*) issued by a particular shaykh to a particular student. The ijāza may have originated as a device for securing the accurate transmission of ḥadīth, but quickly became the standard means by which all Muslim learning was passed on, from teacher to pupil, and from one generation to another. Ultimately, the ijāza took many forms, including that of a general permission which might be granted by a teacher to individual students of advanced standing to teach jurisprudence (*tadrīs*) or issue legal opinions (*iftāʾ*). For most individuals, however, Islamic education continued to focus on particular books or texts and their simple transmission. Consequently, in its most common form, the ijāza certified that a student had studied a particular book or collection of traditions with his teacher: the student had heard the teacher dictate the work and had transcribed what he had heard, or he had himself read his transcription to the teacher, who corrected any mistakes in the student's recitation and copy. The ijāza acted in turn as a license to its recipient to transmit the text, on the authority of his teacher, his teacher's teachers, and all those in a chain of authority (*sanad, isnād*) reaching back to the author of the book or, in the case of ḥadīth, to the Prophet himself or his Companions.[43]

To be sure, the ijāza system grew subject to abuse over the course of the Middle Ages.[44] The chains of authority on which an ijāza's value depended might contain fictive transmissions: chronological gaps between the death of one transmitter and the birth of the next, or transmitters who, because of their youth or geographical distance, could not possibly

[42] Ibn Khaldūn, *Muqaddimah*, 2:426–30, ed. Quatremere, 2:376–79.

[43] A significant body of literature discusses the concept and practice of the ijāza. See especially: Ignaz Goldziher, *Muslim Studies*, trans. C. R. Barber and S. M. Stern (London, 1971), 2:175–80; Tritton, *Materials*, 40ff; Ibrahim Salama, *L'Enseignement islamique en égypte* (Cairo, 1938), 90–96; Pedersen, *Arabic Book*, 31–36; Ṣubḥī al-Ṣāliḥ, *ʿUlūm al-ḥadīth wa-muṣṭalaḥuhu*, 3rd edition (Beirut, 1965), 95ff; Makdisi, *Colleges*, 140–52; *Encyclopedia of Islam* 2nd edition, s.v. "Idjāza." Makdisi, *Colleges*, 148, notes the deeply *personal* character of the ijāza, whether it refers to a particular text or confers a general license to teach or issue legal opinions. Aḥmad b. ʿAlī al-Qalqashandī, *Ṣubḥ al-aʿshā fī ṣināʿat al-inshāʾ* (Cairo, 1914–28), 14:322–35, gives examples of several different types of ijāzas.

[44] For an excellent discussion of the degeneration of the ijāza, see Goldziher, *Muslim Studies*, 2:176–78.

have received a genuine personal authorization from the shaykh who formed the preceeding link in the chain.[45] Such abuses stretched back to the earliest Islamic periods, when the transmission of ḥadīth was in its early, formative stages. Distinguishing genuine from spurious chains of authority formed one of the principal tasks for those who studied ḥadīth, and an elaborate science to secure the authenticity of transmissions developed; one of its lasting contributions to Muslim civilization was the genre of the "biographical dictionary," which allows us to reconstruct in such fine detail the world of learning in the Middle Ages. But with the general reliance on ijāzas to certify the transmission of all texts in virtually all fields of Muslim intellectual endeavor, the system grew subject to a diminished discipline and rigor. Ijāzas were issued that were not so much disingenuous as they were diluted, deprived of meaning. A shaykh might issue a blanket ijāza for every book or subject that he himself was authorized to transmit. He might authorize an ijāza for a student whom he had encountered only briefly, or who had never actually heard his dictation; ijāzas might be issued simply on the basis of a written request and the pupil's reputation (or that of his family) for scholarship. Such was the inflation of ijāzas that even leading scholars of the Mamluk period, such as Ibn Ḥajar al-ʿAsqalānī, saw little shame in reporting having received ijāzas from transmitters whom they had not met, or with whom they had had only the most fleeting contact.[46]

Moreover, it became routine for scholars to bring their children with them to sessions in which a collection of ḥadīth or some other book was being recited, and for the presiding shaykh to issue ijāzas to the children as well. It was not at all unusual for men or women to have received ijāzas at ages as young as four, three, or even two years. A man born at the end of the fourteenth century received an ijāza "in the year of his birth."[47] Jalāl al-Dīn al-Suyūṭī, the prominent and controversial scholar who was born in 1445, recorded that "I have no doubt that I have an ijāza from [Ibn Ḥajar al-ʿAsqalānī, who died in 1449], since my father often attended his teaching circles."[48] Especially in the transmission of ḥadīth, ijāzas issued to very young boys and girls became quite valuable in the pupils' later lives for two interconnected reasons. In the first place, an ijāza held by a young child from an elderly person would, ceteris paribus, rely upon an isnād with fewer names than one received from a younger

[45] Georges Vajda, "La liste d'autorités de Manṣūr Ibn Sālim Waǧīh al-Dīn al-Hamdānī," *Journal Asiatique* 253 (1965), 346.

[46] Ibn Ḥajar, in his *al-Majmaʿ al-muʾassas biʾl-muʿjam al-mufahras*, Dār al-Kutub al-Miṣriyya, "Muṣṭalaḥ" Ms. 75, p. 33, reports first meeting a scholar in Mecca who had previously issued him an ijāza from Damascus. Cf. Tritton, *Materials*, 43.

[47] Al-Sakhāwī, *al-Ḍawʾ*, 1:355; cf. ibid., 5:46.

[48] Al-Suyūṭī, *Taḥadduth*, 45, 50; cf. Sartain, *Jalāl al-Dīn al-Suyūṭī*, 174, note 9.

man or woman; and the fewer names an isnād contained, the stronger it seemed to contemporaries, on the theory that with fewer links in the chains of authority, errors in transmission were less likely to occur. In addition, a child who received an ijāza at a young age might live to become the last surviving person to transmit a work on the authority of some respected shaykh who had died several decades before.

Medieval Muslims themselves, of course, were aware of the dangers implicit in the liberal issuing of ijāzas, and responded accordingly. Concerning the science of ḥadīth, for example, they devised elaborate hierarchies consisting of as many as eight different levels on which ḥadīth might be transmitted. Always, however, the highest estimation was reserved for those who had personally heard the recitation of some text from a recognized transmitter, and who possessed a license (*samāʿ* or *ijāzat al-samāʿ*, literally a "hearing" or a "license of hearing") that attested to the student's having received the text directly from the mouth of the shaykh.[49]

The important element was thus one of personal contact, of entering through the teacher an unbroken chain of authority linking the student to the author of a work of scholarship or, in the case of ḥadīth, to the Prophet or his Companions. Even when ijāzas were issued to strangers, those living in distant locales, or infants, they still represented the transmission of a text from one individual to another, independent of any institutional structure. Consequently, scholars of the Mamluk period continued the practice, developed earlier in the history of Muslim scholarship, of composing *muʿjams* (also called *mashyakha, fahrasa, thabat*, and *barnāmaj*), book-length lists of those with whom they studied and on whose authority they recited ḥadīth.[50] These muʿjams vary some-

[49] Al-Ṣāliḥ, *ʿUlūm al-ḥadīth*, 88–104; Georges Vajda, "De la transmission orale du savoir dans l'Islam traditionnel," *L'Arabisant* 4 (1975), 2–3; Jalāl al-Dīn ʿAbd al-Raḥmān al-Suyūṭī, *Tadrīb al-rāwī fī sharḥ taqrīb al-nawāwī* (Cairo, 1966), 2:4–63.

[50] Scholarship on these muʿjams is vast but scattered; the subject awaits more systematic study. The most important work is that of Georges Vajda, many of whose articles were gathered together in *La transmission du savoir en Islam (VIIe-XVIIIe siècles)*, ed. Nicole Cottart (London, 1983). Al-Sakhāwī, in his *al-Iʿlān biʾl-tawbīkh li-man dhamma ahl al-tawārīkh* (Damascus, A.H. 1349), 118–19, gave a list of muʿjams and mashyakhas, many of which date from the Mamluk period; the passage is translated in Franz Rosenthal, *A History of Muslim Historiography* (Leiden, 1952), 376–78. Several muʿjams were examined during the course of the present research, including Ibn Ḥajar al-ʿAsqalānī's *al-Majmaʿ al-muʾassas liʾl-muʿjam al-mufahris*, organized by the names of his shaykhs, as was the usual custom, and his *al-Muʿjam al-mufahris*, Dār al-Kutub al-Miṣriyya, "Muṣṭalaḥ" Ms. 82, which is organized around the *books* that he studied; that of Tāj al-Dīn ʿAbd al-Wahhāb b. ʿAlī al-Subkī, *Muʿjam al-Subkī*, Dār al-Kutub al-Miṣriyya, Aḥmad Taymūr Pāshā Collection, "Tārīkh" Ms. 1446 [= Maʿhad Iḥyāʾ al-Makhṭūṭāt al-ʿArabiyya, "Tārīkh" Ms. 490]; that of Muḥammad b. Abī Bakr Ibn Zurayq, B.M. Or. 9792; and several others published or summarized by Vajda or his student Jacqueline Sublet. For a more complete bibliogra-

what in form and in the amount of detail they record about an individual's education, but organized as they are around the names and qualities of particular teachers, they all implicitly stress the importance of the personal element in the transmission of Islamic knowledge.

Individual teachers thus transmitted to their students less an abstract body of knowledge embodied in particular texts than a personal authority over those texts, an authority that in the case of promising students was enhanced by the long and close personal relationship indicated by the Arabic word *ṣuḥba*. The concept of ṣuḥba lay at the core of Islamic higher education.[51] The word means "companionship," although often the word "discipleship," with its implication of an authoritative relationship, is probably a better translation. The term described a pattern of personal relationship that permeated medieval Near Eastern society. It described the relationship between a prominent transmitter of the Prophetic traditions and his Mamluk patron, an avid student himself who employed his scholarly friend as a reader of ḥadīth.[52] The model was one of close friendship, but could also indicate more precisely the relationship of master and disciple, as in the case of a young trader who performed commercial services for an older merchant who had previously initiated him into the practices of the business world.[53]

In the context of education, ṣuḥba implied an extremely close personal and intellectual relationship between teacher and student, one fostered over the course of many years. Applied principally in the fields of ḥadīth and jurisprudence, ṣuḥba and its synonyms (especially *mulāzama*) could in fact characterize a master-disciple relationship in any subject of instruction as well as in initiation to Sufi mysticism. But it is especially in its effect on the relationship between teacher and student that the concept interests us. In the Mamluk period, ṣuḥba continued to be the model for Islamic education, so that students were urged not to move "from one shaykh to another before mastering what was begun with the first, for to do so would be to tear down that which had been built up."[54] Not all students were counted among the disciples (*ṣaḥāba*, sing. *ṣāḥib*) of a teacher, only those who devoted themselves to intensive study under him.[55]

---

phy on this genre of Muslim traditional literature, see *Encyclopedia of Islam*, 2nd edition, s.v. "Fahrasa" and "Idjāza."

[51] The most important work on this subject, and indeed on all aspects of Islamic education, is that of George Makdisi. See especially his "*Ṣuḥba* et *riyāsa* dans l'enseignement médiévale," in *Recherches d'islamologie. Recueil d'articles offert à Georges C. Anawati et Louis Gardet par leurs collègues et amis* (Louvain, 1977), 207–21, and the corresponding sections of his book, *Colleges*, esp. 128–29.

[52] Al-Sakhāwī, *al-Ḍaw'*, 4:46–47.

[53] Goitein, *Mediterranean Society*, 5:275–77.

[54] Al-Anṣārī, *al-Lu'lu'*, 7.

[55] Makdisi, "*Ṣuḥba*," 208–10. The verbs corresponding to the nouns ṣuḥba and mulāzama

Such a close relationship could extend over many years, as it must have for Shihāb al-Dīn Aḥmad ibn Asad (d. 1468), who attached himself to Ibn Ḥajar al-ʿAsqalānī "until he had heard from him most of what was recited on his [authority] and most of his writings."[56] Ibn Ḥajar himself proudly recalled that he had been the disciple of the prominent ḥadīth scholar Zayn al-Dīn al-ʿIrāqī (d. 1403) for a period of ten years.[57] On the other hand, as the biographical dictionaries attest, it was possible, and not altogether unusual, for a student to become the ṣāḥib of more than one shaykh. The prominent Syrian *muḥaddith* (transmitter of the Prophetic traditions) Ibrāhīm Sibṭ Ibn al-ʿAjamī (d. 1438), for example, is said to have "studied intensively" with three different shaykhs.[58] Very often those who did so were especially bright and promising students, themselves destined for remarkable academic careers, such as Zayn al-Dīn al-ʿIrāqī, Ibn Ḥajar's teacher, or Ibn Ḥajar himself, who developed this relationship with at least five different shaykhs, several of them in the same subject (jurisprudence).[59]

For all their intimacy, however, instructional relationships were also characterized by the absolute authority of the shaykh, an authority that created an almost insuperable psychological gulf between teacher and student. It may be that any educational model implies some sort of power relationship between instructor and instructed. Certainly, however, the instructional framework envisaged by medieval Islamic texts on pedagogy reinforced an authoritative relationship between a shaykh and his students, a relationship whose way had been prepared during the course of a student's primary education. A passage in Ibn Khaldūn's *Muqaddimah* strikingly highlights in no uncertain terms the subservient relationship of a primary school student to his teacher. The great Mālikī scholar and jurist urged that teachers not punish their students "with injustice and (tyrannical) force." Such severe punishment "makes them lazy and induces them to lie and be insincere, because they are afraid that they will have to suffer tyrannical treatment (if they tell the truth)." Sound advice, but what is significant is the scope of Ibn Khaldūn's admonition: it is directed to the masters, not only of students, but of servants and slaves.[60] Psychologically speaking, the relationship between more advanced students and their teachers was not altogether different. The shaykh was the

were: *ṣahiba* and especially *ṣāḥaba*, and *lazima* and *lāzama*; another used not infrequently was *ittabaʿa*. Makdisi, "*Ṣuḥba*," 209, and idem, *Colleges*, 128–29.

[56] Al-Sakhāwī, *al-Ḍaw'*, 1:228–29.

[57] Ibn Ḥajar, *Inbā' al-ghumr*, 5:172.

[58] Ibn Ḥajar, *al-Majmaʿ al-mu'assas*, 355–56.

[59] Al-Sakhāwī, *al-Ḍaw'*, 2:37, 4:172. For other examples of students who were the disciple of more than one teacher, see ibid., 1:251–52; 2:11, 81, 108; 3:115, 265; 4:120, 280, 282, 331. In each of these cases the operative verb used is that apparently preferred by al-Sakhāwī, *lāzama*.

[60] Ibn Khaldūn, *Muqaddimah*, 3:305, ed. Quatremere, 3:264–65.

possessor of a certain authority that he could, through various devices, transmit to his students. As we shall see, this had practical consequences for the society of the learned elite in the Mamluk period.

The very language and images of those Muslim scholars who wrote self-consciously about education reflect patterns of relationship built on the absolute authority of the teacher. Ibn Jamāʿa, in his treatise on education, employed a metaphor drawn from the world of medicine to describe the student-teacher relationship. A student, he wrote, should respect and obey his shaykh in all matters, "as the patient [obeys] the skillful doctor."[61] More common, however, was the metaphor of a father and child.

> Every student and teacher should show respect for the other, especially the former [i.e., the student especially should be respectful], because his teacher is like the father, or even greater, since his father brought him into the world of perdition, [while] his teacher leads him to the world of eternal life.[62]

A shaykh should treat his students gently, since, in their devotion to him in the pursuit of knowledge, they are "like his children."[63] Teachers certainly saw their obligations to their closest students in parental terms. Some went as far as to provide their students with food and sweets on special occasions, or even to distribute to them their own salaries.[64] Of course, the almost filial devotion expected from students went even deeper. In all respects a student was expected to behave toward his shaykh as a dutiful son to his father. His responsibilities extended to: physically shielding his shaykh from pressing crowds of people; approaching him only with clean clothing, clipped nails, and trimmed hair, and without unpleasant bodily odors; caring for his teacher's children and descendants; and, as a virtual member of his extended family, visiting the dead shaykh's tomb. Insubordination to a teacher, as to a father, drew especial reprobation, and if a student was rude to his shaykh, it was incumbent on his classmates to come quickly to the shaykh's defense, and to censure their ungrateful colleague.[65]

By the same token, a shaykh possessed a broad license to supervise his

[61] Ibn Jamāʿa, *Tadhkirat al-sāmiʿ*, 87.

[62] Al-Anṣārī, *al-Luʾluʾ*, 6–7.

[63] Al-Nawawī, *al-Majmūʿ*, 1:31; cf. Tritton, *Materials*, 49. Similarly, students in the medieval Iraqi yeshivas were called "sons of a master," or "sons of the house of a master." Goitein, *Mediterranean Society*, 2:197.

[64] Kamāl al-Dīn Jaʿfar al-Udfūwī, *al-Ṭāliʿ al-saʿīd al-jāmiʿ asmāʾ nujabāʾ al-ṣaʿīd* (Cairo, 1966), 709; al-Nuʿaymī, *al-Dāris*, 1:103. Makdisi, *Colleges*, 180, lists a number of other examples.

[65] Ibn Jamāʿa, *Tadhkirat al-sāmiʿ*, 90, 93ff, 110, 153–56.

students' lives with the firmness but also the sensitivity of a concerned parent. He was responsible not only for their intellectual growth, but for their moral behavior as well. Ibn Jamāʿa's treatise *Tadhkirat al-sāmiʿ*, on this as on all subjects, displays an awareness of psychological realities that suggests that its author drew on his own extensive classroom experience, and which therefore confirms that the treatise accurately reflects actual classroom situations of the Mamluk period. It was, he wrote, the teacher's duty "to supervise [*yurāqibu*] the circumstances of [his] students in their behavior and direction and morals." If he uncovered an infraction, the shaykh should note and condemn the student's action in his presence, but, at least at first, without singling him out before his peers. If the misbehavior continued increasingly harsh steps were to be taken, culminating with the refractory student's expulsion from the class, especially if the shaykh feared the young man's influence on his fellow students.[66] A teacher's responsibilities toward his students were of course especially important in schools in which many students were actually housed. Ibn Jamāʿa made it clear that the professor of a madrasa had a duty to set an example by his behavior to those who lived in the school, for example by diligently performing his prayers.[67]

The authoritative character of educational relationships was evident in the very form of classroom arrangements.[68] In describing the prescribed behavior of students in class, Ibn Jamāʿa made it clear that those who are to sit nearest the shaykh are those who are worthiest by virtue of their age, learning, or righteousness.[69] But a significant physical, and immense psychological gap separated the teacher from even his most advanced students. According to a twelfth-century treatise on education that circulated widely in the Mamluk period, "it further behooves the student not to sit near the teacher during the lecture except under necessity, rather it is essential that the pupils sit in a semi-circle at a certain distance from the teacher, for indeed this is more appropriate to the respect due [the teacher]."[70] The successful transmission of knowledge required the maintenance of a proper distance between the teacher and his pupils, and concerns for this prompted taboos that restricted the slightest physical contact. Respect for the teacher, according to Ibn Jamāʿa, required that a student carefully refrain from touching his shaykh's body, garment, or even the cushion on which he sat, with any part of his own body or clothing.[71] Ibn al-Ḥājj, in his long fourteenth-century treatise describing con-

[66] Ibid., 60–61.

[67] Ibid., 202.

[68] On this point, see Makdisi, *Colleges*, 91–92.

[69] Ibn Jamāʿa, *Tadhkirat al-sāmiʿ*, 147.

[70] Al-Zarnūjī, *Taʿlīm*, 26, von Grunebaum and Abel, *Instruction*, 36–37.

[71] Ibn Jamāʿa, *Tadhkirat al-sāmiʿ*, 109. Oddly, in a passage somewhat at odds with the

temporary practices of which he disapproved, condemned those scholars who, when delivering their lectures, sat on a raised dais or platform. Such behavior, he thought, smacked of conceit and an inappropriate sense of self-importance (*taraffuʿ*).[72] But in fact the act of teaching from an elevated position must not have been unusual, or else Ibn al-Ḥājj would hardly have bothered to fulminate against it. The practice only reinforced an authority and awareness of superiority already implicit in the teacher-student relationship.

The burdens of such a relationship could at times prove inconvenient or embarrassing to the student. For example, the authority and importance of the teacher also justified his "glorification and veneration" by those who sought instruction from him, effected by such practices as kissing the shaykh's hand. Certain humiliations had to be borne by the student; in particular, flattering one's teachers was inevitable. "Flattery [*al-tamalluq*] is blameworthy except in the quest for knowledge," wrote al-Zarnūjī, author of a treatise on education widely read and copied in the Middle Ages. "In order to learn from them, flattery of one's professor and associates is inevitable."[73] Students might find the flattering of their teachers humiliating, but this and much more had to be borne in the pursuit of the greater goal, knowledge and the license to transmit it. Like other writers of educational treatises, Ibn Jamāʿa never ceased to counsel patience. A student must be patient in quarrels with his shaykh, or when the shaykh is of a bad disposition (*sū' khulq*), and he must always give his shaykh's actions the best possible interpretation, for that "is most beneficial for the student in this world and the next."[74] The student, he wrote, "should not tire of long companionship [ṣuḥba] with his professor, for he [i.e., the shaykh] is like a date palm, under which you wait for something to drop on you."[75]

The problem was that it might take some time for the dates to fall. It is clear from Ibn Jamāʿa's repeated advice to the students of incompetent, slow-witted, or forgetful shaykhs that medieval Islamic educational models and patterns, while producing the authoritative relationship I have been describing, did not guarantee quality of instruction. If the shaykh began to recite something the student had already memorized,

---

rest of his text, Ibn al-Ḥājj urged students to crowd around their teacher, "so that the robes of the students touch the robe of the professor." Ibn al-Ḥājj, *Madkhal al-sharʿ al-sharīf* (Cairo, A.H. 1329), 1:198.

[72] Ibn al-Ḥājj, *Madkhal*, 1:197–98. Cf. Tritton, *Materials*, 49–50.

[73] Al-Zarnūjī, *Taʿlīm*, 63; I have here altered somewhat the translation of von Grunebaum and Abel, *Instruction*, 52. See also al-Zarnūjī, *Taʿlīm*, 21, von Grunebaum and Abel, *Instruction*, 32; ʿAbd al-Karīm b. Muḥammad al-Samʿānī, *Kitāb adab al-imlā' wa'l-istimlā'*, ed. Max Weisweiler (Leiden, 1952), 134–37, 139–40.

[74] Ibn Jamāʿa, *Tadhkirat al-sāmiʿ*, 91.

[75] Ibid., 142.

the student should listen attentively, and try to convey his great joy at hearing the recitation, as if for the first time. If asked if he has memorized the text, the student should not say simply "yes," which would imply he no longer needed his teacher's instruction on the point, nor should he say "no," for that would be untrue; he should instead respond by saying "I prefer to hear it from the shaykh," or "[I memorized it] long ago," or "from you it is more correct," or with some such delicate phrase extricate the shaykh from potential embarrassment. Again, if the shaykh made an error, the student should not point it out, but should gently give him an opportunity to correct the mistake, for example by repeating the error himself in the shaykh's presence; if the teacher persisted in his error, the confused student should simply take the question to another shaykh.[76]

Within this general framework, actual patterns of classroom authority were complicated by a number of factors. In the first place, of course, some "students" might in fact be individuals of comparatively advanced age. A shaykh who transmitted a particular text through an especially reputable chain of authorities might find others of his own age, or even older, attending his recitations and lectures in order to receive an ijāza from him, even for a work they had already studied with another scholar. We shall later encounter an individual who, although himself over the age of forty, nonetheless was installed as a student of ḥadīth in one of Cairo's leading schools. In addition, under some circumstances teaching assistants compensated for but also reinforced the psychological gap between instructor and instructed. The professor, ideally, was to do more than recite a text, or listen to and correct his students' recitations. He should also make himself available at an appointed hour every day and remain for a time after class, to listen to the students as they studied their lessons, correct their mistakes, and answer their questions.[77] But it seems that much of his responsibilities in that regard in fact devolved upon advanced students and young teachers, scholars whose careers had not yet advanced to the point where they could teach authoritatively on their own, and who therefore were not offered valuable professorships and whose reputations would not attract a sizeable body of students.

These "teaching assistants" were accorded a variety of titles: *mustamlī*, *mufīd*, and *muʿīd*. The mustamlī, usually an advanced and trusted student of a shaykh, was primarily associated with the transmission of the Prophetic traditions. In large circles in which ḥadīth were recited, he repeated in a loud voice what the professor himself had dictated, and

[76] Ibid., 104–5, 124–25. Al-Nawawī, *al-Majmūʿ*, 1:37–38, also gives instructions for how students should deal gently with teachers who, for example, fall asleep in class.

[77] Ibn Jamāʿa, *Tadhkirat al-sāmiʿ*, 202–4; cf. Tritton, *Materials*, 49.

elucidated his words to the listeners.[78] A previous scholar noted that by the fifteenth century, the term, although still in use, was not common.[79] In fact, the biographical dictionaries of the period rarely employ the word, although the infrequency of its appearance may reflect only the writers' concern with other, more prominent aspects of students' and ḥadīth transmitters' careers.

Far more common in the sources at our disposal were the terms mufīd (and its verbal noun, *ifāda*, "to benefit" or "to be of use," and by extension "to inform") and especially muʿīd (and *iʿāda*, "to repeat"), terms similar in meaning to those describing teaching assistants in the medieval Jewish academies of the Near East.[80] In the Mamluk period at least, the sources suggest no clear distinction of function and responsibility between the mufīd ("one who benefits [another]") and the muʿīd (literally, "repetitor"). Both terms indicated teaching assistants who were deeply involved in repeating the professor's lesson, listening to the students repeat it from memory, and explaining obscure parts of the lesson to them. It is true that Tāj al-Dīn al-Subkī, himself an experienced educator, discussed muʿīds and mufīds separately in his treatise *Muʿīd al-niʿam wa-mubīd al-niqam* (The Repetitor of Blessings and the Destroyer of Misfortunes), a work devoted to defining the proper behavior of those employed in a variety of academic, religious, bureaucratic, and economic tasks. Regarding the muʿīd, al-Subkī wrote: "His responsibilities go beyond listening to the lesson, and include explaining [it] to some of the students, being of use to them, and doing what the term iʿāda requires"—that is, repeating and explaining the lessons dictated by the professor until the students under his charge had mastered them. By contrast, al-Subkī outlined the mufīd's duties as "to employ what he derives from the lesson as a benefit [*fāʾidatan*, i.e., to others?] from study beyond that of most [students]."[81] But it is clear from the usual language in the biographical dictionaries that to be a mufīd—*afāda 'l-ṭalaba*—was, like the muʿīd, to participate actively in the transmission of knowledge to students.

The practical distinction between the terms muʿīd and mufīd arose in

[78] On the role of the mustamlī, see al-Suyūṭī, *Tadrīb al-rāwī*, 2:132–36; Pedersen, *Arabic Book*, 26; Tritton, *Materials*, 35–37; Makdisi, *Colleges*, 213–14; al-Samʿānī, *al-Imlāʾ*, esp. 84–108.

[79] Tritton, *Materials*, 37.

[80] On the muʿīd and mufīd, see Tāj al-Dīn ʿAbd al-Wahhāb al-Subkī, *Muʿīd al-niʿam wa-mubīd al-niqam*, ed. David Myhrman (London, 1908), 154–55; Ibn Jamāʿa, *Tadhkirat al-sāmiʿ*, 150, 160, 201; Makdisi, *Colleges*, 193–96. Similarly, teachers of the lowest grade in Jewish schools were called *tannāʾīm*, "repetitors." Their duties, too, were to help young students memorize their lessons, since the oral pronunciation of Hebrew texts was also critical to their accurate transmission. Goitein, *Mediterranean Society*, 2:199–200.

[81] Al-Subkī, *Muʿīd al-niʿam*, 154–55.

relation to their connection to the various institutions of education. The iʿāda was usually a paid position, a *waẓīfa*, for which the endowments of particular schools made provisions, and the biographical dictionaries frequently refer to it as such. By contrast, the sources comment simply that a mufīd "benefited students," using a transitive form of the verb (*afāda 'l-ṭalaba*). If he did so, however, the mufīd must have functioned "informally," as a private assistant to a professor. The surviving deeds of endowment suggest that no institution in the Mamluk period ever supported an endowed position called ifāda. Pointedly, al-Subkī described the iʿāda as a waẓīfa, but only referred to the "compensation" that a mufīd might receive.[82]

A number of Cairene schools of the Mamluk period made specific provisions for the appointment of muʿīds, provisions that shed some light on the muʿīd's responsibilities in the transmission of knowledge to students.[83] At the mosque of Sūdūn min Zāda, for example, the muʿīds were to sit with the students either before or after the professor's lectures in order to "explain to [the students] what they had memorized from their books and to elucidate what was obscure to them from [the teachings of] their rite."[84] At the madrasa of Ṣarghitmish, the muʿīds apparently assumed even more responsibilities for the actual instruction, not surprisingly, since that school's professor faced at least sixty students of Ḥanafī jurisprudence, an exceptionally high ratio. During the class in that institution, each of three muʿīds was to read a "lesson" (*dars*) from a book chosen by the professor. The latter was then to provide the students with answers to any questions they might have, but the responsibility for more intimate intellectual contact was left to the muʿīds: each was to come to the majlis before the professor, and to remain after his departure, in order to help students with their problems or questions.[85]

[82] Al-Subkī, *Muʿīd al-niʿam*, 155.

[83] A number also did not. Even leaving aside those "madrasas" such as al-Ghawrī's and al-Sayfī Baybars' that, as noted in the previous chapter, did not make provisions for stipends for either students or teachers, several large schools such as the mosque of al-Mu'ayyad Shaykh and the madrasa of Barsbāy did not have provisions in their deeds of endowments for the appointment of muʿids. See *Waqfiyyat* al-Mu'ayyad Shaykh, Wizārat al-Awqāf o.s. No. 938; *Waqfiyyat* al-Ashraf Barsbāy, Dār al-Wathā'iq No. 173. From this one might conclude that the post of the iʿāda did not exist in those institutions. I think, however, it is more likely that in the fluid world of Islamic education in this period, the *functions* of the iʿāda were undertaken by advanced students, possibly called mufīds, or others whose appointments were less formal and who served more directly at the convenience of the professor.

[84] *Waqfiyyat* Sūdūn min Zāda, Dār al-Wathā'iq No. 58.

[85] *Waqfiyyat* Ṣarghitmish, Wizārat al-Awqāf o.s. No. 3195, published by ʿAbd al-Laṭīf Ibrāhīm ʿAli, "Naṣṣān jadīrān min wathīqat al-amīr ṣarghitmish," pts. 1 and 2 in *Jāmiʿat al-qāhira. Majallat kulliyat al-ādāb* 27 (1965), 121–58, and 28 (1966), 143–200; in the published version, the muʿids' responsibilities are described in pt. 1, 147–48.

These teaching assistants occupied a stage in an individual's academic career intermediary between that of student and teacher; not surprisingly, therefore, many muʿīds were themselves perfectly competent scholars. Aḥmad Ibn Ismāʿīl al-Ḥanafī (d. 1489), for example, at some point in his career held the assistantship in Ḥanafī law at the large congregational mosque of Ibn Ṭūlūn.[86] Ibn Ismāʿīl was an exemplary, if not outstanding scholar of his time. He studied with a number of prominent ulama of the late Mamluk period, including ʿAlam al-Dīn al-Bulqīnī, al-Amīn al-Aqṣarāʾī, the historian al-Sakhāwī, and others, taught informally or as substitute for the professors in various institutions, and held in his own right several teaching posts. From all appearances, his appointment at Ibn Ṭūlūn represented simply a normal early step in the career of a successful late medieval scholar.[87] Other prominent scholars who were muʿīds at early stages in their careers included ʿIzz al-Dīn ʿAbd al-Salām al-Baghdādī (d. 1455), who assisted in Ḥanafī jurisprudence at the mosque of Ibn Ṭūlūn and the Jānibakiyya madrasa, and the famous judge and jurist Sirāj al-Dīn al-Bulqīnī (d. 1403), who was muʿīd at the Kharrūbiyya madrasa before becoming its professor of Shāfiʿī jurisprudence.[88]

Teaching assistants, by whatever term they were described, thus functioned as intermediaries between the shaykh on the one hand and his pupils and any others who might attend his classes on the other. Nonetheless, the authority that was passed was that of the shaykh himself. It was upon this authority, and the personal relationships established between individual teachers and particular students, rather than any formal affiliation to an institution, that Islamic education rested. An education was judged primarily by the number and character of the links that a student forged with prominent transmitters of the Islamic sciences. Those relationships were close and intense, at least in the case of advanced and promising students, even though their authoritative nature could produce a significant psychological barrier between the pupil and his teacher. But the ties were persistent, and followed a student beyond the close of his formal education. Indeed, they shaped not only the character of instruction and pedagogy, but also the course of a student's later academic career, an issue that we shall address in a later chapter.

[86] Presumably in Ḥanafī jurisprudence, although the source is not clear on that point. Moreover, in the absence of any precise dates, we cannot tell from the biographer's account at what age Ibn Ismāʿīl held this post, although presumably the appointment came at a relatively early stage in his career; but this informational gap is typical of the biographical dictionaries. Al-Sakhāwī, *al-Ḍaw'*, 1:234–35.

[87] Cf. Carl Petry, *The Civilian Elite of Cairo in the Later Middle Ages* (Princeton, 1981), 246–48.

[88] Al-Sakhāwī, *al-Ḍaw'*, 4:198–203 (on al-Baghdādī); al-Maqrīzī, *al-Mawāʿiẓ wa'l-iʿtibār bi-dhikr al-khiṭaṭ wa'l-āthār* (Būlāq, 1853–54), 2:369, and al-Sakhāwī, *al-Ḍaw'*, 6:85–90 (on al-Bulqīnī).

The overwhelming preference for oral transmission, and the weight of personal connections in evaluating an individual's academic training, should suggest to us the need to look beyond the formal outlines of particular institutions of learning—one scholar even gave his lessons while walking with his students up and down the main street of Cairo. The social consequences of this aspect of Islamic culture were immense. We shall see in later chapters how the prejudices of the system—for example, the value accorded to an ijāza issued by an elderly man to a young pupil, and the personal authority such an act conveyed—facilitated the participation of disparate segments of the Muslim population in the transmission of Islamic learning. The social horizons of education in late medieval Cairo were very broad indeed, and were limited not by institutional structure, but by the informal system of which the various schools were a part. Despite this caveat, however, it is also true that many teachers in late medieval Cairo taught, and most students studied, in one or more of the city's many institutions of learning, and it is to those schools that we now turn our attention.

III

INSTITUTIONS

THE PERSONAL and informal system described in the previous chapter characterized Islamic education from its inception through the end of the Middle Ages, and in fact survived intact into the twentieth century. Built upon the personal authority of the shaykh, channeled through relationships established between students and teachers, certified by the ijāza, and regulated by the contacts and networks that shaped the educated elite into a coherent social group, the transmission of religious knowledge never came to rely on an institutional structure or a formal system of degrees. Its very informality, as we shall see, guaranteed its vigor, and imparted a measure of openness missing from Western institutions of higher learning until a comparatively recent period.

By the Mamluk period, however, much education transpired in the context of particular institutions established and endowed for the pious purpose of aiding the transmission of Muslim learning. This marked a profound change, for instruction in the earlier Islamic centuries, although occasionally supported on an ad hoc basis by wealthy individuals and important personages in the state, had generally relied upon the independent means, or voluntary poverty, of those committed to learning and teaching. By contrast, Cairo in the fourteenth and fifteenth centuries was a city architecturally dominated by structures—madrasas, mosques, and Sufi convents—designed and constructed to provide shelter and accommodations for students and teachers and a forum for their classes. In many cases blessed with considerable endowments, they dispensed to the educated classes, and to other sectors of the urban community, cash stipends and payments in kind to support the work of passing on the vast corpus of traditional learning from one generation to the next.

The spread of such institutions never resulted in any formalization of the educational process. There is little suggestion in the sources that particular schools ever acquired any lasting identity or mission within the academic sphere distinct from that of the individuals who taught within them: Islamic law allowed them no corporate identity; no method of granting institutional degrees was established; the whole system remained, as it were, thoroughly nonsystematic. The phenomenon of an extensive network of schools—buildings and endowments—became, however, a constant and significant presence in the life of the academic community and profoundly affected the social history of the learned elite of Mamluk Cairo. To give an example: the availability of stipends in particular schools might lead to competition, sometimes fierce, between prospective students and teachers for succession to a lucrative post. When, in 1365–66, the Mamluk amir Yalbughā al-ʿUmarī endowed a new course for Ḥanafīs in the mosque of Ibn Ṭūlūn in Cairo, a number of Shāfiʿī students switched allegiance to the Ḥanafī rite, apparently to take advantage of the liberal stipends dispensed by Yalbughā's endowment.[1] For a scholar such as the famous judge and traditionist Ibn Ḥajar al-ʿAsqalānī (d. 1449), to whose example we shall have frequent occasion to return, endowed professorships—he held well over a dozen at one point or another during his career—came to represent a source of income taken largely for granted. They also introduced an element of patronage into the professional relationship between teachers and their brighter students, a subject we shall examine in detail in the following chapter.

The Variety of Institutional Types

Late medieval Cairo was, as much as anything else, a city of schools. Writing in the early fifteenth century, the historian al-Maqrīzī, in his descriptive treatise on Cairo, mentioned seventy-three madrasas that were then or had at one time since the late twelfth century been in operation.[2] Not all were still open when he wrote. The madrasa of Sultan al-Ashraf Shaʿbān, for example, built on the spot just below the Citadel where the ruins of the Mu'ayyadī hospital stand to this day, had been razed to the ground because it had so often been used by rebellious Mamluks as a staging ground for attacks upon the Citadel, the seat of government. Moreover, al-Maqrīzī's list is hardly exhaustive. Clearly others were built after al-Maqrīzī completed his *Khiṭaṭ*, including some of the more important madrasas of the Mamluk period, such as that of Sultan al-Ghawrī in the central section of medieval Cairo to which it lent its name. He seems also to have neglected to mention several madrasas, such as that of his rival, the historian, judge, and market inspector Badr al-Dīn al-ʿAynī, that were in operation in his day.[3] The lacunae in al-

[1] Taqī 'l-Dīn Aḥmad al-Maqrīzī, *al-Mawāʿiẓ wa'l-iʿtibār bi-dhikr al-khiṭaṭ wa'l-āthār* (Būlāq, A.H. 1270; reptd. Beirut, n.d.), 2:269.

[2] Al-Maqrīzī, *Khiṭaṭ*, 2:362–405.

[3] Oddly, al-Maqrīzī apparently also excluded from his list a number of madrasas mentioned in the earlier work of his teacher, the historian Ibn Duqmāq, *al-Intiṣār li-wāsiṭat ʿiqd al-amṣār*, 4:16, 18, 94, 95, 99. Al-Ḥasan b. ʿUmar Ibn Ḥabīb, too, in his history of the Qalāwūnid dynasty, although primarily concerned with events in Syria, mentioned at least two madrasas founded in Cairo in the first half of the Mamluk period that seem to have escaped al-Maqrīzī's notice; see *Tadhikirat al-nabīh fī ayyām al-manṣūr wa-banīh*

Maqrīzī's work, however, present only the initial obstacle to an attempt to outline the institutional framework of higher education in late medieval Cairo. As we will see, even those terms by which the chroniclers, scholars, and scribes of Mamluk Cairo described the schools in which they studied and taught reflect an ambiguity about the precise characteristics of those schools, an ambiguity that will, however, help us to understand the breadth and diversity of the underlying system of education.

The Egyptian capital's first institution specifically called a madrasa had been founded in al-Fusṭāṭ by Saladin in 1170. Under the Ayyubid regime, construction of madrasas proceeded apace. By the middle of the thirteenth century—by the first years, that is, of the Mamluk sultanate—Cairo and the neighboring city of al-Fusṭāṭ between them boasted at least thirty-two institutions known as madrasas, established principally for instruction in jurisprudence and its ancillary sciences, especially ḥadīth and exegesis.[4] By the early years of the fifteenth century, as we have seen, that number had increased to more than seventy, and dozens more were established over the last century of Mamluk rule. Well over a hundred institutions devoted largely or exclusively to the inculcation of the religious and legal sciences opened their doors in Cairo at one point or another during the Mamluk period. The precise number functioning at any one time is probably impossible to fix. In part this results from oblique references in the sources to schools of which little or nothing is known.[5] More importantly, however, since education remained grounded in the personalities of individual teachers, madrasas conceived in a broader, functional sense could exist wherever a professor taught—in a mosque or congregational mosque, a *khānqāh* (Sufi convent), a private house, or in those institutions specifically labeled madrasas. Several of the more than one hundred schools were simply preexisting mosques or private houses for which a wealthy individual provided endowments to support one or more courses.

Before we can begin to analyze the institutional structure of higher religious and legal education in Mamluk Cairo, we must come to grips with a confusion in the meaning and application of the terms used to

(Cairo, 1976–86), 2:158, 198. Cf. Ibrahim Salama, *L'Enseignement islamique en égypte* (Cairo, 1938), 59–60.

[4] Gary Leiser, "The Restoration of Sunnism in Egypt: Madrasas and Mudarrisūn, 495–647/1101–1249," dissertation, University of Pennsylvania (1976), passim.

[5] For example, we have almost no information concerning the following madrasas, which are given only passing mention in the sources: that of Ibn Yaʿqūb, see Ibn Duqmāq, *al-Intiṣār*, 4:95; Ibn al-Sukrī, see ibid., 4:41; al-Kahhāriyya, see al-Maqrīzī, *Khiṭaṭ*, 2:41, cf. Leiser, "Restoration," 303; al-Nābulusiyya, see al-Maqrīzī, *Khiṭaṭ*, 2:80; al-Shirābshiyya, see ibid., 1:375. Carl Petry, "A Paradox of Patronage," *The Muslim World* 73 (1983), 190, attests, on the basis of his own research, that there were at least 130 "religio-academic institutions" functioning during the later Mamluk period.

describe those institutions. The "madrasa," as classically formulated and as developed first in Baghdad and the East and, later, in the Muslim cities of Syria, was an institution devoted principally to instruction in Islamic law and the other religious sciences, providing salaries and, in some cases, accommodations for a group of teachers, students, and support staff. But increasingly over the course of the Mamluk period such a precise definition of the institution will simply not suffice. Not all madrasas were exclusively or even principally educational institutions, and, as in earlier periods, much serious legal and religious instruction took place outside of madrasas.

One of the institutions that dominated the educational scene in late medieval Cairo was that known as the Ashrafiyya. Constructed and endowed by Sultan al-Ashraf Barsbāy within a few years of his accession to the throne in 1422, the Ashrafiyya, which took its name from its founder, resembled many other institutions of learning in the city. Built on the so-called "cruciform" plan, each of the four open, recessed halls (*īwāns*) surrounding the central courtyard provided the venue for an organized daily class in jurisprudence in each of the four rites of Sunni law; the largest īwān, that facing Mecca and in which the prayer niche (*miḥrāb*) was embedded, was reserved for the Ḥanafī class, to which rite Barsbāy himself, as well as most of the Mamluks, belonged. Separate professors were appointed to lead each class; the Ḥanafī professor doubled as Sufi shaykh. The institution's endowment provided monthly salaries for the school's instructional staff, as well as stipends for between ten and twenty-five students in each class. The school complex included rooms or cells (*ḥalāwī*) that served as a "hospice" (*ribāṭ*) for its students. But the mission of the institution was by no means limited to formal instruction. The complex of buildings included a *sabīl-kuttāb*, a multistory structure containing both a public fountain and a primary school, increasingly common features of Mamluk-period schools, as well as a tomb chamber for the burial of members of the sultan's family. Its minaret clearly advertised its character as a place of public worship, and consequently the school's employees included a number of purely religious functionaries, including a prayer leader (*imām*), preacher (*khaṭīb*), and several teams of Quran readers.[6]

The Ashrafiyya, like many other Mamluk-period schools, was obviously a highly complex institution. Not surprisingly, contemporaries sometimes had trouble knowing what exactly to call it. In 1426, reported the historian Ibn Iyās, "the construction of the madrasa of the sultan [al-

[6] *Waqfiyyat* al-Ashraf Barsbāy, Dār al-Wathā'iq No. 173; Ahmad Darrag, *L'Acte de waqf de Barsbāy* (Cairo, 1963); idem., *L'Égypte sous le règne de Barsbāy*, 825–841/1422–1438 (Damascus, 1961), 406–8; cf. Leonor Fernandes, *The Evolution of a Sufi Institution in Mamluk Egypt: The Khanqah* (Berlin, 1988), 83–85.

Ashraf Barsbāy], which he established in the khānqāh in the street [Bayn al-Qaṣrayn, the principal thoroughfare of the city], was completed." To be sure, this institution, by traditional definitions, was clearly both a madrasa, an institution devoted to instruction in Islamic law and its ancillary sciences, and a khānqāh, a convent housing and making provisions for sixty-five Sufis, and inscriptions on the building itself describe it in those terms. Yet the institution's endowment deed—which described its buildings, enumerated the properties the income from which supported it, and established guidelines that regulated the activities of its beneficiaries—routinely referred to the institution as a *jāmi*ʿ, a "congregational mosque." By contrast, a "madrasa" in the desert outside Cairo, also established by Sultan Barsbāy and provided for in the same document, supported four Ḥanafī students, but was embedded in an institution that served primarily as a convent for Sufis of the Rifāʿiyya order.[7]

This confusion reflected an evolution in the usage of the various terms by medieval Muslim writers. Etymologically, of course, the word madrasa derives from an Arabic verb meaning "to study," and at first the word indicated unambiguously a place for education. Sultan Barsbāy's institutions were constructed and endowed in the early fifteenth century, more than 150 years after the founding of the Mamluk state. By contrast, Cairene institutions called madrasas established during the thirteenth and early fourteenth centuries seem to have been explicitly, and often exclusively, centers of religious and legal education providing salaries for professors of the various legal sciences and stipends for their students. These included several madrasas on Bayn al-Qaṣrayn, the main thoroughfare that bisected the medieval city of Cairo, such as that of Sultan al-Ẓāhir Baybars (al-Ẓāhiriyya), with its courses in Shāfiʿī and Ḥanafī jurisprudence, ḥadīth, and the variant Quran readings, that of al-Manṣūr Qalāwūn (al-Manṣūriyya), with classes in all four rites of law as well as ḥadīth and Quranic exegesis, and that of al-Nāṣir Muḥammad ibn Qalāwūn (al-Nāṣiriyya), with endowed professorships and student stipends in Mālikī, Shāfiʿī, Ḥanafī, and Ḥanbalī jurisprudence. These early Mamluk madrasas resembled in their essentials a neighboring school established at the end of the Ayyubid period by Sultan al-Malik al-Ṣāliḥ (al-Ṣāliḥiyya), the first in Egypt to provide classes for all four rites of law.

By the third decade of the fourteenth century, clear functional distinc-

[7] Ibn Iyās, *Badāʾiʿ al-zuhūr fī waqāʾiʿ al-duhūr* (Cairo, 1984), 2:115. *Waqfiyyat* al-Ashraf Barsbāy, Dār al-Wathāʾiq No. 173, fol. 143r–151r. On the inscriptions in the Ashrafiyya, see Max van Berchem, *Matériaux pour un corpus inscriptionum arabicarum*, pt. 1 [= *Mémoires publiées par les membres de la mission archéologiques françaises au Caire*, vol. 19] (Paris, 1903), 298. The small madrasa in the desert is discussed in Leonor Fernandes, "Three Sufi Foundations in a Fifteenth Century Waqfiyya," *Annales islamologiques* 17 (1981), 141–56.

tions between institutions labeled madrasas on the one hand, and those called jāmiʿs, *masjids* (mosques), and khānqāhs on the other, began to break down. Terms such as madrasa, jāmiʿ, and khānqāh, as applied to particular institutions, *seem* to have been used with less and less precision. An early example is the khānqāh established by a Mamluk amir in 1329, whose shaykh was to lead twenty Sufis not only in their devotional exercises, but in a daily class in Ḥanafī jurisprudence as well. By contrast, the madrasa of Sultan Ḥasan, built in the middle of the fourteenth century, was also known as and functioned as a jāmiʿ, providing for the recitation of a *khuṭba* (sermon) during Friday congregational prayers.[8]

The accounts of contemporary Muslim chroniclers and biographers themselves reflect an uncertainty as to how to describe particular institutions. Increasingly, writers used different terms to refer to the same establishments; not infrequently, one and the same chronicler would himself use different terms. The historian and scholar al-Maqrīzī, for example, in his topographical history of Cairo, called the institution established by the amir Aṣlam al-Nāṣirī in 1345–46 a jāmiʿ, while his younger contemporary Ibn Taghrī Birdī, an equally important historian and biographer, labeled it a madrasa. In another example, Ibn Taghrī Birdī reported that Jānibāk al-Dawādār was, in January 1428, buried in the madrasa he had established; yet both al-Maqrīzī and Ibn Taghrī Birdī himself in another passage called the institution housing Jānibak's tomb a jāmiʿ.[9]

Comparing the terms used by historians and chroniclers with those in the surviving endowment deeds creates even greater confusion. The institution established by the amir Fakhr al-Dīn ʿAbd al-Ghanī in the early fifteenth century made provisions for professors of the Shafiʿī, Ḥanafī, and Mālikī rites, and in its deed is clearly labeled a madrasa, yet al-Maqrīzī calls it a jāmiʿ and discusses it in a section of his survey describing

[8] Leonor Fernandes has discussed the khānqāh of Mughulṭāy al-Jamālī in *The Khanqah*, 34–35, 73. Cf. the madrasas founded by the amirs ʿAlāʾ al-Dīn Aqbughā al-Ustādār, ʿAlāʾ al-Dīn Sanjar al-Jāwulī, and Shihāb al-Dīn Aḥmad b. Aqqūsh al-Mihmandār, all of which al-Maqrīzī discusses in both the madrasa and khānqāh sections of his topographical history of Cairo, the *Khiṭaṭ*. A good sense of the chronology of the gradual breakdown of institutional identity during the Mamluk period can be found in Doris Behrens-Abouseif, "Change in Function and Form of Mamlūk Religious Institutions," *Annales islamologiques* 21 (1985), 73–93. Max van Berchem discussed the confusion of institutional terms in his *Matériaux*, 361–62, although his comments should be read in conjunction with the critique by George Makdisi in *The Rise of Colleges* (Edinburgh, 1981), 296–301.

[9] For Aṣlam al-Nāṣirī's jāmiʿ/madrasa, see al-Maqrīzī, *Khiṭaṭ*, 2:309, and Jamāl al-Dīn Yūsuf Ibn Taghrī Birdī, *al-Manhal al-ṣāfī waʾl-mustawfī baʿd al-wāfī* (Cairo, 1984), 2:457. For that of Jānibāk al-Dawādār, see Ibn Taghrī Birdī, *al-Nujūm al-zāhira fī mulūk miṣr waʾl-qāhira* (Cairo, 1929–72), 14:309, 15:148, and al-Maqrīzī, *Kitāb al-sulūk li-maʿrifat duwal al-mulūk* (Cairo, 1934–73), 4:786. Other examples are legion.

mosques.[10] In the large khānqāh of Jamāl al-Dīn Yūsuf, as we shall see, the principal activities of the Sufis who inhabited the building were educational. The confusion of terms is almost complete: we have jāmiʿs that principally supported Sufis, madrasas whose deeds of endowment made no provisions for academic courses, and khānqāhs that, under the terms by which they were established, functioned primarily as schools.

What are we to make of this apparent confusion in the terms used to describe particular establishments? It is important that we, as late twentieth-century historians, not reify terms such as madrasa, jāmiʿ, masjid, or khānqāh, terms to which medieval Muslims might have attached more abstract meaning. To popular perception, they signified less a particular place, institution, or building than a *function*, and as such their meaning as applied to specific institutions might change over time. Thus, the apparent confusion of terms should be viewed, in the first place, through the lens of that flexible, personal system that characterized Islamic education and the transmission of Muslim knowledge. That a student's authority derived from that of his teacher, and not from the venue in which his education had transpired, meant that no institution, not even the madrasa, could ever establish a monopoly over the inculcation of the Muslim sciences. Any open space—the floor of a mosque, a Sufi cell, a private living room, as well as a chamber in a madrasa—offered a suitable site for instruction. But it suggests also that education in this society cannot be considered in isolation; rather, it must be seen as one element in the broader continuum of Islamic piety and worship. The organized and rigorous transmission of those texts that constituted the body of the Muslim sciences was not accomplished in a hermetic environment. On the contrary, it took place alongside, and sometimes as a part of Sufi activities, public sermonizing, and popular religious celebration, and those who devoted themselves to education did not necessarily see their efforts as something fundamentally distinct from public worship.

Mosques as Centers of Education

It should first be made clear that organized and endowed instruction in Islamic jurisprudence and its ancillary sciences was by no means limited to institutions known as madrasas, and that a study of that education and of those active as students or teachers must encompass other institutions as well. The biographer of Sultan Jaqmaq, a pious individual who reigned for more than a decade in the mid-fifteenth century, noted that although he did not build a madrasa, he nonetheless restored a number of

[10] *Waqfiyyat* Fakhr al-Dīn ʿAbd al-Ghanī, Dār al-Wathāʾiq No. 72; al-Maqrīzī, *Khiṭaṭ*, 2:328.

mosques, including one in the famous market Khān al-Khalīlī, at which he endowed separate classes for Shāfiʿī and Ḥanafī students.[11] Between 1250 and 1517, Cairo saw the establishment or endowment of a large number of institutions principally or exclusively referred to as jāmiʿs or masjids that provided not only space for but income to support courses in jurisprudence, ḥadīth, exegesis, or other religious subjects, identical to those offered in madrasas.

Included in this group were several of the large congregational mosques constructed during earlier phases in Cairo's history, among them al-Azhar in the heart of the city, the mosque of al-Ḥākim near Bāb al-Futūḥ, that of Ibn Ṭūlūn south of the city, and the mosque of ʿAmr ibn al-ʿĀṣ, sometimes referred to as *al-jāmiʿ al-ʿatīq* ("the ancient mosque") in al-Fusṭāṭ.[12] The great mosque of al-Azhar, of course, experienced something of a revival early in the Mamluk period. Al-Azhar, originally constructed by the Fatimid caliphs as the principal mosque of their new royal city of Cairo and as a center for the propagation of Ismāʿīlī Shiʿi doctrine, was largely ignored by the rigorously Sunni sultans of the Ayyubid dynasty, who suspended its role as a center of Friday congregational prayers for ideological reasons. The Mamluk sultan Baybars al-Bunduqdārī (reigned 1260–77) restored to the mosque some if not all of its former glory, and provided again for the recitation there of a public sermon on Fridays. The mosque was not yet the premier establishment of traditional Muslim learning it was to become in later centuries, but it did boast a number of independent endowments that supported teachers and students in a variety of subjects. In 1266–67, a Mamluk amir named Badr al-Dīn Bīlīk al-Khāzindār endowed a course for Shāfiʿīs in one of the *maqṣūras*, here meaning one of the separate compartments or stalls set aside for educational or devotional activities that lined the walls of the building, and thereby provided for a professor of law and a number of students. Each compartment provided space for instruction or study, so that when, a century later, the eunuch Saʿd al-Dīn Bashīr al-Nāṣirī carried out extensive renovations in the mosque, he endowed in another a course for Ḥanafī students and their teacher. Sultan Ḥasan (reigned 1347–51 and 1354–61), too, endowed a course for Ḥanafīs, insisting, however, that it be held in front of the mosque's principal *miḥrāb*, the prayer niche indicating the direction of Mecca.[13]

[11] Shams al-Dīn Muḥammad al-Sakhāwī, *al-Ḍawʾ al-lāmiʿ li-ahl al-qarn al-tāsiʿ* (Cairo, 1934), 3:250.

[12] Cf. Makdisi, *Colleges*, 20–21, where he recognized the role of the larger congregational mosques in higher education in Cairo.

[13] Al-Maqrīzī, *Khiṭaṭ*, 2:275–76; cf. idem., *al-Sulūk*, 1:557. On the meaning in context of the term *maqṣūra*, see *Encyclopedia of Islam*, 1st edition, s.v. "Masdjid," and Bayard Dodge, *al-Azhar: A Millenium of Muslim Learning* (Washington, D.C., 1961), 60–61.

The situation at the mosque of ʿAmr in al-Fusṭāṭ was similar. Al-Maqrīzī listed at least six *zāwiyas*, here meaning particular corners of or spaces in that large mosque, in which endowments supported organized classes in Islamic jurisprudence. Among the more important was that known as the zāwiya al-Majdiyya, next to the miḥrāb, established by Majd al-Dīn al-Ḥārith al-Bahnasī al-Shāfiʿī (d. 1230 or 1231), *wazīr* (minister) to a minor Ayyubid prince in Harrān. As late as the early fifteenth century, the teaching post attached to this zāwiya was "considered [to be] among the splendid positions [to which a scholar might be appointed]." The zāwiya named for the imām al-Shāfiʿī had benefited from lucrative endowments supplied by the Ayyubid sultan al-Malik al-ʿAzīz ʿUthmān, the son of Saladin, and in al-Maqrīzī's day its teaching post remained in the hands of "eminent jurists and important scholars." A zāwiya endowed by Tāj al-Dīn Muḥammad b. Muḥammad b. ʿAlī Ibn Ḥannā, scion of a prominent bureaucratic family, supported courses led by two teachers, one in Mālikī and the other in Shāfiʿī jurisprudence. Again, however, al-Maqrīzī's account in the *Khiṭaṭ* is not exhaustive, since we know of other endowed zāwiyas supporting courses that he failed to mention.[14]

Possibly even more important, from the standpoint of education, were the large congregational mosques of Ibn Ṭūlūn, south and west of the Citadel, and of al-Ḥākim bi-Amr Allāh, just inside the northern gates of the walled city. Both of these mosques, originally constructed in the ninth and early eleventh centuries respectively, benefited from extensive renovations financed and supervised by important Mamluks—the former by Sultan Ḥusām al-Dīn Lājīn shortly after his accession to the throne in 1297, and the latter by the amir (later Sultan) Baybars al-Jāshnakīr following an earthquake in 1303. Sultan Lājīn, in restoring the derelict mosque of Ibn Ṭūlūn, provided salaries for professors and stipends for students in jurisprudence according to the four Sunni rites, as well as courses in ḥadīth, Quranic exegesis, and medicine. Ibn Ṭūlūn, as restored and endowed by Lājīn, became in fact one of the principal centers of higher education in Cairo; since the deed of endowment containing Lājīn's instructions survives, we shall have occasion to refer to it often.[15] Similarly,

[14] For example, the zāwiya al-Khashshābiyya, which in the late fourteenth century employed members of the famous al-Bulqīnī family of scholars; al-Maqrīzī, *al-Sulūk*, 3:814. On the zāwiyas in the mosque of ʿAmr, see al-Maqrīzī, *Khiṭaṭ*, 2:255–56.

[15] Lājīn's restoration work is described in some detail in al-Maqrīzī, *Khiṭaṭ*, 2:268; the deed of endowment will be discussed more thoroughly below; see *Waqfiyyat* Lājīn, Dār al-Wathā'iq No. 17, dated 21 Rabīʿ al-Thānī, A.H. 697 (February 1298). In 1365–66, Amir Yalbughā al-ʿUmarī al-Khāṣṣakī established another course for Ḥanafīs; al-Maqrīzī reports that it provided for "seven teachers [mudarrisīn] for Ḥanafīs," which is likely a mistake for "seven students." Al-Maqrīzī, *Khiṭaṭ*, 2:269.

Baybars al-Jāshnakīr spent more than 40,000 gold dīnārs in restoring al-Ḥākim's mosque, and in the process established in it professors of Shāfiʿī, Ḥanafī, Mālikī, and Ḥanbalī jurisprudence, and of ḥadīth, Quranic recitation, and Arabic grammar, as well as "a large number of students." Al-Ḥākim's mosque, as restored by Baybars al-Jāshnakīr, remained a major center of instruction and was the equal of any Mamluk madrasa: its first four professors of law were all prominent jurists, including the famous Shāfiʿī judge Badr al-Dīn Muḥammad Ibn Jamāʿa.[16]

Other, smaller congregational mosques benefited from restoration work undertaken by Mamluk amirs and sultans, and in the process became centers for higher religious and legal education. At the jāmiʿ al-Māridānī next to the Khaṭṭ al-Tibāna outside Bāb Zuwayla, the southern gates to the city, a mosque first built between 1337 and 1340, the powerful amir Ṣarghitmish (d. 1358) established a class in Ḥanafī jurisprudence before building his own important madrasa near the mosque of Ibn Ṭūlūn. At the institution known as the ribāṭ al-Āthār, a hospice and mosque housing certain relics of the Prophet that was originally established by the same Ibn Ḥannā who endowed a course in the mosque of ʿAmr, the sultan al-Ashraf Shaʿbān (reigned 1363–76) created "a class for Shāfiʿī jurists, and established in it a professor and a number of students." Both the Ḥanafī course at the al-Māridānī mosque and that in Shāfiʿī law at the ribāṭ al-Āthār operated throughout the fifteenth century, and their professorships were held at times by a number of prominent legal scholars.[17]

Other Mamluk-period institutions specifically and consistently called jāmiʿs housed endowed classes in jurisprudence from the moment of their foundation. These include the jāmiʿ al-Khaṭīrī in Būlāq (established ca. 1336–37), which in addition to a large library housed a course for Shāfiʿīs; the jāmiʿ al-Maghribī, not to be confused with a never-completed madrasa of the same name; the jāmiʿ of Āq Sunqur al-Salārī (d. 1343) near the Citadel; and that of Bahāʾ al-Dīn Aṣlam al-Silāḥdār (d. 1346).[18] The mosques of Sūdūn min Zāda (established 1402) and al-Shiblī

[16] Al-Maqrīzī, *Khiṭaṭ*, 2:278; Jalāl al-Dīn al-Suyūṭī, *Tārīkh al-khulafāʾ* (Cairo, 1976), 484; Carl Petry, *The Civilian Elite of Cairo in the Later Middle Ages* (Princeton, 1981), 333–34.

[17] On the al-Māridānī mosque itself, see al-Maqrīzī, *Khiṭaṭ*, 2:308. Al-Maqrīzī makes no mention of the institution's professorship; for that, see al-Sakhāwī, *al-Ḍawʾ*, 3:250, under the biography of Saʿd al-Dīn Ibn al-Dīrī, one of the scholars who held the post. Al-Sakhāwī does not specifically say it was a Ḥanafī professorship, but all those known to have held it were in fact Ḥanafīs, and of course Ṣarghitmish himself was a partisan of that rite. On the ribāṭ al-Athār, see al-Maqrīzī, *Khiṭaṭ*, 2:429.

[18] See al-Maqrīzī, *Khiṭaṭ*, 2:309–10, 312, 328. To these might be added the jāmiʿ of Uzbak al-Ẓāhirī, established at the end of the fifteenth century. Al-Sakhāwī states categorically that he provided for Sufis and "teachers" (*mudarrisīn*, or possibly "two teachers," *mudarrisayn*) as well as Quran readers and a library; al-Sakhāwī, *al-Ḍawʾ*, 2:272. The endowment

Kāfūr (1414) provided salaries and stipends for a number of teachers and students, and were sometimes known as madrasas; but their endowment deeds survive, and identify them, respectively, as a jāmiʿ and a masjid.

Institutional "types," therefore, can not fully delineate the boundaries of the world of higher education in late medieval Cairo. From an instructional or curricular viewpoint, there is nothing to distinguish these jāmiʿs and masjids from other institutions commonly called madrasas. The same subjects—principally jurisprudence according to one or more of the four rites of law, and occasionally the other religious sciences as well—were taught in the jāmiʿ of Ibn Ṭūlūn or the ribāṭ al-Athār as in madrasas, and by the same people. Shihāb al-Dīn Aḥmad b. Muḥammad, of the famous al-Bulqīnī family of scholars, held teaching posts in Shāfiʿī jurisprudence at the al-Maghribī mosque, that of Ibn Ṭūlūn, and at the ribāṭ al-Athār, but also at the Ḥijāziyya madrasa. Similarly, Badr al-Dīn Muḥammad Ibn Jamāʿa, the author of an important treatise concerning education, was professor at the mosque of al-Ḥākim, but also at such prestigious madrasas as the Ṣāliḥiyya in Bayn al-Qaṣrayn and the Nāṣiriyya (also known as the Ṣalāḥiyya) next to the tomb of the imām al-Shāfiʿī.[19] Madrasas and mosques drew their teaching talent from the same pool of scholars. There was, in fact, little to distinguish them.

Nothing in this is, or should be, surprising. For centuries before the advent of the madrasa, mosques were the only public venue for higher Islamic education. Scholars taught in them informally, gratis or in exchange for payments from their students, and no doubt continued to do so through the twelfth and thirteenth centuries, when institutions called madrasas began to be established in the Egyptian capital. In the Mamluk period, however, mosques came to resemble madrasas in that—through the munificence of the original builder or that of a later benefactor—they offered formal, endowed courses in the Islamic religious sciences.

But the two institutions drew closer still. A jāmiʿ was, literally, a "congregational mosque" in which the communal Friday prayers were said and a sermon was recited by a preacher. According to some legal opinions, Friday prayers should be held at only one location in each Muslim community. This principle had begun to break down well before the Mamluk period, but by the time al-Maqrīzī wrote his topographical and historical description of Cairo in the fifteenth century, the number of

deed for this institution survives, although I was unable to consult it; Doris Behrens-Abouseif, however, reports that while it mentions twenty Sufis and their shaykh, as well as a prayer leader (imām) and a preacher (khaṭīb), it makes no provisions for academic classes. Behrens-Abouseif, "Change," 91, and idem., *Azbakiyya and Its Environs from Azbak to Ismāʿīl, 1476–1879* (Cairo, 1985), 34.

[19] For Shihāb al-Dīn al-Bulqīnī, see al-Sakhāwī, *al-Ḍawʾ*, 2:119–20; for Badr al-Dīn Ibn Jamāʿa, see al-Maqrīzī, *Khiṭaṭ*, 2:278, and idem, *al-Sulūk*, 1:771, 798.

Cairene institutions at which Friday prayers were said had reached 130. Many of these were known as madrasas, and by the fifteenth century it had become a standard practice to provide for a preacher to deliver the Friday sermons in these schools.[20]

The process was a gradual one, but began early in the Mamluk period. The madrasa of Sultan Ḥasan, established in the middle of the fourteenth century, has been identified as "the first to be attached to a congregational mosque, i.e., the first to be a madrasa at the same time as a jāmiʿ."[21] In fact, however, given the essential similarity between institutions known as madrasas and certain teaching mosques, the educational function of the academic class and the exhortatory function of the sermon had been brought into close spatial proximity several decades before the construction of the Ḥasaniyya madrasa: at the congregational mosques of Ibn Ṭūlūn and al-Ḥākim, and at the smaller mosques of Āq Sunqur, Āl Malik, al-Khaṭīrī, and al-Māridānī. Moreover, other, older madrasas had in the interim become venues for the Friday prayers: in 1330, after the approval of the *qāḍīs* (judges) and the creation of a supplementary endowment to support a preacher, muezzins (*mu'adhdhins*) to deliver the call to prayer, and Quran readers, they were said in the Ṣāliḥiyya madrasa for the first time.[22] To be sure, there was resistance to this innovation. As late as 1373, when a pious amir wished to construct a pulpit (*minbar*) and provide for a preacher in the Manṣūriyya, a madrasa established in the late thirteenth century by Sultan al-Manṣūr Qalāwūn, one group of legal scholars successfully objected to the planned restoration on the grounds that one could see the minbar of the Ṣāliḥiyya from the door of Qalāwūn's school.[23] But the very fact that the objection was phrased on such narrow grounds indicates that already the functional fusion of madrasa and mosque was a fait accompli.

The blurring of the distinction between madrasa and mosque should remind us that the transmission of knowledge was, for medieval Muslims, first and foremost an act of piety. Study, like prayer, was an activity that could only be undertaken effectively in a state of ritual purity. Before attending a class, a scholar must "cleanse himself of ritual impurities and wickedness"; only in this way would he achieve "the glorification of

[20] Al-Maqrīzī, *Khiṭaṭ*, 2:244–45. Among the fifteenth-century madrasas that employed a khaṭīb were those of Sultan Barsbāy, Zayn al-Dīn al-Ustādār, Sultan Qaytbāy, Qānī Bāy Qarā, al-Sayfī Baybars, and Sultan al-Ghawrī. On the provision of Sufi convents with preachers for the Friday prayers, compare Muḥammad M. Amīn, *al-Awqāf wa'l-ḥayāt al-ijtimāʿiyya fī miṣr* (Cairo, 1980), 206, with Fernandes, *The Khanqah*, 95–96.

[21] Behrens-Abouseif, "Change," 78.

[22] Al-Maqrīzī, *al-Sulūk*, 2:317.

[23] Al-Maqrīzī, *al-Sulūk*, 3:206.

knowledge and the veneration of the holy law."[24] Physically, madrasas and mosques were often indistinguishable, and madrasas invariably included those architectural features commonly associated with private and public prayer. Indeed, when in the early sixteenth century a woman with the unusual name of Khadīja bint al-Dirham wa Niṣf decided to convert her house into a "madrasa," she added to it those architectural features necessary for the holding of private worship and congregational prayers: a prayer-niche, a minaret, and a pulpit.[25] She understood clearly what men and women of the post-Enlightenment world may easily forget: that education, and the very process of transmitting religious knowledge, was above all a way to worship God.

Sufi Convents as Centers of Education

In refurbishing her house for use as a madrasa, Khadīja added one other architectural feature besides those necessary for public prayer: cells for the residence and private worship of Sufis. The particular forms of worship associated with Sufi mystics, like the communal prayers and public sermons of Friday gatherings, were increasingly common features of educational institutions over the Mamluk period, a trend reflected in the gradual breakdown of any meaningful distinction between the terms madrasa and khānqāh. The Ashrafiyya, which Ibn Iyās had described as a madrasa "in" a khānqāh, is only the most glaring instance of the frequent inability of late medieval writers positively to identify particular institutions as belonging to one category or the other.

This is not to say that, in all cases, institutions called madrasas and khānqāhs were identical. Especially in the thirteenth and early fourteenth centuries, a khānqāh was primarily, if not exclusively, an institution providing accommodations, meals, and cash stipends to Sufi mystics to support their daily performance of ritual Sufi worship (*ḥuḍūr*): prayers, the unison chanting of portions of the Quran, and the recitation of mystical poems. The great khānqāh established by Saladin known as Saʿīd al-Suʿadāʾ, the large complex constructed by the order of Sultan al-Nāṣir Muḥammad at Siryāqūs north of Cairo, and that established in the heart of the city by al-Nāṣir's rival Baybars al-Jāshnakīr, for example, all fall into this category: built before the first quarter of the fourteenth century, they included no organized and endowed classes among their devotional activities.[26] Nor were these institutions ever known as madrasas. Simi-

[24] Badr al-Dīn Muḥammad Ibn Jamāʿa, *Tadhkirat al-sāmiʿ wa'l-mutakallim fī adab al-ʿālim wa'l-mutaʿallim* (Hyderabad, A.H. 1353), 30–31.

[25] Ibn Iyās, *Badāʾiʿ al-zuhūr*, 5:336.

[26] On these institutions and their activities, see Fernandes, *The Khanqah*, 16–32, 54–58. Baybars al-Jāshnakīr did stipulate that an instructor in ḥadīth be appointed to give classes

larly, early Mamluk madrasas such as those built by Sultans Baybars al-Bunduqdārī, al-Manṣūr Qalāwūn, and Qalāwūn's son al-Nāṣir Muḥammad were exclusively devoted to educational concerns, and made no provisions for Sufi exercises.

Such clear distinctions, of course, soon began to break down. Particular institutions, whether known as madrasas or khānqāhs, increasingly made provisions for the support of both formal instruction and Sufi worship.[27] An early example was the institution founded by Mughulṭāy al-Jamālī in the third decade of the fourteenth century. Clearly labeled a khānqāh in its deed of endowment, its principal beneficiaries were a shaykh and twenty Sufis who were also "students of the religious sciences," all of them specifically of the Ḥanafī school of law.[28] Increasingly over the years of Mamluk rule, institutions were established in which Sufi and student not only functioned side by side, but were in fact one and the same. An institution established in the middle of the fifteenth century by Zayn al-Dīn al-Ustādār, made provisions for twenty Sufis and their shaykh, with the stipulation that the Sufis were to receive instruction in Shāfiʿī jurisprudence.[29] The famous khānqāh of Jamal al-Dīn Yūsuf al-Ustādār, an early fifteenth-century establishment, provided a much greater array of courses—in jurisprudence according to all four of the Sunni rites, ḥadīth, exegesis, and the variant Quran readings—but again, almost all the students were required to be Sufis and the professor of Shāfiʿī law was responsible also for leading the Sufi devotional exercises.[30]

One measure of the change may be gleaned from a comparison of a series of royal institutions constructed over the course of the Mamluk period. Sultan al-Nāṣir Muḥammad, of course, in the early fourteenth century established two separate institutions, a madrasa in Bayn al-Qaṣrayn providing classes in all four rites of jurisprudence, and a khānqāh

in the *qubba* (the domed burial chamber) attached to his khānqāh, but there is no indication that this class necessarily involved any of the institution's Sufis. Al-Maqrīzī, *Khiṭaṭ*, 2:417.

[27] A phenomenon first noticed by Muḥammad Amīn; see his *al-Awqāf*, 238; cf. Fernandes, *The Khanqah*, passim, although the meaning of her comment that "it is not clear whether [the institution founded by Sanjar al-Jāwulī] was a khanqah-madrasa or a khanqah and a madrasa grouped in the same complex" is not entirely clear.

[28] *Waqfiyyat* Mughulṭāy al-Jamālī, Wizārat al-Awqāf, o.s. No. 1666, ll. 378–95; cf. Fernandes, *The Khanqah*, 34–35. Several other institutions dating to the early decades of the fourteenth century were clearly both madrasas and khānqāhs: for example, the Aqbughāwiyya, the Jāwuliyya, and the Mihmandāriyya; each is listed by al-Maqrīzī both in that section of his *Khiṭaṭ* dealing with madrasas and that dealing with khānqāhs.

[29] *Waqfiyyat* Zayn al-Dīn al-Ustādār, Dār al-Wathā'iq No. 110, ll. 1219–32, 1237–43.

[30] *Waqfiyyat* Jamāl al-Dīn Yūsuf al-Ustādār, Dār al-Wathā'iq No. 106, ll. 1–93; cf. Fernandes, *The Khanqah*, 38–39. From the terms of the endowment, it would appear that, for an unexplained reason, the students of Quranic exegesis were not required to be Sufis.

for Sufis outside of Cairo in Siryāqūs. By contrast, al-Ẓāhir Barqūq established only one institution, the Ẓāhiriyya, in 1386, and provided therein for sixty Sufis in addition to a large number of students of jurisprudence, ḥadīth, and the variant Quran readings. Slightly more than a generation later, the Ashrafiyya not only combined madrasa and khānqāh functions in the same institution, but, as we have seen, combined them in the same people: Sufis and students were identical, and the school's Ḥanafī professor was also the shaykh of the Sufis.[31]

But Sufism in the later Middle Ages was a diverse and polymorphic phenomenon. The formal institutional structure of khānqāhs could hardly contain the activity and energy of the growing numbers of men and women who identified themselves in some way as Sufis. Informal groups of Sufis and their shaykhs would often gather in institutions known as *zāwiyas*. The term "zāwiya" was especially flexible—it could mean, as we have seen, a particular corner of a large mosque, but it often referred to small mosques providing forums for the performance of popular Sufi worship and rituals. Al-Maqrīzī's description of the zāwiyas of Cairo in the early fifteenth century makes it clear that the zāwiyas themselves by no means conformed to a single pattern: some were specially endowed, some were not; some were established by Mamluk sultans or amirs, some by the shaykhs who presided over them; some housed mostly Sufis from foreign lands, some attracted principally local Muslims. Consequently, we would do well not to insist that the zāwiya was a distinct *type* of institution, but rather to see it as one end of a continuous institutional spectrum that included khānqāhs, madrasas, and mosques. Some housed men revered by the masses for the outrageousness of their religious practices, but the shaykhs of others were pious, sober, and learned men. The term "shaykh" of course meant teacher as well as Sufi master, and the shaykhs of the zāwiyas listed by al-Maqrīzī sometimes taught ḥadīth, jurisprudence, and other subjects in those very institutions. A zāwiya might even provide stipends for students of the religious sciences, much as did more formal institutions such as madrasas and khānqāhs. Through institutions known as zāwiyas, education and the transmission of knowledge reached ever deeper into the Muslim population of Cairo.[32]

[31] On al-Nāṣir Muḥammad's madrasa, see al-Maqrīzī, *Khiṭaṭ*, 2:382, and the summary of the institution's endowment deed from al-Nuwayrī's *Nihāyat al-arab fī funūn al-adab*, published as an appendix to al-Maqrīzī, *al-Sulūk*, 1:1041ff; on his khānqāh, see al-Maqrīzī, *Khiṭaṭ*, 2:422–23, and Fernandes, *The Khanqah*, 29–32. On the Ẓāhiriyya, see *Waqfiyyat* al-Ẓāhir Barqūq, Dār al-Wathā'iq No. 51; on the Ashrafiyya, see *Waqfiyyat* al-Ashraf Barsbāy, Dār al-Wathā'iq No. 173.

[32] On the zāwiya, see al-Maqrīzī, *Khiṭaṭ*, 2:430–36; Leonor Fernandes, "Some Aspects of the *Zāwiya* in Egypt at the Eve of the Ottoman Conquest," *Annales islamologiques* 19 (1983), 9–17. The zāwiya of Zayn al-Dīn Ṣidqa provided stipends for four Shāfi'ī students;

The gradual blending of educational and Sufi activities in the same institutions reflected a deeper transformation, the social and intellectual assimilation of Sufis and Sufism into the mainstream of Muslim intellectual life.[33] Although the establishment of endowed institutions—khānqāhs—may have relieved the initial suspicion of some elements of the educated elite regarding the orthodoxy of Sufism and its adherents, the unease felt by men such as the strict Ḥanbalī jurist Ibn Taymiyya lingered well into the Mamluk period. Tāj al-Dīn al-Subkī, himself a scholar and judge of the Shāfiʿī rite, writing in the fourteenth century, still found room to criticize those who "mock the Sufis and who do not believe in them."[34] But the growing respectability of Sufism proved irresistible. Even Ibn Taymiyya, for all the scorn he poured onto certain excesses of mystical enthusiasm, was himself a member of a Sufi order. In the course of the fifteenth century, most institutions of higher learning established in Cairo made provisions for their students and teachers to perform Sufi rites as well as carry out their lessons in legal or traditional subjects.

But the rapprochement between madrasa and Sufi convent, or more precisely between their educational and devotional functions, may also have reflected a fundamental similarity between the mystical and intellectual approaches to religious texts. Consider, for example, the striking description of the class in Ḥanafī law in the endowment deed of the convent of Mughulṭāy al-Jamālī, and the way in which it was to blend naturally and almost imperceptibly into the devotional exercises that preceded it. The shaykh was

> to gather with the Sufi students [*al-fuqarā'*] each day in the *qiblī īwān* [the covered hall, facing the direction of Mecca] of this khānqāh, in the middle of which is the prayer-niche, after morning prayers, and distribute pages from the holy book to them. They are to read from it, and to pray after their reading for the founder [of the khānqāh] and for Muslims [generally], and [then the shaykh] is to recite to them a lesson from the holy sciences . . . ,

and this, the deed noted, "according to the custom of madrasas."[35] The *ḥuḍūr*, the Sufi group exercises, were constructed around the audible "pronunciation" or "remembering" (*dhikr*) of texts—the Quran, ḥadīth, mystical and devotional poems—whether by individuals or by the group. Formal lessons in one of the religious sciences, of course, often focused

---

Waqfiyyat Zayn al-Dīn Ṣidqa, Dār al-Wathā'iq No. 59, the third document on the scroll, dated 25 Rabīʿ al-Awwal, A.H. 807, beginning in the margin.

[33] On this subject generally, see Fernandes, *The Khanqah*, 33ff, 97–108.

[34] Tāj al-Dīn ʿAbd al-Wahhāb al-Subkī, *Muʿīd al-niʿam wa-mubīd al-niqam*, ed. David Myhrman (London, 1908), 124.

[35] *Waqfiyyat* Mughulṭāy al-Jamālī, Wizārat al-Awqāf o.s. No. 1666, ll. 381–89.

on other texts—works of exegesis, legal commentaries—but there, too, the oral element was, as we have seen, paramount: instruction and learning required the actual pronunication of texts and their committal to memory. Lessons, not altogether unlike Sufi ritual, provided an opportunity to worship God, and so routinely began with prayers for the Prophet and others, and with group readings of portions of the Quran. In this the prescriptive deeds of endowment reflected carefully the guidelines established by Ibn Jamāʿa, who wrote a long treatise outlining the forms and processes of education.[36] But increasingly, it was stipulated that the students and their teacher begin by chanting particular *ṣūras* (chapters) of the Quran frequently associated with worship in the Sufi convents.[37] Ibn Jamāʿa may have revealed more than he intended when he urged students, when preparing their teacher's prayer carpet, to fold back its left rear edge "in the manner of the Sufis."[38]

The Organization of Schools of Higher Education

Instruction in the religious sciences and the transmission of knowledge was thus not limited to institutions known as madrasas, nor did it occur in isolation from other religious activities. Indeed, the institutional structure of higher education was extraordinarily diverse, its lack of uniformity brought on by several factors. In the first place, of course, it resulted from the complete absence of any overarching state or ecclesiastical authority responsible for shaping Islamic education, or indeed any aspect of Islamic religious culture. Norms might be established, in practice as in belief, by consensus within the Muslim community. After the death of the Prophet, however, Islamic law, custom, and doctrine grew and developed without either the practical advantages or potential liabilities of a central authority, personal or institutional, capable of imposing definitive rules to guide either the thoughts or practice of individual Muslims. Secondly, and more instrumentally, the Islamic law of charitable endowments (*waqf*, pl. *awqāf*) allowed individual benefactors to fashion schools

[36] Ibn Jamāʿa, *Tadhkirat al-sāmiʿ*, 34–35. See, for example, the following deeds of endowment: *Waqfiyyat* Ṣarghitmish, Wizārat al-Awqāf o.s. No. 3195, p. 26, published by ʿAbd al-Laṭīf Ibrāhīm ʿAlī, "Naṣṣān jadīrān min wathīqat al-amīr Ṣarghitmish," *Jāmiʿat al-qāhira. Majallat kulliyat al-ādāb* 27 (1965), 147; *Waqfiyyat* Qalamṭāy, Dār al-Wathāʾiq No. 68, ll. 247–50; *Waqfiyyat* Sūdūn min Zāda, Dār al-Wathāʾiq No. 58, ll. 244–59.

[37] The chapters were al-Ikhlāṣ, al-Falaq, and al-Nās (known collectively as al-Muʿawwidhatān), and the beginning of al-Baqara. See, for example, *Waqfiyyat* Zayn al-Dīn Ṣidqa, Dār al-Wathāʾiq No. 59, ll. 77–86, and *Waqfiyyat* Khushqadam al-Zimam, Wizārat al-Awqāf n.s. No. 188, ll. 49–57. Cf. Fernandes, *The Khanqah*, 57.

[38] Ibn Jamāʿa, *Tadhkirat al-sāmiʿ*, 109.

according to their preferences or means.[39] Since there was no church responsible for supporting education or building the institutions in which it transpired, the Mamluk period saw, in the words of one scholar, a "broadening of the base of architectural patronage." Educational and religious institutions were established not by the state, but by individuals—Mamluks, merchants, bureaucrats, or scholars—who paid for their construction and created endowments to meet the salaries of their beneficiaries and provide for their maintenance.[40]

The Mamluk elite, possessing as it did enormous resources of wealth and significant sources of income, undertook the construction and endowment of the lion's share of religious and educational institutions. At least twenty-two Mamluk-period institutions of higher learning owed their existence to the munificence of sultans or their families, including those older mosques restored and provided with lessons. The first Mamluk sultan, al-Muʿizz Aybak, established in al-Fusṭāṭ a madrasa about which little is known.[41] It was al-Ẓāhir Baybars, however, who ascended the throne in 1260, who established a pattern emulated by later sultans by building an imposing madrasa in the main street of Cairo, Bayn al-Qaṣrayn. Because its deed of endowment has not survived we do not know the number of teachers, students, and other stipendiaries provided for in this institution; clearly, however, the Ẓāhiriyya was a significant institution, with endowed courses in jurisprudence according to the Shāfiʿī and Ḥanafī rites, ḥadīth, and the science of reciting the seven variant Quran readings (*qirā'āt*).[42] Until the fall of Cairo to the Ottomans in 1517, most important Mamluk sultans—including al-Manṣūr Qalāwūn (d. 1290), his son al-Nāṣir Muḥammad (d. 1340) and grandson al-Nāṣir al-Ḥasan (d. 1361), al-Ẓāhir Barqūq (d. 1399), al-Mu'ayyad Shaykh (d. 1421), and al-Ashraf Qānṣūh al-Ghawrī (d. 1516)—continued to build and endow major establishments of religious education.

In physical size and in the breadth of the activities they supported,

[39] Makdisi, *Colleges*, 35–74.

[40] The phrase is from Oleg Grabar, "The Architecture of the Middle Eastern City from Past to Present: The Case of the Mosque," in *Middle Eastern Cities*, ed. Ira M. Lapidus (Berkeley, 1969), 39. R. S. Humphreys, "The Expressive Intent of Mamluk Architecture in Cairo," *Studia Islamica* 35 (1972), 92, suggested that the sultan as benefactor and founder (*wāqif*) can be seen, not as a representative of governmental authority, but simply as the richest and most powerful patron.

[41] Ibn Duqmāq, *al-Intiṣār*, 1:92–93; al-Maqrīzī, *Khiṭaṭ*, 1:345, 346, 347.

[42] Al-Maqrīzī, *Khiṭaṭ*, 2:378–79. Note that al-Qalqashandī, in his administrative manual *Ṣubḥ al-aʿshā*, states that classes were provided for students in all four Sunni schools of law. Aḥmad b. ʿAlī al-Qalqashandī, *Ṣubḥ al-aʿshā fī ṣināʿat al-inshā'* (Cairo, 1914–28), 3:364. Another madrasa called "al-Ẓāhiriyya" was constructed in Damascus on behalf of Baybars and as his tomb; see Gary Leiser, "The Endowment of the al-Zahiriyya in Damascus," *Journal of the Economic and Social History of the Orient* 27 (1983), 33–55.

these royal institutions generally dwarfed all others. Certainly al-Ḥasan's was the largest, providing within its immense physical structure endowed professorships in a variety of religious and legal subjects, as well as scholarships for 506 students, not to mention support for a wide variety of greater and lesser religious functionaries. Yet it was not wholly atypical of these royal institutions. Sultan Lājīn, for instance, established in the restored mosque of Ibn Ṭūlūn endowed professorships in the four rites of law, exegesis, ḥadīth, and even medicine, and provided stipends for a total of 150 students. The madrasas or teaching mosques of al-Nāṣir Muḥammad, al-Ẓāhir Barqūq, al-Mu'ayyad Shaykh, and al-Ashraf Barsbāy all boasted endowed courses in Shāfiʿī, Ḥanafī, Mālikī, and Ḥanbalī jurisprudence, to which Barqūq's and al-Mu'ayyad Shaykh's added courses in ḥadīth and the variant Quran readings, the latter offering a class in exegesis as well.

But sultans and their families by no means established all, or even most of the schools built in Cairo between 1250 and 1517. From the origin of the Mamluk sultanate to its fall, more than sixty institutions of learning (or endowments providing for classes in previously established institutions) have been identified that owe their creation to Mamluk amirs, army officers, and government officials who were not themselves sultans, or to members of their immediate families.[43] These amiral institutions included a number of important centers of religious learning, such as the Mankūtimuriyya, Ṣarghitmishiyya, and Aqbughāwiyya madrasas, the Shaykhūniyya khānqāh, and the mosque of Sūdūn min Zāda. Another fifty or more were founded by non-Mamluk government bureaucrats and administrators, scholars, doctors, or merchants. Most of these institutions were smaller, less prestigious, and less well-endowed than those built by Mamluks, although there were exceptions, such as the great khānqāh of Jamāl al-Dīn al-Ustādār, one of the leading civilian bureaucrats of the early fifteenth century.

The schools established by such men (and several women) were multifaceted institutions: educational forums, centers of public worship, tombs for their founders, and often wealthy establishments providing housing, food, and cash stipends for large numbers of teachers and pupils. But although instruction may have been their principal function, teachers and students made up only a fraction, albeit a large one, of the community of individuals they employed. At the huge teaching mosque established by Sultan al-Mu'ayyad Shaykh in the early fifteenth century

[43] Compare the figures compiled for all religious institutions in Damascus during the Mamluk period by Ira Lapidus, *Muslim Cities in the Later Middle Ages* (Cambridge, Mass., 1967), 73. Not surprisingly, royal institutions accounted for a greater percentage of the total in Cairo; but in both metropolises, the total contribution of the Mamluks (both sultans and amirs) was paramount.

just inside Bāb Zuwayla, for example, teachers and students constituted just under half of the institution's four hundred stipendiaries. Not all Cairene schools were so large, even those established by sultans, but they all provided employment for large numbers of men in educational, religious, administrative, and support positions.

In particular, it is important to recall that virtually every school was also a center of worship. Consequently, schools of higher education provided for a host of religious functionaries of varying degrees of importance, among them, very often, a preacher to deliver a sermon on Fridays. Almost every institution included among its stipendiaries a prayer leader as well as a number of muezzins to summon the faithful to prayer. Frequently the schools' founders felt strongly enough to require that the imām, although serving a diverse community, belong to a particular rite: occasionally the Shāfiʿī, as at the mosque of Ibn Ṭūlūn; more commonly the Ḥanafī, as at the madrasas of Ṣarghitmish and Barqūq and the mosque of Barsbāy. An exceptionally large institution might require the services of several imāms—the mosque of al-Mu'ayyad Shaykh employed four, one for each rite—while complexes that included domed chambers (*qubbas*) for the burial of the founder and his family often provided that space with a separate prayer leader. The presence of an imām and preachers helped to transform the school into a center of prayer and worship for the broader Muslim community, since Muslims other than those receiving stipends from the institution's endowments came to the schools to pray and to hear the Friday sermon.

Indeed, great attention was paid to the spiritual as well as intellectual needs of an institution's stipendiaries and others who frequented it. Founders provided for virtually every aspect of corporate religious life, in particular the public recitation of the Quran, ḥadīth, and other pious works. The mosque of Barsbāy in Bayn al-Qaṣrayn was by no means unusual in supporting fifteen Quran readers, organized into five groups (*jawqāt*) to read from the holy book after each of the five daily prayers, and to pray for Muḥammad, and then for the founder and his family. Especially where the complex included a burial chamber for the interment of the founder and members of his family, the public recitation of the Quran took on a special significance, as at the madrasa of the amir Ṣarghitmish. There, under the dome covering the burial spot of the madrasa's founder, forty-eight men (*muqri'ūn*) read continually from the Quran, day and night, in groups of four. Recitation of the Quran and communal acts of worship provided one of the links that bound schools to the urban community around them. At the khānqāh of Jamāl al-Dīn al-Ustādār, twelve *qurrā' shubbāk* were hired to read portions of the Quran from the window in the eastern wall overlooking the street outside so that the recitation might be heard by passersby, and "refresh whoever hears it, and soften his heart."[44] At the mosque of Sultan al-Mu'ayyad Shaykh, a total of fifty-seven readers were hired to recite passages from the Quran and pray for the Prophet, the sultan and his descendants, and for Muslims generally, twenty-four hours a day.

But institutions of the size and complexity of many of these schools required a considerable support staff as well. Some held jobs that directly supported educational and devotional pursuits. Any school that housed a library, for example, had to provide for a librarian (*khāzin al-kutub*) to supervise the distribution of books and ensure that they were safely returned. Larger schools, such as the madrasa of Sultan al-Ghawrī, housed extensive collections in books of "Quranic exegesis, ḥadīth, jurisprudence, language, rhetoric, the roots of jurisprudence and religion, logic, and other [sciences] such as grammar and morphology and others."[45] The duties of others, though of importance to the schools' religious functions, were more menial. Virtually all schools hired at least one, and often several *waqqāds*, men in charge of cleaning, lighting, and extinguishing the lamps and candles in the building and on its minaret. A few late Mamluk schools in which Friday services were held also hired a *mubakhkhir* to burn incense. An important figure in every school was the gatekeeper (*bawwāb*), whose job it was to "prevent the entry of suspicious and iniquitous men."[46] His duties may have included a general supervision over at least the younger students, since endowment deeds sometimes required the gatekeeper to be "chaste" (*dhū ʿiffa*), a requirement made explicitly of no other stipendiary except the primary school instructor (*mu'addib*).[47] Other employees undertook the supervision and maintenance of the institution's physical plant: a *farrāsh* to handle a variety of tasks, a *kannās* to sweep the floors, even a *rashshāsh* to sprinkle water on the street in front of the building to keep down the dust. An exceptionally large institution such as al-Mu'ayyad Shaykh's might even provide employment for a doctor (*ṭabīb*) and eye specialist (*kaḥḥāl*), and for men to maintain the building itself (e.g., its marble and plumbing).

In a second category were those who administered the properties forming the endowment that supported the complex and who distributed its income. General supervision of the institution was of course in the hands of the general financial and administrative controller, the *nāẓir*. Supporting his work, at least in those large institutions the supervision of whose properties required considerable attention, was an array of administrative officials. Consider, for example, the mosque of Sultan Barsbāy.

[44] *Waqfiyyat* Jamāl al-Dīn al-Ustādār, Dār al-Wathā'iq, No. 106, ll. 181–91.

[45] *Waqfiyyat* Qānṣūh al-Ghawrī, Wizārat al-Awqāf o.s. No. 882, p. 188. For "rhetoric," the text includes the Arabic terms *maʿāni*, *bayyān*, and *badīʿ*.

[46] *Waqfiyyat* al-Ẓāhir Barqūq, Dār al-Wathā'iq No. 51, ll. 884–85.

[47] See, for example, *Waqfiyyat* Jamāl al-Dīn al-Ustādār, Dār al-Wathā'iq No. 106, l. 158.

There, at least nine men assisted the controller in his administrative duties. A collector (*jābī*) and his assistant (*shādd*) supervised "the extraction of the income of the endowed [property], and its disbursement." A separate administrative officer (*ʿāmil*) kept the accounts; two notaries (*shāhids*), executors of minor legal affairs, were hired to distribute stipends to the endowment's beneficiaries; a *bardadār* acted as an all-around assistant to the administrative staff; and another official held *waẓīfat tawqīʿ al-awqāf*, to secure from the qāḍīs periodic confirmations of the endowment's permanence and legal execution (*al-thubūt wa'l-tanfīdh*). In addition, a separate controller and jābī supervised the endowment's extensive Syrian properties.[48]

The administrative apparatus at a school such as Barsbāy's did more, however, than provide remunerative employment for numerous bureaucrats; it helped to safeguard the substantial investment that a founder made in establishing his school, and to ensure the proper performance of its educational and devotional tasks. Elaborate instructions were accordingly drawn up to regulate appointment to the powerful position of controller. Most often, the deeds of endowment stipulated that the founder himself was to hold the controllership (*naẓar*) while he lived, although he had the right to assign its duties to one of his choosing. After his death, control of the school was generally left in the hands of his children and descendants, often in conjunction with certain powerful political, military, or religious officials who were associated with the institution in order to discourage tampering with or confiscation of its endowments.[49] Thus, for example, the controllership of the mosque of al-Mu'ayyad Shaykh was to devolve, after his death, to "the most rightly guided" (*al-arshad*) of his male descendants, who was to be assisted by a powerful amir and a high-ranking government bureaucrat.[50] Other endowments made similar provisions. The deed of endowment of the madrasa of Sultan Barqūq, established toward the end of the fourteenth century, set out complicated but precise stipulations regarding its controllership. Its terms may offer a clearer insight into the unstated objectives of the founders in assigning control of their institutions to one group of individuals or another. The founder himself was to administer the endowments for

[48] *Waqfiyyat* al-Ashraf Barsbāy, Dār al-Wathā'iq No. 173, fol. 126a–131b. On the work of the controller and his assistants, see Amīn, *al-Awqāf*, 303–20, and Fernandes, *The Khanqah*, 60–64.

[49] Amīn, *al-Awqāf*, 117–18.

[50] *Waqfiyyat* al-Mu'ayyad Shaykh, Wizārat al-Awqāf o.s. No. 938. The two officers to be appointed to assist in the controllership were the *kātib al-sirr* and the *dawādār kabīr*, in the later Mamluk period one of the highest offices to which a Mamluk amir could aspire. On the office of the dawādār, see David Ayalon, "Studies on the Structure of the Mamluk Army—III," *Bulletin of the School of Oriental and African Studies* 16 (1954), 62–63.

the duration of his life, allowing him to keep a watchful eye on his most significant charitable endeavor. After his death, his children—more precisely, the "most rightly guided" of his male children and descendants—were to undertake the supervision of the school and its endowments in return for a monthly payment of 430 dirhams. Should they for any reason no longer be able or competent to hold the post, it became the joint responsibility of three men. The first was to be a powerful Mamluk official, whose participation was secured by a payment of 300 dirhams per month, although of that sum he was to pay "whatever [amount] he thinks proper" to a prominent and reputable Ḥanafī scholar to assist him, or substitute for him in his duties.[51] Both the secretary of the chancellery (*kātib al-sirr*), a prominent government official and advisor to the sultan, often appointed from among the learned elite, and the institution's own Ḥanafī shaykh were to share in the controllership in association with the amir, in exchange for payments of one hundred dirhams and thirty dirhams respectively.[52] The overriding concern in this case, as in others, seems to have been to associate with the administration of the school some combination of powerful men who might, in times of need, rise to the institution's defense, plus those who by virtue of their training and office might be relied upon to understand and respond to the institution's educational and religious needs.

The Range of Institutional Size and Academic Program

Those who founded institutions of higher education, such as the sultans Barqūq and al-Mu'ayyad Shaykh, wisely devoted careful attention to the appointment of men to supervise the administration and financial opera-

[51] The amir to be chosen was to be in one of three powerful political positions: either the dawādār, or the *ḥājib kabīr*, the amir responsible for justice among the Mamluks, or the *ra's nawbat al-umarā' al-jamdāriyya*. It is difficult to know exactly which office this last phrase refers to, unless it is the *ra's nawbat al-umarā'* mentioned by Ayalon, "Studies—III," 60, 70. Presumably his responsibilities involved in some way the supervision of the royal Mamluks; certainly the position was one of authority and power.

[52] *Waqfiyyat* al-Ẓāhir Barqūq, Dār al-Wathā'iq No. 51, ll. 1066ff. Should the participation of the amir become impossible, "for any legal reason," the kātib al-sirr and the Ḥanafī shaykh were to hold the controllership themselves, in conjunction with one of the founder's *'utaqā'* (freed slaves), should any be available and suitable. A later document, however, the last in a series on the verso side of the scroll and which has no date, but immediately follows one dated 3 Sha'bān, A.H. 797, made two amendments to these terms. First, it rescinded the preliminary interest of the founder's children and descendants in the controllership, and vested it directly in the "committee of three." Second, it altered the list of Mamluk amirs from among whom the principal controller was to be drawn, adding to it the *āmīr ākhūr* (the superviser of the royal stables) and the *amīr majlis* (who guarded and arranged the sultan's audiences), a political office of increasing importance from the reign of Barqūq. On the amīr akhūr and the amīr majlis, see Ayalon, "Studies—III," 59, 63, 69.

tion of their endowments. Founding any school required a substantial outlay of funds, although only sultans and the very rich commanded the resources necessary to finance the construction and endowment of the large schools so frequently mentioned in the chronicles and biographical dictionaries. So much might be expected. What the surviving deeds of endowment reveal, however, is the extraordinary range of different types of institutions. Schools differed significantly from each other, not on the basis of the terminology by which they were known, but according to their physical size, the strength and income of the endowments that financed them, and more importantly the number of professors and students and the breadth of the activities they supported.

The imposing facade of the school of Sultan Ḥasan, established in the second half of the fourteenth century, dominates the Cairene neighborhood south and west of the Citadel in which it sits.[53] Even in the Middle Ages it was recognized as the city's "greatest madrasa," as al-Qalqashandī put it.[54] The madrasa complex (see Figure 1) consists of a large inner courtyard (A) surrounded by four covered *īwāns* (B, C, D, and E), halls or recessed chambers, each of which was assigned to the professor and students of a particular rite for holding their classes. Here the Shāfiʿī rite held pride of place, and its professor and his students claimed the privilege of occupying the *qiblī* īwān, the largest of the four recessed halls and that facing the direction of Mecca. Each of the tall, multistoried edifices between the īwāns (F, G, H, and J) formed separate madrasas set aside for the Shāfiʿī, Ḥanafī, Mālikī, and Ḥanbalī students supported by the institution's endowments. Each distinct madrasa contained a small mosque (masjid) for the use of the students, and a myriad of private cells for their residence. Behind the qiblī īwān was a spacious domed tomb chamber (K) intended for the burial of Sultan Ḥasan and his children and descendants.

As the building dominated its surroundings, so the school must have loomed large in the minds of medieval Cairene students and educators. The scope of the religious and academic activities it supported dwarfed that of all other schools. Of its 506 students, 400 studied law according to one of the four rites. But the school also supported separate courses in Quranic exegesis, ḥadīth, the variant Quran readings, the foundations of

[53] The following information is drawn from the institution's deed of endowment, *Waqfiyyat* al-Nāṣir Ḥasan, Dār al-Wathā'iq No. 40 and Wizārat al-Awqāf o.s. No. 881, published by Muḥammad M. Amīn in Ibn Ḥabīb, *Tadhkirat al-nabīh*, 3:339–449. Architectural descriptions of the building can be found in the report of the Comité de Conservation des Monuments de l'Art Arabe, *Rapport de la deuxième commission. Exercice 1893*, 10:104–9, in Louis Hautecoeur and Gaston Wiet, *Les mosquées du Caire* (Paris, 1932), vol. 1, and Osman Rostem, *The Architecture of the Mosque of Sultan Hasan* (Beirut, 1970).

[54] Al-Qalqashandī, *Ṣubḥ al-aʿshā*, 3:363.

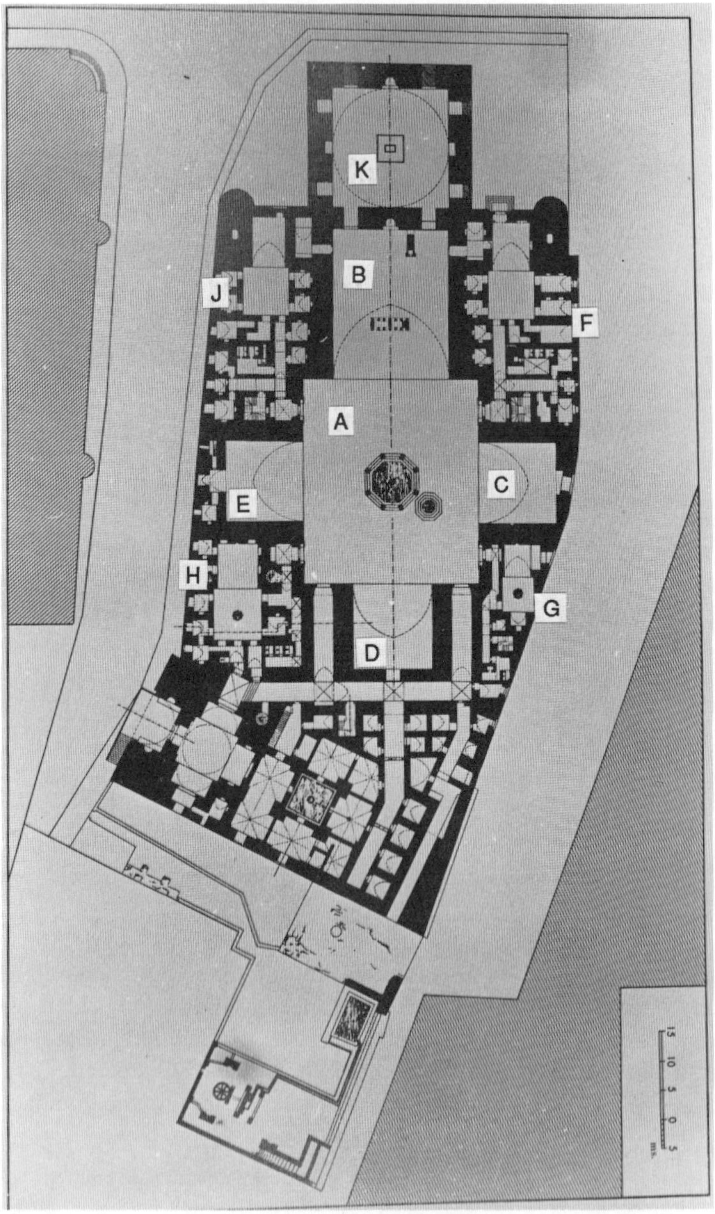

Figure 1. The madrasa of Sultan Ḥasan, ground plan (from a drawing by Max Herz)

jurisprudence, the Arabic language, medicine, and even—it was a small class, with only six students—the science of determining the times of prayer. Its formal academic program was supplemented by a full range of religious and devotional activities. Individual imāms led prayers in the main sanctuary, in the tomb chamber, and in the smaller mosques attached to each separate madrasa. A preacher delivered the Friday sermon to the assembled congregation from the *minbar* (pulpit) at the back of the qiblī īwān. And no fewer than 120 Quran readers kept up a constant recitation of the Muslim holy book.

Impressive as it was, the madrasa of Sultan Ḥasan corresponded in its essentials to a group of large and prominent schools. These schools at the top of the educational pyramid of the Mamluk period typically provided endowed stipends for professors to lead courses in jurisprudence according to all four rites, stressing thereby the supremacy of the study of the holy law. The other religious sciences were not forgotten, however, and larger schools often boasted separate courses in subjects such as Quranic exegesis, ḥadīth, and the variant Quran readings as well. While none were as large as that of Sultan Ḥasan, several institutions supported sizeable populations of students: 145 at the madrasa of Sultan Barqūq, and 175 at the mosques of al-Muʾayyad Shaykh and (as renovated by Sultan Lājīn) Ibn Ṭūlūn.[55]

Naturally, larger institutions required more substantial endowments to fund their diverse programs. A full analysis of the financial assets and economic impact of the endowed madrasas, teaching mosques, and khānqāhs of Mamluk Cairo lies beyond the scope of this work, but it may be useful to convey some sense of the size of their incomes and expenditures. Among larger schools, total monthly expenses ranged from 6,500 dirhams at the madrasa of Sultan Barqūq, established at the end of the fourteenth century, to 46,000 at the Ḥasaniyya, built and endowed several decades earlier.[56] Consequently, most of these larger institutions were established by sultans, including: al-Manṣūr Qalāwūn (reigned

[55] In addition to the institutions mentioned in the text, the larger schools included the Nāṣiriyya of Sultan al-Nāṣir Muḥammad, the madrasa of al-Fakhr ʿAbd al-Ghanī, the mosque of al-Ashraf Barsbāy, and the khānqāh of Jamāl al-Dīn al-Ustādār. These schools are by no means the only examples that might be mentioned. They are meant rather as models, chosen in large part simply because their deeds of endowment survive, so that we possess considerably more detailed information on their internal constitutional arrangements than for other institutions.

[56] These sums refer only to the monthly stipends paid to the endowment's beneficiaries; they do not, therefore, take into account various daily, monthly, seasonal, and annual expenses (not always delineated precisely) for clothing, water, oil, candles, soap, bread, sweets, and sacrifices for the Islamic holidays provided to some or all of the *arbāb al-waẓāʾif* (the institution's employees and students), let alone the original costs of constructing the buildings.

1280–90), founder of an important madrasa-hospital complex on Bayn al-Qaṣrayn in the heart of the city; al-Manṣūr Lājīn (1297–99), who restored the mosque of Ibn Ṭūlūn; al-Nāṣir Muḥammad (reigned intermittently between 1294 and 1340), whose madrasa dates to the early years of the fourteenth century; al-Mu'ayyad Shaykh (1412–21), who constructed a teaching mosque in 1420; and al-Ashraf Barsbāy (1422–37), whose mosque in Bayn al-Qaṣrayn was established in 1424. Occasionally, however, other individuals acquired the means necessary to endow a substantial institution, such as the Jamāliyya khānqāh, built in the early fifteenth century by Jamāl al-Dīn al-Ustādār, a wealthy bureaucrat who, according to the chroniclers, grew so powerful that he lacked only the title of sultan.[57]

Nonetheless, the importance of large institutions in the history of education in late medieval Cairo should not obscure the fact that many smaller schools also existed and flourished during the two and a half centuries of Mamluk rule. In many respects these schools resembled their larger cousins: both, for example, routinely included tombs for the burial of their founders and their descendants. Yet in other characteristics they differed from the schools we have, until now, been reviewing. The number and structure of the classes these institutions provided, and by extension their role in the broader system of education, sometimes suggest that, in certain cases, the quality of the instruction they supported was inferior to that in the larger schools.

In an intermediary category fall a number of institutions that, although perhaps devoted to scholars of a particular rite, still provided prestigious teaching posts and supported a large number of students. Among them was the madrasa or mosque of the amir Sūdūn min Zāda,[58] located on a street leading from the square in front of the Ḥasaniyya to Bāb Zuwayla, the southern gate of the city of Cairo (see Figure 2).[59] Architecturally, this institution, built around an open central courtyard (A) somewhat smaller than that at the Ḥasaniyya, and lacking the tall recessed īwāns of the latter, was clearly a jāmiʿ, a congregational mosque. A miḥrāb, the prayer-niche indicating the direction of Mecca (B), was constructed in the

[57] Al-Maqrīzī, *al-Sulūk*, 4:129.

[58] The deed of endowment refers to the institution as a jāmiʿ, but contemporary historians routinely called it a madrasa. See, for example, al-Sakhāwī, *al-Ḍaw'*, 1:150, 3:96, 4:233, 6:302, and Ibn Iyās, *Badā'iʿ al-zuhūr*, 2:47, 5:297.

[59] Information concerning this mosque is taken from its deed of endowment, *Waqfiyyat* Sūdūn min Zāda, Dār al-Wathā'iq No. 58. Little remains of the mosque today. In the late nineteenth century, the Comité de Conservation des Monuments de l'Art Arabe recorded its plan (see Figure 2); see its report in *Rapport de la deuxième commission. Exercice 1903*, vol. 20. See also Ḥusnī Nuwayṣar's architectural reconstruction of the mosque, based largely on its waqfiyya, *Madrasa jarkasiyya ʿalā namaṭ al-masājid al-jāmiʿa: Madrasat al-amīr sūdūn min zāda bi-sūq al-silāḥ* (Cairo, 1985).

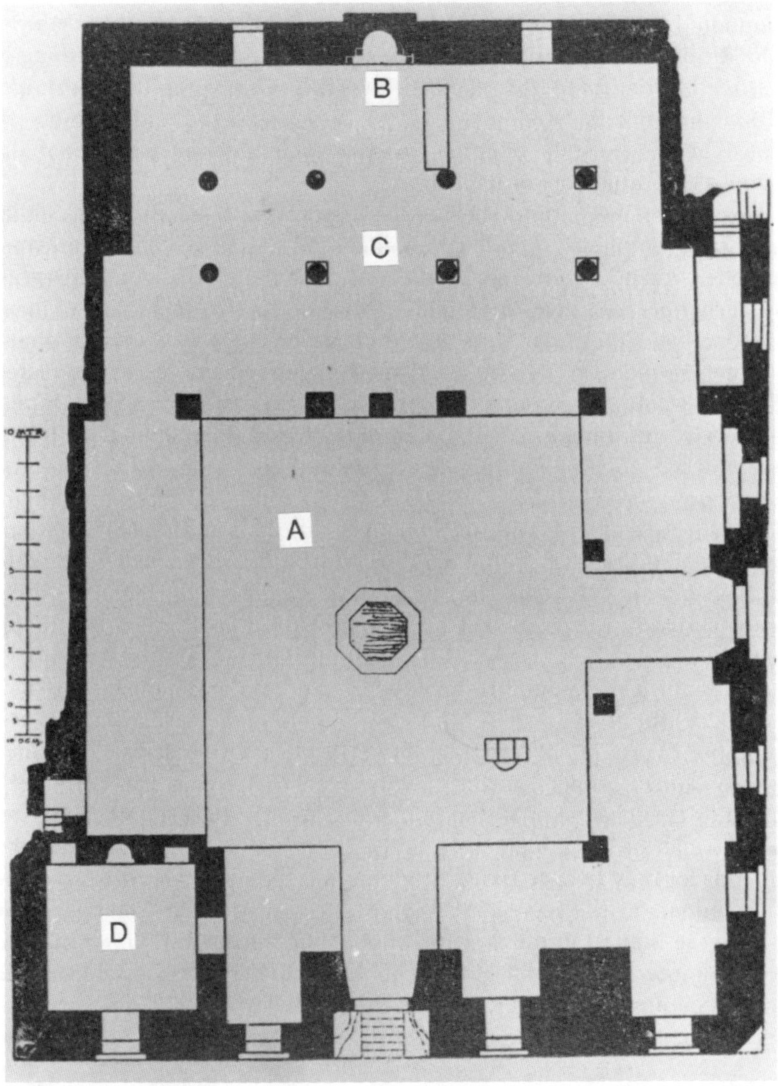

Figure 2. The mosque of Sūdūn min Zāda, ground plan (from Louis Hautecoeur and Gaston Wiet, *Les mosquées du Caire*, Fig. 23)

southern wall, while in front of it was a roofed area (C), measuring approximately thirteen by twenty meters, in which the institution's Ḥanafī and Shāfiʿī professors and their students were to hold their classes. A tomb (D) to the left of the entrance was built for the burial of the founder's children. Across the street, another complex housed a primary school (*maktab*) for orphans and a public fountain (*sabīl*), increasingly common appendages to schools of higher education in the Mamluk period. Unlike the Ḥasaniyya and some other madrasas, there is nothing in the deed of endowment to indicate that this school provided accommodations for its forty students of Ḥanafī and Shāfiʿī law, although a residence in the mosque building was set aside for housing one of the school's two professors or its imām.

Like larger institutions such as the Ḥasaniyya, the mosque of Sūdūn min Zāda employed a full complement of religious functionaries—a preacher, imām, Quran and ḥadīth readers, a number of muezzins—but it clearly operated as an academic institution. Its two professors of jurisprudence and their assistants and students collectively received almost as much in monthly salaries as all the religious functionaries associated with the tomb and mosque, the primary-school teacher and his pupils, the service personnel, and the administrative staff combined. In this it resembled a number of other medium-sized academic institutions. Architecturally, the madrasa of the amir Ṣarghitmish resembled more closely the Ḥasaniyya, with its four recessed īwāns and accommodations for most of its students.[60] The Ṣarghitmishiyya, however, was devoted to students of only one Sunni rite, supporting a professor of Ḥanafī jurisprudence and sixty pupils, as well as an instructor of ḥadīth and fifteen students of the Prophetic traditions. Despite their more limited focus, both the Sūdūniyya and Ṣarghitmishiyya were important institutions, and over the last century and a half of Mamluk rule both of these schools included a number of prominent jurists and traditionists on their staffs.

Not all institutions, however, were even as large as the Ṣarghitmishiyya or the mosque of Sūdūn min Zāda. We have already encountered the khānqāh of Mughulṭāy al-Jamālī, established in 1329 and providing stipends for only twenty Ḥanafī students and their shaykh. Similarly, the Sufi students at the mosque[61] of Zayn al-Dīn al-Ustadār (established in 1451) were limited in number to twenty.[62] Other institutions were positively minute. The madrasa of Jawhar al-Lālā (Figure 3), established in 1430, occupies a prominent spot on the hill below the Citadel overlooking the madrasa of Sultan Ḥasan.[63] Its central courtyard (A)—covered,

[60] See the institution's deed of endowment, *Waqfiyyat* Ṣarghitmish, Wizārat al-Awqāf o.s. No. 3195, published by ʿAbd al-Laṭīf Ibrāhīm ʿAlī, "Naṣṣān jadīrān min wathīqat al-amīr ṣarghitmish" (pts. 1 and 2), in *Jāmiʿat al-qāhira*. *Majallat kulliyat al-ādāb* 27 (1965), 121–58, and 28 (1966), 143–200.

[61] The institution's waqfiyya generally refers to it as a jāmiʿ; the terms khānqāh and madrasa, however, also appear.

[62] Information on the endowment and constitution of these smaller schools is drawn primarily from a sample of those whose waqfiyyas have survived: *Waqfiyyat* Mughulṭāy al-Jamālī, Wizārat al-Awqāf o.s. No. 1666; *Waqfiyyat* Zayn al-Dīn al-Ustādār, Dār al-Wathāʾiq No. 110.

[63] Information is drawn from the institution's deed of endowment, *Waqfiyyat* Jawhar al-

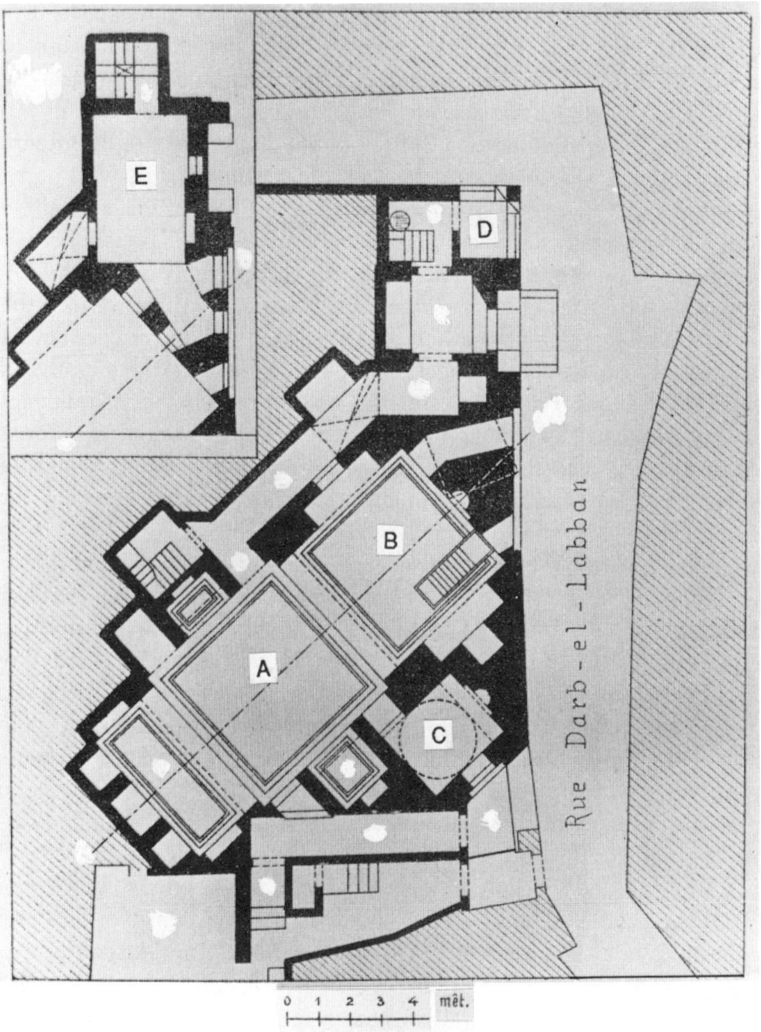

Figure 3. The madrasa of Jawhar al-Lālā, ground plan (from Comité de Conservation des Monuments de l'Art Arabe, *Rapport de la deuxième commission. Exercice 1892*, Pl. 7)

unlike those at the Ḥasaniyya or the mosque of Sūdūn—measures barely twenty-five square meters. The principal (qiblī) īwān (B), with its mihrāb and pulpit, is even smaller. The complex included a tomb (C) for the

Lālā, Dār al-Wathā'iq No. 86. The madrasa was described by the Comité de Conservation des Monuments de l'Art Arabe in *Rapport de la deuxième commission. Exercice 1892*, vol. 9.

burial of the founder, as well as a public fountain (D) and, above it, a primary school (E), but there is no indication that permanent residences were provided for any of the madrasa's stipendiaries. Not surprisingly, the staff of this madrasa was also considerably reduced. The students enrolled in the school doubled as Sufis, but they numbered only fifteen. One man acted as both Sufi shaykh and professor in Ḥanafī law; if possible, he was also to serve as librarian. This school, like others, was also a mosque, and an imām was hired to lead daily prayers. Religious functionaries executed the other devotional tasks: three muezzins issued the call to prayer from the school's minaret; a *ḥāfiẓ* (one who had memorized the Quran) recited sections of the holy book following noon prayers; and a traditionist read particular collections of ḥadīth during the months of Rajab, Shaʿbān, and Ramaḍān. But the tiny burial chamber could not accommodate nearly as many Quran readers as the large domed tomb at the Ḥasaniyya, and so they were limited here to five separate troops of three readers each, to read continually from the Quran and to pray for the soul of the institution's founder.

From the level of the Jawhariyya, the number of religious and academic functionaries hired by some schools, and in particular the number of students supported by the institutions, tapered to a handful. At a khānqāh established in the large cemetery outside Cairo (the Qarāfa) by Zayn al-Dīn Ṣidqa, the Sufi students numbered only ten. Five Ḥanafīs comprised the entire student body at the madrasa of Qalamṭāy, and five Shāfiʿīs at the mosque of al-Shiblī Kāfūr. As few as four Shāfiʿī students were provided with stipends at a separate zāwiya established by the same Zayn al-Dīn Ṣidqa.[64] In these smaller schools, restrictions on the endowments' income resulted in a corresponding reduction in the number of nonacademics hired to supplement the institutions' educational functions. Of the smaller schools whose endowment deeds survive, only the mosque of Zayn al-Dīn al-Ustādār, established in the mid-fifteenth century by a wealthy and powerful bureaucrat,[65] provided for a full complement of religious, administrative, and service positions: an imām, preacher, and twelve muezzins; Quran readers, a reciter of ḥadīth, and another to recite poems in praise of the Prophet; bawwābs, farrāshes, waqqāds, and a mubakhkhir; and several others to administer the endowment's properties. At smaller institutions, certain employees naturally undertook responsibilities that, at larger establishments, fell to a more specialized work force. Thus, for example, the bawwāb of the madrasa of Qalamṭāy also cleaned the building, supervised the provision of water,

[64] *Waqfiyyat* Zayn al-Dīn Ṣidqa, Dār al-Wathāʾiq No. 59; *Waqfiyyat* Qalamṭāy, Dār al-Wahtāʾiq No. 68; and *Waqfiyyat* al-Shiblī Kāfūr, Dār al-Wathāʾiq No. 76.

[65] See his biographical sketch in al-Sakhāwī, *al-Ḍaw*ʾ, 10:233–34.

and acted as *kātib al-ghayba*—recording, that is, unexcused absences on the part of the five Ḥanafī students and the six Quran readers assigned to the tombs of Qalamṭāy and his children. At the zāwiya of Zayn al-Dīn Ṣidqa, the imām not only led those assembled for daily prayers, but first issued the call to prayer. Every day of the week except Friday, he taught Quran and writing to the orphans in the primary school attached to the zāwiya; and after both the morning and evening prayers, he led the zāwiya's four Shāfiʿī students in reciting Quranic passages, chanting the words "there is no god but God," and praying for the soul of the zāwiya's founder. At the madrasa of Jawhar al-Lālā the imām was required, if possible, to supervise the library, and for his pains received a supplement of one hundred dirhams to his monthly salary. The madrasa of al-Sayfī Baybars hired a separate librarian, but also delegated to him the task of reciting, during the months of Rajab, Shaʿbān, and Ramaḍān, the famous collection of ḥadīth, the *Ṣaḥīḥ* of al-Bukhārī.[66]

A Hierarchy of Educational Institutions

It should be clear, then, that organized legal and religious education flourished in a variety of settings in Mamluk Cairo, and that if terms such as "madrasa," "khānqāh," and "jāmiʿ" by themselves tell us increasingly little about the character of particular institutions, we can identify a wide range of schools differentiated by size and the number of classes they supported. It remains to be seen, however, whether these distinctions correspond to meaningful criteria by which we can map out a hierarchy of institutions of higher education. Not surprisingly, as we shall see, not all Mamluk schools were created equal.

Studies of Cairene society in the later Middle Ages have recognized the dominance of a group of large and wealthy schools, founded primarily by sultans and wealthy amirs, corresponding to the larger institutions, and others like them, described above. It was these schools, one researcher suggested, that "*trained* the majority of those persons who became entrenched within the civilian elite."[67] While the assertion is correct in stressing that these institutions loomed large in the minds of late medieval students and educators, it is also, in the strictest sense, problematic. By itself, it is virtually impossible to prove, since the biographical sources on which a study of medieval Islamic education must largely be based provide almost no details about the venue of a given scholar's

[66] *Waqfiyyat* Qalamṭāy, Dār al-Wathā'iq No. 68, ll. 270–79; *Waqfiyyat* Zayn al-Din Ṣidqa, Dār al-Wathā'iq No. 59, ll. 77–86; *Waqfiyyat* Jawhar al-Lālā, Dār al-Wathā'iq No. 86, ll. 315–19; *Waqfiyyat* al-Sayfī Baybars, Dār al-Wathā'iq No. 313, the third document on the scroll, dated 20 Shawāl, A.H. 921, ll. 39–42.

[67] Petry, *Civilian Elite*, 160 and passim; emphasis added.

education.[68] Moreover, of course, the institutions themselves did no real training: that was left to individual instructors. As we have seen, despite the proliferation of endowed institutions of learning, venue remained at best a secondary issue in the fundamentally personal system of late medieval Islamic education. But the larger schools, whether called madrasas, mosques, or khānqāhs, blessed with larger endowments and the increased visibility of having a sultan or prominent amir as patron, clearly surpassed smaller and less wealthy schools, both in terms of the quality of their teaching talent and the guidelines by which their classes were conducted.

In the first place, founders of the larger and more prominent schools, while leaving teachers a relatively free hand in shaping the curriculum of individual classes, might structure the provisions of their endowments so as to ensure (or so they hoped) the excellence of those chosen as the schools' professors. The deed establishing al-Mu'ayyad Shaykh's school, for example, delineated in general but forceful terms the requisite qualifications of the institution's academic staff. The Ḥanafī professor of law, for example, was to be

> expert [lit. "one who knows by heart," *ḥāfiẓ*] in the writings of the legal scholars, interpretation of the ulama, the difference[s] in the schools of law, and the texts of the imām Abū Ḥanīfa, may God be pleased with him, and of his companions who followed him, may God be pleased with them, knowledgeable too of all the books of the Ḥanafī [scholars] and of [how to] elucidate their issues and make clear their questions . . . competent to teach and issue legal opinions, equal to the best of the scholars and teachers devoted to instruction in holy knowledge.

Sensitive to the peculiar demands of particular subjects, that same document expressed a special concern that the institution's professor of Quranic exegesis be expert and fluent in "the language of the Arabs" to ensure his capacity to understand and explain the archaic language of the Quran, and that the professor of ḥadīth be "knowledgeable of the names of the men of the Prophetic tradition[s] and their transmitters, a grammarian, holder of a strong chain of authority [i.e., for the traditions that he recited]."[69] Amir Ṣarghitmish went further and stipulated that the

[68] While the medieval biographers did in fact provide comprehensive information on the institutions in which scholars held endowed teaching posts, their accounts are considerably scantier in relation to the *places* in which individuals received their education. Indeed, Petry's own results reflect this discrepancy. Consider his figures 3 through 8; note the paucity of references in the sources to "educational sites" in comparison to "occupational sites."

[69] *Waqfiyyat* al-Mu'ayyad Shaykh, Wizārat al-Awqāf o.s. No. 938, ll. 520–24, 555–56, 562; cf. the required qualifications of the shaykh al-ḥadīth at the madrasa of Barqūq, *Waqfiyyat* al-Ẓāhir Barqūq, Dār al-Wathā'iq No. 51, ll. 806–7.

controller of the madrasa that bore his name was to appoint as professor "the Ḥanafī in Egypt [who is] most learned in the law."[70]

If the laws of competitive markets applied, the Ṣarghitmishiyya may well have attracted the premier teaching talent in the country, since the 300 dirhams the Ḥanafī professor was paid was perhaps the highest monthly salary available to a teacher in Egypt at the time of the madrasa's construction and endowment in the middle of the fourteenth century.[71] Fulfilling the endowment's stipulation may have soon become more difficult, since within a few years the madrasa of Sultan Ḥasan was offering its Ḥanafī professor an equivalent sum, and by the start of the next century other schools paid even more. But in general the larger institutions offered their students and especially teachers a level of remuneration beyond the reach of smaller, less well-endowed schools, and so probably retained a qualitative edge. Al-Sakhāwī recognized as much in his description of Barsbāy's madrasa which, he candidly noted, was in his day "the most splendid place [of instruction] in terms of [its] remuneration [of its stipendiaries]."[72]

Against such wealth, smaller schools simply could not compete. Comprehensive comparisons are of course difficult, given three interrelated problems: stipends are set in different deeds of endowment using different currency units—silver dirhams (*dirham nuqra*), copper dirhams (*dirham fulūs*), half dirhams (*niṣf*); both currency values and prices fluctuated over time; that in most cases we cannot determine whether and by how much stipends were raised to compensate for inflation, or lowered to reflect a decline in the revenue of an endowment.[73] But in cases where direct comparisons can be made—for example, between schools established within a few years of each other—the evidence suggests, not surprisingly, that the same institutions that limited the number of their students and other stipendiaries paid those they did support considerably less.

Consider three telling comparisons. At the khānqāh of Mughulṭāy al-Jamālī, established in 1329, the Ḥanafī shaykh received a total of 100 silver dirhams per month, only half the salary of the four professors of law at the madrasa of al-Nāṣir Muḥammad constructed only a few years

[70] *Waqfiyyat* Ṣarghitmish, Wizārat al-Awqāf o.s. No. 3195, p. 26; ʿAbd al-Laṭīf Ibrāhīm ʿAlī, "Naṣṣān jadīrān," pt. 1, 147.

[71] By contrast, the Ḥanafī professor at the mosque of Ibn Ṭūlūn, endowed by Sultan Lājīn at the end of the thirteenth century, received 200 dirhams per month, as did his counterpart at the madrasa of al-Nāṣir Muḥammad. Instructors at smaller, less well-endowed institutions were paid considerably less.

[72] *Aḥsan al-amākin ṣarfan*. Al-Sakhāwī, *al-Ḍaw'*, 3:9–10.

[73] On currencies and prices, see Eliyahu Ashtor, *Histoire des prix et des salaires dans l'orient médiéval* (Paris, 1969), 267–381, esp. 274–82.

before. The Shāfiʿī shaykh at the khānqāh of Zayn al-Dīn Ṣidqa (dating from the first years of the fifteenth century) might have received as much as 120 dirhams per month, depending upon his qualifications;[74] yet the Ḥanafī and Shāfiʿī professors at the mosque of Sūdūn min Zāda, built and endowed in the same period (the deed dates from 1402), were paid 250 dirhams each. By the fifteenth century, a debased copper dirham was the principal currency in circulation, and the Ḥanafī shaykh at the madrasa of Jawhar al-Lālā received 500 copper dirhams (worth approximately 25 silver dirhams) for his services, according to the deed of endowment dated 1431. His colleague at the grand mosque of Sultan Barsbāy, however, was from 1424 paid 3,000 copper dirhams, six times the salary paid to the shaykh of the smaller institution. Out of these isolated comparisons a pattern emerges suggesting a noticeable discrepancy between salaries in large and small institutions of learning, and which must have affected the ability of the smaller schools to attract the most prominent and highly respected teachers.

Salaries may have reinforced a hierarchy, but other provisions in the deeds of endowment may also have ensured that the quality of education would vary considerably from one school to another. For example, stipulations in the deeds of the larger schools regarding the academic classes demonstrate that they formed the schools' primary activity, and reflect the concern of the founders to guarantee a stable environment and quality instruction. In some cases, this involved ensuring that the rite to which the founder himself adhered was given pride of place. In madrasas of the so-called cruciform shape, in which four recessed īwāns surrounded an open courtyard, the īwān oriented in the direction of Mecca was routinely reserved for the classes of the rite to which the founder wished to grant special honors. In most Mamluk schools, the rite thus favored was, as at Sultan Barqūq's, the Ḥanafī, but a preference for others was not unheard of. At al-Nāṣir Muḥammad's madrasa, the Mālikīs were favored; at Jamāl-al-Dīn al-Ustādār's, the Shāfiʿīs.[75]

[74] As imām and shaykh of the khānqāh, which was the principal object of the original document in Zayn al-Dīn's waqfiyya (dating from 13 Jumādā al-Awwal; the year, however, is obscured), he received 60 dirhams per month. A second document (dated 3 Muḥarram, A.H. 803) provided 30 dirhams for a Shāfiʿī professor to give a daily class, presumably in Shāfiʿī jurisprudence; the document further stipulates that the shaykh was to hold this post if he was competent to do so. He was also to receive another 30 dirhams provided by a third document (dated 25 Rabīʿ al-Awwal 807) as compensation for teaching a course in a separate zāwiya, established outside Bāb Zuwayla.

[75] The founder of a school had several other means at his disposal by which he might favor one rite over another, and given the frequent adherence of the Mamluks to the Ḥanafī rite, it was usually Ḥanafī scholars and students who reaped the benefits. At the madrasa of Barqūq and the mosques of Barsbāy and al-Mu'ayyad Shaykh, the Ḥanafī professor was also appointed Sufi shaykh, a position from which he exercised greater responsibility, and

More generally and more importantly, the founders of these larger and ultimately more prestigious institutions left precise instructions as to when, and for how long, class sessions should be held. Writers on educational matters, such as Burhān al-Dīn al-Zarnūjī, the author of a treatise on education that circulated widely in the Mamluk period, felt that the best time for instruction was the period after dawn.[76] According to Badr al-Dīn Muḥammad Ibn Jamāʿa, the entire day was to be devoted to the pursuit of knowledge, but early morning was especially appropriate for organized study (*al-baḥth*); the period before daybreak was better suited to memorization, the middle of the day to writing, and the nighttime to reading and group study (*al-muṭālaʿa wa'l-mudhākara*).[77] Most endowment deeds therefore stipulated that teachers and students meet for their classes between sunrise and noon.[78] The early morning air must have been filled with the sound of students reciting and teachers correcting their lessons, especially at those institutions that offered multiple classes, such as the khānqāh of Jamāl al-Dīn al-Ustādār where the professors of all four rites were to hold their classes "at any time between the rising of the sun and the call to noon prayers."[79] But whenever they were held, sufficient time was allocated to them. Thus, at the madrasa of Sultan Barqūq, while the class in Ḥanafī jurisprudence met for three and a half hours after sunrise, those of the Shāfiʿī, Mālikī, and Ḥanbalī professors met for an equivalent time between noon and the afternoon prayers.[80] At most of these schools, classes were held at least five times

in which he earned considerably more: at the mosque of al-Mu'ayyad Shaykh, for example, he received 500 dirhams niṣf compared to 150 for the Shāfiʿī professor, and 100 each for those of Mālikī and Ḥanbalī law.

[76] Burhān al-Dīn al-Zarnūjī, *Taʿlīm al-mutaʿallim, ṭarīq al-taʿallum* (Cairo, 1977), 47, trans. G. E. von Grunebaum and Theodora M. Abel, *Instruction of the Student, the Method of Learning* (New York, 1947), 58; al-Zarnūjī added to this the period between sunset and the evening prayers (*al-ʿashā'*).

[77] Badr al-Dīn Muḥammad Ibn Jamāʿa, *Tadhkirat al-sāmiʿ wa'l-mutakallim fī adab al-ʿālim wa'l-mutaʿallim* (Hyderabad, A.H. 1353), 72–73.

[78] For example, *Waqfiyyat* al-Manṣūr Lājīn, Dār al-Wathā'iq No. 17, ll. 332–49, where these hours are specified for the four classes in jurisprudence; the classes in ḥadīth and exegesis were similarly assigned to "the start of the day" (*awwal al-nahār*). See also: *Waqfiyyat* Ṣarghitmish, Wizārat al-Awqāf o.s. No. 3195, p. 27, and ʿAbd al-Laṭīf Ibrāhīm ʿAlī, "Naṣṣān jadīrān," pt. 1, 148, where the class in Ḥanafī law met from sunrise to noon, while the appointed hours for the class in ḥadīth were between noon and afternoon prayers. At the Mu'ayyadī mosque, the precise times of the classes were left to the discretion of the controller; morning seems to have been the most likely hour, however, since the Sufi exercises, which all were required to attend, were to take place after afternoon prayers. *Waqfiyyat* al-Mu'ayyad Shaykh, Wizārat al-Awqāf o.s. No. 938, l. 529.

[79] *Waqfiyyat* Jamāl al-Dīn al-Ustādār, Dār al-Wathā'iq No. 106, ll. 54–55ff; here the class in exegesis met at a different time, from noon prayers until the call to afternoon prayers.

[80] *Waqfiyyat* al-Ẓāhir Barqūq, Dār al-Wathā'iq No. 51. No particular times were set aside

per week, with Tuesdays and Fridays as holidays, although occasionally students were excused from formal instruction on Mondays as well.[81]

By contrast, formal stipulations in smaller schools' deeds of endowment often allotted considerably less time to organized study than did those of larger institutions. At the mosque of al-Shiblī Kāfūr, for example, the Shāfiʿī students gathered with their shaykh on Sundays and Wednesdays only. To be sure, it was not always the case that students at smaller and less prestigious schools received an abbreviated education, at least in terms of formal instruction. The endowment deed for the madrasa of Qalamṭāy stipulated that the institution's five Ḥanafī students were to gather with their shaykh "on those days on which instruction customarily takes place"—which, as we have seen, may have included every day except Tuesday and Friday.[82] But the usual pattern was for smaller, less well-endowed schools to make less stringent demands on their students. At the madrasa of Jawhar al-Lālā they met on Saturdays, Sundays, and Wednesdays. The Shāfiʿī professor and his students gathered at the zāwiya of Zayn al-Dīn Ṣidqa on four days of the week, but for only "thirty minutes of a sandglass."[83]

Instruction, and the hours of reading and memorization that students required to prepare for their classes, may have been taken more seriously at the larger schools. Consider, for example, the somewhat idiosyncratic stipulation at the madrasa of Barqūq and the Jamāliyya khānqāh that none of the institution's stipendiaries be appointed from among the *shuhūd* (sing., *shāhid*), the notaries who sat in shops (*al-ḥawānīt*) transacting minor legal affairs.[84] Employment as a shāhid was one means by which an advanced but impecunious student might finance his continuing education. Muḥammad b. ʿAlī b. Muḥammad al-Qāyātī al-Shāfiʿī (d. 1446), for example, who eventually held prestigious and well-paid teaching posts in the Ẓāhiriyya (Barqūq) and Ashrafiyya (Barsbāy) madrasas, worked as a shāhid in the mosque of al-Ṣāliḥ outside Bāb Zuwayla before his appointment as a paid student in the Muʾayyadī mosque.[85] Such em-

---

for that institution's classes in ḥadīth, the variant Quran readings, and exegesis, although they were to be equivalent to the time between noon and the afternoon prayers.

[81] Classes were held five days per week at the khānqāh of Jamāl al-Dīn al-Ustādār and at the madrasa of Barqūq, and only four days at the mosque of Sūdūn and the madrasa of Ṣarghitmish.

[82] *Waqfiyyat* Qalamṭāy, Dār al-Wathāʾiq No. 68, l. 248.

[83] *Waqfiyyat* al-Shiblī Kāfūr, Dār al-Wathāʾiq No. 76, ll. 75–77; *Waqfiyyat* Jawhar al-Lālā, Dār al-Wathāʾiq No. 86, ll. 292–95; *Waqfiyyat* Zayn al-Dīn Ṣidqa, Dār al-Wathāʾiq No. 59, the third document on the scroll (dated 25 Rabīʿ al-Awwal, A.H. 807), ll. 121–25, where the class was stipulated to last *miqdār thalāthīn daraja ramliyya*.

[84] On the shāhid, see Emile Tyan, *Histoire de l'organisation judiciaire en pays d'islam*, 2nd edition (Leiden, 1960), 236–52, and *Encyclopedia of Islam*, 1st edition, s.v. "Shāhid" (by W. Heffening).

[85] Ibn Taghrī Birdī, *al-Nujūm al-zāhira*, 15:513; cf. al-Sakhāwī, *al-Ḍawʾ*, 8:213.

ployment, however, might also distract a student from his studies, and was consequently frowned upon by Islamic theorists of education. It was best to pursue one's studies without a break, and to submit only to the most urgent necessities: eating, drinking, sleep, severe pain, short rests, and "the discharge of conjugal duties."[86] Thus, again, the endowment deeds bowed to the advice of the ulama and insisted that a shāhid give up his outside employment before being appointed to a position in a school, so that, as one document put it, external obligations would not encroach on the time to be devoted to study and Sufi exercises.[87]

By contrast, the increased extracurricular demands imposed on students at the smaller schools must have diminished, if not the total number of hours spent in class, then the amount of time spent in private study, and consequently the effectiveness of formal instruction. To a certain extent, this was true at any institution that combined Sufi devotional exercises with educational functions, even at the mosque of Sultan Barsbāy, where the Sufi students held their academic classes in the morning and their Sufi worship in the late afternoon (*baʿd ṣalāt al-ʿaṣr*), and reflected simply the changing norms of piety that saw Sufism and academic instruction as complementary activities.[88] The demands on a student's time could increase, however. The day entirely devoted to study, as envisioned by Ibn Jamāʿa, must have seemed a distant ideal to the Sufi students at the small khānqāh of Zayn al-Dīn Ṣidqa. The ten of them received instruction in Shāfiʿī jurisprudence "every day of the week except Fridays" and the usual holidays, but the deed of endowment also saddled them with a variety of nonacademic responsibilities: one was to be the servant (*khādim*) responsible for the prayer carpets; another doubled as instructor in the institution's primary school; others were to read and pray in the attached tomb and to act as muezzin and gatekeeper; still others held administrative positions.[89]

[86] Ibn Jamāʿa, *Tadhkirat al-sāmiʿ*, 27; al-Zarnūjī, *Taʿlīm*, 43, von Grunebaum and Abel, *Instruction*, 54.

[87] *Waqfiyyat* Jamāl al-Dīn al-Ustādār, Dār al-Wathāʾiq No. 106, ll. 148–54; cf. *Waqfiyyat* al-Ẓāhir Barqūq, Dār al-Wathāʾiq No. 51, ll. 1008–12. A secondary objective of this prohibition may have been to exclude those whose devotion to the pursuit of religious knowledge was dubious, and whose loyalties and interests might have been tainted by association with the Mamluks, since in both institutions it also excluded those who were *mubāshiran ʿind al-umarāʾ*; but as the deed of Jamāl al-Dīn makes clear, the principal concern was less a conflict of interest than of time: if they were willing to forgo their outside employment, there was to be no objection to their appointment to the madrasa.

[88] *Waqfiyyat* Barsbāy, Dār al-Wahtāʾiq No. 173. Cf. *Waqfiyyat* Zayn al-dīn al-Ustādār, Dār al-Wathāʾiq No. 110, where the students gathered for their class in law in the early afternoon (*baʿd ṣalāt al-ẓuhr*), and their Sufi devotional exercises later in the day (*baʿd ṣalāt al-ʿaṣr*).

[89] *Waqfiyyat* Zayn al-Dīn Ṣidqa, Dār al-Wathāʾiq No. 59; a similar regime was in place at

More importantly, the capacity of larger schools of higher religious and legal education to support endowed courses in separate subjects—the jurisprudence of a particular rite or of several rites, Quranic exegesis, ḥadīth, or the variant Quran readings—provided a framework that encouraged, if it did not absolutely guarantee, a serious attention to the subject at hand. The science of jurisprudence remained the jewel in the crown of the madrasas and other religious schools—subjects such as exegesis, ḥadīth, and grammar seem often to have held a secondary place, or to have played a supportive role. One measure of the prominence given to law may be seen in the range of salaries at those institutions hiring instructors in the different subjects. Frequently teachers of jurisprudence were paid as much as two times the salary of the teachers of ḥadīth, as at the madrasa of Barqūq, where the four professors of law received 300 dirhams to 150 for the professor of ḥadīth, and 100 for the professor of the variant Quran readings.[90] At that same school, a special provision in the deed of endowment gave preference to students of the class in the variant Quran readings to advance to the class in jurisprudence according to their rite when they had completed their Quranic studies, as if to emphasize both the distinct nature of the subjects and the more advanced character of the study of *fiqh* (jurisprudence).[91] At the mosque of Ibn Ṭūlūn, Sultan Lājīn's endowment deed provided, in addition to four professors of jurisprudence and one each of exegesis and ḥadīth with between twenty and thirty students each, instructors in the Quran, its variant readings, and Arabic grammar, to work with students individually or in groups, clearly as an adjunct to their studies in the other subjects.[92]

But in many schools, the choice of subject for any particular class, let alone the text, was left to the discretion of the professor, even for those ostensibly devoted to the study of jurisprudence. Indeed, with regard to the internal arrangements of each particular class (as opposed to the for-

---

the large khānqāh of Jamāl al-Dīn al-Ustādār, where the Sufi students were to hold the majority of the institution's religious, service, and administrative posts.

[90] Cf. the situation at the madrasa of Ṣarghitmish, where the professor of Ḥanafī jurisprudence was paid 300 dirhams, compared to 100 for the shaykh al-ḥadīth. There were, of course, exceptions. At the khānqāh of Jamāl al-Dīn al-Ustādār, all the professors were paid the same amount (300 dirhams) regardless of their subject, while at the mosque of al-Mu'ayyad Shaykh, the professors of exegesis, ḥadīth, and the variant Quran readings were paid 50 dirhams more than their colleagues in Mālikī and Ḥanbalī jurisprudence (although considerably less than the Ḥanafī professor, and the same as that in Shāfiʿī law).

[91] *Waqfiyyat* al-Ẓāhir Barqūq, Dār al-Wathā'iq No. 51, ll. 976–81.

[92] *Waqfiyyat* Lājīn, Dār al-Wathā'iq No. 17, ll. 318–22. The man hired to teach the Quran (*talqīn kitāb allāh al-ʿazīz*) is "for whoever desires it [i.e., instruction];" and the instructor in the variant Quran readings and grammar is "to sit from the start of the day so that students may study with him the seven [variant Quran] readings, singly or as a group, and grammar." The endowment did not provide stipends for students in these subjects.

mal guidelines under which schools were administered), the most striking aspect of the endowment deeds is their flexibility. Tāj al-Dīn al-Subkī complained about professors who strayed in their lectures from the subjects stipulated in the deeds of endowment for the schools in which they taught; professors who, for example, held endowed teaching positions in jurisprudence according to one of the four rites but gave classes in "Quranic exegesis or ḥadīth or grammar or the foundations [of law?] or some other subject because of their lack [of comprehension] of jurisprudence." Teachers should teach the subject stipulated by the deed, he opined; otherwise they are "eaters of forbidden things" (*ākil al-ḥarām*).[93] In fact, however, the deeds of endowment themselves left a good deal of latitude to the schools' professors. Often they left even the choice of subject matter to the teacher, even at the madrasa of Barqūq where, for example, the Ḥanafī professor was to teach "whatever he chooses from the jurisprudence of his rite and its foundations and Quranic exegesis and grammar and the foundations of religion [*uṣūl al-dīn*] and other subjects."[94]

But the "broadening of the base of architectural patronage"—the rush to construct schools by members of the military and political elites less wealthy than the sultans and the most powerful amirs—resulted in a bifurcation among institutions of learning that largely corresponded to distinctions of size and level of salary, but that was even more fundamental. While the larger and better-endowed schools attracted teaching staffs and students of a decidedly elite, cosmopolitan, international character,[95] the comparative poverty of the smaller schools' endowments effectively prohibited them from restricting, even in theory, the choice of their instructors to "the most learned" ulama. While it is, of course, impossible to judge with absolute certainty the quality of classes from the guidelines set by the deeds of endowment, their terms make it more difficult to identify these smaller schools as institutions primarily devoted to serious study.

Consider, for example, the following. We noted a tendency even in some of the larger and better-endowed institutions, such as the madrasa of Barqūq, to leave the choice of subject for individual classes to the discretion of the professor. In the smaller schools, the financial considerations that made it impossible to hire separate teachers of jurisprudence, ḥadīth, and Quranic exegesis only exacerbated the tendency. At the khānqāh of Mughulṭāy al-Jamālī, the Ḥanafī shaykh delivered lectures

[93] Al-Subkī, *Muʿīd al-niʿam*, 153.

[94] *Waqfiyyat* al-Ẓāhir Barqūq, Dār al-Wathāʾiq No. 51, l. 785; cf. *Waqfiyyat* Jamāl al-Dīn al-Ustādār, Dār al-Wathāʾiq No. 106, ll. 59–60; and the waqfiyya of al-Nāṣir Muḥammad as summarized in al-Nuwayrī's *Nihāyat al-arab* and published in al-Maqrīzī, *al-Sulūk*, 1:1043ff.

[95] Petry, *Civilian Elite*, esp. 161–62.

generally "from the sciences and ḥadīth."[96] The professor of the zāwiya of Zayn al-Dīn Ṣidqa instructed "from books of jurisprudence" according to the Shāfiʿi rite and from "other subjects of the legal sciences."[97] Stipulations at the mosque of Zayn al-Dīn al-Ustādār were hardly more explicit; students were to read to the professor from books of jurisprudence, its foundations, Arabic, morphology (*taṣrīf*), "and other subjects."[98]

This dilution in the structural framework of education may well have been an unrecognized consequence of the blending of an increasingly popular Sufism and organized higher education, a point discussed above. This is not to posit any intrinsic antithesis between the mystical nature of Sufi activities and the disciplined study of the Islamic sciences; as we have seen, several schools that were known as khānqāhs, or that combined Sufi and educational functions, were among the most prestigious and rigorous academic institutions of late Mamluk Cairo. Rather, it follows from the freedom allowed to Mamluks and others to construct and endow institutions—whether we identify them as madrasas, khānqāhs, or mosques—and to organize their activities in an idiosyncratic fashion. Thus it emerges from the deeds of endowment of several of these smaller institutions that the *principal* focus was on the Sufi exercises: a class in jurisprudence or another subject may have been added as an afterthought. At the khānqāh of Zayn al-Dīn Ṣidqa, for example, the original deed of endowment made provisions only for ten Sufis and their shaykh, whose duties included organized prayer for the founder, but not systematic instruction. Stipulations regarding a course in jurisprudence "and other subjects" were provided only in a later document, appended to the initial deed, although the later document did stipulate that the shaykh was also to function as the khānqāh's professor, if he were capable of doing so.[99]

Thus, the mixing of Sufism and higher education did not fuse the mystical and rational aspects of Islamic religion into a homogenous, undifferentiated mass, at least as far as education is concerned. Mixed institutions such as the khānqāh of Jamāl al-Dīn al-Ustādār or the Mu'ayyadī mosque, where Sufis and students were identical, may well have maintained academic standards. On the other hand, a madrasa such as that of Jawhar al-

[96] *Min al-ʿulūm wa'l-ḥadīth al-nabawiyya. Waqfiyyat* Mughulṭāy al-Jamālī, Wizārat al-Awqāf o.s. No. 1666, ll. 381–89.

[97] *Wa ghayr al-fiqh min al-ʿulūm al-sharʿiyya. Waqfiyyat* Zayn al-Dīn Ṣidqa, Dār al-Wathā'iq No. 59, ll. 121–25.

[98] *Waqfiyyat* Zayn al-Dīn al-Ustādār, Dār al-Wathā'iq No. 110, ll. 1219–32; the passage stipulates that students read to the professor *mā yaqṣidūn qirā'tahu min kutub al-ʿilm al-sharīf min fiqh wa uṣūl wa ʿarabiyya wa taṣrīf wa ghayr dhālika.*

[99] The later document is dated 3 Muḥarram, A.H. 803 (the date of the first document is obscured). *Waqfiyyat* Zayn al-Dīn Ṣidqa, Dār al-Wathā'iq No. 59.

Lālā, where the Sufis' principal duty consisted of reading the Quran and praying "for the Prophet, may God bless and protect him, and for his honor the [madrasa's] founder and for his honorable brother al-Ṣafawī Jawhar al-Khāzindār, and for all the Muslims," could hardly have made stringent intellectual demands of them in their tri-weekly class in Ḥanafī jurisprudence.[100]

But the wide disparity in the size, character, and focus of educational institutions, reflecting a broad spectrum within the world of organized education, should not be read simply as the cause or consequence of some ominous decline in academic standards; it had an important positive role to play. Instruction, worship, and Sufi devotional exercises were nonexclusive elements in a continuum; the relative weight given to each, as stipulated by the founders of the various institutions, helped to shape the nature of the comprehensive religious experience of those who lived or studied in them. If the base of architectural patronage expanded, so too did the number of those Muslims who could participate actively and in some sustained fashion in the educational process and the transmission of knowledge. The spread throughout the city of schools of varying size, wealth, and character must have served to expand the social horizons of higher education and draw into its world both individuals and groups of people who might otherwise have remained more marginal to it. Since, however, the fundamental educational factor was a personal relationship rather than a building or endowment, even this expanded circle of schools could not contain the full range of those committed, in one way or another, to knowledge and its transmission.

Teaching Unsupported by Institutional Endowments

The many and various schools established or endowed during the Mamluk period contributed significantly to the transmission of religious knowledge by providing income and, often, accommodations and meals for both students and teachers. But as we have seen, education in late medieval Cairo rested on an informal system of personal relationships rather than institutional reputation and affiliation. Not surprisingly, therefore, many shaykhs taught and many pupils studied in classes and venues outside the network of endowed schools. The network of institutions established in Cairo over the course of the later Middle Ages, varied as they were, still did not delineate the boundaries of higher religious

[100] *Waqfiyyat* Jawhar al-Lālā, Dār al-Wathā'iq No. 86, esp. ll. 279–86, describing the Sufis' duties, and ll. 292–95, requiring a class in Ḥanafī jurisprudence on Saturdays, Sundays, and Wednesdays.

education. Here again, developments paralleled those in the contemporary Jewish communities of the Near East since Jewish scholars, too, frequently taught in homes, stores, or synagogues—scholars with no official status but who were nonetheless learned.[101]

Before the rapid spread in the eleventh and twelfth centuries of institutions known as madrasas, endowed schools providing stipends and living accommodations for teachers and students, instruction in the Islamic religious sciences transpired on a more ad hoc basis. In some circumstances individuals were appointed to "official" teaching posts in important mosques, or received from Islamic rulers and wealthy notables some form of financial support. In general, however, teaching circles gathered less formally, with instructors routinely collecting fees from those students who attended their classes.[102] It has been recognized that this informal system survived the establishment and spread of madrasas providing structured forums for education, but the attention demanded by the prevalence of endowed institutions of learning in medieval Syria and Egypt has perhaps obscured the degree to which the Islamic teaching system remained informal and unaffected by its institutional framework down to the end of the Middle Ages.[103]

Clearly, informal teaching circles built around individual teachers survived the growing popularity of madrasas and other institutions devoted by the terms of their endowment to higher Islamic education. Al-Maqrīzī tells us that until the great plague of 1348 the ancient Mosque of ʿAmr in al-Fusṭāṭ hosted more than forty teaching circles (*ḥalqa*) for the study of the religious sciences (*iqrāʾ al-ʿilm*).[104] Some of these were certainly endowed, thereby providing stipends for teachers and students in the manner of the typical madrasa, but very likely many more were private, in which teachers taught gratis or in exchange for payments from their students. At al-Azhar, too, several teaching circles were established and endowed by wealthy amirs and others. But al-Maqrīzī described that mosque as a thriving center for the educational activities of more than seven hundred men, for "reading the Quran and studying it and teaching it, for the study of the different religious sciences, jurisprudence, ḥadīth, Quranic exegesis, and grammar,"[105] much of which must have been or-

[101] S. D. Goitein, *A Mediterranean Society: The Jewish Communities of the Arab World as Portrayed in the Documents of the Cairo Geniza* (Berkeley, 1971), 2:205.

[102] Johannes Pedersen, *The Arabic Book*, trans. Geoffrey French (Princeton, 1984), 20; Makdisi, *Colleges*, 10ff, 159–62; *Encyclopedia of Islam*, 2nd edition, s.v. "Masdjid" and "Madrasa."

[103] Makdisi, *Colleges*, 161. Compare A. L. Tibawi's critique of Makdisi's early work on madrasas, in "Origin and Character of Al-Madrasah," *Bulletin of the School of Oriental and African Studies* 25 (1962), 230–31.

[104] Al-Maqrīzī, *Khiṭaṭ*, 2:256.

[105] Al-Maqrīzī, *Khiṭaṭ*, 2:276.

ganized informally, unsupported and unrestricted by any formal endowments.

Even in schools that made specific provisions for classes in particular subjects, the support of students of a particular rite, and the appointment of paid professors to lead them, scholars often taught on their own, outside the confines of the institution's endowments. The pious Shāfiʿī scholar Ibrāhīm b. Aḥmad b. ʿAlī al-Bījūrī (d. 1421), for example, was "very poor," and held few paying appointments for religious or educational employment in endowed institutions. He was at last appointed to the chair in Shāfiʿī jurisprudence in the Fakhriyya madrasa, but accepted the post only reluctantly, upon the insistence of his students. Yet "a large number of students studied with him, as did most of the scholars of our age," clearly more than those who received instruction from him at the Fakhriyya. Al-Bījūrī may have resisted employment, but he taught jurisprudence informally in several Cairene schools, including the Nāṣiriyya and the Sābiqiyya madrasas, *iḥtisāban*, "seeking a reward from God," that is, gratis.[106] Ibn Ḥajar al-ʿAsqalānī, too, although holding at various times teaching appointments in more than a dozen Cairene institutions, "volunteered" to teach or deliver lectures at a number of institutions, among them the Mankūtimuriyya, which was next to his house, and the *dār al-ḥadīth* (a school devoted to the study of the Prophetic traditions) al-Kāmiliyya.[107] Majd al-Dīn Ismaʿīl b. Abī 'l-Ḥasan al-Birmāwī al-Shāfiʿī (d. 1430), whose pupils included several generations of Shāfiʿī students, never held a paid teaching post, although he did give lectures in an "obscure school" (*madrasa khāmila*) outside of Cairo.[108]

We saw above that instruction in the Islamic sciences might be provided by a number of institutions, mosques and khānqāhs as well as madrasas. Yet it is clear that the scope of education in the Mamluk period was by no means bounded by the institutions, of whatever name, established to facilitate it. According to Ibn al-Ḥājj, a jurist of the early fourteenth century, teaching could take place not only in madrasas but in mosques and private homes (*buyūt*, sing. *bayt*).[109] Ibn al-Ḥājj expressed

[106] Jamāl al-Dīn Yūsuf Ibn Taghrī Birdī, *al-Manhal al-ṣāfī wa'l-mustawfī baʿd al-wāfī* (Cairo, 1984), 1:43–47; al-Sakhāwī, *al-Ḍaw'*, 1:20. On the meaning of the term iḥtisāban in relation to teaching, see Makdisi, *Colleges*, 180.

[107] Sabri K. Kawash, "Ibn Ḥajar al-ʿAsqalānī (1372–1449 A.D.): A Study of the Background, Education, and Career of a ʿĀlim in Egypt," dissertation, Princeton University (1969), 135–37; the list of schools in which Ibn Ḥajar held teaching appointments can be found in al-Sakhāwī, *al-Ḍaw'*, 2:38–39.

[108] Al-Sakhāwī, *al-Ḍaw'*, 2:295–97.

[109] Ibn al-Ḥājj, *Madkhal al-sharʿ al-sharīf* (Cairo, 1929; reptd. Beirut, 1981), 1:85–86. At this early date, Ibn al-Ḥājj was still able to conceive of a difference between a madrasa and a mosque. He preferred the latter for several reasons, most notably because the common people, to benefit whom is the principal purpose of Islamic education, were more likely to

a preference for instruction in mosques, and a positive distrust of education in private homes, "unless the scholar permits the entrance to his house of all who come." But his comment confirms that much instruction did transpire informally, in private teaching circles in homes or in the more public forum of a well-attended mosque. Moreover, his concern was that education in the law and other subjects be open to all; he made no distinction between the *character* or focus of classes given in a madrasa, mosque, or private home.[110]

It was a simple fact that the supply of individuals licensed to teach or to transmit the basic books on which learning rested exceeded the number of paying teaching posts available. The biographical dictionaries of the period are littered with references to men (and, under certain circumstances, women) who taught, but very often we are told nothing about teaching appointments. Some of the sources, such as Ibn Ḥajar al-ʿAsqalānī's compilation of the biographies of famous personages who died during the eighth *hijrī* century (corresponding roughly to the fourteenth century C.E.), *al-Durar al-kāmina fī aʿyān al-miʾa al-thāmina* (The Secret Pearls concerning the Notables of the Eighth Century), contain accounts that are comparatively cursory; it is impossible, therefore, to conclude from the silence of any particular biographical entry that the scholar in question never held an endowed teaching post. Other Mamluk-period historians, however, in particular al-Sakhāwī in his immense biographical dictionary *al-Ḍawʾ al-lāmiʿ li-ahl al-qarn al-tāsiʿ* (The Brilliant Light concerning the People of the Ninth Century), were scrupulous in including all available information regarding appointments to paying instructional posts. When, therefore, we are told that a man such as Shihāb al-Dīn Aḥmad b. ʿĪsā b. Aḥmad al-Ṣanhājī al-Azharī al-Mālikī (d. 1423) taught, but are told nothing regarding any particular academic appointments, we are tempted to conclude that his teaching focused on informal teaching circles—perhaps, as his name suggests, in the al-Azhar mosque. Al-Ṣanhājī was accomplished in Quranic studies, the Arabic language, and jurisprudence; he was "diligent in teaching [*al-iqrāʾ*] from dawn to dusk"; and he counted among his students such later luminaries as Shams al-Dīn Muḥammad b. Aḥamd b. ʿUmar al-Qarāfī (d. 1463), whom he instructed in Arabic grammar and the foundations of jurisprudence. Yet despite his active involvement in the transmission of learning, neither al-Sakhāwī nor any other contemporary historian indicates that he ever held a paying teaching post.[111]

attend a mosque than a "madrasa." After the first decades of the fourteenth century, such a distinction must have appeared increasingly meaningless.

[110] Tritton, *Materials*, 34–35, and Pedersen, *Arabic Book*, 20–21, cite examples, primarily from the early medieval period, of instruction in private homes.

[111] Al-Sakhāwī, *al-Ḍawʾ*, 2:59; cf. Aḥmad Ibn Ḥajar al-ʿAsqalānī, *Inbāʾ al-ghumr bi-abnāʾ*

The opportunity to teach informally, unsupported by any charitable endowment, allowed many to participate actively in the transmission of Muslim learning who for various reasons were unable to attain or unwilling to accept a paying position. Some, for example, taught informally while waiting for an appointment to a well-paid instructional post. This was especially true of those who, like ʿIzz al-Dīn ʿAbd al-Salām b. Aḥmad al-Baghdādī, came to Cairo from a distant home. ʿAbd al-Salām, a prominent Ḥanafī scholar from Iraq, arrived in the Egyptian capital in 1407–08. Eventually he became professor of jurisprudence at a number of prominent Cairene schools, including the Aqbughāwiyya, the Ashrafiyya, the Mankūtimuriyya, and the Nāṣiriyya in Bayn al-Qaṣrayn. These appointments, however, were not immediately forthcoming, and although approaching the age of forty, he was installed as a student of ḥadīth at the new Jamāliyya khānqāh. ʿAbd al-Salām, however, had already made a name for himself in a variety of academic fields, including jurisprudence, exegesis, and the variant Quran readings, and while still a student at the Jamāliyya "people drew near to him and studied with him."[112]

Alternatively, a prominent scholar might teach in one of these informal instructional circles at the end of his career. The famous legal scholar and transmitter of the Prophetic traditions Walī 'l-Dīn Aḥmad Ibn al-ʿIrāqī had held teaching posts in ḥadīth at the Ẓāhiriyya, the Qānibayhiyya, the Qarasunquriyya, and the mosque of Ibn Ṭūlūn, and in Shāfiʿī jurisprudence at the Fāḍiliyya and the Jamāliyya.[113] But after he resigned as qāḍī in 1422 he retired to his house, where he devoted himself to teaching and writing until his death the following year.[114] In 1426, Kamāl al-Dīn Muḥammad b. ʿAbd al-Wāḥid, known as Ibn al-Humām, one of the leading Ḥanafī scholars of his generation, was appointed shaykh and Ḥanafī professor at the Ashrafiyya madrasa, one of the most visible and lucrative teaching posts in Cairo. Four years later, however, he resigned after a dispute with a leading Mamluk over the appointment of one of his pupils to a student fellowship in the institution. Hardly ready at the age of forty to end his teaching career, he retired to his house outside of Cairo and, in the words of one of his biographers, "continued to devote himself to teaching."[115] By 1443, however, Ibn al-Humām began to miss the in-

al-ʿumr (Hyderabad, 1975; reptd. Beirut, 1986), 8:50; see also the biography of Shams al-Dīn al-Qarāfī in al-Sakhāwī, *al-Ḍaw'*, 7:27–28.

112 *Aqbala al-nās ʿalayhi fa-akhadhū ʿanhu.* Al-Sakhāwī, *al-Ḍaw'*, 4:198–203, esp. 199.

113 Al-Sakhāwī, *al-Ḍaw'*, 1:338.

114 *Istamarra mulāziman li-baytihi mukibban ʿalā 'l-ishghāl wa'l-taṣnīf.* Ibn Taghrī Birdī, *al-Manhal al-ṣāfī*, 1:334.

115 *Dāma mulāziman li'l-ishghāl.* The phrase is Ibn Taghrī Birdī's, from his obituary notice of Ibn al-Humām in *al-Nujūm al-zāhira*, 16:187; other details of Ibn al-Humām's life are taken from his biography in al-Sakhāwī, *al-Ḍaw'*, 8:127–32.

come of a formal teaching post, and went so far as to seek the assistance of two other scholars in securing for him the appointment as shaykh and professor at the Shaykhūniyya khānqāh.

Others, while holding nonacademic jobs, managed nevertheless to participate actively in the transmission of Muslim learning. Shihāb al-Dīn Aḥmad al-Qanā'i al-Qāhirī (d. 1454), a Shāfiʿī scholar with an impressive list of teachers and demonstrated accomplishments in such fields as jurisprudence and Arabic, clearly taught, since we are given the names of several of his students. His biographer, however, states that he held only two posts: that of a Sufi stipendiary in the Fakhriyya, and of imām and Sufi shaykh in the Quṭbiyya.[116] Similarly, Zayn al-Dīn Khālid al-Azharī al-Shāfiʿī (d. 1466), after a thorough education in jurisprudence and other subjects, eventually held the post of Sufi shaykh at the khānqāh Saʿīd al-Suʿadā', a position that as far as we know involved no teaching responsibilities; yet he too "applied himself to being of use to students, and a number studied with him."[117] In the late fourteenth century, a young student who had recently completed his primary studies at the *maktab* (primary school) associated with the Ṣarghitmishiyya madrasa began to frequent the nearby Shaykhūniyya; there, he studied a little jurisprudence with the imām before joining the institution's formal class in the subject.[118] Others earned an income from less lofty employment. Quite a few were employed as shāhids, notaries who acted as professional witnesses before the qāḍīs and transacted various basic legal affairs, or in other low-ranking religious or legal employment, and yet "instructed students in jurisprudence and other subjects."[119]

The issue can also be approached, of course, from the opposite side. If teachers taught privately in their homes, or publicly in mosques or even madrasas without necessarily receiving stipends from established endowments, they did so because many students were eager to attend, even though these pupils would not necessarily receive payments or accommodations to reward their efforts. To be sure, most Cairene schools did provide financial support, residences, and board to groups of students of varying size, in accordance with the common understanding of the madrasa's function. Consider, for example, the Ashrafiyya, the school established in Cairo by Sultan al-Ashraf Barsbāy (reigned 1422–37). Its stipendiaries included professors of all four rites of law as well as sixty-five Sufi students of jurisprudence: twenty-five Ḥanafīs, twenty Shāfiʿīs, ten Mālikīs, and ten Ḥanbalīs. Each was provided with a monthly stipend, as

[116] Al-Sakhāwī, *al-Ḍaw'*, 1:320–21.

[117] *Wa taṣaddā li-nafʿ al-ṭalaba fa-akhadha ʿanhu jamāʿa*. Al-Sakhāwī, *al-Ḍaw'*, 3:170–71.

[118] Al-Sakhāwī, *al-Ḍaw'*, 4:100.

[119] Al-Sakhāwī, *al-Ḍaw'*, 1:156.

well as a daily ration of bread, thereby freeing both students and teachers from the necessity of pursuing outside employment to finance their studies.[120] Just as important for our present purposes, the institution provided cells—*khalāwī*—intended to be residences for its students. Such a setting provided the opportunity to establish a strict, rigorous, and isolated environment for instruction in the Islamic sciences, and it seems that some, at least, conceived of this as the specific role of the madrasa.

However, accommodations at many of these schools may have served principally as residences for students who came to Cairo from other cities or countries for their education. A number of schools provided residences specifically for those students who came to the Egyptian capital from distant homes, and who would not therefore have family residences in the city. This was most notable at the Ḥanafī madrasa established by Amir Ṣarghitmish in the mid-fourteenth century; its endowment deed expressly restricted the school to "foreign Ḥanafī students."[121] Similarly, of the 113 students of jurisprudence, exegesis, ḥadīth, and the variant Quran readings at the khānqāh of Jamāl al-Dīn al-Ustādār, only 20 were specifically given a place of residence (*sakan*) in the institution; those thus accommodated were to be "free of marital ties and worldly attachments, and foreign to the lands of Egypt."[122]

Cairo was, in fact, a cosmopolitan center of study and instruction in the Islamic sciences, attracting students and scholars from virtually every corner of the Muslim world.[123] This situation is reflected in the endowment deeds of several of the more important schools that provided their students with leaves of absence to facilitate visits to their families in distant lands. At the madrasa of Sultan Barqūq, for example, it was stipulated that

> if someone travels for reasons other than the *ḥajj* [the pilgrimage to Mecca], and if his journey is for [the purpose of] visiting his family or relatives, then a journey of three months' duration shall be allowed him, [although] during his absence he shall not receive his stipend; and when he returns, he shall

[120] The monthly stipends varied considerably. The highest salary was paid to the Ḥanafī professor who also functioned as the institution's Sufi shaykh; he was paid 3,000 copper dirhams per month. By contrast, the Shāfi'ī professor was paid 100 silver dirhams per month, his Mālikī and Ḥanbalī colleagues 50 silver dirhams each. As for the students, the Ḥanafīs were to receive 300 copper dirhams per month, the others 10 silver dirhams each. *Waqfiyyat* al-Ashraf Barsbāy, Dār al-Wathā'iq No. 173, fol. 116r–119v.

[121] *Al-ṭalaba al-ḥanafiyya al-ghurabā'*. *Waqfiyyat* Ṣarghitmish, Wizārat al-Awqāf o.s. No. 3195, p. 26; cf. 'Abd al-Laṭīf Ibrāhīm 'Alī, "Naṣṣān jadīrān," pt. 1, 147. Leonor Fernandes, "Mamlūk Politics and Education: The Evidence from Two Fourteenth Century Waqfiyya," *Annales islamologiques* 23 (1987), 91.

[122] *Waqfiyyat* Jamāl al-Dīn al-Ustādār, Dār al-Wathā'iq No. 106, ll. 29ff.

[123] Petry, *Civilian Elite*, 79–80.

receive his stipend; but if he stays away longer than three months, he shall be dismissed and another appointed to his position.[124]

While the original deed of endowment for the mosque of al-Mu'ayyad Shaykh included much more stringent provisions, a later document altered the terms governing excused absences for the institution's staff and students, so that they would conform to those at Barqūq's madrasa: that is, all of the school's stipendiaries were granted three months' unpaid leave per year to visit "family and relations" (*al-ahl wa'l-aqārib*).[125] It may be significant, however, that all those schools, the terms of whose endowments allowed absences for visiting family and relatives, were among the larger and more prominent schools of Cairo, such as the madrasas of Barqūq and Barsbāy, the khānqāh of Jamāl al-Dīn al-Ustādār, and the mosque of al-Mu'ayyad Shaykh. While less wealthy and less prestigious institutions routinely allowed their stipendiaries to perform the pilgrimages to Mecca or Jerusalem, they do not seem to have excused lengthy visits to distant relatives. This may suggest that their students were, primarily, local.[126]

On the other hand, it is clear that even in madrasas that specifically provided stipends, daily food rations, and living accommodations for some number of students, many attended classes who did not live in the school, or who in some cases did not even receive a stipend from its endowments. This is largely obscured by our sources, by the apparent lack of concern of the biographical dictionaries to reveal *where* medieval Muslims studied, and by the natural preoccupation of the deeds with those who lived in and received stipends from the institutions. But the few glimpses we do receive suggest a world in which students came and went to classes with a fair degree of fluidity.

In a few cases, such as at the madrasa of Ṣarghitmish, most students were expected to reside in the institution itself: there, a limited number of students who received stipends were given permission to live outside the madrasa, presumably in order to allow them to marry.[127] But the situation at the madrasa of Sultan al-Ẓāhir Barqūq may have been more typical. There, one particular residence hall (*qāʿa*) was set aside for the Ḥanafī professor and Sufi shaykh, but the rest of the school's accommodations were to be assigned to stipendiaries at the discretion of the institution's controller. Among them, 167 student residences (buyūt) were

[124] *Waqfiyyat* al-Ẓāhir Barqūq, Dār al-Wathā'iq No. 51, ll. 991–93; cf. *Waqfiyyat* al-Ashraf Barsbāy, Dār al-Wathā'iq No. 173, fol. 137v.

[125] *Waqfiyyat* al-Mu'ayyad Shaykh, Wizārat al-Awqāf o.s. No. 938, in a document in the margin at the bottom of the scroll.

[126] Cf. Petry, *Civilian Elite*.

[127] *Waqfiyyat* Ṣarghitmish, Wizārat al-Awqāf o.s. No. 3195, p. 28; cf. ʿAbd al-Laṭīf Ibrāhīm ʿAlī, "Naṣṣān jadīran," pt. 1, 148. Ṣarghitmish's waqfiyya specifically granted six of sixty students, to be chosen by the professor, the right to live outside the madrasa.

provided. The Ẓāhiriyya's endowment deed made provisions for stipends for 125 students—forty in Ḥanafī jurisprudence, twenty for each of the Shāfiʿī, Mālikī, and Ḥanbalī rites, fifteen students of ḥadīth, and ten of the seven variant Quran readings—in addition to sixty Sufis (who also lived in the student residences). The controller of the institution was specifically empowered to permit some students receiving stipends and entitled to accommodations to live outside the confines of the school. In addition, any student who wished to take the cash equivalent of his daily food rations could do so. More importantly, the endowment deed made explicit reference to students who regularly came to the madrasa but did not live there (called *al-mutaraddidūn*). If one of those who lived in the madrasa wished to marry, the deed stipulated, "let him do so, and let his room [*mabītuhu*] be given to an unmarried man from among those who frequent [*al-mutaraddidīn*] this madrasa for the purposes of study."[128]

Other deeds of endowment, while understandably preoccupied with those actually living in the schools or receiving stipends from them, also indicated that students unaffiliated with the institutions themselves would regularly attend lessons. At the Jamāliyya, for example, the controller was to permit no one other than the institution's stipendiaries to live in the school, unless that person was a Sufi and a student, and one who frequented the khānqāh (*mutaraddidan li'l-khānqāh*). Moreover, he was to be given the first stipendiary position that became available.[129] The mosque of al-Shiblī Kāfūr provided stipends for only five Shāfiʿī students, but the class that took place there on Sundays and Wednesdays was also for "those students who participate with them in the [class]."[130] The deed of Khushqadam al-Zimām, too, acknowledged that "outsiders" would attend the classes that he endowed at al-Azhar, which he intended to move to a separate institution, apparently never built.[131]

In a similar vein, it was also the case that some lived in the schools who were *not* regular, salaried students or professors. Ibn Jamāʿa was of the opinion that if the founder of an institution had stipulated that the inhabitants of his madrasa be restricted to those who received stipends (*al-murattabūn*), then his wishes should be respected.[132] In fact, however, the actual deeds suggest that founders did not routinely make such a stipulation. Recognizing this, Ibn Jamāʿa further opined that those who

[128] *Waqfiyyat* al-Ẓāhir Barqūq, Dār al-Wathāʾiq No. 51, ll. 749–50, 926–27, 971–75.

[129] *Waqfiyyat* Jamāl al-Dīn al-Ustādār, Dār al-Wathāʾiq No. 106, ll. 307–10.

[130] *Li-man shārakahum fi'l-ḥuḍūr min ṭalabat al-ʿilm. Waqfiyyat* al-Shiblī Kāfūr, Dār al-Wathāʾiq No. 76, l. 76.

[131] I am indebted to ʿAbd al-Ghanī Maḥmūd ʿAbd al-ʿAṭī's book, *al-Taʿlīm fī miṣr zaman al-ayyūbiyyīn wa'l-mamālīk* (Cairo, 1984), 220, for this reference. By the time I myself read the document (*Waqfiyyat* Khushqadam al-Zimām, Wizārat al-Awqāf n.s. No. 188), the critical passage was obscured by a piece of opaque tape; only later, through reading ʿAbd al-ʿAṭī's book, did I become aware of the full meaning of this comment in the waqfiyya.

[132] Ibn Jamāʿa, *Tadhkirat al-sāmiʿ*, 210.

lived in madrasas who were not stipendiaries should attend the institution's classes; if they did not, then they should leave the building during the time of instruction; if they would not leave, then they should not leave their rooms, or walk around the madrasa, or raise their voices, or lock or open their doors noisily.[133]

Many of those who simply lived in the schools without regularly participating in the academic functions were no doubt serious scholars and students in their own right. Some were minor academics who, while having attained a minimal level of education, had not reached a rank from which they could expect preferments to paid instructional posts. Badr al-Dīn Ḥusayn Ibn al-Naḥḥāl (d. 1443), for example, received a solid if unexceptional education in the Quran, jurisprudence, and other subjects, but as far as we can tell never held a teaching post, although he did transmit ḥadīth. Yet late in life, after being blinded by an eye disorder, he retired to a cell in the Sayfiyya madrasa, a relatively obscure school for Shāfiʿīs.[134] Still others who resided in the schools had even more tenuous connections to the world of education. For example, Abū 'l-ʿAbbās al-Ḥijāzī (d. 1436 or 1437) lived in the Ẓāhiriyya madrasa on Bayn al-Qaṣrayn. He clearly never held any academic post there—his biographers tell us virtually nothing about his education, and do not even indicate to which Sunni rite he belonged. On the contrary, his fame rested on his composition and recitation of poems in praise of local notables.[135]

Clearly, then, the schools became magnets attracting a variety of intellectuals and hangers-on. Their most important gift to the Muslim community was the most basic one: a permanent forum for instruction and the transmission of knowledge. But human nature and the necessities of living being what they are, the academic community also came to value, and expect, the cash stipends and other forms of support provided by the schools. The establishment and endowment of institutions of learning over the course of the later Middle Ages did not transform the character of education, but it did introduce a new and somewhat disturbing element into the social relationship of teachers and students, as we shall see in the following chapter.

[133] Ibid., 216.

[134] Al-Sakhāwī, *al-Ḍaw'*, 3:154. Other nonacademics lived in this madrasa at other times. Gary Leiser identified a Sufi who lived (but apparently did not teach) here in the early thirteenth century, during the Ayyubid period; see "Restoration," 310.

[135] Ibn Ḥajar, *Inbā' al-ghumr*, 8:434–35; al-Sakhāwī, *al-Ḍaw'*, 2:72–73. Cf. the case of Ibn al-Amīn al-Kātib (d. 1482) who, despite a decent education in the religious sciences, was best known for his poetic compositions in three languages (Arabic, Persian, and Turkish), a skill that brought him into close contact with several Mamluks. When he died, in his sixth decade, he lived in a cell (khalwa) in the Ṣarghitmishiyya madrasa. Al-Sakhāwī, *al-Ḍaw'*, 4:72–73.

IV

PROFESSORS AND PATRONS

CAREERS IN THE ACADEMIC WORLD

MUḤAMMAD IBN AL-ḤĀJJ, a jurist who died in 1336, composed a treatise that, in the words of his biographer, "exposed the vices and heretical innovations" in which the Muslim population of Cairo indulged. Always a fierce critic of contemporary standards and practices, he deplored what he perceived to be the increasing concern of the ulama for wealth and worldly status. Ibn al-Ḥājj summed up his criticism with the pithy observation that "whereas before, a man spent his money in order to acquire knowledge, now he acquires money through his knowledge."[1] Modern secular academics in the West, too, anxious to maintain the "purity" of intellectual activity, have from time to time maintained the ideal of a strict separation of learning from potentially corrupting financial reward, but to the eye of a pious medieval Muslim the matter was far more urgent. The mixing of lucre and learning rankled this fourteenth-century jurist (who was, admittedly, prone to rather vituperative complaining) because of the essential holiness of the task of acquiring and transmitting knowledge.

What bothered Ibn al-Ḥājj was not wealth per se. Not a few Muslim scholars, of course, earned or inherited fortunes through family business connections. Indeed, the medieval Islamic world generally avoided that radical division of intellectual and commercial labor that has at times impoverished both the academy and the corporation in the West. The overall attitude of Islamic law and culture to wealth and worldly comforts is more favorable, and less ambivalent, than that of the Christian West, in which the ascetic and monastic ideals were always available as powerful alternative models. In Islam, all the heavy weight of tradition served to extol the value of religious knowledge and encourage its acquisition and transmission—by and to all members of society. Consequently, Islam had never known a sharp social divide between men of religious learning and men of commerce, and Mamluk Egypt produced no exception to that rule. Even Ibn Ḥajar al-ʿAsqalānī, the famous Shāfiʿī jurist and possibly

[1] Muḥammad Ibn al-Ḥājj, *Madkhal al-sharʿ al-sharīf* (Cairo, 1929; reptd. Beirut, 1981), 2:126. Cf. Ibn Ḥajar al-ʿAsqalānī, *al-Durar al-kāmina fī aʿyān al-miʾa al-thāmina* (Cairo, 1966–67), 4:355–56.

the single most important scholar of the later Middle Ages, probably came from a merchant family, and may himself have participated in commercial activities.[2]

However, the phenomenon of the "merchant-scholar," and more broadly of the social mixing of academic and commercial elites, does not concern us directly. Rather, the immediate issue is framed by the complaint of Ibn al-Ḥājj: that religious scholars were now *exploiting* their knowledge to acquire wealth. Higher religious education had always aimed, at least in part, at forming a cadre of men qualified to discharge certain religious and legal duties, most notably as judges of the Islamic courts, and to this extent had always served as a means, at least for a few, to gainful employment. But it was not this limited phenomenon that annoyed Ibn al-Ḥājj. Rather, his complaint was a response to certain consequences of the proliferation since the twelfth century of endowed institutions that disbursed their substantial income to the academic elite in the form of salaries, stipends, meals, and accommodations. It was not that educated men performed new functions; rather, those functions became the obligation of hired functionaries in the multitude of new institutions. An education in the religious sciences now provided access to a whole host of regular employment opportunities: as professors and educators, assistants in instruction, Quran and ḥadīth readers, and prayer leaders and preachers. The establishment of these institutions did not alter the process of instruction and the transmission of knowledge; by creating numerous new sources of employment, however, it did have profound consequences for the character of social relations among the ulama.

The Control of Appointments to Academic Posts

In the world of higher Islamic education in late medieval Cairo, a learned and well-placed man certainly could acquire a fair amount of money. Holding a single teaching appointment in one of the many schools of Mamluk Cairo by itself would not make a scholar rich. The stipends attached to professorships varied considerably from one institution to another, but a scholar might compensate for a comparatively small salary in one by holding more than one post. Sirāj al-Dīn ʿUmar, known as Qāriʾ al-Hidāya, the leading Ḥanafī jurist of the early fifteenth century, was professor of jurisprudence or ḥadīth in over half a dozen of Cairo's leading madrasas and teaching mosques, and "grew rich from the large num-

[2] Ira Lapidus, *Muslim Cities in the Later Middle Ages* (Cambridge, Mass., 1967), 108–9. Sabri K. Kawash, "Ibn Ḥajar al-ʿAsqalānī (1372–1449 A.D.): A Study of the Background, Education, and Career of a ʿĀlim in Egypt," dissertation, Princeton University (1969), 20–23, 218–41.

ber of his appointments."[3] Another scholar earned the reprobation of Cairo's academic community by brazenly wresting a prominent and lucrative professorship from an infirm, aged man, whose son was nevertheless successfully discharging his father's teaching duties. The usurper's behavior, according to his biographer, suggested an unscrupulous character, just the type whose mixing of mercenary motives and academic pursuits angered Ibn al-Ḥājj, since he had a habit of frequenting Mamluk amirs and "did not refrain from collecting money from any source."[4]

As if to confirm Ibn al-Ḥājj's complaint, appointments to academic employment became in the Middle Ages objects for sale. The practice was not necessarily confined to Mamluk Cairo: it was widespread in Syria, as a sixteenth-century history of Damascene madrasas suggests.[5] It followed in fact a widespread pattern of demanding payment in exchange for appointment to religious or legal positions: sultans routinely accepted sizeable gratuities from those seeking office as judges, market inspectors, or other legal functionaries appointed by the state. Contemporary historians and biographers at times treated it almost as a commonplace, blandly remarking that a particular scholar paid 400 (dinars, presumably) for the post of Sufi shaykh and Ḥanafī professor at the Shaykhūniyya. Others besides sultans benefited from the practice: in particular, a scholar who held appointment to an institutional post might trade his professorship for cash. The jurist and historian Ibn Ḥajar al-ʿAsqalānī is said to have resigned his professorship in ḥadīth at the Jamāliyya madrasa to one of his students for a payment of 50 dinars. On occasion, a note of criticism creeps into the narratives of contemporary observers. Ibn Iyās, for example, remarked that a certain scholar paid Sultan Qayt Bāy "a large amount of money" to replace Badr al-Dīn Ibn al-Dīrī as shaykh and Ḥanafī professor of the Mu'ayyadiyya, even though the founder of the institution had stipulated that the post was always to be held by a member of the al-Dīrī family. Another historian used the word *rishwa*, "bribery," in relating the succession of an incompetent scholar to professorships at the Ṣarghitmishiyya and elsewhere. But such pejorative remarks must have reflected peculiar circumstances or personal rivalries, factors that were frequently present but are not always detectable in the surviving source material, because on the whole the practice was common. If it had not been, al-Sakhāwī, the great fifteenth-century historian who probably knew more about the academic establishment than any other writer,

[3] Shams al-Dīn Muḥammad al-Sakhāwī, *al-Ḍaw' al-lāmiʿ li-ahl al-qarn al-tāsiʿ* (Cairo, 1934; reptd. Beirut, n.d.), 6:109–10.

[4] Ibn Ḥajar al-ʿAsqalānī, *Inbā' al-ghumr bi-abnā' al-ʿumr* (Hyderabad, 1975; reptd. Beirut, 1986), 5:322, 6:122–23.

[5] ʿAbd al-Qādir b. Muḥammad al-Nuʿaymī, *al-Dāris fī tārīkh al-madāris* (Damascus, 1948), for example, 1:255; cf. George Makdisi, *The Rise of Colleges* (Edinburgh, 1981), 171.

would not have bothered to note that a particular individual relinquished a number of his lesser teaching posts to a group of worthy scholars "free of charge" (*majjānan*).[6] If teaching posts might be "sold," appointments to them were necessarily a desirable commodity. Who actually controlled the appointment of scholars to teaching positions in the various schools of Mamluk Cairo? The question is certainly not an idle one, since some of the professorial "chairs" carried substantial emoluments. To control appointments to them was to control a valuable form of patronage.

There is in fact no direct and definitive answer to the question. Even in theory, Islamic law did not provide an unequivocal response. In a *fatwā*, an authoritative but nonbinding legal opinion analogous to the Jewish *responsum*, Taqī 'l-Dīn ʿAlī al-Subkī (d. 1355) noted that some legal scholars held that, while the financial controller (*nāẓir*) of a madrasa and its endowments had authority over the building and its financial affairs, it was up to the *ḥākim*, here probably meaning the qāḍi, or, possibly, the ruler, to appoint the professors. Al-Subkī and others disagreed, however, and confirmed the general right of the controller to make appointments to teaching posts, although he did believe that it was the prerogative of the ḥākim to determine who was fit to hold a teaching appointment, and to forbid the installation of incompetent shaykhs.[7]

The actual practice in Mamluk Cairo presents a confusing pattern of overlapping authority. From at least the time of Sultan al-Ẓāhir Baybars (reigned 1260–77), pure *khayrī* endowments—those, that is, of an exclusively charitable nature, such as endowments established to support the

[6] References are to: al-Sākhāwī, *al-Ḍaw'*, 4:48, 100 (citing Badr al-Dīn al-ʿAynī, who used the word "rishwa"), and 6:303; Kawash, "Ibn Ḥajar," 124, citing a still unpublished portion of al-Sakhāwī's detailed biography of his teacher, *al-Jawāhir wa'l-durar fī tarjamat shaykh al-islām Ibn Ḥajar*; Muḥammad Ibn Iyās, *Badā'iʿ al-zuhūr fī waqā'iʿ al-duhūr*, ed. Muḥammad Muṣṭafā (Cairo, 1982–84), 3:243; al-Sakhāwī, *al-Ḍaw'*, 6:303. On payments and bribery for academic and religious posts in the Mamluk period, see Aḥmad ʿAbd al-Rāziq, *al-Badhl wa'l-barṭala zaman salāṭīn al-mamālīk* (Cairo, 1979), esp. 124–26.

[7] Taqī 'l-Dīn ʿAlī al-Subkī, *Fatāwā 'l-Subkī* (Cairo, A.H. 1356; reptd. Beirut, n.d.), 2:150–54. For a discussion of the legal literature surrounding the law of *waqf* (charitable endowments) as it related to institutions of learning, see Makdisi, *Colleges*, 35–74. Certain points emerge from Makdisi's discussion—to which we shall have occasion to return—but even there, the picture is far from clear. The character of the institutions and their endowments, and the nature of the literary evidence, limit the possibility of making generalizations. The endowment deeds (*waqfiyyas*) themselves could differ significantly, and some might be more strictly adhered to than others, for social, economic, and political reasons, rather than legal ones. Moreover, the *fatwās* of medieval jurists on which much of Makdisi's discussion is based were, as he himself notes, nonbinding legal opinions, and therefore cannot necessarily be assumed consistently to reflect actual medieval practice. Particularly useful in the specific context of Mamluk Egypt, and a starting point for any study of the actual administration of endowments in late medieval Cairo, is the important work of Muḥammad M. Amīn, *al-Awqāf wa'l-ḥayāt al-ijtimāʿiyya fī miṣr* (Cairo, 1980), esp. 107–25.

poor of Mecca and Medina—had been under the direct supervision of the Shāfiʿī chief judge (*qāḍī 'l-quḍāt*), the senior legal official in the Mamluk state. Private (*ahlī*) endowments instituted solely for the benefit of the founder and/or his family, as well as those which combined both charitable and private purposes, likewise "were subject to the superintendence [*ishrāf*] of the Shāfiʿī qāḍī, although each of these endowments also had its private controller [*nāẓir*], according to the stipulation of the founder."[8] Virtually all of the endowments supporting institutions of learning in Mamluk Cairo fell into this last category, providing income both for a school as well as for the founder's family and descendants. Appointments to their teaching posts were the prerogative, in the first place, of the founder himself, or of the controller appointed by him or succeeding to his reponsibilities after his death, according to stipulations in the deed of endowment.[9] Appointments, however, were at least nominally subject to the review of the Shāfiʿī chief qāḍī, who had the responsibility of a "general supervision" (*naẓar ʿāmm*) over endowments, because he was the "senior judge" (*kabīr al-quḍāt*) in Egypt.[10] But in practice the appointment process was also subject to the intervention of the reigning sultan and, especially, to the suggestions and nominations of the educated elite themselves.

When the founder and benefactor of an institution of learning wished to appoint particular men as professors or students, he encountered little resistance. Not infrequently do the biographical dictionaries and chronicles report that a scholar was appointed professor in a particular school by the founder of the institution. The qāḍī Zayn al-Dīn ʿUbāda al-Anṣārī (d. 1346), for example, held the professorship in Mālikī law at the mosque of Sultan al-Ashraf Barsbāy "from the founder upon the opening of the school." The founder retained an interest in appointments to his institution well after its opening, and could name successors to his original appointees after their death or resignation, as did Zayn al-Dīn ʿAbd al-Bāsiṭ, who appointed at least the first two shaykhs of the madrasa that he founded, the Bāsiṭiyya.[11]

Sultan al-Ashraf Barsbāy (reigned 1422–37), for example, seems to

[8] Amīn, *al-Awqāf*, 113–16ff.

[9] On the stipulations providing for succession to the *naẓar* (the controllership of the endowment), see Chapter Five.

[10] Tāj al-Dīn ʿAbd al-Wahhāb al-Subkī, *Muʿīd al-niʿam wa-mubīd al-niqam*, ed. David Myhrman (London, 1908), 78–79; cf. Makdisi, *Colleges*, 55–57.

[11] On the appointment of al-Anṣārī, see al-Sakhāwī, *al-Ḍaw'*, 4:17, and ʿAbd al-Ḥayy Ibn al-ʿImād, *Shadharāt al-dhahab fī akhbār man dhahab* (Cairo, A.H. 1350; reptd. Beirut, 1979), 7:258. The first shaykh of the Bāsiṭiyya, ʿIzz al-Dīn ʿAbd al-Salām al-Qudsī, left the position sometime before his death in 1446 to become shaykh at the Ṣalāḥiyya in Jerusalem; upon his resignation, ʿAbd al-Bāsiṭ appointed Shihāb al-Dīn Aḥmad al-Adhrāʿī to his Cairene madrasa. Al-Sakhāwī, *al-Ḍaw'*, 1:276, 4:203–6.

have taken a keen and continuing interest in the school he constructed. In 1424 he "bestowed a robe of honor [*khalaʿa*] on ʿAlāʾ al-Dīn ʿAlī al-Rūmī al-Ḥanafī, [marking] his appointment as Sufi shaykh and professor of Ḥanafī law at the Ashrafiyya madrasa." Less than two years later, however, the Sultan was forced to demand the resignation of al-Rūmī because of the discovery that the shaykh had been appropriating to himself the stipends assigned to several of the institution's Sufi students who had died. Barsbāy then appointed Kamāl al-Dīn Ibn al-Humām Ḥanafī shaykh. Ibn al-Humām's tenure, however, lasted only until 1430, when he resigned after a dispute over the appointment of one of his favored students as a stipendiary in the school. At this point Barsbāy once again intervened, and after failing to persuade Ibn al-Humām to remain as shaykh and professor, appointed Amīn al-Dīn al-Aqṣarāʾī to the position.[12]

The wealthy Mamluks and others who built and endowed institutions of learning often made certain that scholars to whom they were connected by personal ties received employment in their schools. Given the incomplete nature of the literary record, it is an open question as to whether most founders of educational institutions took an active personal interest in these appointments. It may well be that they responded to the suggestions of trusted advisers or influential scholars, who would of course have been in a better position to know who among the ulama was especially fitted for a given post. In particular cases, however, we can certainly discern specific ties of patronage between the wealthy benefactors of educational institutions, very often Mamluk amirs or sultans, and those scholars holding academic appointments. The Ḥanafī qāḍī Badr al-Dīn Maḥmūd al-ʿAynī's close relationship with Sultan al-Muʾayyad Shaykh (reigned 1412–21), for example, is well known. The Turkish-speaking jurist and historian was among the ruler's "intimate companions and friends," and was rewarded with an appointment as professor of the Prophetic traditions at the Muʾayyadiyya when it first opened, a post that he held until his death in 1452. Humām al-Dīn al-Khawārizmī (d. 1416), a Shāfiʿī scholar who came to Cairo at the end of the fourteenth century, developed an equally close relationship with Jamāl al-Dīn Yūsuf al-Ustādār, a powerful figure in the Mamluk kingdom until his execution in late 1409. When the construction of Jamāl al-Dīn's khānqāh was completed in 1408, the founder appointed Humām al-Dīn to be the school's professor of Shāfiʿī law, granting him a residence in the institution and bestowing on him stipends and gifts in addition to his official salary.[13]

[12] The quotation is from Jamāl al-Dīn Yūsuf Ibn Taghrī Birdī, *al-Nujūm al-ẓāhira fī mulūk miṣr wa'l-qāhira* (Cairo, 1929–72), 14:266. See also ibid., 14:285, 16:187–88, and al-Sakhāwī, *al-Ḍaw'*, 6:41–42, 8:127–32, 10:240–43.

[13] On Badr al-Dīn al-ʿAynī, see al-Sakhāwī, *al-Ḍaw'*, 10:132–33. Badr al-Dīn was also an

Urban society in the Mamluk period was characterized by a web of patronage that bound the ulama as a group to the military elite. In exchange for protection from external enemies and income from bureaucratic and legal appointments, the educated elite legitimized the Mamluk regime by enjoining obedience on the local population, mediating the government's needs for tax revenues, and performing a host of tangible and intangible services to the state.[14] Such patronage, however, like the transmission of knowledge itself, depended at least as much on personal relationships as on corporate identities and interests. The pattern of appointment to positions of academic employment in the schools suggests that such patronage was experienced by many as a personal tie between an individual Mamluk and a particular scholar. There must, for example, have been some sort of strong personal connection between Amīn al-Dīn al-Aqṣarā'ī and the Mamluk amir Jānibak al-Ẓāhirī (d. 1463). According to al-Aqṣarā'ī's biographer, not only did the Mamluk himself appoint the scholar to the professorship of his madrasa, but "it is said that [Jānibak] would not have built the madrasa were it not for [al-Aqṣarā'ī]."[15] The fact that several of the foundation deeds for Cairene schools specified that particular scholars were to be appointed to teaching posts within the institution suggests that the benefactors had these scholars in mind when making the decision to undertake the massive expenditures that founding a school involved. Information in the deeds is by no means complete, however, so that the failure of any particular document to record the names of academic appointees did not mean that the founder remained indifferent as to who was to teach in his institution. The foundation deed for the Jamāliyya khānqāh, for example, records the appointment of Humām al-Dīn al-Khawārizmī as Shāfiʿī professor, but neglects to mention that the founder, Jamāl al-Dīn Yūsuf, also appointed the institution's other original instructors.[16] Whether or not most founders actually built and endowed their institutions for the benefit of particular scholars, most did take an active interest in the process of making appointments to academic positions in their schools.

---

intimate of the sultans al-Ẓāhir Ṭaṭar (reigned 1421) and al-Ashraf Barsbāy (reigned 1422–37). On Humām al-Dīn al-Khawārizmī, see ibid., 7:128.

[14] The locus classicus of this argument is Lapidus, *Muslim Cities*, esp. 130–41.

[15] Al-Sakhāwī, *al-Ḍaw'*, 10:241.

[16] Taqī 'l-Dīn Aḥmad al-Maqrīzī, *al-Mawāʿiẓ wa'l-iʿtibār bi-dhikr al-khiṭaṭ wa'l-āthār* (Būlāq, A.H. 1270), 2:401–2, in his account of the opening of the school, makes it clear that Jamāl al-Dīn "sat" (*ajlasa*) Humām al-Dīn down on a carpet representing his appointment as Shāfiʿī professor and Sufi shaykh. For the other original appointees, al-Maqrīzī simply used the word *qarrara*, "he appointed," which of course could be *qurrira*, "he [the professor] *was* appointed." Other accounts, however, specify that the founder actively appointed the others: for example, "Jamāl al-Dīn appointed him [Badr al-Dīn Maḥmūd ibn al-Shaykh Zāda] as Ḥanafī professor in his madrasa." Al-Sakhāwī, *al-Ḍaw'*, 10:136; cf. ibid., 7:6.

It is worth bearing in mind that the ties that bound the Mamluks and the ulama were concrete and intensely personal, and were subject to the strains and vicissitudes of any personal relationship. In one deed dating to the early sixteenth century, we can trace at least the outlines of the tempestuous course taken by the relationship between a Mamluk amir and the shaykh he had appointed to his madrasa. Al-Sayfī Baybars, a high-ranking military and political officer in the last years of the Mamluk state, in the first of two documents, dated 3 Jumādā al-Awwal, A.H. 921 (June 1515), appointed someone named Shihāb al-Dīn Abū 'l-ʿAbbās Aḥmad b. Ismāʿīl al-Saftī as the Sufi shaykh of his madrasa, as well as its prayer leader and preacher. According to the document, Shihāb al-Dīn's son Badr al-Dīn Muḥammad held the posts in tandem with his father. In the following document on the scroll, however, dated five months later, the founder altered somewhat the terms under which his madrasa was to be administered. Among other matters, he stripped Shihāb al-Dīn of all his posts except that of Sufi shaykh, and "expelled" (*akhraja min waqfihi*) his son Badr al-Dīn altogether, forbidding him to hold any post within the institution, and stipulating that Shihāb al-Dīn's children and descendants were permanently excluded from inheriting his position. Al-Sayfī Baybars' feelings toward Shihāb al-Dīn himself must have been degenerating rapidly, however, since later in the same document the founder stipulated that "the name of Shaykh Shihāb al-Dīn Aḥmad al-Saftī al-Mālikī be dropped," and that, at least for the present, no one was to be appointed Sufi shaykh.[17]

After the death of a founder, a controller was appointed to administer the endowment and the institutions it supported, according to stipulations laid down in the deed of endowment. He, of course, like the founder, had particular responsibility for the hiring of an academic institution's staff.[18] The literary sources—the chronicles and biographical dictionaries—rarely, however, bother to record a scholar's appointment at the hands of an institution's controller. This lacuna may simply indicate that the practice was routine, and therefore unworthy of comment. But it is clear that in actual practice the situation was quite fluid. Despite a controller's responsibilities for an institution, lines of authority were not always drawn precisely, and qāḍīs, amirs, and sultans all had a hand in the appointment of the teaching staff of Cairo's schools.

In particular, the reigning sultan enjoyed a special prerogative in the

[17] The deed in question is that of al-Sayfī Baybars (Dār al-Wathā'iq No. 313, specifically the second and third documents on the scroll, dated 3 Jumādā al-Awwal and 20 Shawāl, A.H. 921), the construction of whose madrasa was completed in late 1515; cf. Ibn Iyās, *Badā'iʿ al-zuhūr*, 4:477. I have been unable to identify the Shihāb al-Dīn al-Saftī to whom this deed refers.

[18] Cf. Makdisi, *Colleges*, 47–48.

appointment of professors to paid teaching positions. According to al-Qalqashandī's encyclopedic guide to bureaucratic and chancery practice, *Ṣubḥ al-aʿshā*, "the sultan does not make appointments to teaching posts, except in those [schools] of great importance and high prestige, [and] which are not [under the supervision] of a controller."[19] He then listed several schools in which the sultan did routinely make appointments, including the Ṣalāḥiyya madrasa next to the tomb of the imām al-Shāfiʿī, the teaching circle (*zāwiya*) in the mosque of ʿAmr known as the Khashshābiyya, the Manṣūriyya madrasa established by al-Manṣūr Qalāwūn in the late thirteenth century, the "lesson" (*dars*) in the mosque of Ibn Ṭūlūn,[20] and "others like them." Later in his administrative handbook, he gave examples of documents of appointment (*tawqīʿ*, pl. *tawāqīʿ*) to teaching positions that were drafted by scribes in the royal chancellery; they included appointments to the zāwiya of al-Shāfiʿī in the mosque of ʿAmr, the Ṣalāḥiyya and the Qamḥiyya madrasas, the "Qubbat al-Ṣāliḥ" in the Manṣūriyya complex,[21] and the Ḥākimī mosque.

Al-Qalqashandī's remarks notwithstanding, the exact parameters of the sultan's authority in the distribution of academic posts is difficult to determine. Many royal "appointments" may have been purely formal, making official the naming of a candidate chosen in fact through some more informal mode of selection. On the other hand, the monarch was certainly privileged to make appointments to particular important schools. The chronicles and biographical dictionaries provide many examples of sultans assigning to scholars academic positions in the institutions listed by al-Qalqashandī, such as the Ṣalāḥiyya or Qamḥiyya madrasas, sometimes specifying that the appointments were made "by noble decree" (*bi*

[19] Aḥmad b. ʿAlī al-Qalqashandī, *Ṣubḥ al-aʿshā fī ṣināʿat al-inshāʾ* (Cairo, 1914–28), 4:39.

[20] It is difficult to know what this refers to. The most important courses in Ibn Ṭūlūn were those in jurisprudence according to the four *madhāhib* (Sunni rites), the traditions, exegesis, and other subjects endowed by Sultan al-Manṣūr Lājīn at the end of the thirteenth century; clearly, however, these were more than one "lesson." Moreover, the institution had its own controller; al-Maqrīzī, *Khiṭaṭ*, 2:269, listed a large number of Shāfiʿī qāḍīs and amirs who consecutively held the controllership of the institution from the late thirteenth until the early fifteenth century, and others after the time of al-Maqrīzī can be identified (for example, in al-Sakhāwī, *al-Ḍawʾ*, 1:77–78, 4:228–29, 292–94). It is possible that the reference might be to a course in Ḥanafī jurisprudence endowed by the amir Yalbughā al-ʿUmarī in 1356; see al-Maqrīzī, *Khiṭaṭ*, 2:269.

[21] Al-Qalqashandī refers to this institution simply as *qubbat al-Ṣāliḥ*. The reference, however, is presumed to refer to the courses established in the *qubba* (domed burial chamber) of the Manṣūriyya madrasa and hospital complex on behalf of al-Manṣūr Qalāwūn's grandson al-Ṣāliḥ Ismāʿīl; see al-Maqrīzī, *Khiṭaṭ*, 2:380. Al-Sakhāwī used the phrase "qubbat al-Ṣāliḥ" to refer to these courses; see, for example, *al-Ḍawʾ*, 4:146, in which the historian Ibn Khaldūn was appointed to the Mālikī professorship *bi-qubbat al-ṣāliḥ biʾl-bimāristān*.

tawqīʿ sharīf).[22] From other sources, too, we know that Sultan al-Ẓāhir Barqūq, shortly before his death, altered the terms of the endowment for his madrasa so that its controllership would always be held by the reigning sultan.[23]

But sultans also intervened directly and personally to appoint professors at schools besides those in which they had the stipulated right to do so. The controller at the madrasa of al-Ashraf Barsbāy was selected according to precise rules laid down by the founder in his deed of endowment. Yet at some point it seems to have become the prerogative of the sultan to appoint at least the institution's Sufi shaykh and Ḥanafī professor, since Sultan Qayt Bāy routinely did so in the late fifteenth century. At the Māridānī mosque, Saʿd al-Dīn Ibn al-Dīrī (d. 1462) at one point held the professorship in Ḥanafī law. However, "after delivering one lesson, [Sultan] al-Ashraf Barsbāy wrested the post from him [*intazaʿahu minhu*] and gave it to his imām al-Muḥibb al-Aqṣarāʾī." Al-Aqṣarāʾī was clearly somewhat embarrassed by the illegitimacy of his appointment, but lamely "excused himself by [his] inability to refuse to accept [the position]." At the Muʾayyadiyya, Qayt Bāy in 1471 appointed as Sufi shaykh and Ḥanafī professor a man who was not a member of the al-Dīrī family, to which the founder had specifically assigned the post in perpetuity. By doing so, he not only meddled in the appointment process of a school that had its own controller, but did so in direct contravention of the terms of the school's endowment.[24]

The extent of effective royal influence is suggested by instances in which sultans acted as arbitrators of disputes among the educated elite themselves as to who was to receive well-paid professorships. When, for example, the famous Ḥanafī jurist known as al-Sirāj Qāriʾ al-Hidāya died in 1426, a number of scholars competed for the post he had held as shaykh and professor of law at the Shaykhūniyya. To settle the dispute, Sultan Barsbāy ordered the contestants to assemble before the Sufis and students of the khānqāh. When they had gathered, "a group from among the people of the khānqāh sided with [*taʿaṣṣaba*] Zayn al-Dīn al-Tafahanī," and so the sultan appointed him to the post.[25]

[22] For an example of an appointment "bi-tawqīʿ sharīf," see Taqī ʾl-Dīn Aḥmad al-Maqrīzī, *al-Sulūk li-maʿrifat duwal al-mulūk* (Cairo, 1934–73), 1:700. More commonly, the historians simply report that a sultan "appointed" (*qarrara*) a particular scholar to a post: for example, Sultan Barqūq "appointed" the historian Ibn Khaldūn professor of Mālikī law at the Qamḥiyya, and later Sultan Qaytbāy "appointed" Taqī ʾl-Dīn al-Ḥuṣnī professor at the Ṣalāḥiyya; al-Sakhāwī, *al-Ḍawʾ*, 4:146, and Ibn Iyās, *Badāʾiʿ al-zuhūr*, 3:45.

[23] Al-Maqrīzī, *al-Sulūk*, 3:849; Amīn, *al-Awqāf*, 116.

[24] On the Ashrafiyya, compare *Waqfiyyat* al-Ashraf Barsbāy, Dār al-Wathāʾiq No. 173, fol. 139r–v with Ibn Iyās, *Badāʾiʿ al-zuhūr*, 3:108, 193, 376. On the incident at the Māridānī mosque, see al-Sakhāwī, *al-Ḍawʾ*, 3:250. On the appointment at the Muʾayyadiyya, see Ibn Iyās, *Badāʾiʿ al-zuhūr*, 3:62.

[25] Ibn Ḥajar, *Inbāʾ al-ghumr*, 8:95. For al-Sirāj's biography, see ibid., 8:115–16; al-Sa-

In the selection process, the sultan could even overrule the judgment of the chief qāḍī, as another dispute brought to the attention of Barsbāy demonstrates. When al-Sirāj Qāri' al-Hidāya died, he held teaching posts in Ḥanafī law not only in the Shaykhūniyya, but also at several other Cairene institutions. By his request, these positions passed upon his death to his son. Because the boy was too young to teach, or for some other reason, ʿIzz al-Dīn ʿAbd al-Salām al-Baghdādī (d. 1455) taught for him as a substitute (*nā'ib*). It happened, however, that while ʿIzz al-Dīn was absent from Cairo, the son of Qāri' al-Hidāya died. The chief qāḍī ʿAlam al-Dīn Ṣāliḥ al-Bulqīnī[26] "seized the opportunity" to appoint several other scholars to the posts that the deceased boy had, officially, held, and thus the stage was set for an unpleasant confrontation.

When ʿIzz al-Dīn al-Baghdādī returned from his journey and discovered that he had, in effect, been deprived of several valuable teaching positions, he "shouted and pleaded for help, and let it be known that he had no choice but to complain of the qāḍī's [actions] to the sultan." As he was ascending to the Citadel for his audience with the sultan, ʿIzz al-Dīn encountered the qāḍī, who inquired after his rival's intentions. The deprived scholar confidently announced that he had in his sleeve a copy of *al-Ḥāwī*, a popular treatise in Ḥanafī law, and that he would present it to the sultan and ask him to open it to any page. "From this," he said, "you and I will settle [the matter], and thus my just claim will be exposed." Whether ʿIzz al-Dīn's demonstration was intended to signify that the law was entirely on his side, or whether it represented some act of bibliomancy, apparently it impressed the sultan, who ordered ʿIzz al-Dīn to be reinstated to all the posts, which he then held in his own right for a number of years.[27]

In an earlier case involving the professorship in ḥadīth at the Manṣūriyya madrasa, the sultan intervened in a dispute involving the institution's controller and the Shāfiʿī qāḍī, and in the process effectively

khāwī, *al-Ḍaw'*, 6:109–10. For the biography of Zayn al-Dīn ʿAbd al-Raḥmān al-Tafahanī, see al-Sakhāwī, *al-Ḍaw'*, 4:98–100.

[26] In al-Sakhāwī's account—which as far as I know is the only record of the dispute—the qāḍī is referred to only as " ʿAlam al-Dīn." The only qāḍī with the *laqab* ʿAlam al-Dīn in the period following Sirāj al-Dīn's death in 1426 was ʿAlam al-Dīn Ṣāliḥ al-Bulqīnī, who was Shāfiʿī chief qāḍī on several occasions between the death of Sirāj al-Dīn and that of ʿIzz al-Dīn al-Baghdādī; see Ibn Iyās, *Badā'iʿ al-zuhūr*, 2:127, 137, 176, 184, 256, 258, 265, 275, 304, and Kamal Salibi, "Listes chronologiques des grands cadis de l'égypte sous les mameloukes," *Revue des études islamiques* 25 (1957), 81–125. Al-Sakhāwī said that, at the time of the incident, ʿAlam al-Dīn was "in office"—literally, that he was *mutawallī*, a word that can mean the same as *nāẓir* (controller) and that, here, might be intended to signify the Shāfiʿī chief qāḍī's "general supervision" (*naẓar ʿāmm*) over charitable endowments. For ʿAlam al-Dīn's biography, in which the dispute with ʿIzz al-Dīn is not mentioned, see al-Sakhāwī, *al-Ḍaw'*, 3:312–15.

[27] The story is found in al-Sakhāwī's biography of ʿIzz al-Dīn al-Baghdādī, *al-Ḍaw'*, 4:201.

passed judgment on the qualifications of a scholar for the post. The altercation arose when, in 1338, the controller of the institution, Sanjar al-Jāwulī, appointed Shihāb al-Dīn Aḥmad al-ʿAsjadī to the post. Sanjar, although a Mamluk amir, was himself a scholar of ḥadīth, and might have been relied upon to have chosen a fitting transmitter of the Prophetic traditions. Others vehemently disagreed with the choice, however. In particular, the Shāfiʿī qāḍī ʿIzz al-Dīn Ibn Jamāʿa objected to the appointment of al-ʿAsjadī. Ibn Jamāʿa's father had previously been professor of ḥadīth at the Manṣūriyya, and in his words, the appointee "was not worthy of the post," for it was "too important a position for the likes of al-ʿAsjadī."

The reigning sultan, al-Nāṣir Muḥammad ibn Qalāwūn, at first ordered a council to be held in the Manṣūriyya madrasa to resolve the dispute. Ibn Jamāʿa and Sanjar al-Jāwulī were the principal disputants, but "[all] the qāḍīs and many scholars" participated in the debate, including the Manṣūriyya's students themselves, who complained to Sanjar that "you have appointed over us one who is not worthy. We only want [a teacher] from whom we will benefit." The Ḥanafī chief qāḍī testified to al-ʿAsjadī's qualifications, but another scholar claimed that, when the appointee read *Sūrat al-Fātiḥa*, the opening chapter of the Quran, he would make as many as three mistakes in his pronunciation.

The dispute grew more heated, the participants using "indecent language," and eventually it broke up in anger. At last the affair was brought again to the sultan, who was forced to intervene personally in the matter. Sanjar al-Jāwulī swore to his appointee's fitness for the post, and produced a document written by the Ḥanafī qāḍī attesting to al-ʿAsjadī's competence and giving him the honorific title "the outstanding scholar" (*al-ʿālim al-fāḍil*). Ibn Jamāʿa retorted that "[such] honorifics attached to a person do not establish either his knowledge or his ignorance." The parties to the dispute remaining adamant in their contradictory assessments of al-ʿAsjadī's abilities, the sultan was forced to choose between them. He agreed, finally, with the opinion of Ibn Jamāʿa, and forbade the appointment of al-ʿAsjadī as professor of ḥadīth at the school.[28]

The sultan's choice in this particular instance, however, is not at issue. What claims our attention is the dynamics of the dispute, and the role of the sultan as arbitrator of contradictory professional assessments among the ulama. It is clear that no single individual held effective and absolute authority over appointments at the Manṣūriyya, a condition characteristic of institutions of learning in medieval Cairo. The process of making ap-

[28] The story is told in substantially similar versions by al-Maqrīzī, *al-Sulūk*, 2:449, and Ibn Ḥajar, *al-Ḍurar*, 1:288–89. Al-Maqrīzī, in his account, names the Manṣūriyya as the venue for the discussion; Ibn Ḥajar says it was the Ṣāliḥiyya, across the street.

pointments to paid teaching positions in academic institutions was in practice extremely fluid. Lines demarcating the limits of authority were not necessarily clear. The founders of the schools, and after them the controllers who oversaw the functioning and finance of the institutions, constituted a group that, prima facie, was responsible for academic appointments. But in practice, other individuals, qāḍīs and especially the reigning sultan, enjoyed some vaguely defined influence over the appointment process, especially in the larger and more prestigious schools of the city.

The Educated Elite as Patrons

Patronage can be a contagious game, and the story of patronage in the academic world of late medieval Cairo is incomplete if it confines itself to the more or less obvious ties that bound the ulama to wealthy members of the military elite. In the absence of clear guidelines to regulate the appointment process, those most likely to benefit were those well-connected in the world of education: those, that is, whose personalities and reputations shaped the matrix of personal relationships through which knowledge was transmitted, and which in effect defined the academic hierarchy. In other words, much was left to the initiative of the ulama themselves, and in particular to the most reputable and powerful among them. Indeed, insofar as the availability of teaching positions provided an opportunity for patronage and the dispensing of favors, such patronage was practiced not so much by the Mamluks as by the educated elite. High-ranking scholars in effect appropriated to themselves the right to hold professorial "chairs" and then distributed them to their students, their friends, and especially their sons.

The extent to which the ulama managed to control access to remunerative employment in the schools and mosques cannot be overemphasized. Even in cases where an appointment was nominally made by some individual in a position of authority, it is likely that influence wielded behind the scenes by the scholarly community proved decisive. When Fakhr al-Dīn ʿAbd al-Ghanī built and endowed a madrasa in the early fifteenth century, he appointed as its first shaykh and professor of Shāfiʿī law Shams al-Dīn Muḥammad al-Birmāwī. In 1420, Shams al-Dīn moved to Damascus in the company of his friend Najm al-Dīn ʿUmar Ibn Ḥajjī, who paid him an undisclosed sum and "ordered him to resign from the post [in favor of] Burhān al-Dīn al-Bījūrī." Al-Bījūrī was persuaded to accept the position, but it only became official when Zayn al-Dīn ʿAbd al-Qādir, the son of the founder of the madrasa and apparently still its controller, "signed" the order effecting the transfer (*amḍā 'l-nuzūl*) and "made" al-Bījūrī (*jaʿalahu*) professor.[29]

Some evidence of the decisive influence of the ulama even appears in one of the few copies of a royal appointment preserved by al-Qalqashandī. ʿIzz al-Dīn Ibn Jamāʿa was appointed professor at the "zāwiyat al-Shāfiʿī" in the mosque of ʿAmr in al-Fusṭāṭ early in the year 1330, but it is clear from the rather florid language of the document of appointment that he owed his appointment to his father Badr al-Dīn, the previous professor of Shāfiʿī law there. "His father [Badr al-Dīn]," the document reads, "believes that what must be said extolling [his son], and what is instructive regarding his standing, [indicates] his worthiness [for the post], and therefore he deems advisable the transferral to his son of the teaching post of the zāwiya in the mosque of al-Fusṭāṭ (the Protected by God) so that [his son] will occupy his place."[30]

The intervention of the ulama went beyond simply making recommendations regarding who was appropriate for a particular teaching post. Scholars sometimes intervened in the appointment process to secure positions for their friends and students. A brief excursus into the language of the Arabic sources will make the point clearer. The terms that the chroniclers and biographers used to describe the practice include "through the mediation of" (*bi-wāsiṭa*) and "through the concern of" (*bi-ʿināya*). Thus, for example, a scholar named Taqī 'l-Dīn ʿAbd al-Laṭīf Ibn al-Amāna was appointed, following the death of his father in 1436, to the latter's professorships in ḥadīth and Shāfiʿī law in two Cairene madrasas "through the concern of" ʿAlā' al-Dīn ʿAlī al-Qalqashandī, a prominent jurist and ḥadīth transmitter who himself held a number of important teaching positions. Kamāl al-Dīn Ibn al-Humām, a Ḥanafī jurist, angrily resigned from his prestigious teaching posts at the Ashrafiyya and Manṣūriyya madrasas in 1430, for reasons that were discussed above. A little more than a decade later, however, his temper had cooled enough so that he wished to secure new employment. An experienced academic, Ibn al-Humām knew what he must do; to secure a teaching appointment to the Shaykhūniyya khānqāh he "sought the help of" (*istaʿāna bi*) two prominent Ḥanafī scholars.[31]

[29] Jamāl al-Dīn Yūsuf Ibn Taghrī Birdī, *al-Manhal al-ṣāfī wa'l-mustawfī baʿd al-wāfī*, ed. Muḥammad M. Amīn (Cairo, 1984–), 1:45–46.

[30] A rather loose translation of the convoluted Arabic in the document of appointment: *Wa-ra'ā wāliduhu 'l-mushār ilayhi min istiḥqāqihi mā aqtaḍā an yunawwihu bi-dhikrihi wa-yunabbihu ʿalā 'l-maʿrifa bi-ḥaqq qadrihi, fa-āthara 'l-nuzūl lahu ʿammā bi-'smihi min tadrīs al-zāwiya bi-jāmiʿ miṣr al-maḥrūsa li-yaqūmu maqāmahu.* Al-Qalqashandī, *Ṣubḥ al-aʿshā*, 11:228.

[31] On Ibn al-Amāna's appointment, see al-Sakhāwī, *al-Ḍaw'*, 4:332. Taqī 'l-Dīn may well have needed support in order to succeed to his father Badr al-Dīn Muḥammad's posts, since he was only nineteen years old when his father died. There is nothing in al-Sakhāwī's bi-

Scholars could also in effect pass on their professorships to their friends and students. The appointment might be subject to the ratification of a controller, as it was in the case of Burhān al-Dīn al-Bījūrī's succession to the chair at the Fakhriyya madrasa. The very language of the contemporary sources, however, suggests that the choice of a successor might lie with the sitting professor. The sources often report that A "resigned a post in favor of" B (*nazala lahu ʿanhu*), or "left it to him" (*tarakahu lahu*). Most commonly used was the phrase "he relinquished it to him" (*raghiba lahu ʿanhu*); alternatively, B might be said to have been appointed "upon A's relinquishing of the post to him" (*bi-raghbatihi lahu ʿanhu*). Each of these expressions was, in substance, synonymous with the others.[32]

Phrases such as *raghiba ʿanhu* or *nazala ʿanhu* by themselves, of course, simply meant that a professor resigned his post, and imply nothing regarding the choice of a successor.[33] But when they consciously used the terms in conjunction with the prepositional phrase *lahu* ("to him," or "on behalf of him," or "in favor of him"), the biographers and historians seem to have implied a decided act on the part of a teacher holding an endowed teaching post in selecting a particular successor. Almost all of such instances involved two individuals united by some close relationship: fathers and sons, uncles and nephews, brothers, or teachers and pupils.[34] A professor of Ḥanafī law at the Ṣarghitmishiyya, for example,

ographies of any of these men to indicate why ʿAlāʾ al-Dīn al-Qalqashandī should take such an interest in the career of the young man, except perhaps that Taqī ʾl-Dīn's brother Jalāl al-Dīn had once studied with ʿAlāʾ al-Dīn. On Ibn al-Humām, see al-Sakhāwī, *al-Ḍawʾ*, 8:130. Cf. A. S. Tritton, *Materials on Muslim Education in the Middle Ages* (London, 1957), 45.

[32] The parallel meanings of the terms are, in context, clear. Occasionally, however, we find different writers, or even the same writer, using some combination of the three basic terms to describe the same event. For example, in his intellectual autobiography *al-Majmaʿ al-muʾassas biʾl-muʿjam al-mufahras*, p. 447, Ibn Ḥajar al-ʿAsqalānī tells us that "I left the teaching post [in ḥadīth]" (*taraktu lahu al-tadrīs*) at the Jamāliyya madrasa to his friend and student Kamāl al-Dīn Muḥammad al-Shumunnī (an account and choice of words quoted by al-Sakhāwī, *al-Ḍawʾ*, 9:75); in his historical chronicle *Inbāʾ al-ghumr*, 7:340, he wrote: "I resigned the post in favor of him" (*nazaltu lahu ʿanhu*). Similarly, Ibn Ḥajar wrote, regarding the lesson in Shāfiʿī jurisprudence at the Shaykhūniyya, that Nūr al-Dīn al-Abyārī "left it to me" (*tarakahu lī*); *al-Majmaʿ*, 411. His pupil al-Sakhāwī, however, recorded that "he relinquished [the post] to our shaykh," (*raghiba ʿanhu . . . li-shaykhinā*), here meaning Ibn Ḥajar; *al-Ḍawʾ*, 5:230. Kawash, Ibn Ḥajar, 121, suggests that the term *nazala lahu* was used only where the holder of an office was dismissed; for such a reading, however, he cites no authority, and in fact its use in contexts such as that cited above suggests that it indicated a voluntary action on the part of the holder.

[33] For examples, see al-Sakhāwī, *al-Ḍawʾ*, 3:237, 4:90, 201. Cf. E. W. Lane, *Arabic-English Lexicon* (London, 1963), 1110, col. 3.

[34] For examples of fathers passing their teaching positions to sons, see al-Sakhāwī, *al-Ḍawʾ*, 2:119–20, 4:106–13; al-Maqrīzī, *al-Sulūk*, 3:814, 4:74; for uncles to nephews, see al-

suffered from a protracted illness but did not die until "after he had relinquished his teaching post to his son." When Ibn Ḥajar resigned the professorship of ḥadīth at the Manṣūriyya to Badr al-Dīn Ibn al-Amāna, and that in Shāfiʿī law at the Shaykhūniyya to Shihāb al-Dīn Ibn al-Muḥammira, someone complained that each of his successors was better suited for the other's post. Ibn Ḥajar responded that his choice had been deliberate, that, "on the contrary, I wished to extend the capabilities of each of the two men in that [field of study] for which he was not famous." The great scholar and jurist thus explicitly acknowledged that the choice of his successors—those to whom he relinquished his posts—had been his alone.[35]

The exercise by professors of this form of patronage—of effectively selecting, if not officially installing, their successors—was apparently a matter of routine. Most historical and biographical sources of the period provide precious little information about the employment of individual scholars in particular schools on specific occasions. In those that do systematically preserve some record of the appointment process, however, especially al-Sakhāwī's biographical dictionary of fifteenth-century personages, the observation that one teacher stepped down from his post in favor of another is extraordinarily common. It is possible to identify scholars all or most of whose academic appointments were secured in such a fashion. Shihāb al-Dīn Aḥmad Ibn Asad (d. 1467), for example, found employment as prayer leader in one madrasa through the intervention of his teacher, the famous jurist and traditionist Ibn Ḥajar; later, professorships in the variant Quran readings at three prestigious Cairene schools were passed to him from those who had formerly held them, including at least one scholar under whom Ibn Asad had studied. Similarly, Shihāb al-Dīn Aḥmad Ibn Taqī (d. 1440) owed professorships in Mālikī law or ḥadīth in five different schools to those who had previously taught in them, including a cousin and at least one of his teachers.[36]

Very often, of course, such patronage was exercised on behalf of a scholar's children, more specifically his sons, an issue to which we shall return. But the kind of close personal and intellectual relationships forged by the intimate association of teacher and student, relationships reinforced by the system's overwhelming preference for the oral transmission of knowledge, frequently had this practical consequence: that masters passed their academic positions on to their "intellectual sons," that is, to their pupils. Kamāl al-Dīn Muḥammad al-Shumunnī (d. 1418),

---

Sakhāwī, *al-Ḍaw'*, 2:119–20, 10:240–43; for brothers to brothers, see ibid., 3:313, 4:46–48, 134; for teachers to pupils, see ibid., 1:227–31, 235, 2:78–80, 4:150–52, 5:230–31, 6:302, 7:5–8, 8:127–32.

[35] Al-Sakhāwi, *al-Ḍaw'*, 4:99, 6:320.

[36] Al-Sakhāwī, *al-Ḍaw'*, 1:229–30, 2:78–80.

although a slightly older contemporary of Ibn Ḥajar al-ʿAsqalānī, had been a student in his class in ḥadīth at the Jamāliyya khānqāh. When the famous traditionist resigned the post in 1416, he left it to his student al-Shumunnī, who held it for two years until his death. Ibn Ḥajar also transferred his professorship in Quranic exegesis at the grand madrasa of Sultan Ḥasan to his friend and "disciple" (*ṣāḥib*) Zayn al-Dīn ʿAbd al-Raḥmān al-Sandabīsī (d. 1448). Another Zayn al-Dīn ʿAbd al-Raḥmān, known as al-Tafahanī (d. 1432), became the disciple of Badr al-Dīn Maḥmūd al-Kulustānī (d. 1398) and, when his teacher was appointed an important administrative official in the government, took over his teaching duties at the Aytamishiyya madrasa.[37]

The transfer of employment in such a manner from friend to friend or teacher to pupil was a commonplace in Mamluk Cairo. There may be some evidence of resistance to the practice, and thus to the power and prerogatives of the ulama, in the deeds of endowment for several Cairene schools. A rather obscure stipulation in the deed of the Jamāliyya, for example, forbade that "anyone [be appointed] to a position in the khānqāh, or be given a residence in it, because of status or intercession or one possessed of power and might."[38] It is difficult to know precisely what such a stipulation, and one similar to it in the endowment deed of Sultan Barqūq's madrasa, signified. The general idea is clear: that no one is to be appointed to a paying position within the institution through outside intervention. But whether the prohibition applied to the practice of professors naming their successors is doubtful; and in any case, the institutional histories of both the Jamāliyya and the Ẓāhiriyya include a number of instances of professors "relinquishing" their posts to sons, friends, or students.[39]

Indeed, so common was the practice that a professor's refusal to select his successors could elicit a comment and surprise. A scholar named Zayn al-Dīn ʿAbd al-Raḥmān al-Fāraskūrī, for example, held the professorship, presumably in Shāfiʿī jurisprudence, at the Manṣūriyya and Ẓāhiriyya madrasas in the early fifteenth century. As he neared death from some undisclosed illness, he was asked to "resign" his teaching posts in favor of his chosen companions; he refused to do so, however, claiming

[37] See, respectively, Ibn Ḥajar, *Inbāʾ al-ghumr*, 7:339–40, and al-Sakhāwī, *al-Ḍawʾ*, 4:152, 98.

[38] The incomplete passage in *Waqfiyyat* Jamāl al-Dīn al-Ustādār, Dār al-Wathāʾiq No. 106, ll. 348–49, reads: *wa-sharaṭa ayḍan an lā [ ] aḥad biʾl-khānqāh al-madhkūra fī waẓīfa wa-lā yuʿṭī fīhā bayt bi-jāh wa-lā bi-shifāʿa wa-lā bi-dhī quwwa wa-shawka*. Cf. a similar passage in the endowment deed of Sultan al-Ẓāhir Barqūq, Dār al-Wathāʾiq No. 51, ll. 1007–8.

[39] Examples for the Jamāliyya can be found in Ibn Ḥajar, *Inbāʾ al-ghumr*, 7:339–40, and al-Sakhāwī, *al-Ḍawʾ*, 1:235, 4:163, 203–6, 280–81, 9:74–75; for the Ẓāhiriyya, in al-Maqrīzī, *al-Sulūk*, 3:814, and al-Sakhāwī, *al-Ḍawʾ*, 1:227–31, 3:313, 4:280–81.

that "I do not command them [i.e., the teaching posts], in life or in death."[40] Most scholars, however, were naturally less reluctant to exercise this important form of patronage. Kamāl al-Dīn ʿUmar Ibn al-ʿAdīm, for example, during the illness that finally cost him his life in 1408, only followed a common pattern in relinquishing his teaching posts at the Manṣūriyya madrasa and the Shaykhūniyya khānqāh to his son.[41]

Scholars thus took advantage of a system that allowed them in effect to pass on opportunities for academic employment to their friends and pupils. That they felt free to do so may have resulted from another commonplace in the history of appointments to teaching positions in Mamluk Cairo, and one that concentrated power and wealth in the hands of a few: namely, the tendency of important scholars to hold employment in several different institutions. Ibn Ḥajar al-ʿAsqalānī, for instance, may have willingly surrendered his professorships at the Jamāliyya khānqāh and the madrasa of Sultan Ḥasan to his pupils; but the great jurist and traditionist at one time or another held appointments in more than a dozen other schools as well.[42]

The practice of holding appointments to several academic institutions at the same time was not a new one. It was common in Syria, where the spread of madrasas had begun early in the twelfth century, and was not unknown in schools established in Cairo during the Ayyubid period.[43] The extent to which scholars in late medieval Cairo took advantage of the opportunity to hold several professorships simultaneously cannot be determined precisely since, although the sources often name those institutions in which a particular individual taught, only rarely do they give us the precise dates of a teacher's tenure. Even so, however, it can be said with confidence that the practice was widespread. Particular circumstances sometimes reveal the multiple holdings of an individual professor. When, for example, the Shāfiʿī chief qāḍī Taqī ʾl-Dīn Ibn Bint al-Aʿazz was summarily dismissed in 1291, "none of the positions [*waẓāʾif*] [that he held] were left in his hands." The total number of appointments that he held amounted to seventeen: they included, besides the judgeship, the post of preacher at the mosque of al-Azhar and at least four

[40] *Fa-qāla lā ataqalladuhā ḥayyan wa-mayyitan.* Ibn Ḥajar, *Inbāʾ al-ghumr*, 5:326–27.

[41] Al-Maqrīzī, *al-Sulūk*, 4:74; cf. Ibn Ḥajar, *Inbāʾ al-ghumr*, 6:122–23, and al-Sakhāwī, *al-Ḍawʾ*, 6:65–66.

[42] Al-Sakhāwī, *al-Ḍawʾ*, 2:38–39, lists the institutions in which Ibn Ḥajar taught. Kawash, "Ibn Ḥajar," 120–34, basing his study largely on al-Sakhāwī's detailed, but only partially published biography of his teacher, *al-Jawāhir waʾl-durar*, provides a far more detailed account of Ibn Ḥajar's professional history, giving, for example, the dates on which Ibn Ḥajar was appointed to many of his teaching postions.

[43] Makdisi, *Colleges*, 167–68, drawing primarily on Syrian sources, provides a concise discussion of the practice and of reactions against it; on Ayyubid Cairo, see Leiser, "Restoration," 412.

administrative or bureaucratic functions, but also "a number of professorships." Taqī 'l-Dīn ʿAlī al-Subkī was called in the mid-fourteenth century to be qāḍī in Damascus, and the teaching positions that he held in Cairo at that time were transferred, at his request, to his son Bahā' al-Dīn Aḥmad; the schools included the Manṣūriyya, Sayfiyya, and Kahhāriyya madrasas, the mosque of Ibn Ṭūlūn, "and others." Similarly, when Sirāj al-Dīn ʿUmar, the famous Ḥanafī jurist known as Qāri' al-Hidāya, died in 1426, his biographer records that his professorship in jurisprudence at the Shaykhūniyya was filled by one scholar, while "his son was appointed to the rest of the positions held by Sirāj al-Dīn at his death," including professorships at the Aqbughāwiyya, Ashrafiyya, and Nāṣiriyya madrasas and at the mosque of Ibn Ṭūlūn.[44]

The practice of holding multiple teaching appointments became all but institutionalized in the tendency to attach a number of important professorships to the offices of the chief qāḍī of the various rites of law. For example, at the same time that Jalāl al-Dīn Muḥammad al-Qazwīnī was called from Damascus to Cairo to assume the office of Shāfiʿī chief qāḍī in 1326, he was also appointed to professorships at the Nāṣiriyya and Ṣalāḥiyya madrasas and at the *dār al-ḥadīth* al-Kāmiliyya. What was sauce for the goose was sauce for the gander, and the chief judges of the other schools of law also held teaching posts incidental to their judicial office. For example, ʿIzz al-Dīn Aḥmad al-ʿAsqalānī (not to be confused with his more famous namesake, Ibn Ḥajar al-ʿAsqalānī) held the office of chief Ḥanbalī qāḍī in Cairo for almost twenty years until his death in 1471, as well as professorships in the Ṣāliḥiyya, Ashrafiyya, and Nāṣiriyya madrasas and the mosque of Ibn Ṭūlūn "adjoined to the judgeship" (*al-muḍāfa li'l-qaḍā'*). The practice seems to have been one of custom rather than a formal requirement of any institution's endowment. The lessons in Shāfiʿī, Ḥanafī, Mālikī, and Ḥanbalī jurisprudence at the *qubba* (dome) of the Manṣūriyya madrasa were, al-Maqrīzī tells us, originally supported by valuable endowments, and the professorships were held only by the four chief qāḍīs. By the first decades of the fifteenth century, however, the endowments had deteriorated, and by the time al-Maqrīzī wrote his history of Cairo, those who taught at the qubba were "not competent."[45]

[44] The final quotation is from Ibn Ḥajar, *Inbā' al-ghumr*, 8:116; see also al-Sakhāwī, *al-Ḍaw'*, 4:201. On Ibn Bint al-Aʿazz, see al-Maqrīzī, *al-Sulūk*, 1:773; on the al-Subkīs, compare the accounts in Ibn Ḥajar, *al-Durar*, 1:225–26, and Ibn Taghrī Birdī, *al-Manhal al-ṣāfī*, 1:409. Many other examples could be cited; see al-Maqrīzī, *al-Sulūk*, 3:357.

[45] See, respectively, al-Maqrīzī, *al-Sulūk*, 2:283; al-Sakhāwī, *al-Ḍaw'*, 1:205–7; and al-Maqrīzī, *Khiṭaṭ*, 2:380. On the subject of the chief qāḍīs as teachers, see Joseph H. Escovitz, *The Office of the Qāḍī al-Quḍāt in Cairo under the Baḥrī Mamlūks* (Berlin, 1984), 192–206.

Occasionally, scholars simultaneously held appointments to two professorships in the same institution. In late 1377 or early the next year, Ḍiyā' al-Dīn ʿUbayd Allah al-Qaramī, who was already shaykh at a prominent Sufi convent, was placed in charge of the classes in Shāfiʿī law and the Prophetic traditions at the Manṣūriyya madrasa. Zayn al-Dīn ʿAbd al-Raḥmān al-Tafahanī succeeded the famous historian Ibn Khaldūn as instructor in ḥadīth at the Ṣarghitmishiyya madrasa, and later added to it the institution's professorship in Ḥanafī law. In 1365, ʿIzz al-Dīn Ibn Jamāʿa was dismissed as Shāfiʿī qāḍī, but found himself appointed professor of jurisprudence and of traditions at the mosque of Ibn Ṭūlūn, as well as controller of its endowments.[46]

The practice of simultaneously holding academic employment in two or more institutions, or two professorships in the same school, excited some controversy and a little opposition among the learned elite. Tāj al-Dīn al-Subkī, a prominent Shāfiʿī jurist of the fourteenth century, after pointing out that it was "not permissible" for one man to be the imām in two mosques since he could not simultaneously lead prayers at both places, noted that the same objection applied to professors employed to teach in two institutions, if the deeds of endowment stipulated that the lessons were to be held at the same hour.[47] Stipulations in the deeds of endowment of a few Mamluk schools may have attempted to forestall such conflicts, by forbidding those drawing stipends from the institutions' endowments to hold a second paid position (*waẓīfa*) in that school or in any other, at least if they involved duties that were to be discharged at the same hour.[48] A sixteenth-century history of schools in Damascus suggests that multiple employment was a problem there, too, and records that several madrasas in the Syrian capital also forbade their teachers to "combine two posts."[49] But complaints about the practice and efforts to prevent it were only sporadic, and stood little chance of forestalling a

[46] See, respectively, al-Maqrīzī, *al-Sulūk*, 3:320; al-Sakhāwī, *al-Ḍaw'*, 4:98; and al-Maqrīzī, *al-Sulūk*, 3:99.

[47] Al-Sūbkī, *Muʿīd al-niʿam*, 164.

[48] The passages in the three deeds that contained such a prohibition differed only slightly. The deed of the Jamāliyya khānqāh reads: *an lā yajmaʿa aḥad min ahlihā wa'l-munazzalīn fī waẓīfa bi-hā bayna waẓīfatayn bi-hā wa-lā bi-ghayrihā bi-taʿāruḍ fī waqt wāḥid yaḥṣulu al-khalal fī aḥad minhumā li'l-ishtighāl fī'l-ukhrā illā man qarrarahu al-wāqif*; *Waqfiyyat* Jamāl al-Dīn al-Ustādār, Dār al-Wathā'iq No. 106, ll. 313–35. That of Sultan Barsbāy: *wa-an lā yajmaʿa aḥad min arbāb al-waẓā'if bi'l-jāmiʿ bi'l-ḥarīriyyīn wa'l-madrasa wa'l-turba wa'l-qubba al-kā'in dhālika bi'l-ṣaḥrā' bayna waẓīfatayn illā man ʿuyyina lahu an yajmaʿa*; *Waqfiyyat* al-Ashraf Barsbāy, Dār al-Wathā'iq No. 173, fol. 137v. And the deed of Zayn al-Dīn al-Ustādār: *an lā yajmaʿa aḥad fī'l-jāmiʿ al-madhkūr bayna waẓīfatayn wa-lā bayna waẓīfa fīhi wa-waẓīfa [fī] ghayrihi taʿāraḍahā sawā'a 'l-shaykh al-musammī bi-aʿālihi wa-man ʿuyyina maʿahu fīhi*; *Waqfiyyat* Zayn al-Dīn al-Ustādār, Dār al-Wathā'iq No. 110, l. 1461.

[49] Al-Nuʿaymī, *al-Dāris*; see, for example, 1:34, 206, 369, 592.

custom widely accepted among the academic elite, and one that, after all, principally benefited those successful scholars who wielded the greatest moral and intellectual authority. Of three Cairene schools whose deeds of endowment theoretically restricted the "outside employment" of their stipendiaries, at least one hired some individuals as professors who nevertheless held instructional posts in other institutions.[50] Moreover, one of the other deeds specifically exempted the "shaykh"—that is, the professor of jurisprudence—from the restriction regarding additional employment.[51]

Did the practice of holding multiple appointments create difficulties? Al-Subkī apparently saw in it the violation either of a teacher's obligations to his students, or of the stipulations imposed upon him by the terms of the endowments supporting the schools. Classes in the various institutions were, of course, usually held at the same time, most commonly for several hours either in the morning or in the afternoon, at least according to the prescriptive deeds. Zayn al-Dīn al-Tafahanī, without violating the terms of the Ṣarghitmishiyya's endowment, could have discharged his duties as professor both of Ḥanafī jurisprudence and ḥadīth, since the school's deed set aside the morning for the lesson in law and the late afternoon for that in the traditions.[52] On the other hand, ʿIzz al-Dīn Ibn Jamāʿa (who, as we have seen, was professor both of ḥadīth and Shāfiʿī jurisprudence at the mosque of Ibn Ṭūlūn) would have found it difficult to fulfill the stipulations that governed the school's operations. The deed named "the beginning of the day" (*awwal al-nahār*) as the appointed time for the lesson in ḥadīth, but also required the Shāfiʿī professor to sit with his students "between the rising of the sun and noon."[53] When the lessons to be taught were in different institutions, the tension between duties stipulated in the deeds and what was humanly possible was even greater. One scholar held apppointments in both the Nāṣiriyya and Ṣalāḥiyya madrasas. Because of their close proximity, he could deliver his lecture in one and then run across the street to the other.[54] But others simultaneously held teaching posts in schools scattered about the city. Many, as we have seen, relinquished their appointments to their friends or students. But Ibn Ḥajar al-ʿAsqalānī, who held several other posts

[50] For several years until his death in 1423, Majd al-Dīn Sālim al-Maqdisī held professorships in Ḥanbalī law at the Jamāliyya and also the Ḥasaniyya and the madrasa of Umm al-Sultan; al-Sakhāwī, *al-Ḍaw'*, 3:241. Ibn Ḥajar al-ʿAsqalānī, as we know, was professor of ḥadīth at the Jamāliyya from 1408 until 1416; during that time, however, he was also professor in at least three other institutions. See Kawash, "Ibn Ḥajar," 120–25.

[51] *Waqfiyyat* Zayn al-Dīn al-Ustādār, Dār al-Watha'iq No. 110, l. 1461.

[52] *Waqfiyyat* Ṣarghitmish, Wizārat al-Awqāf o.s. No. 3195, pp. 27, 30.

[53] *Waqfiyyat* al-Manṣūr Lājīn, Dār al-Watha'iq No. 17, ll. 327ff., 332ff.

[54] Al-Sakhāwī, *al-Ḍaw'*, 4:138.

while also holding forth as professor at the Mu'ayyadiyya, apparently resolved his conflicting obligations by limiting his teaching at that important school to Wednesdays of every week.[55]

But the popularity and success of the practice of holding multiple teaching posts rested primarily on the fact that it allowed leading scholars to exercise yet another form of patronage over their students and lesser colleagues. It was not always necessary that they definitively "relinquish" their jobs to others; they could appoint junior scholars to discharge their duties as "deputies" or "substitutes" (*nā'ib*, pl. *nuwwāb*). The holder of a professorial chair apparently would himself select the substitute, and assign to him some portion of the stipend attached to the post. Such a system was clearly subject to abuse, since a scholar might collect a number of appointments and hire substitutes for those in which he himself could not teach, and in fact the practice did lead to some criticism.[56] Complaints aside, however, it also became a common feature of schools in the Mamluk period, and professors not infrequently appointed their students as their substitutes. For years, apparently, Ibn Ḥajar al-ʿAsqalānī left his teaching duties at one school to a succession of his pupils.[57]

Substitute teaching played a recognized role in the transmission of the Islamic religious sciences. Al-Qalqashandī's administrative manual even preserves a document officially appointing a certain Tāj al-Dīn Muḥammad al-Ikhnā'ī as the substitute for a teaching post in the mosque of ʿAmr that was held by his uncle. According to the document, Tāj al-Dīn was to teach as substitute so long as his uncle lived, but would then hold the position "in his own right" (*istiqlālan*) after the latter's death.[58] Scholars with relatively undistinguished academic records might spend much of their teaching careers substituting for others, receiving appointments in their own names, if at all, only at the end of their lives.[59] In exchange for their services, substitute teachers received the *maʿlūm al-niyāba*, some portion of the post's stipend, although individuals are occasionally mentioned who substituted gratis (*majānan*).[60] It is not known precisely how much a substitute was routinely paid—presumably his wages were set on an ad hoc basis by the official holder of the post—but in at least one case a substitute grew dissatisfied with the level of his remuneration. Muḥyī al-Dīn ʿAbd al-Qādir Ibn Taqī (d. 1490) substituted for the son of a fa-

[55] Kawash, "Ibn Ḥajar," 126.

[56] Makdisi, *Colleges*, 167, 188–89, and passim.

[57] Kawash, "Ibn Ḥajar," 125. Such instances were common enough to be frequently mentioned by the biographers without comment; see, for example, al-Sakhāwī, *al-Ḍaw'*, 1:46, 224, 4:38, 165, 6:302.

[58] Al-Qalqashandī, *Ṣubḥ al-aʿshā*, 11:229–31.

[59] See, for example, al-Sakhāwī, *al-Ḍaw'*, 3:264–65, 4:80–82.

[60] Al-Sakhāwī, *al-Ḍaw'*, 1:162–63.

mous scholar at the Ẓāhiriyya madrasa, but, his biographer reports, he "grew dissatisfied with the nā'ib's stipend" and desired to be officially appointed to the post himself. His behavior raised eyebrows, as his contemporaries compared his apparent greed with the magnanimity of another scholar who substituted gratis; the biographer excused him, however, commenting wryly that "the difference between the two [substitutes], especially in jurisprudence, is obvious."[61]

A substitute might be appointed for a perfectly legitimate reason. In particular, a professor might appoint one to teach his classes while he was absent performing a pilgrimage. The deeds of endowment that governed the operation of Cairo's schools routinely made provisions for the appointment of substitutes if a teacher left to perform the pilgrimage to Mecca, or to visit the holy sites in Jerusalem, or, in some cases, to visit his relatives outside of Cairo. Thus, for example, when al-Khaṭīb al-Wazīrī made his pilgrimage, Sharaf al-Dīn Ibn ʿAbd al-Ḥaqq substituted for him as professor of Quranic exegesis at the Mu'ayyadiyya, because he was "the most accomplished student in the class."[62] When Taqī 'l-Dīn al-Ḥuṣnī went to Mecca in 1472, he named his student ʿAbd al-Raḥīm al-Abnāsī as his substitute for the professorship in Shāfiʿī law at the Ṣalāḥiyya madrasa. ʿAbd al-Raḥīm's lessons were highly praised, but he unsuccessfuly sought to use the opportunity to secure a permanent appointment to the post.[63]

On other occasions, substitutes taught on a more indefinite and extended basis. When, for example, a professor grew old or weak, he might appoint his son or a promising student as his substitute rather than formally relinquish his post. In this way, ʿIzz al-Dīn Aḥmad al-ʿAsqalānī (d. 1471), a student who went on to hold some of the most prominent professorships in Ḥanbalī law, while yet in his late teens or early twenties substituted for his aging teacher Majd al-Dīn Sālim al-Maqdisī in at least four different professorships.[64] Sulaymān ibn Shuʿayb al-Azharī, who apparently never held a teaching post in his own name, must have substituted at the mosque of Ibn Ṭūlūn for years, since at some point in the late fifteenth century he was substitute in the class in Mālikī law for both his teacher Sirāj al-Dīn ʿUmar Ibn Ḥarīz (d. 1487) and, after him, for Ibn Ḥarīz's son.[65]

[61] Al-Sakhāwī, *al-Ḍaw'*, 4:263. "He grew dissatisfied with the nā'ib's stipend" would seem to me to be the sense of al-Sakhāwī's statement *shāḥaha* [lit., "he was stingy"?] *fī maʿlūm al-niyāba*.

[62] Al-Sakhāwī, *al-Ḍaw'*, 4:38. For another example, see ibid, 3:177.

[63] Al-Sakhāwī, *al-Ḍaw'*, 4:165. Here the term used is *istakhlafahu*, meaning "he appointed him as substitute;" cf. Makdisi, *Colleges*, 189.

[64] Al-Sakhāwī, *al-Ḍaw'*, 1:206; for other examples, see ibid., 3:231–32, 4:33–35.

[65] See, respectively, al-Sakhāwī, *al-Ḍaw'*, 1:206, 3:265; for other examples, see ibid., 3:231–32, 4:33–35.

Above all, however, mature scholars substituted for boys who, despite their young age and lack of preparation, were formally appointed to professorships in the various institutions of learning in Mamluk Cairo. Most commonly, this resulted from the dominant tendency for sons, no matter what their age, to inherit their fathers' posts, a point on which we will shortly have more to say. For the present, however, what is important is the opportunity this presented to scholars to teach in madrasas and mosques to which they might not otherwise receive a formal appointment. We have already seen how ʿIzz al-Dīn al-Baghdādī was substitute for the son of the famous Ḥanafī scholar al-Sirāj Qāri' al-Hidāya, after the latter's death and his son's succession to most of his teaching posts, in several of Cairo's premier academic institutions. Similarly, Burhān al-Dīn Ibrāhīm al-Laqānī filled in for the son of one of his teachers as professor of Mālikī law in three important schools.[66] As in the case of ʿIzz al-Dīn al-Baghdādī, it was quite possible for a substitute formally to succeed to the professorship after the death or resignation of the young incumbent.[67] If the boy's minority were a long one, several successive substitutes might be required. When, for example, a scholar who held the professorship in Quranic exegesis at the Manṣūriyya madrasa died in 1483, his son, who succeeded him at the post, was apparently too young to do the teaching himself. His responsibilities were discharged by Jamāl al-Dīn al-Kūrānī, one of his father's teachers, until Jamāl al-Dīn's own death in 1489, at which point another substitute was appointed who eventually succeeded, in his own name, to the post.[68] In another instance, an accomplished scholar substituted for his young pupil who had, at far too tender an age, succeeded to the post of Sufi shaykh and professor of Ḥanafī law at the prestigious Shaykhūniyya khānqāh.[69]

The point of all this is that the pattern of assignments to paid teaching positions in Cairene schools left much to the discretion and patronage of the educated elite themselves. The creation and endowment of an extensive network of schools providing permanent employment for a significant number of scholars may not have changed the methods or the content of higher education, but it did establish a new form of patronage by which the senior ulama could effectively control access to prestigious pro-

[66] Al-Sakhāwī, *al-Ḍaw'*, 1:162.

[67] For example, al-Sakhāwī, *al-Ḍaw'*, 1:47. See also the incident recounted in Jalāl al-Dīn al-Suyūṭī, *al-Taḥadduth bi-niʿmat allāh*, ed. E. M. Sartain (Cambridge, 1975), 91; cf. al-Sakhāwī, *al-Ḍaw'*, 2:68.

[68] The story can be pieced together from three separate biographies in al-Sakhāwī, *al-Ḍaw'*, 4:37–39, 5:48–49, 10:252–54. For a similar example, see ibid., 3:265, 4:263.

[69] Sirāj al-Dīn ʿUmar Qāri' al-Hidāya briefly substituted for his young pupil Nāṣir al-Dīn Muḥammad Ibn al-ʿAdīm who, in his late teens and early twenties, was shaykh and professor at the Shaykhūniyya. See their biographies in al-Sakhāwī, *al-Ḍaw'*, 6:109–10, 8:235.

fessorships. If others held the formal right to make appointments in the various schools, the decisive influence was in fact often wielded by the ulama. They might intervene to help secure a post for their friends, or leave particular employment to individuals of their own choosing. Individually, they might collect a considerable number of separate academic appointments and select their favorite students as substitutes, for themselves or for their sons. Teaching posts were valuable commodities, and it is no surprise that individuals highly placed in the academic hierarchy sought to control them. Ibn Ḥajar al-ʿAsqalānī exhibited no special venality when he sought the appointment as professor of ḥadīth at the great mosque of Sultan Ḥasan for his thirteen year-old son, and then, because the boy was so young, taught in his place.[70] His paternal concern for his son's position in the world of learning does, however, reflect the extraordinary importance of family connections to academic success. It is to this aspect of the professional life of the ulama that we now turn.

Family Connections and Academic Careers

It was the opinion of medieval educational theorists that poverty should be no excuse, for one of sound mind and body, for failing to strive after knowledge. After all, wrote al-Zarnūjī in his treatise on education and learning, no one was poorer than Abū Yūsuf, the seminal Ḥanafī jurist of the eighth century. Yet financial independence has always been a factor in allocating higher educational resources, since it creates opportunities for leisure and free time for the purpose of study. Even al-Zarnūjī was forced to admit that having wealth could be of great service to a fledgling scholar: "It was said to a learned man, 'By what means did you acquire knowledge?' He said: 'Through a rich father. Because by means of his [riches] he supported virtuous and learned men and so was the cause of an augmentation of learning.' " More practically, with wealth one could purchase books, or have them copied, and "this is a help in [attaining] knowledge and learning."[71]

But the most significant nonintellectual factor contributing to the success of an academic career in Mamluk Cairo was not wealth per se, but having as one's father a prominent scholar and teacher. To a certain degree, this may be viewed as a thoroughly natural phenomenon: the son of a scholar was more likely to be introduced early and attracted to the academic profession, and indeed, fathers are often listed in the biographical dictionaries as the first of an individual's many teachers. But certain

[70] Kawash, "Ibn Ḥajar," 61.

[71] Burhān al-Dīn al-Zarnūjī, *Taʿlīm al-mutaʿallim, ṭarīq al-taʿallum* (Cairo, 1977), 40, 41, trans. G. E. von Grunebaum and Theodora M. Abel, *Instruction of the Student, the Method of Learning* (New York, 1947), 51, 52.

peculiarities of the Islamic teaching system, as well as certain institutional developments in late medieval Cairo, contributed to hardening significantly career patterns among the ulama and to making success in the academic field almost a matter of inheritance.[72]

The education of Aḥmad b. ʿAbd al-Raḥīm, known as Ibn al-ʿIrāqī (d. 1422), provides a measure of the care with which ulama families undertook the instruction of their offspring. The son of another prominent scholar also known as Ibn al-ʿIrāqī, Aḥmad was born in Cairo in 1360 and before the age of three was brought before ʿIzz al-Dīn Ibn Jamāʿa and other prominent scholars in the Egyptian capital. In 1363–64, his father traveled to Syria and took Aḥmad with him, presenting the young boy before the leading scholars and ḥadīth transmitters of Damascus and Jerusalem. In particular, the father requested that these traditionists issue to his son ijāzas, licenses empowering him to transmit ḥadīth on their authority. Especially in the field of ḥadīth transmission, such experiences could prove valuable for Aḥmad Ibn al-ʿIrāqī and others like him in their later academic careers: three-year-olds may not have understood the lessons or traditions recited in their presence, but they could later in life claim to have studied directly with prominent shaykhs of previous generations.[73] Back in Cairo, Aḥmad began a more systematic education in law, grammar, and other subjects, as well has ḥadīth. Here, too, family connections proved invaluable. He studied jurisprudence with Burhān al-Dīn Ibrāhīm al-Abnāsī (d. 1399), an intimate companion of his father who, "because of the close friendship" that they shared, secured for Aḥmad student fellowships in several schools.[74] His father took him to Mecca and Medina, where Aḥmad studied ḥadīth with the leading scholars of the Hijaz, and later he traveled again to Syria, this time in the company of another friend of his father, where he heard traditions from the next generation of transmitters.

[72] For studies of family "dynasties" of scholars, see Kamal Salibi, "The Banū Jamāʿa: A Dynasty of Shāfiʿite Scholars," *Studia Islamica* 9 (1958), 97–109, and William Brinner, "The Banū Ṣaṣrā: A Study in the Transmission of a Scholarly Tradition," *Arabica* 3 (1960), 167–95. The "family connection" was crucial to education, and more particularly to one's recognition as a valuable teacher, in other medieval Islamic societies as well; Richard Bulliet, *The Patricians of Nishapur: A Study in Medieval Islamic Social History* (Cambridge, Mass., 1972), esp. 55–60, and Roy Mottahedeh, *Loyalty and Leadership in an Early Islamic Society* (Princeton, 1980), 135ff. Cf. Dale Eickelman, *Knowledge and Power in Morocco: The Education of a Twentieth-Century Notable* (Princeton, 1985), 87–88.

[73] The biographies of almost all famous scholars and teachers from the Mamluk period contain similar accounts. These early educational experiences proved invaluable for women scholars, as well; see Chapter Six.

[74] The actual term used was *waẓāʾif*. The word could refer either to student fellowships, or, of course, to employment as a teacher or other religious functionary. In context, the former seems the most likely interpretation. Al-Sakhāwī, *al-Ḍawʾ*, 1:338; cf. al-Abnāsī's biography in ibid., 1:174.

The care and attention with which a prominent scholar could direct the studies of his sons could also, of course, act as a catalyst for their careers. In Cairo, Aḥmad Ibn al-ʿIrāqī gave lessons "in the lifetime of his father and of his teachers," which led Zayn al-Dīn to compose the verses: "the lessons of Aḥmad are better than those of his father, / Which gives his father the greatest satisfaction." Consequently, when Zayn al-Dīn was appointed qāḍī of Medina in 1383, Aḥmad, who was as yet in his mid-twenties, took up his father's teaching responsibilities in a number of Cairene schools.[75] Similarly, the famous traditionist and Ḥanafī scholar Sirāj al-Dīn ʿUmar al-Bulqīnī granted to his son Jalāl al-Dīn ʿAbd al-Raḥīm permission to teach and to issue *fatwās* (legal opinions) at the extraordinarily young age of seventeen, attesting to the brilliance of his son and pupil in the science of Islamic jurisprudence.[76]

Not surprisingly, the concerns of the ulama extended to securing for their sons prominent, lucrative, and secure teaching posts. In this the institutional framework of education in Mamluk Cairo proved to be of great assistance. The tendency for sons to inherit the teaching posts occupied by their fathers was, of course, by no means new. It had in fact manifested itself early in the development of institutions supporting classes in the legal and religious sciences, and long before the onset of the Mamluk regime.[77] But in the later Middle Ages, the tendency became hard and fast, and was eventually codified in the deeds of endowment establishing madrasas and cognate institutions of learning.

The most obvious means by which a prominent scholar could secure for himself and his progeny a secure teaching post was by establishing a school himself. The founder could then stipulate, in the institution's deed of endowment, that he and his descendants were to hold the professorship, so long as they were themselves competent scholars.[78] Taqī 'l-Dīn al-Subkī discussed, in a fatwā dating from the mid-fourteenth century, a madrasa in Damascus that made precisely such a stipulation.[79] Scholars seem to have been responsible for a greater share of the schools constructed in the provinces of Upper Egypt than in the metropolitan capital; since many of these scholar-benefactors went on to teach in the insti-

[75] Al-Sakhāwī, *al-Ḍaw'*, 1:338–39. Aḥmad was successfully challenged for the post of professor of ḥadīth at the Kāmiliyya, however, by his teacher Ibn al-Mulaqqin; ibid., 4:174. Similar verses are ascribed to Taqī 'l-Dīn ʿAlī al-Subkī regarding his son Aḥmad; Ibn Ḥajar, *al-Durar*, 1:225, and Ibn Taghrī Birdī, *al-Manhal al-ṣāfī*, 1:409.

[76] Al-Sakhāwī, *al-Ḍaw'*, 4:108.

[77] Makdisi, *Colleges*, 170.

[78] Makdisi, *Colleges*, 170, notes, with reference especially to the eleventh and twelfth centuries, that the tendency of sons to inherit posts from fathers was especially pronounced in madrasas that had been established by professors.

[79] Al-Subkī, *Fatāwā*, 2:43–44.

tutions that they founded, we may assume that their own sons not infrequently inherited their posts.[80]

In Cairo, apparently, relatively few scholars built schools specifically to perpetuate their own academic dynasties. One who did was Bahā' al-Dīn ʿAlī b. Muḥammad b. Salīm Ibn Ḥannā (d. 1278–79), the founder of the madrasa al-Ṣāḥibiyya al-Bahā'iyya in al-Fusṭāṭ. Ibn Ḥannā was in fact a bureaucrat who rose to the rank of *wazīr*, but his family had a demonstrated interest in education. From its foundation, the professorship of this institution was held by members of the Ibn Ḥannā family. The first to teach there was Fakhr al-Dīn Muḥammad, the founder's son, followed by a succession of other descendants of the founder over at least six generations. The professorship remained in the hands of family members until, in the early years of the fifteenth century, the school, plundered of its endowments and even of the marble with which it was constructed, with only two or three pupils remaining of its once significant student body, ceased to function.[81]

Few scholars had the means or, if they did, the inclination to establish for themselves and their offspring institutions of the size of al-Ṣāḥibiyya al-Bahā'iyya. One who did build and endow a madrasa was Sirāj al-Dīn al-Bulqīnī. We know very little concerning this madrasa other than the fact that Sirāj al-Dīn and many of his family members and their descendants were buried here. The institution still survived as a mosque when, in the nineteenth century, ʿAlī Pāshā Mubārak completed his topographical survey of Cairo. Although Sirāj al-Dīn and his sons did hold informal sessions for public instruction in the madrasa, there is no indication that the institution's endowments, the deeds for which have not survived, ever provided organized lessons, with student stipends and paid professorial chairs, in Islamic law or its ancillary sciences.[82] The madrasa known as the Majdiyya, located in al-Fusṭāṭ, was established by the shaykh Majd al-Dīn Abū Muḥammad ʿAbd al-ʿAzīz b. al-Ḥusayn al-Khalīlī al-Dārī (d. 1281). Again, its deed of endowment is lost, but we know that Majd al-Dīn established in it a Shāfiʿī professor, two teaching assistants (*muʿīds*), and twenty students, as well as a prayer leader and a muezzin. Moreover, al-Maqrīzī tells us that Majd al-Dīn's son Fakhr al-Dīn ʿUmar, though he

[80] Jean-Claude Garcin, *Un centre musulman de la haute-égypte médiévale: Qūṣ* (Cairo, 1976), 268–69. For examples of scholars who built and then taught in madrasas in the south, see Kamāl al-Dīn Jaʿfar al-Udfūwī, *al-Ṭāliʿ al-saʿīd, al-jāmiʿ asmāʾ nujabāʾ al-ṣaʿīd* (Cairo, 1966), 514, 699–700.

[81] Al-Maqrīzī, *Khiṭaṭ*, 2:370–71.

[82] Al-Maqrīzī gives a brief account of this madrasa in his *Khiṭaṭ*, 2:52. See also ʿAlī Pāshā Mubārak, *al-Khiṭaṭ al-tawfīqiyya al-jadīda li-miṣr wa'l-qāhira* (Būlāq, A.H. 1306), 5:66, 6:5. Al-Sākhāwī mentions several members of the Bulqīnī family who were buried in this madrasa; see *al-Ḍaw'*, 3:313, 4:40–41, 112, 6:89, 12:55, 94, 118.

successfully pursued a bureaucratic career and became wazīr on four separate occasions, held the professorship of this institution until his death in 1312.[83] Such schools, however, represented only a tiny fraction of those established and functioning in Cairo during the later Middle Ages.

Alternatively, scholars retired to smaller institutions, often called *zāwiyas* (in this context indicating a small mosque), that they constructed and/or provided with endowments, and in which they taught. For example, Burhān al-Dīn Ibrāhīm al-Abnāsī, the same man who was instrumental in the education of Aḥmad Ibn al-ʿIrāqī, after holding a number of teaching positions in Cairo, established his own zāwiya on the island of al-Maqas outside of Cairo. Here, he taught jurisprudence and attracted to his side many of the best students in the city, offering them food and "subsistence" (*rizq*). We know that al-Abnāsī provided an endowment to support a lesson and a library, but cannot be certain whether any descendants inherited the post after him.[84]

But even in other schools, in those established by Mamluks or nonacademic civilians, it became common practice for a child to inherit his father's teaching posts. That this was so is evident from even a cursory reading of biographical dictionaries such as al-Sakhāwī's *al-Ḍaw' al-lāmiʿ*. Examples are legion. The Aḥmad Ibn al-ʿIrāqī who began his education in his third year eventually succeeded to his father's teaching posts after the latter's death. If a scholar left more than one son, they might share his posts. Bahā' al-Dīn Aḥmad (d. 1422) and Badr al-Dīn Muḥammad, the sons of ʿUthmān b. Muḥammad al-Manāwī al-Shāfiʿī, inherited a number of teaching posts in Cairene schools from their father, including those at the Jāwuliyya, Saʿdiyya, Sukriyya, Quṭbiyya, and Majdiyya, as well as the shrine of the Prophet's grandson al-Ḥusayn.[85]

The inheritability of teaching posts became, in fact, a leitmotif of the institutionalized side of higher education in medieval Cairo. The biogra-

[83] Al-Maqrīzī, *Khiṭaṭ*, 2:400. On Fakhr al-Dīn ʿUmar Ibn al-Khalīlī, see Ibn Ḥajar, *al-Durar*, 3: 246–47. That Ibn Duqmāq called the madrasa that of the "Banū Khalīlī" may also suggest that its professors were drawn from that family. Ibrāhīm b. Muḥammad Ibn Duqmāq, *al-Intiṣār li-wāsiṭat ʿiqd al-amṣār* (Paris, 1893; reptd. Beirut, n.d.), 4:28.

[84] Al-Sakhāwī, *al-Ḍaw'*, 1:173. A certain Burhān al-Dīn Ibrāhīm b. Ḥajjāj al-Abnāsī (d. 1432) lived in this zāwiya, and his son ʿAbd al-Raḥīm (d. 1486) was nā'ib (substitute professor) here; Ibn Ḥajar, *Inbā' al-ghumr*, 8:286–87, and al-Sakhāwī, *al-Ḍaw'*, 4:165. There is no indication, however, that these two scholars were directly related to the Burhān al-Dīn al-Abnāsī for whom the zāwiya was named, although they shared a *nisba*. Several other scholars established schools about which even less is known, including: Aḥmad b. Ibrāhīm b. Naṣr Allāh (d. 1471), Ḥanbalī chief judge from 1453 until his death, who established "a mosque and madrasa and public fountain and cistern [*sabīl wa-ṣahrīj*];" and Ibrāhīm b. ʿAlī b. Aḥmad al-Niʿmānī (d. 1492), who established along the Nile across from the Nilometer a zāwiya that, according to al-Sakhāwī, was really a madrasa, and in which Friday prayers were said and a sermon read; al-Sakhāwī, *al-Ḍaw'*, 1:207, 78–79.

[85] Al-Sakhāwī, *al-Ḍaw'*, 1:380, 8:149.

phers almost took the practice for granted, and sometimes blandly remark that so-and-so "taught after his father in several places," without bothering to name the institutions.[86] For at least a century from its construction in 1329, the professorship in Ḥanafī law at the Jamāliyya khānqāh was the preserve of several generations of the family of its first incumbent.[87] Not all institutions were so closely tied to one particular family, but the histories of most schools of the period yield at least one, and many several, instances of sons succeeding fathers in their academic employment.

So accepted was the practice that a deviation from the rule might engender a dispute. When Burhān al-Dīn Ibrāhīm al-Bījūrī died in 1422, none of his children were considered his equal in intellectual accomplishment. Consequently, a colleague of al-Bījūrī was appointed to his post in the Fakhriyya madrasa. So incensed was his son at being passed over for the post that he refused in anger his father's jobs at other Cairene schools. A more hostile confrontation embroiled the Shaykhūniyya khānqāh when, at the beginnng of the fifteenth century, its respected professor of Ḥanafī law, al-Shaykh Zāda al-ʿAjamī, grew weak with age. His son Maḥmūd substituted for him, and apparently expected to inherit his father's position. Just before Zāda's death, however, a rival scholar, Kamāl al-Dīn ʿUmar Ibn al-ʿAdīm, successfully challenged the competence of the aged shaykh and received the appointment himself. Kamāl al-Dīn's peers apparently deplored his actions, but nonetheless Maḥmūd "was excluded from his father's post."[88]

The extreme youth of their sons did not always prevent scholars from actively seeking their appointment to academic employment. Very often, sons succeeded to their fathers' teaching positions at tender ages, before they could successfully shoulder full academic responsibilities. The same Ibn al-ʿAdīm who prevented Maḥmūd b. Zāda from succeeding his father as professor at the Shaykhūniyya in 1407 invited his own young son Nāṣir al-Dīn Muḥammad to lecture in his place. Nāṣir al-Dīn was, according to one chronicler, a "youth who may or may not have attained puberty," although it appears that he must have been seventeen years of age. In any case, Ibn al-ʿAdīm saw in his son's lecturing "the means of advancing him to employment in the post, despite his young age, and the complete absence of hair on his face." His ploy was successful, and when Ibn al-ʿAdīm died the following year, his son was appointed in his place.[89] In situations where the holder of a professorial chair was simply

[86] For example, al-Sakhāwī, *al-Ḍaw'*, 1:368, 4:121.

[87] Al-Maqrīzī, *Khiṭaṭ*, 2:392.

[88] See, respectively, al-Sakhāwī, *al-Ḍaw'*, 1:20, and Ibn Ḥajar, *Inbā' al-ghumr*, 5:322.

[89] Al-Maqrīzī, *al-Sulūk*, 4:52, 74; Ibn Ḥajar, *Inbā' al-ghumr*, 7:245.

too young to teach, a substitute might be appointed, as we have seen, to fulfill the boy's instructional duties.

The routine transfer of teaching posts from father to son was a practice that benefited primarily the educated elite itself. When the decisive influence of the ulama generally is recalled, it will be seen that they not only formed the group through which Islamic learning was transmitted from one generation to the next, but also created the conditions allowing them to replicate their own power, wealth, and position in their offspring. This replication became a widely accepted pattern, and consequently, the endowment deeds of many late Mamluk madrasas and cognate institutions included stipulations that appointments in them were to be hereditary, that is, that sons were to be allowed to succeed their fathers in their posts. At the mosque of Barsbāy, for example, if one of the institution's professors or other appointees died and left a son who was qualified (*ṣāliḥ*) to asssume the responsibilities of his father's post, he was to be appointed to it.[90] Similarly, the endowment deed of Khushqadam al-Zimām, which provided for fifty-nine Sufis and their shaykh, Shāfiʿī and Ḥanafī professors and ten students each, as well as a number of minor functionaries, stated:

> The founder stipulates that if one of the aforementioned appointees dies and has a son of legal age [*bāligh*] who is from among the people of the Blessed Quran and [who is] worthy [*ṣāliḥ*] for the post, the controller should appoint him to his father's place and disburse to him his [father's] salary [*rizq*].[91]

The ties of blood were broad as well as deep, and so a school's endowment deed might provide that, if the deceased officeholder had no son, a relation (*qarīb*) might be appointed to his post.[92]

Naturally, many sons would not be considered capable of assuming their fathers' posts and discharging their duties because of their youth: they may have been perfectly competent students, showing every sign of intellectual promise, but not yet advanced enough in their studies to justify their appointment to professorial chairs. Not to be forestalled, the hereditary clauses in the endowment deeds often made provisions for this contingency. If the deceased professor's son was not qualified at the time of his father's death, but was expected to become so at some later date, a substitute might be appointed to teach in the son's place until his deficiencies were overcome.[93]

[90] *Waqfiyyat* al-Ashraf Barsbāy, Dār al-Wathā'iq No. 173, fol. 134r-v.

[91] *Waqfiyyat* Khushqadam al-Zimām, Wizārat al-Awqāf n.s. No. 188, ll. 135–37.

[92] *Waqfiyyat* al-Shiblī Kāfūr, Dār al-Wathā'iq No. 76, ll. 50–51.

[93] See, for example, *Waqfiyyat* al-Ashraf Barsbāy, Dār al-Wathā'iq No. 173, fol. 134r–v; *Waqfiyyat* Sūdūn min Zāda, Dār al-Wathā'iq No. 58, ll. 365–67; *Waqfiyyat* Jawhar al-Lālā,

Of course, as we have seen, the practice of sons inheriting their fathers' teaching posts had a long pedigree, predating the Mamluk period considerably. What clauses such as that in the deed for the madrasa of Sultan Barsbāy represent, however, is the regularization of the practice, and confirmation of the privilege accruing to prominent scholars and teachers of ensuring that control of well-paid teaching positions remained in their families' hands. The clauses were not a gratuitous formality, but a conscious device to secure a privilege, as witnessed by the fact that they were sometimes included in documents augmenting or modifying endowments established several years earlier.[94] Clauses such as that at Barsbāy's madrasa became more frequent over the last century of Mamluk rule. The documentary evidence for the thirteenth and fourteenth centuries is much scantier, so that it may be dangerous to rely too heavily upon the silence of early Mamluk deeds of endowment. It is, however, notable that the first instance of such a clause in a surviving deed for a Mamluk-period school is found in the endowment deed for the mosque of the amir Sūdūn min Zāda, dating from 1402. Thereafter, they became quite common, a feature of most endowment deeds for late Mamluk institutions of education.[95]

To be sure, the deeds of endowment for late Mamluk institutions of learning suggest that some shared a reluctance to codify the practice of allowing sons to inherit their fathers' posts. In the endowment established by Sultan Khushqadam, for example, a hereditary clause similar to those above was conspicuously absent; rather, the controller was pointedly instructed to replace the institution's deceased functionaries with

Dār al-Wathā'iq No. 86, ll. 389–93; *Waqfiyyat* Zayn al-Dīn al-Ustādār, Dār al-Wathā'iq No. 110, ll. 1459ff.

[94] *Waqfiyyat* al-Shiblī Kāfūr, Dār al-Wathā'iq No. 76, specifically the fifth document on the roll, dated 1 Dhū 'l-Ḥijja, A.H. 818, ll. 50–51; *Waqfiyyat* Qānī Bāy Qarā, Wizārat al-Awqāf o.s. No. 1019, specifically the third document on the roll, dated 3 Rajab, A.H. 920 (Muḥammad Amīn, in his *Fihrist wathā'iq al-qāhira* [Cairo, 1981], 242, gives this date as A.H. 910, but the correct date appears to be 920), ll. 879–80.

[95] *Waqfiyyat* Sūdūn min Zāda, Dār al-Wathā'iq No. 58, ll. 365–67 is the earliest such waqfiyya uncovered during research for this book. It is possible that earlier examples escaped my attention. Even if thirteenth- or fourteenth-century examples exist, however, I believe that the general pattern—that such clauses became more frequent, almost de rigueur, over the course of the fifteenth century—is valid. In addition to those cited above, see the following deeds of endowment: *Waqfiyyat* Jawhar al-Lālā and Jawhar al-Qunuqbā'ī, Dār al-Wathā'iq No. 89, ll. 66–67; *Waqfiyyat* Qānī Bāy Qarā, Wizārat al-Awqāf o.s. No. 1019, ll. 879–90. The deed of endowment for the madrasa and khānqāh of Sultan al-Ghawrī has a similar clause, applying to the institutions' Sufis and Quran readers *wa ghayrihim min arbāb al-waẓā'if al-madhkūra*. As noted above, this institution actually provided no salaried teaching positions, but the language of this clause would seem to apply not simply to the Sufis and readers but to all the other *arbāb al-waẓā'if* provided for in the endowment. *Waqfiyyat* al-Ghawrī, Wizārat al-Awqāf o.s. No. 882, ll. 225–26.

"whoever is suitable" for the post.[96] More importantly, while numerically few, those schools whose endowment deeds did not specifically stipulate the inheritability of posts included several of the largest and most important schools founded over the latter half of the Mamluk period, such as the madrasa of Sultan Barqūq and the khānqāh of Jamāl al-Dīn al-Ustādār.[97] Yet the fact that the deeds for some institutions included no hereditary clause did not mean that, in practice, their posts would not be transferred to the posterity of those who held them. Between 1388 and 1475, for example, the Ḥanafī professorship at the madrasa of Sultan Barqūq was the preserve of several generations of the al-Sīrāmī family, despite the fact that the school's endowment deed carried no stipulation that sons were to succeed their fathers. Particular professors of Shāfiʿī law and Quranic exegesis at the same institution successfully transferred their posts to their sons.[98]

In this way, the proliferation of endowed institutions of learning served above all the interests of the educated elite, and afforded them the opportunity to guarantee their progeny's succession to their academic honors—and income. It should be stressed that the social phenomenon of sons inheriting the rank and employment of their scholarly fathers did not necessarily affect the character of education itself, the means and channels through which religious knowledge was transmitted. From a social perspective, the phenomenon is nonetheless significant. In the first place it may suggest that the social world of the higher-ranking ulama of the Mamluk period was not entirely fluid. The overall situation was far from one of caste, but the tendency for—and later the provisions in deeds of endowment allowing—sons to inherit their fathers' teaching posts may have contributed to a restriction of social movement and the concentration of career opportunities in the hands of particular families. The spread of institutions with endowments devoted specifically to education certainly suited the interests of those already resting at the top of the academic hierarchy, and proved to be a financial windfall for them.

[96] *Waqfiyyat* Khushqadam, Wizārat al-Awqāf o.s. No. 809, ll. 144–45. Like other late Mamluk "madrasas," this institution made no actual provisions for appointing professors; this clause was apparently to apply to the preacher, prayer leader, muezzin, ḥadīth readers, etc.

[97] Other schools that were apparently not bound by such a stipulation included that of Sultan al-Mu'ayyad Shaykh and the madrasas of Qalamṭāy and al-Sayfī Baybars.

[98] On the Sīrāmī family, see al-Sakhāwī, *al-Ḍaw'*, 4:158–59, 10:266, 327. The son of Nūr al-Dīn ʿAlī must have succeeded to his father's professorship in Shāfiʿī jurisprudence since several of Nūr al-Dīn's students substituted for the young boy; see ibid., 3:263, 4:264–65, 5:249–51. Similarly, Sirāj al-Dīn ʿUmar passed the professorship in exegesis to his son Jalāl al-Dīn ʿAbd al-Raḥmān; al-Maqrīzī, *al-Sulūk*, 3:814, cf. al-Sakhāwī, *al-Ḍaw'*, 4:109, 6:86.

V

RELIGIOUS EDUCATION AND THE MILITARY ELITE

IN ONE SENSE, the world of higher religious education in late medieval Cairo was utterly dependent on the rambunctious, mostly Turkish-speaking, dubiously Muslim Mamluk soldiers who monopolized political and military power. Mamluk sultans and amirs, between them, were responsible for the creation and endowment of most institutions of higher religious education, and perhaps inevitably so, since they controlled a disproportionate share of income-producing property.[1] Given the absence of an organized church and anything resembling ecclesiastical corporations as known in the West, scholars and religious functionaries, as well as the wider Muslim society that they served, relied heavily on individual members of the ruling military elite to take an interest in religious and educational affairs. Their interest, of course, did not necessarily affect the transmission of knowledge itself, but it did make possible the network of schools and paying professorships that, as was seen in the previous chapter, the educated elite managed to manipulate to their own advantage.

The extent of the Mamluks' financial contribution to religious education cannot be overemphasized. Despite the increasingly violent political struggles and the generally deteriorating economic conditions of the last century of Mamluk rule, they continued, through the early decades of the sixteenth century, actively to support the religious interests of Muslim society and, in particular, to construct educational institutions. A previous study has suggested that the Mamluks, distracted by internal dissension and a reduction of their disposable income, lost interest in the founding of new educational and religious institutions and that, in Syrian cities at least, the civilian elite established and endowed an increasing proportion of schools and mosques.[2] In the case of Cairo, however, the Mamluks continued to account for the lion's share of new schools. At least seventy-four teaching institutions can be shown to have been constructed or endowed during the Turkish period (1250–1389), covering roughly the

[1] On the wealth of Mamluks generally, see Ira Lapidus, *Muslim Cities in the Later Middle Ages* (Cambridge, Mass., 1967), passim, esp. 50–51, 59ff.

[2] Lapidus, *Muslim Cities*, 37. On the economic problems of Egypt and Syria in the late Middle Ages, see ibid., 36, and A. L. Udovitch et al., "England to Egypt, 1350–1500: Long-term Trends and Long-distance Trade," in *Studies in the Economic History of the Middle East*, ed. Michael Cook (Oxford, 1970), 115–28.

first half of the Mamluk sultanate: twelve by Mamluk sultans, thirty-six by Mamluk amirs or their families, and twenty-six by non-Mamluk civilians, scholars, and bureaucrats. Despite the general economic decline of the Circassian period (1389–1517) and the corresponding reduction in the income of individual Mamluks, there was only a minor slowdown in the construction and endowment of new schools. From the end of al-Ẓāhir Barqūq's first reign in 1389 until the Ottoman conquest of Egypt, at least sixty institutions were constructed or endowed, eleven by sultans, thirty by Mamluk amirs, and nineteen by others.[3] Schools dating from the Circassian period did tend on the whole to be financially less substantial institutions, for example providing salaries and stipends for fewer students and professors—or, indeed, none at all—as Mamluk benefactors, reacting to their weakened economic position, confined themselves to constructing the buildings, providing for their upkeep, and supporting a range of religious functionaries.[4] But the essential point is that the Mamluks' interest in things educational and religious, as measured by their decision to construct or endow the schools of Cairo, did not wane over the final decades of their rule. The period witnessed less a decline in the numbers of new foundations of learning than it did in the founders' capacities to provide amply for them.

Institutions devoted to higher religious and legal education came, of course, in a variety of forms and sizes. Still, it should be clear that establishing a madrasa, khānqāh, or teaching mosque, even a small one, required a good deal of wealth. The building that housed classes had to be

[3] These figures are based on my own survey of the literature, especially the major published chronicles and biographical dictionaries. Determining when each individual school was established is at times a difficult task, since the precise date of their construction and endowment, especially for smaller and less prestigious schools, is not always known. For the figures given here, when the precise date of establishment of any given institution is not known, the *terminus ante quem* is taken as the date of founding. Figures for the number of new schools established during the Circassian period are especially tentative; the actual number may well be higher than the figures given here. Al-Maqrīzī's topographical description of Cairo, *al-Mawāʿiẓ wa'l-iʿtibār bi-dhikr al-khiṭaṭ wa'l-āthār*, provides a useful, although not exhaustive, list of religious and educational institutions founded in the Turkish Mamluk period. However, since it was written in the first decades of the fifteenth century, and since no comparable work was written until ʿAlī Pāshā Mubārak's *al-Khiṭaṭ al-tawfīqiyya al-jadīda* in the mid-nineteenth century, we possess no contemporary source listing late Mamluk schools that even pretends to be comprehensive. We must rely, therefore, on scattered references in the chronicles and biographical dictionaries in compiling a catalog of Cairene schools founded between al-Maqrīzī's death in 1442 and the Ottoman conquest in 1517.

[4] See Chapter One. Doris Behrens-Abouseif, "Change in Function and Form of Mamluk Religious Institutions," *Annales islamologiques* 21 (1985), 88, notes the decline in endowments' economic strength over the last years of Mamluk rule, as does Lapidus, *Muslim Cities*, 37, 69, although the latter suggests that, at least in Syrian cities, the decline represented "growing neglect [of religious and educational affairs] by the Mamluk regime."

built and maintained, and endowments had to be created that provided sufficient income for the salaries of the school's beneficiaries. Given the pattern of foundation of new institutions, it would seem that the wealthy elements of medieval Cairene society, and especially the Mamluk elite, retained to the end the interests and concerns that led them to endow institutions of learning. What motivations prompted men—and a few women—of the Mamluk period to make the expenditures necessary to endow a school? In particular, what ties of interest bound the Mamluk soldiers to the transmission of Muslim religious knowledge?

Endowing a School: Political Considerations

The madrasas and mosques of medieval Cairo were, for the most part, not insubstantial buildings. Not all were as imposing as the fortress-like structure established by Sultan Ḥasan below the Citadel, but most were prominent architectural features of the streets and quarters in which they were located; a few even lent their names to the surrounding neighborhoods. Constructing such an institution in some respects represented, for those wealthy enough to make the necessary outlays, a form of conspicuous consumption through which some sort of message was communicated to the population of the city. Some have discerned in the very architecture of the Cairene madrasas—in their massive facades, and the tall deep portals so reminiscent of the palaces and houses inhabited by the amirs—a systematic symbolic linking of the power of the educated establishment to the political interests of the ruling elite.[5] But did the Mamluks, in endowing institutions of higher religious and legal education, really act with the profound sense of their collective political interests such an interpretation implies?

It has often been assumed that the rise and spread of the madrasa in the Fertile Crescent and, later, in Egypt was linked to the efforts of the new Sunni regimes of the twelfth century to combat the religious and political propaganda of the Shiʿi regimes—the Fatimids in Egypt, for example—that had dominated the central Islamic world during the eleventh.[6] This may well have been the case in the early years of the "Sunni revival," that period which saw the organization of an effective and conscious Sunni response to both Shiʿi political ascendancy and the challenge of the Latin crusaders. A key element of that response lay in the

[5] R. Stephen Humphreys, "The Expressive Intent of Mamluk Architecture in Cairo," *Studia Islamica* 35 (1972), esp. 78, 111.

[6] See, for example, A. S. Tritton, *Materials on Muslim Education in the Middle Ages* (London, 1957), 103; a more recent work coming to the same conclusion specifically in the Egyptian context is Muḥammad M. Amīn, *al-Awqāf wa'l-ḥayāt al-ijtimāʿiyya fī miṣr* (Cairo, 1980), 235.

efforts of the new Sunni rulers, such as Nūr al-Dīn Maḥmūd b. Zangī in Syria (d. 1174) and his successor, Ṣalāḥ al-Dīn b. Ayyūb (d. 1193, better known to the West as Saladin), to establish madrasas and other institutions to train a new Sunni religious elite. It would be difficult to see in any other light the first madrasa established in Aleppo, a Shāfiʿī institution that the angry Shiʿi residents of the city saw fit promptly to demolish.[7]

In Egypt, too, such concerns may have informed the decisions of those who, in the twelfth and early thirteenth centuries, chose to construct Sunni madrasas. Until the collapse of the Fatimid caliphate in 1171, their Cairene establishments such as the great mosque of al-Azhar served as training centers for the men sent out to propagate the Fatimids' radical Ismāʿīlī brand of Shiʿism. The first Egyptian madrasas, established several decades before the fall of the Fatimids, must have represented to contemporaries a renaissance of Sunni learning in the face of institutions devoted to Ismāʿīlī propaganda. Ridwān ibn al-Walākhshī, the first of a series of Sunni *wazīrs* (ministers) to the late Fatimid caliphs, in 1137–38 founded one of the earliest Egyptian madrasas, a school for students of Mālikī law in Alexandria; fourteen years later another Sunni wazīr, Ibn al-Sallār, established a second school in the port city, this one for Shāfiʿīs. Their schools, and especially those built and endowed by Saladin toward the end of the twelfth century, constituted a conscious attempt to establish a political base among the Sunni residents of Alexandria and al-Fusṭāṭ in opposition to the Shiʿi regime.[8]

The political context in which institutions of traditional Muslim learning were constructed, however, did not remain static. By the middle of the thirteenth century—by the time, that is, of the coup that brought the Mamluks to power—the Shiʿi presence in Egypt had all but been extinguished. The Ismāʿīlī Fatimids had never succeeded in converting large numbers of Egyptians to Shiʿism. Even under the Ayyubid sultans who ruled Egypt during the late twelfth and early thirteenth centuries, threats to the legitimacy and power of the new Sunni regime may have stemmed less from any residual Shiʿism than from the still large Christian population of the country, which had adopted a more assertive stance under a series of Christian ministers to the later Fatimid caliphs. Indeed, recent research has suggested that even Ayyubid madrasas were constructed more to organize the Sunni community against the Christian

[7] Dominique Sourdel, "Réflexions sur la diffusion de la madrasa en orient du XIe au XIIIe siècle," *Revue des études islamiques* 44 (1976), 173.

[8] Gary L. Leiser, "The Restoration of Sunnism in Egypt: Madrasas and Mudarrisūn 495–647/1101–1249," dissertation, University of Pennsylvania (1976), 131–51, 151–52ff., 189–90.

residents of Egypt than to combat a realistic Shiʿi menace.[9] It is difficult, therefore, to see in the munificence of the Mamluk military elite in establishing and endowing institutions of higher religious education an attempt to confirm Sunnism's "new role as the one orthodoxy within their realms," at least if the "heretical" enemy is identified as Shiʿism.[10] No other "orthodoxy" was even conceivable.

But it may be misleading to search for an explanation of the remarkable proliferation of schools under the patronage of the Mamluks exclusively, or even primarily, in broad political considerations. It is true that the Mamluks had extinguished, almost by accident, the respected Ayyubid regime, but the circumstances surrounding the endowment of each school reveal little trace of any attempt, conscious or unconscious, to confirm the political role of the Mamluks *as a group* in medieval Egyptian society. Even though the behavior of many superficially Islamicized Mamluks was not such as to win the approbation of the legal and religious authorities, those same scholars recognized the contributions of the Mamluk system as a whole to the defense and vitality of the Muslim community—Ibn Khaldūn, after all, credited the "Turks" with nothing less than the salvation of Islam. Thus the pattern of endowment should probably not be read as an attempt to overcome any perceived illegitimacy to their rule. Rather, the very fact that individuals, and not the state, undertook the construction of schools, mosques, and Sufi convents suggests that individual concerns governed the decision to establish a charitable endowment. Insofar as the Mamluks' efforts to establish and endow schools were "political," they reflect the intensely *personal* character of Egyptian politics during the Mamluk period, in which bitter and mutually hostile political factions coalesced principally around the leading personalities of the Mamluk corps.

Intimate and lasting ties bound each individual school to the reputation, or memory, of the individual who founded it. In a recurrent pattern, Mamluks built schools in the immediate vicinity of their personal dwelling places in the city. The official opening of a new school, especially those constructed by sultans, was routinely marked by a vast public banquet at which courtiers, judges, and scholars gathered together to eat a meal, listen to the recitation of the Quran or ḥadīth, or even a formal lesson in jurisprudence or exegesis, pray, and distribute alms to the institution's stipendiaries and the local poor. The name of a religious or academic establishment generally derived from that of its founder—the Ẓāhiriyya of al-Ẓāhir Barqūq, for example, or the Ṣarghitmishiyya of the

[9] Ibid., passim, and Gary Leiser, "The *Madrasa* and the Islamization of the Middle East: The Case of Egypt," *Journal of the American Research Center in Egypt* 22 (1985), 29–47.

[10] Humphreys, "Expressive Intent," 94. Despite the criticisms offered here, Humphreys' article remains a brilliant analysis of the meaning of Mamluk architecture.

amir Ṣarghitmish—and the Mamluks seem to have been eager to acquire the prestige within the community associated with the construction of a school devoted to religious learning. Consider, for example, the fate of the khānqāh known as the Baybarsiyya built and endowed by Sultan Baybars al-Jāshnakīr in the first years of the fourteenth century. By the time it was completed, Baybars was dead, deposed by his rival al-Nāṣir Muḥammad, who promptly closed the institution and confiscated its endowments—and, for good measure, ordered the obliteration of Baybars' name from the institution's inscriptions. Ultimately, al-Nāṣir Muḥammad permitted the khānqāh to reopen, and even restored its endowments, but only after the completion of his own convent in Siryāqūs, north of the city, and its elevation to the status of premier khānqāh in the Egyptian capital.[11]

A good deal, it seems, resided in a name. In the fiercely competitive world of Mamluk politics, the establishment of a prominent institution of learning, which took its name from its founder, provided him with a potent symbol of political legitimacy. After the disgrace, arrest, and execution of Jamāl al-Dīn Yūsuf al-Ustādār, a rich and powerful civilian bureaucrat of the early fifteenth century, Sultan al-Nāṣir Faraj ibn Barqūq sought, through a legal maneuver involving Jamāl al-Dīn's endowments, to reconstitute the school he had founded and to rename it the Nāsiriyya. This sultan, too, had Jamāl al-Dīn's name effaced from the building's inscriptions, and replaced with his own, so that "the name of the Sultan was inscribed on top of [the walls] surrounding the courtyard and upon the school's candles and carpets and ceilings." Faraj's triumph, however, proved short-lived. After the succession of his rival al-Mu'ayyad Shaykh to the sultanate, the endowments of Jamāl al-Dīn, who had formerly been a client of the new sultan, were restored to his heirs. And of course the institution Jamāl al-Dīn founded is, to this day, known as the Jamāliyya.[12]

Thus, to medieval observers, the establishment of a school of higher education served an important commemorative function. By retaining the names of their founders, sultans and amirs and, in cases like that of Jamāl al-Dīn Yūsuf, powerful civilian bureaucrats, religious establishments provided individual benefactors with a symbolic capital that redounded to their credit. This, after all, was a society that treasured knowledge, especially religious knowledge, knowledge of the revelation of God and the law to which it gave rise. Through the establishment of institutions devoted to its transmission, the Mamluks were able to link

[11] Al-Maqrīzī, *Khiṭaṭ*, 2:417; Leonor Fernandes, *The Evolution of a Sufi Institution in Mamluk Egypt: The Khanqah* (Berlin, 1988), 25–29.

[12] Al-Maqrīzī, *Khiṭaṭ*, 2:402–3; Shams al-Dīn Muḥammad al-Sakhāwī, *al-Ḍaw' al-lāmiʿ li-ahl al-qarn al-tāsiʿ* (Cairo, 1934; reptd. Beirut, n.d.), 10:297.

their names to the most valued asset of the society over which they ruled. The decision to build or endow an institution of learning was thus, in the broadest sense, a political act, but one that responded not to any external or ideological threat, but to the desire of individual Mamluks to integrate themselves into the local Muslim culture.

Endowing a School: Financial Considerations

If Mamluk politics were primarily personal, then the victims of that political process were not ideas or ideologies so much as the individual Mamluks whose factions lost power. In this world, the construction and endowment of a school—or, for that matter, of other religious institutions—provided the Mamluks with more than *symbolic* capital. Despite the vast expenditures necessary to establish a school, the Mamluks paradoxically found in the endowment of madrasas and cognate institutions an opportunity to protect their wealth and provide for a steady income to their heirs. In the early fifteenth century, Ibn Khaldūn noted that educational establishments had flourished in Egypt under the Mamluk regime because of the attempt by members of the ruling elite to preserve for their children some of their wealth, otherwise subject to confiscation at their deaths. It was possible, of course, simply to establish an endowment designed specifically to benefit one's heirs. In theory the property of such legal instruments was inalienable, but in fact these endowments remained vulnerable to confiscation. A safer bet was to establish an endowment in favor of a madrasa, khānqāh, or mosque, or for some other charitable purpose, and to ensure that its income would exceed the charity's requirements. Any surplus, then, could be earmarked for the founder and his heirs.[13]

Such endowments, for mixed charitable and private purposes, remained for most of the Mamluk period the safest way of ensuring the orderly transferral of a Mamluk's wealth to his heirs. The reluctance of the regime to tamper with the endowments of religious institutions was palpable. In the month of Dhū 'l-Qaʿda of the year A.H. 872 (May–June 1468), Sultan Qayt Bāy summoned a council consisting of the caliph, the four chief qāḍīs, a group of leading religious scholars, and several prominent amirs. The sultan detailed to the assembled notables the military threat posed by a restive Turkoman principality on the empire's Syrian-Anatolian border, and the insufficiency of government funds to outfit an

[13] Ibn Khaldūn, *The Muqadimmah*, trans. Franz Rosenthal (New York, 1958), 2:435; cf. Lapidus, *Muslim Cities*, 74. On mixed endowments, which he identifies as a third type intermediary between purely private (*ahlī*) and purely charitable (*khayrī*) waqfs, see Amīn, *al-Awqāf*, 72–73ff. Amīn's book is, in fact, the definitive study of charitable endowments in Mamluk Egypt and their impact on, among other things, religious institutions.

army to confront it. He proposed, therefore, to raise the necessary money from the people and from the endowments of mosques and other religious institutions which, he noted, recently "had increased in number." Arriving late, but in time to express his opinion, a prominent Ḥanafī shaykh, Amīn al-Dīn Yahyā al-Aqṣarā'ī, expostulated on the wickedness of the plan, at which, apparently, the sultan backed down.[14]

Over the last decades of Mamluk rule, as external threats pressed more heavily and civil disorders in Cairo became more frequent, attempts to raid charitable endowments continued and, increasingly, succeeded. In 1500–1501, rebellious young Mamluks ascended en masse to the Citadel, demanding from the new sultan Qānṣūh al-Ghawrī the customary payment in celebration of his accession. When they returned to the city below, the rumor quickly spread that the sultan planned to distribute to them lands belonging to the endowments of mosques and madrasas. Again, in council the four chief qāḍīs rejected the sultan's plan. This time, however, the Ḥanafī qāḍī returned to the sultan at the end of the day, and together they reached a compromise: the endowments were to be left intact, but were to surrender to the sultan a full year's income.[15]

At least until the end of the fifteenth century, however, such endowments were generally safe; not surprisingly, therefore, many of the deeds establishing schools also made provisions for regular payments to the founder and his descendants from the income of the endowment. The sums involved could be substantial. One school's endowment provided for a fixed payment of 2,000 dirhams per month to the children and descendants of the founder, as well as a certain proportion of the endowment's residual income, compared to 250 dirhams per month for the mosque's professors of Ḥanafī and Shāfi'ī law.[16] Most commonly, a founder's children were provided for out of what was left of the endowment's income after expenditures on the school or other object of charity. Amir Qalamṭāy, for example, after setting aside one-third of the residual income of his endowment for the upkeep and repair of his madrasa, stipulated that the remaining two-thirds be distributed among his children and their descendants.[17] Several founders went further and insisted that the residual income be divided among their children and descendants equally, without regard to gender, thereby circumventing the laws of Islamic inheritance that required a male to receive double a female's por-

[14] Muḥammad b. Aḥmad Ibn Iyās, *Badā'i' al-zuhūr fī waqā'i' al-zuhūr* (Cairo, 1984), 3:13–15.

[15] Ibn Iyās, *Badā'i' al-zuhūr*, 4:14–15. On Mamluk expropriations from charitable endowments, see Lapidus, *Muslim Cities*, 40, 77.

[16] *Waqfiyyat* Sūdūn, Dār al-Watha'iq No. 58, ll. 327–34, 342–53.

[17] *Waqfiyyat* Qalamṭāy, Dār al-Watha'iq No. 68, ll. 310ff.

tion.[18] A Mamluk's feelings of responsibility might extend beyond the bounds of his immediate family circle: one, for example, provided that half of the residual income of his endowment be set aside for his wife (as long as she remained unmarried), his children, and their descendants, but allotted another eighth for his two sisters and their heirs.[19] Bonds of devotion in medieval Muslim families included other members of a household, such as emancipated slaves (*ʿatīq*, pl. *ʿutaqāʾ*), whom many Mamluks also named residual beneficiaries.[20]

The law governing charitable endowments provided wealthy individuals a second means to ensure the regular disbursement of money to their offspring. Each endowment required the services of a controller (*nāẓir*), one to oversee the administration of the endowment and the distribution of funds to its beneficiaries. Usually the founder reserved to himself the right to hold the controllership during his lifetime, but after his death could pass the post on to his children. The endowment deeds outlined in considerable detail the criteria by which future controllers were to be appointed, and in most cases—more than three quarters of the deeds that survive and which give the relevant information—the founder's children and descendants, or, in some cases his freed slaves and their descendants, were to hold or at least share in the controllership of the institution.[21] The sums passed on to heirs in this manner, if not colossal, were

[18] For example, *Waqfiyyat* al-Mu'ayyad Shaykh, Wizārat al-Awqāf o.s. No. 938, ll. 720–40; *Waqfiyyat* Jamāl al-Dīn al-Ustādār, Dār al-Wathā'iq No. 106, ll. 366–98; *Waqfiyyat* Mughulṭāy al-Jamālī, Wizārat al-Awqāf o.s. No. 1666, ll. 449–77; *Waqfiyyat* Sūdūn, Dār al-Wathā'iq, No. 58, ll. 327–34, 342–53.

[19] *Waqfiyyat* Mughulṭāy al-Jamālī, Wizārat al-Awqāf o.s. No. 1666, ll. 449–92.

[20] See, for example, *Waqfiyyat* Mughulṭāy al-Jamālī, Wizārat al-Awqāf o.s. No. 1666, ll. 516–26, where he specifically assigns one eighth of his waqf's residual income to his ʿutaqāʾ. More commonly, the founder's manumitted slaves were made residual beneficiaries only after his direct descendants had died out. See, for example, *Waqfiyyat* Jamāl al-Dīn al-Ustādār, Dār al-Wathā'iq No. 106, ll. 366–98, and *Waqfiyyat* al-Mu'ayyad Shaykh, Wizārat al-Awqāf, o.s. No. 938, ll. 720–40. Much more frequently, a founder's emancipated slaves were entrusted with the controllership (naẓar) of the institution, which itself was a paying proposition; on this point, see below.

[21] See the following deeds: that of al-Nāṣir Muḥammad ibn Qalāwūn, a summary of which is preserved in Shihāb al-Dīn Aḥmad al-Nuwayrī's encyclopedic treatise *Nihāyat al-arab fī funūn al-adab*, the relevant sections printed as an appendix to Taqī 'l-Din Aḥmad al-Maqrīzī's *Kitāb al-sulūk li-maʿrifat duwal al-mulūk* (Cairo, 1934–73), 1:1043ff.; Mughulṭāy al-Jamālī, Wizārat al-Awqāf o.s. No. 1666, ll. 530–44; Sultan Ḥasan ibn Muḥammad ibn Qalāwūn, as published by Muḥammad M. Amīn in al-Ḥasan ibn Ḥabīb, *Tadhikirat al-nabīh fī ayyām al-manṣūr wa banīh*, (Cairo, 1976–86), 3:339ff.; Ibn Badīr al-ʿAbbāsī, Dār al-Wathā'iq No. 43, ll. 338–42; al-Ẓāhir Barqūq, Dār al-Wathā'iq No. 51, ll. 1065ff.; Zayn al-Dīn Ṣidqa, Dār al-Wathā'iq No. 59, ll. 86ff.; Sūdūn min Zāda, Dār al-Wathā'iq No. 58, ll. 367–73; al-Shiblī Kāfūr, Dār al-Wathā'iq No. 76, ll. 97–100; al-Fakhrī ʿAbd al-Ghānī, Dār al-Wathā'iq No. 72, ll. 328–35; al-Mu'ayyad Shaykh, Wizārat al-Awqāf o.s. No. 938, ll. 740–49; al-Ashraf Barsbāy, Dār al-Wathā'iq No. 173. fol. 139r–v; Jamāl al-Dīn al-Ustādār, Dār

not insubstantial. Most often the controller was paid a monthly stipend comparable to that of the senior instructor or religious official in the institution. At the madrasa of Ṣarghitmish, for example, the controller received 200 dirhams per month, the professors of Ḥanafī jurisprudence and ḥadīth 300 each. At the madrasa of Sultan Ḥasan, the Shāfiʿī professor also received 300 dirhams per month, but the controller was paid 1,000 for his services.

Even in the case of those institutions for which deeds have not survived, the circumstances surrounding their foundation and the creation of endowments for their upkeep strongly suggest that Ibn Khaldūn was right, and that the protection of personal and family wealth lay close to, if not absolutely at the front of, a founder's list of priorities. Already in the first years of the Mamluk regime, schools were established by public figures who had previously suffered arrest and the confiscation of their wealth, and who might therefore be inclined to seek out ways to protect what wealth remained to them. The founder of the Marzūqiyya, Ṣafī 'l-Dīn Ibrāhīm Ibn Marzūq (d. 1261), a prominent Syrian merchant, ḥadīth scholar, and adviser to governors, had been arrested and mulcted of 500,000 dinars in 1238–39, after which he came to Egypt where, sometime before his death, he established his madrasa.[22] Another who established one of the earliest Mamluk madrasas, Amir ʿAlā' al-Dīn Aydakīn al-Bunduqdārī (d. 1285), had also known imprisonment and confiscation, in this case at the hands of the Ayyubid sultan al-Malik al-Ṣāliḥ Najm al-Dīn, before endowing his madrasa not far from the mosque of Ibn Ṭūlūn.[23]

In later instances, the connection between some sort of crisis in the career of the individual and the decision to endow a school is far less tenuous. Consider, for example, the madrasa established by Amir Sayf al-Dīn Mankūtimur al-Husāmī. Mankūtimur stipulated that the madrasa

al-Wathā'iq No. 106, ll. 399ff.; Zayn al-Dīn al-Ustādār, Dār al-Wathā'iq No. 110, ll. 1471ff.; Qānī Bāy Qarā, Wizārat al-Awqāf o.s. No. 1019, ll. 388–92; al-Sayfī Baybars, Dār al-Wathā'iq No. 313, ll. 180–86; Sultan al-Ghawrī, Wizārat al-Awqāf o.s. No. 882, pp. 222–25.

[22] Not surprisingly, perhaps, Ibn Duqmāq tells us that the waqf of this institution was "insufficient"—*yasīra*. Ibrāhīm b. Muḥammad Ibn Duqmāq, *al-Intiṣār li-wasiṭat ʿaqd al-amṣār* (Paris, 1893; reptd. Beirut, 1966), 4:95. It is not known when exactly this madrasa was constructed and endowed—presumably sometime between Ibn Marzūq's arrest in 1238–39 and his death in 1261. Gary Leiser points out that this madrasa may have been built under the last Ayyubids. Ibn Marzūq became an adviser to the Ayyubid al-Malik al-Ṣāliḥ in Egypt; the latter's death, and the political crisis that followed, may well have played a role in inducing Ibn Marzūq to endow this institution. Leiser, "Restoration," 296–97.

[23] Jamāl al-Dīn Yūsuf Ibn Taghrī Birdī, *al-Manhal al-ṣāfī wa'l-mustawfī ba'd al-wāfī* (Cairo, 1984–), 3:155–56. Little is known of this institution. Ibn Taghrī Birdī calls the building simply a "tomb" (*turba*); others, however, specifically label it a madrasa; al-Maqrīzī, *Khiṭaṭ*, 2:73 and possibly 399, and Ibn Iyas, *Badā'iʿ al-zuhūr*, 1 (pt. 1):415.

offer courses in both Mālikī and Ḥanafī law, and provided a library for the use of the school's students; he endowed the institution with property in Syria and elsewhere. We know nothing about whether the deed of endowment also made provisions for Mankūtimur himself, his descendants, household slaves, or anyone else not directly associated with the madrasa. The date of the institution's establishment is significant, however. The building was completed in 1298–99, but construction could hardly have commenced more than a short time before its completion. Mankūtimur, a Mamluk of Sultan Husām al-Dīn Lājīn, rode to power, as it were, on the coattails of his *ustadh* (master) following Lājīn's coup against Sultan Kitbughā in the month of Ṣafar, A.H. 696 (December 1296). It was not until the next month, Rabīʿ al-Awwal, that Mankūtimur was even made an amir, and not until the end of 696, in Dhū 'l-Qaʿda, that he was appointed viceroy (*nā'ib al-salṭana*).[24] It was in this post, at that time the second highest in the sultanate, that Mankūtimur acquired the kind of income that allowed—and to a prudent man, might encourage—the endowment of an institution such as that which he established. Mankūtimur played a central role in the *rawk*, the redistribution of quasi-feudal *iqṭāʿs* (grants of income from agricultural estates) to the military elite, carried out under Sultan Lājīn. In this sensitive post, the income of this parvenu skyrocketed to over 100,000 dinars per year. Suddenly he possessed the means to build and endow a madrasa or some other religious institution; motivation may have followed quickly. In the course of his administration of the rawk and other matters, Mankūtimur had alienated many of the leading amirs, who grieved that, among other things, the value of their own feudal grants had shrunk. Soon rumors began to circulate of a plot against Mankūtimur and Lājīn; we know that Mankūtimur was aware of them, for at one point he threatened—perhaps disingenuously—to forsake his lucrative and powerful post and "go live among the *fuqarā'* [Sufi ascetics]." The point is that, from an individual perspective, the time was ripe for Mankūtimur's decision to endow a religious institution if he wished thereby to shelter any portion of his wealth from confiscation. By Rabīʿ al-Ākhir of A.H. 698 (January-February 1299), within a few months of his madrasa's construction, Mankūtimur and his patron, Sultan Lājīn, were dead.[25]

[24] On the office of the nā'ib al-salṭāna, see David Ayalon, "Studies on the Structure of the Mamluk Army—III," *Bulletin of the School of Oriental and African Studies* 16 (1954), 57–58.

[25] Al-Maqrīzī gives a succinct account of the circumstances of Mankūtimur's rise to power and his subsequent death in the coup against Lājīn in his account of Mankūtimur's madrasa, in his *Khiṭaṭ*, 2:387–88. More details can be gleaned from his chronicle for those two years, *Kitāb al-sulūk li-maʿrifat duwal al-mulūk*, 1:820–72. Cf. Ibn Taghrī Birdī's account in *al-Nujūm al-zāhira fī mulūk miṣr wa'l-qāhira* (Cairo, 1929–72), 8:85–105.

A quarter of a century later, al-Maqrīzī tells us, in 1323, Amir ʿAlam al-Dīn Sanjar al-Jāwulī established a madrasa in the Khaṭṭ al-Kabash, in the same street as his house, near the mosque of Ibn Ṭūlūn. Sanjar, who died in 1345, had originally been a Mamluk of Jāwul, an amir of Sultan Baybars. After Jāwul's death, Sanjar moved to the service of Sultan Qalāwūn, and after him served under his son al-Nāṣir Muḥammad. Sanjar was an exceptionally pious and learned Mamluk—a point to which we will return—and provided in his endowment for a course in Shāfiʿī jurisprudence and a number of Sufis. Again, we know nothing about what provisions he might have made in the deed of endowment to preserve his own wealth, but the timing of his decision to establish this madrasa was striking: in 1320 Sanjar had been arrested; when his madrasa was established in 1323, he was still imprisoned in Alexandria, facing what must have seemed a very uncertain future.[26]

The evidence for individuals such as Mankūtimur al-Husāmī and Sanjar al-Jāwulī is admittedly circumstantial—without their actual deeds of endowment, or more detailed information from the sources, we cannot prove that their decisions to establish schools were informed by the opportunity to protect their personal wealth behind the shield of the Islamic law of endowment. But the coincidence of a personal crisis, often one threatening arrest and confiscation of wealth, and the decision to endow an institution of religious learning recurred throughout the Mamluk period. As in the previous cases, the decision of Sayf al-Dīn Aljāy al-Yūsufī to build and endow a madrasa for Shāfiʿī and Ḥanafī students coincided suspiciously with his arrest. Sultan Ḥasan had promoted him to the rank of an "amir of 100," the highest military rank to which a Mamluk could aspire. After Ḥasan's assassination and Yalbughā al-ʿUmarī's rise to power as commander-in-chief (*atābak*) of the Mamluk armies under Sultan al-Ashraf Shaʿbān, Aljāy in 1363–64 was confirmed in office as *amīr jandār*, a high-ranking position charged with supervision of a combined arsenal/detention center.[27] By the autumn of 1366, however, matters had begun to unravel. In December of that year, a group of Yalbughā's own Mamluks initiated a revolt against him, on account of his wanton cruelty toward them, and persuaded the fourteen year-old sultan to join them. The coup was successful, and Yalbughā was killed. Over the next several months, high-ranking amirs such as Aljāy must have felt the increasing precariousness of their positions as the new atābak Asundumur concen-

[26] Al-Maqrīzī, *Khiṭaṭ*, 2:398. Ultimately, in fact, Sanjar was released from prison in 1328 and rose to become an amir of 100 and a commander (*muqaddam*) of 1,000, and to hold several important political-administrative posts.

[27] On the "amir of one hundred," see David Ayalon, "Studies on the Structure of the Mamluk Army—II," *Bulletin of the School of Oriental and African Studies* 15 (1953), 467–69. On the atābak and the amīr jandār, see idem, "Structure—III," 58–59, 63–64.

trated power in his own hands, and arrest and banishment was meted out to those formerly associated with Yalbughā. Finally, three months after Yalbughā's demise, a revolt broke out against Asundumur; it was put down, and the leaders, among them Aljāy, were arrested and imprisoned. We know that Aljāy's madrasa was established in that same year. Is it too much to read his decision to endow it against the background of the uncertainty of his personal position?[28]

In the case of the mosque established by Amir Sūdūn min Zāda in 1402, we can be even more precise. Originally a Mamluk of Sultan Barqūq, Sūdūn rose through the ranks of the military elite. By 1400–1401 he was an *amīr tablakhāna*, the second highest officer rank in the Mamluk army, leader of a detachment of soldiers (*ra's nawba*), and, for a period of two months, treasurer to the sultan (*khāzindār*).[29] Tamurlane's invasion of Syria in that year threw the Mamluk military elite into confusion; the details need not concern us here, but one of the consequences was an abortive rebellion of disgruntled amirs that broke out in Ramaḍān, A.H. 804 (April 1402). Sūdūn seems to have been involved in this disturbance in some way, and by the fourteenth day of Shawwāl—that is, by the middle of the following month—he was in custody, and was later moved to prison in Alexandria.[30] Again, the date is worth noting: the deed of endowment establishing the institution that bears his name dates from "the last days of Ramaḍān," 804—just days, that is, before his arrest.[31] It should come as no surprise that the deed provides for a monthly payment of 2,000 dirhams to his descendants, males and females equally, and also that a portion of any remainder after the endowment's stipulated expenditures be paid to them.

The link between a personal crisis and the decision to endow a madrasa holds as well for non-Mamluks who were employed in important governmental or bureaucratic posts. Jamāl al-Dīn Maḥmūd b. ʿAlī b. Aṣfar had begun his career as a minor bureaucrat, but persevered until, under Sultan Barqūq, he became *ustādār*, a position in which he undertook the important responsibility of distributing their pay to the Mamluks.[32] Despite setbacks—during the interregnum of 1389–90, for example, in what

[28] Al-Maqrīzī, *Khiṭaṭ*, 2:399, summarizes the story of Aljāy and his madrasa; further details can be gleaned from Ibn Taghrī Birdī, *al-Nujūm al-zāhira*, 11:24–44.

[29] On the rank of amīr tablakhāna, see Ayalon, "Structure—II," 469–70; on the office of khāzindār, see idem, "Structure—III," 62.

[30] Compare the accounts in al-Maqrīzī, *al-Sulūk*, 3:1084 and passim; Ibn Taghrī Birdī, *al-Nujūm al-zāhira*, 12:286 et passim; al-Sakhāwī, *al-Ḍaw'*, 3:275; and Ibn Iyās, *Badāʾiʿ al-zuhūr*, 1 (pt. 2):650–53. Al-Sakhāwī's abbreviated and relatively late account actually suggests that Sūdūn and the others were imprisoned during Ramaḍān; the other three sources, however, make clear that they were captured on the fourteenth day of Shawwāl.

[31] *Waqfiyyat* Sūdūn min Zāda, Dār al-Wathāʾiq No. 58.

[32] On the office of the ustādār, see Ayalon, "Structure—III," 61–62.

he might well have looked upon as a warning, he was imprisoned and fined—after Barqūq's restoration to the throne he amassed an extraordinary personal fortune. In A.H. 799 (1396–97), Maḥmūd was imprisoned and tortured to death, but his fall from grace had actually begun toward the beginning of A.H. 797 (1394–95)—the year in which he established a madrasa. In Rabīʿ al-Awwal of that year, he was beaten and fined 150,000 dirhams at the orders of the sultan; in Rajab, he lost his post as ustādār; in Shaʿbān, he was dismissed as head of the royal mint in Cairo; and in Ramaḍān he was fined another 150,000 dirhams. His subsequent losses—al-Maqrīzī gives totals of 1,400,000 dinars, 1,000,000 silver dirhams, as well as goods valued at over 1,000,000 silver dirhams—need not concern us; the point is that by the time he built his madrasa, his position was precarious and worsening. Maḥmūd also seems to have attempted, albeit unsuccessfully, a new tack for protecting his wealth in a religious institution: in A.H. 798 (1395–96) the sultan's men discovered and unearthed 6,000 dinars and more than a million silver dirhams from the ground behind his madrasa.[33]

A similar tale could be told concerning Jamāl al-Dīn Yūsuf b. Aḥmad b. Muḥammad al-Ustādār, who founded his famous khānqāh in Jumādā al-Awwal, A.H. 810 (October 1407), the construction of which was completed fourteen months later. In A.H. 809, Jamāl al-Dīn was appointed wazīr and *nāẓir al-khāṣṣ*, in addition to his post as ustādār, a combination of positions that effectively made him responsible for distributing to the army pay, food, and clothing, but that also exposed him to the wrath of the Mamluks should the funds at his disposal fall short. In the first month of A.H. 810 he was still strong enough to appoint his son, an incompetent youth of seventeen, to the position of supervising the annual pilgrimage (*amīr al-ḥajj*). But the economy of Egypt was already in serious disarray, payments to the Mamluk soldiers were in arrears, and apparently much of the blame fell on Jamāl al-Dīn's shoulders. He, too, might have read the writing on the wall: by A.H. 812 he was in disgrace, imprisoned and impoverished. Like Jamāl al-Dīn Maḥmūd, he hid a part of his treasure in his madrasa; like that of Amir Sūdūn, his endowment deed has survived. Consequently we *know* that it stipulated that the remainder of the endowment's income after the expenses of the school were to go to his children and descendants, in equal shares for males and females, and that one of them was to hold the controllership of the endowment, at a stipend of 200 dirhams per month.[34]

[33] Ibn Iyās, *Badāʾiʿ al-zuhūr*, 1 (pt. 2):2, 478. Maḥmūd's story can be found in al-Maqrīzī's account of his madrasa, *Khiṭaṭ*, 2:395–97; further details can be gleaned from his chronicle, *al-Sulūk*, 3:829–55.

[34] *Waqfiyyat* Jamāl al-Dīn Yūsuf al-Ustādār, Dār al-Wathāʾiq No. 106. On the madrasa

Thus the establishment and endowment of schools ostensibly to benefit teachers, students, and the educated class more generally also offered the wealthy elite the opportunity to secure the transferral of at least some of their wealth to their heirs and descendants. From all accounts, it was a mechanism widely employed. Of the seven deeds of endowment considered in this study that neither made provisions for direct payments to designated children nor stipulated that they at least share in the paying post of controller of the endowment, three belonged to eunuchs, who presumably were childless.[35] The Mamluk polity systematically precluded the ruling military elite from transferring their political power to their offspring. Indirectly, however, the endowment of institutions of religious education provided them with a means by which they might pass on their wealth to their descendants, and with it, perhaps, some portion of their status.

Endowing a School: Pious Considerations

We should not, however, be led to believe that only mercenary considerations led medieval men and women to establish and endow madrasas and other religious institutions. On the contrary, financial considerations were only one of a number of highly personal factors that informed the decision of an individual to endow a school or mosque.

Above all, we should not dismiss the possibility that Mamluks and others established schools of higher education out of a genuine interest in their religious and instructional functions. For men such as Sirāj al-Dīn ʿUmar al-Bulqīnī (d. 1403) or Badr al-Dīn Maḥmūd al-ʿAynī (d. 1451), two leading scholars and judges who established institutions known as madrasas, such concerns may be assumed. For the members of the military elite and their families who established the majority of institutions of learning, the connection may be more problematic. Can a pious interest in higher religious education be reconciled with the prevailing image, shared by many of the contemporary historians and biographers, of the Mamluks as wild, ethically lax, and only superficially Islamicized?

Cultural animosity toward the Turks—to which ethnic group, broadly speaking, most Mamluks belonged—and in particular skepticism of their

itself, see al-Maqrīzī, *Khiṭaṭ*, 2:401–3; Jamāl al-Dīn's story can be followed more closely in idem., *al-Sulūk*, 4:28–113.

[35] The founders in question were Khushqadam al-Zimām, Jawhar al-Lālā, and al-Shiblī Kāfūr; see their waqfiyyas, Wizārat al-Awqāf n.s. No. 188, Dār al-Wathā'iq No. 86, and Dār al-Wathā'iq No. 76, respectively. Of these, however, it is worth noting that Jawhar al-Lālā's and al-Shiblī Kāfūr's documents provided for direct payments to themselves and their emancipated slaves—that is, to the members of their households—and that Kāfūr's ʿutaqāʾ were also to have a share in the controllership.

intellectual aptitudes and sensitivity to religious matters, has deep roots in the Arab Islamic societies of the Near East. In the words of Ulrich Haarmann, Arab suspicion of the Turks amounts to the level of an ideology. From at least the ninth century, various Turkish military elites had intermittently ruled or dominated the central Islamic lands of Syria, Iraq, and Egypt, and their political dominance perhaps naturally gave rise to cultural antipathies and ethnic stereotypes among their Arabic-speaking subjects. To be sure, the "Turk" was universally acknowledged to excel in the martial arts, an almost inescapable conclusion given their position in Muslim society. Moreover, at least among some, most notably the perceptive historian Ibn Khaldūn, resentment gradually gave way to a grudging acknowledgement that Turkish-speaking soldiers had performed an incalculable service to the Islamic world by delivering it from the dual threat of pagan Mongols and Christian Crusaders. But to most Muslim Arabs, the Turks in general, and Mamluks in particular, remained boors, alienated from the mainstream culture by their ignorance of Arabic and their indifference to Islam. Many scholars of the religious sciences were especially eager to deny the Mamluks any credit for achievement in academic or literary pursuits, and their prejudice infected the historical and biographical literature of the period.[36]

But as Ulrich Haarmann has suggested, such self-serving attitudes of the religious scholars toward the Mamluks may do the Turkish soldiers an injustice. For a start, it should be remembered that most madrasas, khānqāhs, and other religious institutions established during the two and a half centuries of Mamluk rule were associated with tombs for their founders, their wives and children, their descendants, and sometimes their household slaves.[37] Naturally this was true for non-Mamluk founders—the madrasa of the Bulqīnī family, for example, functioned in fact as a family mausoleum, with many members of the family, both male and female, interred there over the course of the fifteenth century. But Mamluks also laid great stress on burial in a religious or academic institution, and most of the schools of Mamluk Cairo served this secondary purpose, housing the tombs not only of the sultans or amirs who founded the institutions, but of their families as well. During the infighting that fol-

[36] The views of the Muslim Arab scholars, historians, and biographers have also shaped those of modern students of the Mamluks; see, for example, Anne-Marie Schimmel, "Some Glimpses of the Religious Life in Egypt during the Mamluk Period," *Islamic Studies* 4 (1965), 356ff. On the subject of Arab attitudes toward the Turks generally, and the Mamluks in particular, see Ulrich Haarmann, "Ideology and History, Identity and Alterity: The Arab Image of the Turk from the ʿAbbasids to Modern Egypt," *International Journal of Middle East Studies* 20 (1988), 175–96, and "Rather the Injustice of the Turks than the Righteousness of the Arabs—Changing ʿUlamāʾ Attitudes towards Mamluk Rule in the Late Fifteenth Century," *Studia Islamica* 88 (1988), 61–78.

[37] See Humphreys, "Expressive Intent," 113–17.

lowed the assassination of Sultan Lājīn in the late thirteenth century, one of the Mamluk conspirators, Sayf al-Dīn Ṭughjī, was killed and his body unceremoniously carted away from the Citadel in a dung bin; the unflattering conveyance notwithstanding, his corpse was taken directly to his madrasa for burial. After the completion of the Nāṣiriyya, Sultan al-Nāṣir Muḥammad transported the body of his mother to his new madrasa for reburial; Sultan Barqūq also reinterred his deceased children upon the construction of the Ẓāhiriyya.[38] When Zaynab bint Jirbāsh al-Karīmī died in 1460, she too was buried in Sultān Barqūq's madrasa in Bayn al-Qaṣrayn, because her mother, Fāṭima, was the daughter of Qānibāy, the son of Barqūq's sister.[39] Her connection to the sultan, who had died more than half a century earlier, was surely somewhat remote; that she shared his tomb testifies to the strength of the continuing bonds between the families of Mamluks and the institutions of learning their progenitors had founded.

Indeed, so great was the connection in the public mind between institutions of learning and places of burial that the terms madrasa and *turba* (tomb) could be conflated. Several institutions in late medieval Cairo were known as "turbas," but functioned as schools. Al-Shiblī Kāfūr (d. 1427) built a turba outside of Cairo, and made provisions for the recitation in it of a sermon (*khuṭba*) during the Friday prayers. But a contemporary historian noted that "he had another madrasa" (*wa lahu madrasa ukhrā*) in Khaṭṭ Ḥārat al-Daylam, as if the two terms were synonymous.[40] The point is simply to stress the connection, as these things were popularly understood, between the establishment of an institution of learning and the provision of a burial spot for oneself and one's family. The concern of the founder was to secure for himself, and for any buried with him, the *baraka*, or blessing, associated with the holy activities of the school—the study and teaching of law and other religious subjects, performance of the Sufi exercises, recitation of the Quran, prayer. Jawhar al-Lālā spelled out explicitly his concern that his tomb, attached to his madrasa, absorb through a sort of osmosis the blessings somehow connected with pious endeavors. He stipulated in his deed of endowment that, in addition to himself, one should be buried there "who is a man of good deeds and religion and knowledge, and who is famous for [his] righteous-

[38] Al-Maqrīzī, *al-Sulūk*, 1:951, 3:596.

[39] Al-Sakhāwī, *al-Ḍaw'*, 12:40–41.

[40] Ibn Taghrī Birdī, *al-Nujūm al-zāhira*, 15:143. Amir Jānibak al-Ẓāhirī (d. 1463) established outside Bāb al-Qarāfa a "turba" that "included a madrasa and *taṣawwuf* [i.e., provisions for Sufis] and a primary school for orphans." Al-Sakhāwī, *al-Ḍaw'*, 3:57–59. Amir Almās al-Ashrafī (d. ca. 1475) built a "turba" and established in it classes for Ḥanafīs, with provisions for seven students. Ibid., 2:321. On the confusion of institutional terms generally, see Chapter Three.

ness and [in whom the people] believe, so that his blessings may accrue to the founder."[41] Sultan Baybars, we are told, announced piously to the scholars assembled in the madrasa he had built in Bayn al-Qaṣrayn that "I established this place for God, and when I die, do not bury me here, and do not change the character of it." But he was buried in a madrasa nonetheless, albeit one in Damascus built posthumously and especially for that purpose.[42]

Consequently the deeds of endowment often provided prayer leaders, Quran readers, and other minor religious posts specifically for the tombs established in or alongside madrasas, "for formal Quran recitations for the sake of those buried in the tomb," as one late fifteenth-century deed put it.[43] People felt keenly the continuing presence of the entombed founder in the burial structure, as an amusing anecdote concerning the madrasa and tomb of Khawand Tatar al-Ḥijāziyya, a daughter of Sultan al-Nāṣir Muḥammad, suggests. Upon discovering that one of the Quran readers had entered the domed burial chamber (*qubba*) without long drawers (*sarāwīl*), the chief of the eunuchs who guarded and cared for the qubba beat the man and berated him because he "entered into [the presence] of Khawand Tatar without drawers"—that is, disrespectfully, without the proper garments, threatening the efficacy of his pious task.[44]

The presence of entombed founders and their relatives ensured that institutions of higher education would play a part in the broader Muslim phenomenon of the *ziyārāt*, the visitation of the dead in their tombs.[45] Sultan al-Ẓāhir Barqūq specifically set aside the burial chamber next to his madrasa for the benefit of "those who frequent it, Quran readers, [the sultan's] descendants . . . and his relatives," and employed eunuchs to serve and guard the tomb.[46] Not surprisingly, as Barqūq's deed suggests, a founder's descendants might frequent his tomb and the associated madrasa to visit their father, mother, or relatives, and to attend the ongoing religious or educational activities. Other schools provided private accommodations (*mabīt*) for overnight visitors to the tomb from among the founder's families or their descendants. We know from references in the chronicles that schools, or more precisely those buried in them, were routinely visited. Sultan Barqūq used to visit his deceased father Anas,

[41] *Waqfiyyat* Jawhar al-Lālā, Dār al-Wathā'iq No. 86, ll. 230–33.

[42] Al-Maqrīzī, *al-Sulūk*, 1:556, 646. On the Damascene madrasa, see Gary Leiser, "The Endowment of the al-Zahiriyya in Damascus," *Journal of the Economic and Social History of the Orient* 27 (1983), 33–55.

[43] *Waqfiyyat* Qānibāy Qarā, Wizārat al-Awqāf o.s. No. 1019, ll. 253–54.

[44] Al-Maqrīzī, *Khiṭaṭ*, 2:383.

[45] Christopher S. Taylor of Drew University is currently preparing a full-length study of the ziyārāt during the Mamluk period.

[46] *Waqfiyyat* al-Ẓāhir Barqūq, Dār al-Wathā'iq, No. 55.

whom he had buried in his madrasa in Bayn al-Qaṣrayn. His son and successor, Sultan Faraj, also visited the graves of Anas and his own mother in the Ẓāhiriyya; on one such occasion in 1407 he took the opportunity to provide the institution with an endowment to supplement its income.[47] In the rich ceremonial world in which the Mamluks lived, such visits provided both an opportunity for a public display of piety as well as the chance to highlight for personal political purposes a connection to a deceased, respected sultan, especially when the visitor was himself a reigning sultan whose grip on the government was weak. Sultan al-Ashraf Shaʿbān, for example, throughout his reign made a habit of visiting his celebrated grandfather al-Nāṣir Muḥammad's tomb and that of his great-grandfather al-Manṣūr Qalāwūn in the great Manṣūriyya complex on the main street of medieval Cairo.[48] Such institutions represented a confluence of learning, piety, and good government, and Mamluks such as al-Ashraf Shaʿbān eagerly capitalized on the "symbolic capital" that their fathers and predecessors had acquired through the patronage of learning.

Religious Learning among the Mamluks

A desire on the part of individual Mamluks to secure an efficacious burial setting thus fed into the nexus of personal concerns that informed their decisions to endow institutions of learning. By itself the fact that most founders were buried in their madrasas, mosques, or khānqāhs, even that they were buried specifically in order to be the beneficiaries of the baraka of the institutions' activities, does little to broaden our picture of Mamluk piety, except to stress that the Mamluks participated in a religious exercise that lay at the heart of the religious experience of most medieval Muslims. The broader question of piety among the Mamluks is in fact a far more complex issue, an issue whose bizarre and intriguing history has yet to be written.[49] Here we confine ourselves to remarks touching on the surprisingly pervasive interest in Islamic religious and legal learning among the Mamluk elite. The genuineness of any individual's religious experience is an almost impossible matter to judge. But a close look at those Mamluks who did endow institutions of religious education suggests that the image of a rapacious and nonreligious alien military elite, unconcerned with the spiritual and especially the educational affairs of Islam, bears revision.

In theory, at least, all Mamluks were exposed to at least the basics of Muslim religious practice and learning. The conversion to Islam of the

[47] Al-Maqrīzī, *al-Sulūk*, 3:769; Ibn Taghrī Birdī, *al-Nujūm al-zāhira*, 13:68.

[48] Al-Maqrīzī, *al-Sulūk*, 3:190.

[49] For some preliminary comments, see Donald Little, "Religion under the Mamluks," *The Muslim World* 73 (1983), 165–81, esp. 165–72.

young, foreign-born, newly imported slaves was the sine qua non of their training, and so, for example, the education of the royal Mamluks in Cairo's Citadel included a grounding in the fundamentals of Islam. Al-Maqrīzī, in a famous passage in his topographical history of Cairo, described their training. They were schooled in Arabic and Arabic writing, and above all in the Quran, by a local Muslim scholar (*faqīh*) who came to them every day. Their teacher sought to instill in them the "good manners of the holy law" (*ādāb al-sharī'a*), and so they instructed them in the basic rituals of religion, such as prayer, as well as, perhaps, a "bit of jurisprudence." The explicit purpose of the training was their acculturation to the religion and norms of local Muslim society, or as al-Maqrīzī put it, "the mingling of the glorification of Islam and its people in their hearts."[50]

It is becoming clear that the acculturation of the Mamluks into mainstream Muslim society was by no means unsuccessful. The ethical laxity of many Mamluks, and the consequent hostility toward them on the part of the religious scholars and historians of medieval Cairo, should not disguise the extent to which large numbers of adult Mamluks participated in the religious life of the Egyptian capital, and in particular it should not obscure their eagerness to involve themselves in the transmission of Muslim learning. The research of Ulrich Haarmann in the biographical literature of the thirteenth and fourteenth centuries has identified a number of individual Mamluks who exhibited genuine and pious interest in religious and legal learning, and who to that end forged deep personal connections to the ulama of the cities of Egypt and Syria. Over the last century and a half of Mamluk rule, as the Ḥanafī rite to which most Mamluks belonged came to occupy a more prominent place in Cairo's religious and educational institutions, and as more and more Turkish-speaking Ḥanafī scholars from Anatolia, Iran, and more remote Asian provinces flocked to Cairo, the intellectual and personal ties that bound the Mamluks to the world of Islamic learning grew only more intense.[51]

It is against this background that the decision of individual Mamluks to endow institutions of learning must be seen. The chroniclers and biographers report, almost as a matter of course, that many of those amirs who established schools were "religious" (*dayyinan*) and "charitable"

[50] Al-Maqrīzī, *Khiṭaṭ*, 2:213–14.

[51] The pioneering work on this subject is that of Ulrich Haarmann, especially his study of fourteenth-century Mamluks, "Arabic in Speech, Turkish in Lineage: Mamluks and Their Sons in the Intellectual Life of Fourteenth-Century Egypt and Syria," *Journal of Semitic Studies* 33 (1988), 81–114. On the increasing prominence of the Ḥanafī rite in Cairene educational institutions, see Leonor Fernandes, "Mamluk Politics and Education: The Evidence from Two Fourteenth Century Waqfiyya[s]," *Annales islamologiques* 23 (1987), 87–98.

(*khayyiran*). One such was a certain ʿAlāʾ al-Dīn Ṭaybars, who built his madrasa outside the door to the al-Azhar mosque, although the historian does remark that his character was "in contrast to Āqbughā ʿAbd al-Wāhid," a notoriously oppressive and covetous Mamluk with little appreciation for Muslim ethical principles, "who also built his madrasa at the door to al-Azhar."[52] But not a few Mamluks who endowed schools also participated actively in various forms of religious or legal instruction. They include, of course, sultans such as al-Nāṣir Ḥasan, Qaytbāy, and Qanṣūh al-Ghawrī, whose interest in intellectual matters is well known, but also some of the more obscure Mamluk amirs who founded the numerous smaller schools of the city.

ʿAlam al-Dīn Sanjar al-Jāwulī, the Mamluk who, as we have seen, founded a madrasa outside Cairo in 1323, presents a striking example. Al-Maqrīzī called him *al-faqīh al-Shāfiʿī* ("the Shāfiʿī scholar or jurist") who, during the eight years he spent in prison, "copied the Quran and books of ḥadīth and the like." Al-Maqrīzī's high opinion of Sanjar was shared by other chroniclers, such as the Syrian Ibn Ḥabīb, who noted that he "heard ḥadīth and transmitted it, and read jurisprudence according to the Shāfiʿī rite, and issued legal opinions [*fatwās*] and composed books, and met with scholars and was charitable toward them." Among the works he transmitted was the *Musnad* of al-Shāfiʿī, a collection of ḥadīth excerpted from that famous jurist's treatise *al-Mabsūṭ*; he went so far as to compose an arrangement of these traditions in topical order, and wrote a commentary on them in several volumes.[53] For Sanjar our information is more detailed, but he was certainly not unique. Sayf al-Dīn Āl Malik, originally a Mamluk of Sultan Qalāwūn's who rose to become viceroy in Egypt, established both a mosque and a madrasa with a lesson in Shāfiʿī law in the Ḥusayniyya district to the north of the walled city of Cairo. He was known, we are told, for sitting in his mosque all day long without becoming tired or bored. Ibn Taghrī Birdī also reports that he frequently sat with students during their lessons. One scholar even prepared for him a *mashyakha*, a list of those shaykhs on whose authority he was entitled to transmit ḥadīth.[54]

[52] Ibn Taghrī Birdī, *al-Nujūm al-zāhira*, 9:246; cf. idem., *al-Manhal al-ṣafī*, 2:480–82.

[53] Ḥajjī Khalīfa (= Kātib Çelebi), *Kashf al-ẓunūn ʿan asāmī ʾl-kutub waʾl-funūn* (Istanbul, 1941–43), 2:1683; Sanjar's commentary is in fact the first of several that Ḥajjī Khalīfa mentions. A manuscript copy of Sanjar's work apparently still exists; see Joseph Schacht, *Aus Kairiner Bibliotheken*, part 2, in *Abhandlungen der Preussischen Akademie der Wissenschaften*, 1929 (Berlin, 1930), 15. On Sanjar, see al-Maqrīzī, *al-Sulūk*, 2:299, 674, and *Khiṭaṭ*, 2:398; Ibn Ḥabīb, *Tadhkirat al-nabīh*, 3:75–76; Ṣalāḥ al-Dīn Khalīl Ibn Aybak al-Ṣafadī, *al-Wāfī biʾl-wafayāt* (Wiesbaden, 1979), 15:482–84; ʿAbd al-Ḥayy Ibn al-ʿImād, *Shadharāt al-dhahab fī akhbār man dhahab* (Cairo, A.H. 1350; rptd. Beirut, 1979), 6:142–43.

[54] Ibn Taghrī Birdī, *al-Manhal al-ṣāfī, 3:85–88.*

Taghrī Birdī 'l-Bakalmishī (d. 1442), a powerful amir who held several of the most important offices of state in the Mamluk kingdom, built an institution near the mosque of Ibn Ṭūlūn that is variously called a madrasa and a jāmiʿ, but whose endowments certainly supported at least one professor in one of the religious sciences. As *ḥājib al-ḥujjāb*, in which office he held responsibility for the administration of (non-sharīʿa) justice among the Mamluks, he undertook his duties seriously, and "never heard a petition sent [to him] without struggling to do justice, as he saw it." As a member of the ruling military elite, of course, he took an interest in things such as *furūsiyya*, the skills and practical knowledge of horsemanship and the military games that lay at the core of a Mamluk's training and active life. Yet he also "wrote in a hand appropriate to his station and studied jurisprudence and asked questions of the legal scholars and studied various histories." Nor was his interest in legal matters superficial, as he "memorized questions about which the jurists disputed."[55]

A simple suggestion may clarify the situation: namely, that we avoid the assumption that the kind of violent and (from a strict Islamic perspective) unethical behavior in which the Mamluks often indulged precluded a serious interest in religious and educational matters. Ṭūghān al-Ḥasanī al-Ẓāhirī (d. 1415), who built a madrasa near the home of the scholarly Bulqīnī family in the Bahāʾ al-Dīn quarter of Cairo, in his younger days was a drunkard and a reveler, but later changed his ways, and sat and studied with the ulama.[56] Amir Sayf al-Dīn Ṣarghitmish (d. 1358) not only established an important madrasa for Ḥanafīs to the north of the mosque of Ibn Ṭūlūn, but by all accounts studied jurisprudence and other subjects, enjoyed the company of the ulama and frequently sat with them in their study circles, and became an avid partisan of the Ḥanafī rite. Yet "his morals were vicious and his spirit strong, and although he studied jurisprudence and [the Arabic] language, his behavior went beyond the proper bounds."[57]

An intellectual preoccupation with religious sciences thus informed the decision of some Mamluks to build and endow a school or other institu-

[55] Al-Sakhāwī, *al-Ḍaw'*, 3:27–28; Ibn Taghrī Birdī, *al-Nujūm al-zāhira*, 15:496–97, and idem, *al-Manhal al-ṣāfī*, 4:54–56. On the office of the ḥājib al-ḥujjāb, see Ayalon, "Structure—III," 60. There is an extensive literature on furūsiyya and the systematic military training undergone by Mamluks; in particular see the work of David Ayalon, especially his "Notes on the *Furūsiyya* Exercises and Games in the Mamluk Sultanate," *Scripta Hierosolymitana* 9 (1961), 31–62.

[56] Al-Sakhāwī, *al-Ḍaw'*, 4:11.

[57] The words are al-Maqrīzī's, *Khiṭaṭ*, 2:404–5; cf. Ibn Taghrī Birdī, *al-Nujūm al-zāhira*, 10:328, and Aḥmad Ibn Ḥajar al-ʿAsqalānī, *al-Durar al-kāmina fī aʿyān al-miʾa al-thāmina* (Cairo, 1966–67), 2:305–6. Leonor Fernandes discusses Ṣarghitmish, his madrasa, and his almost fanatical partisanship of the Ḥanafī rite in her article, "Mamluk Politics and Education."

tion, but the broader point to be stressed is that a religious education, or at least some familiarity with the texts and traditions of Muslim learning, was not unusual among the Mamluks. To be sure, it is in fact difficult to determine precisely the extent of learning among the Mamluks. Even with a systematic study of the entries for amirs in the biographical dictionaries, we could not be certain that all the information was at our disposal, since the sources do not claim to give the *comprehensive* life stories of their subjects. But the biographical dictionaries in fact abound with tantalizing hints relating to the education of the military class. The historians record nothing unusual in the fact that an amir had "memorized the Quran, and heard [the recitation of] ḥadīth," or that another "participated in [the study of] jurisprudence and history," or that one wrote in a good hand in addition to having studied jurisprudence and the variant Quran readings.[58] Other Mamluks besides Bakalmish al-ʿAlāʾī (d. 1398) were partisans of the Ḥanafī rite, and others besides Arghūn al-Nāṣirī (d. 1331) collected books in the various sciences and wrote out their own copies of the *Ṣaḥīḥ* of al-Bukhārī.[59] Not infrequently do the historians—most of whom, such as al-Sakhāwī, were themselves scholars or from scholarly families—give as a Mamluk's epithet the title "al-faqīh."[60]

All this, however, is more suggestive than definitive, and more nuanced questions must be put to the sources. If many Mamluks, and in particular many Mamluk founders of schools and other religious institutions, were in some sense "learned," what significance can we in fact attach to their education in the Islamic sciences? What was the extent of their learning, and what limitations differentiated it from the education of a fully trained scholar? Above all, did they participate actively in the transmission of the Muslim religious and legal sciences?

The term faqīh (pl. *fuqahāʾ*) means "religious scholar or student" or, more properly, "scholar of the religious law." It is difficult, however, to be certain as to what exactly the biographers intended when they applied the title to particular Mamluks. The sources only rarely provide details of an amir's education, beyond saying that "he studied [religious] knowledge" (*lahu ishtighāl biʾl-ʿilm*), or "he studied jurisprudence" (*tafaqqaha, lahu mushārika fiʾl-fiqh*), or "he read a number of legal treatises" (*wa kāna . . . yaqraʾu fī baʿḍ al-rasāʾil al-fiqhiyya*), although that

[58] Ibn Ḥabīb, *Tadhkirat al-nabīh*, 1:229; al-Sakhāwī, *al-Ḍawʾ*, 2:311; Ibn Taghrī Birdī, *al-Nujūm al-zāhira*, 15:151–52.

[59] Al-Sakhāwī, *al-Ḍawʾ*, 3:17–18; Ibn Ḥabīb, *Tadhkirat al-nabīh*, 2:211–12, Ibn Ḥajar al-ʿAsqalānī, *al-Durar*, 1:374, and Ibn Taghrī Birdī, *al-Manhal al-ṣāfī*, 2:306–8. Cf. Haarmann, "Arabic in Speech," 93–94.

[60] Examples can be found in al-Sakhāwī, *al-Ḍawʾ*, 3:45, 53–54, 276; Ibn Iyās, *Badāʾiʿ al-zuhūr*, 3:148, 202.

is true of many civilians as well.[61] Consequently there is no guarantee that use of the term reflected a significant intellectual achievement. Over the course of the Mamluk period, other valuable appellations, such as "qāḍi" and "amir," also came to be applied more generously than some purists might allow, and the same may well apply to the term "faqīh." But when a Mamluk was accorded and accepted the epithet "al-faqīh," he was in effect appropriating to himself a title of enormous cultural significance that commanded a premium of social respect. Whether or not he deserved the title is almost secondary to his desire to secure it and the willingness of the Muslim community to recognize his appropriation of it.

To be sure, serious limitations prevented many Mamluks from becoming, even if they had desired it, full-fledged scholars. In their encounter with the sophisticated Islamic sciences beyond their rudimentary training in the barracks, many did not penetrate beyond the preliminary layers of learning.[62] Sayf al-Dīn Aqṭūh (d. 1448) studied jurisprudence, but only understood its superficial questions (*ẓawāhir masā'il*). Sayf al-Dīn Sūdūn al-Ẓāhirī (d. 1440) was "an all-round faqīh" (*kāna . . . faqīhan fi'l-jumla*); but although he studied jurisprudence assiduously, he "wasted his time in doing so," according to Ibn Taghrī Birdī, "because of his limited understanding and lack of imagination." Ibn Ḥajar commented of his Mamluk son-in-law, Shāhīn al-ʿAlā'ī (d. 1456), that although he had copied in his own hand *al-Shifā*, a popular treatise on the life and attributes of the Prophet, and Mālik ibn Anas' early law book, the *Muwaṭṭa'*, "it was worth less than the paper, and he did not benefit from it."[63]

Indeed, even comparatively educated Mamluks may not always have fully understood that which they studied—after all, for most of these Turkish-speaking soldiers, Arabic was a second language. Amir Khayr Bak (d. 1482), who established a madrasa in the Zuqaq Ḥalab, wrote well, and "studied the variant Quran readings and jurisprudence and the principles of religion, and in general understood [them];" however, his biographer gently noted, "if he probed more deeply and brought up particular examples, it would have been better for him to avoid them."[64] Uzbak min Ṭuṭukh al-Ẓāhiri, who established a teaching mosque, studied with

[61] Examples can be found in al-Sakhāwī, *al-Ḍaw'*, 2:311, 329, 10:277.

[62] One can even find the verb *ta'addaba*, which usually connoted a primary education, employed to describe the intellectual relationship between a Mamluk and a scholar; see, for example, al-Sakhāwī, *al-Ḍaw'*, 3:10.

[63] Ibn Taghrī Birdī, *al-Nujūm al-zāhira*, 15:525–26; al-Sakhāwī, *al-Ḍaw'*, 3:283, and Ibn Taghrī Birdī, *al-Nujūm al-zāhira*, 15:478–79; al-Sakhāwī, *al-Ḍaw'*, 3:296. The full title of the treatise is *al-Shifā bi-taʿrīf ḥuqūq al-muṣṭafā*, by Abū 'l-Faḍl ʿIyād b. Mūsā al-Yaḥsubī (d. 1149); see Ḥajjī Khalīfa, *Kashf al-ẓunūn*, 2:1052–55.

[64] Al-Sakhāwī, *al-Ḍaw'*, 3:207–8.

several ḥadīth scholars while he was still a young Mamluk in the barracks in the Citadel; yet the man who actually recited the ḥadīth on that occasion, Taqī 'l-Dīn al-Qalqashandī, commented that Uzbak "did not understand a word of Arabic."[65] On the other hand, despite the cultural importance of Arabic, the simple fact that a Mamluk could not communicate effectively in the local language by itself does not indicate an alienation from the various forms of Muslim piety, or even from Islamic religious knowledge and its transmission. In the fertile cultural ground of the Mamluk court, a vibrant Turkish literary tradition also took root, through which the Mamluks were exposed to various religious writings, such as lives of the Prophet, Sufi poetry, and basic legal treatises, as well as to profane literature from Persia and elsewhere.[66]

A little knowledge, when improperly tended, can be dangerous; the rule applies to the Mamluks as well as others, and the tentative immersion of the military elite in the world of higher Islamic learning could engender complications. Amir Azdumur al-Ṭawīl, originally a Mamluk of Sultan al-Ẓāhir Jaqmaq who rose to hold several high offices of state, was eventually banished to Mecca and, in 1480, was strangled by order of Sultan Qayt Bāy. Azdumur studied the Quran intensively and successfully, so much so that he recited it in an organized group. And although he, like Khayr Bak, understood things "in general," his stubbornness led him to "meddle in [matters] that did not concern him, and to [have] evil beliefs [*sū' ʿaqīda*] and [to] make light of matters of religion and mistreat many legal scholars and [to] scorn them."[67]

It is important, however, that we not simply compare the participation of the Mamluks in higher Muslim learning and education to the systematic instruction that produced a fully trained civilian scholar, and then judge the former to be inferior. Their purposes, for a start, were clearly different. Whereas an ʿālim was intensively trained for an academic or judicial career from an early age, a Mamluk's religious or legal education necessarily took a back seat to training in the military arts, which alone could assure him of a successful career. On the whole, a strict consciousness of identities characterized both academic and military elites. Occasionally, an exceptionally well-educated Mamluk might be certified to *hold* an official teaching position, as was Arghūn al-Nāṣirī (d. 1331), dawādār to Sultan al-Nāṣir Muḥammad, who constructed a madrasa in

[65] Al-Sakhāwī, *al-Ḍaw'*, 2:270. We know that Taqī 'l-Dīn al-Qalqashandī, who cast aspersions on Uzbak's comprehension of Arabic, was the official reader (*qāri'*) at these sesssions from the account in Ibn Taghrī Birdī, *al-Manhal al-ṣāfī*, 4:72–73.

[66] Haarmann, "Arabic in Speech," 90–93; see also Barbara Flemming, "Literary Activities in Mamluk Halls and Barracks," in *Studies in Memory of Gaston Wiet*, ed. Myriam Rosen-Ayalon (Jerusalem, 1977), 249–60.

[67] Al-Sakhāwī, *al-Ḍaw'*, 2:273–74.

Mecca and "received permission to issue fatwās and teach [Ḥanafī jurisprudence]."[68] But in general, Mamluks did not teach in or hold endowed chairs in the religious schools of Cairo any more than scholars accepted military commissions.

Many Mamluks may have conceived of the recitation of the Quran and other religious works more as entertainment than as education. The biographical dictionaries reveal that many of these warriors delighted especially in the reading of histories and literature, and Sultan Barsbāy's close relationship with the scholar and judge Badr al-Dīn al-ʿAynī, who translated for him books of history, is well known.[69] Al-Subkī complained bitterly of Quran readers and those who recited poems in praise of the Prophet (*munshid*, pl. *munshidūn*) that they often frequented amirs who clearly derived no spiritual nourishment from the recitations, but rather considered the readings a sort of "background noise" or entertainment:

> Once I saw a munshid at the encampment [*mukhayyam*] of one of the amirs, where many people had gathered. He was reading a poem and reciting the attributes of the Prophet, may God bless and preserve him, but the people were not listening to him; indeed, there was no one there who understood what he was saying. Because of this I experienced a heart-rending pain.[70]

Other Mamluks may have touched the world of education more intimately through some personal circumstance. Mamluks, of course, frequently married the daughters of the educated elite, and through such marriage alliances the soldiers may have been introduced at least to the basics of Islamic learning. Zaynab, the daughter of the prominent fifteenth-century Ḥanafī jurist al-Amīn al-Aqṣarāʾī, married in succession a Mamluk of Sultan al-Ashraf Barsbāy and one of Sultan al-Ẓāhir Jaqmaq. Both took at least elementary steps into the world of education, and both owed their accomplishments to their marriage into a family of learning. The first husband, Jānibak al-Ẓāhirī, wrote in a good hand and copied a number of works such as *al-Shifā*, which he studied with his father-in-law.[71] Jaqmaq al-Ashrafī, who married Zaynab after Jānibak's death, also "was instructed" (*tahadhdhaba*) by his wife's father, and managed successfully to memorize the entire Quran.[72] Al-Aqṣarāʾī was also related by

[68] Ibn Taghrī Birdī, *al-Manhal al-ṣāfī*, 2:306.

[69] Ibn Taghrī Birdī, *al-Nujūm al-zāhira*, 15:110; cf. Petry, *Civilian Elite*, 70.

[70] Tāj al-Dīn ʿAbd al-Wahhāb al-Subkī, *Muʿīd al-niʿam wa-mubīd al-niqam*, ed. David Myhrman (London, 1908), 158.

[71] Al-Sakhāwī, *al-Ḍawʾ*, 3:54. The important phrase reads *qaraʾahu ʿalā* [lit., he read it with] *sihrihi*. The Arabic word *sihr* implies any kinsman of a man's wife; it is therefore of course possible that Jānibak received his education from a brother of Zaynab's, although her father seems the most likely candidate. Cf. E. W. Lane, *An Arabic-English Lexicon* (London, 1863–93), s.v. "*sihr*."

[72] Al-Sakhāwī, *al-Ḍawʾ*, 3:75.

marriage to another prominent Mamluk, Yashbak al-Ẓāhirī al-Ṣaghīr (d. 1480 or 81), who according to al-Sakhāwī also took an interest in the Islamic sciences, collecting books and building three separate madrasas in Cairo.[73] Al-Aqṣarā'ī's efforts to educate his Mamluk relations proved more successful than those of Ibn Ḥajar, but the fact that they all attempted to relate on an academic plane is itself significant.

Yet within the constraints under which they operated, the accomplishments of many Mamluks in the world of Islamic education were by no means trivial. That many would take the time and trouble even to attempt to study Muslim jurisprudence is itself remarkable. And if the efforts of some produced only meager results, others reached a position in which they could actively apply their legal training. Sanjar al-Jāwulī, who established a madrasa in the early fourteenth century, was not the only Mamluk who was accorded the title *muftī*, and who was thereby qualified to issue fatwās on the basis of Islamic law. Others, such as Arghūn al-Nāṣirī, a Mamluk of Sultan Qalāwūn who eventually became viceroy in Egypt and dawādār, also "studied Ḥanafī jurisprudence and excelled in it until he was accounted one who issued fatwās."[74]

Such learning, it seems, was not wholly incompatible with the political and military responsibilities facing a prominent Mamluk. Yashbak al-Faqīh (d. 1473), for example, was an extraordinarily accomplished student of jurisprudence, the variant Quran readings, and ḥadīth. He received private lessons from several scholars, including al-Badr ibn ʿUbayd Allāh, who visited him several days a week, and with whom he studied *al-Hidāya*, a fundamental textbook of Ḥanafī jurisprudence.[75] He also studied with al-Sakhāwī, reading to the scholar and historian parts of the *Ṣaḥīḥ* of al-Bukhārī, and hearing al-Sakhāwī recite several of his own works, including *al-Qawl al-badīʿ fī'l-ṣalāt ʿalā 'l-ḥabīb*, a long treatise on prayers for the Prophet. Al-Sakhāwī was apparently pleased with the progress and understanding of this Mamluk who proclaimed to him: "I will continue to read with you until I encounter God and [become] a student of the religious sciences." Yet Yashbak was no misfit Mamluk. He participated in campaigns against the "Franks," became involved in the political intrigues that plagued the Mamluk government during the fifteenth century, and served as dawādār to Sultan al-Ẓāhir Khushqadam.[76]

Taghrī Birmish al-Nāṣirī (d. 1448), who served Sultan Jaqmaq as deputy of the Citadel, was also known as "the Ḥanafī faqīh." It was said that he was in fact born a Muslim, and that his father (illegally) sold him into

[73] Ibid., 10:272–74.

[74] Ibn Ḥajar al-ʿAsqalānī, *al-Durar*, 1:374.

[75] By Burhān al-Dīn ʿAlī b. Abī Bakr al-Marghīnānī (d. 1197); on this work, see Ḥajjī Khalīfa, *Kashf al-ẓunūn*, 2:2031–40.

[76] Al-Sakhāwī, *al-Ḍaw'*, 10:270–72.

slavery at the age of seven; whatever his origins, he outshone most other Mamluks in the extent of his learning. Both Ibn Taghrī Birdī and al-Sakhāwī listed the names of many of those with whom he studied jurisprudence and especially ḥadīth. Among them were several of the leading scholars of his day, including Ibn Ḥajar al-ʿAsqalānī, Sirāj al-Dīn ʿUmar (known as Qāri' al-Hidāya, who held professorships in Ḥanafī law at prestigious schools such as the Ashrafiyya, the Nāṣiriyya, and the Aqbughāwiyya), and Saʿd al-Dīn al-Dīrī, who taught Ḥanafī jurisprudence at the Fakhriyya madrasa, the mosque of al-Mu'ayyad Shaykh, and other institutions. Taghrī Birmish's active commitment to academic pursuits, in the midst of an otherwise unexceptional military and political career, stands as a sort of benchmark for what an eager Mamluk could achieve. His intellectual association with prominent transmitters of the Muslim sciences suggests the degree to which the academic elite, although it complained about the Mamluks as a group, accepted as routine the participation of individual soldiers in the pursuit of religious knowledge.[77]

Mamluks and the Transmission of Ḥadīth

Above all, Mamluks listened eagerly to the recitation of ḥadīth, and some participated actively in its transmission. The biographical literature frequently mentions amirs who participated in public recitations of the important books of traditions, such as the *Ṣaḥīḥs* of al-Bukhārī and Muslim ibn al-Ḥajjāj, or the *Maṣābīḥ*, a popular collection containing ḥadīth excerpted from the larger and more comprehensive volumes. It was not unusual for Mamluks to hear recitations supervised by prominent transmitters such as Ibn Ḥajar, or to attend sessions in a prominent educational institution such as the Shaykhūniyya khānqāh. Taghrī Birmish al-Faqīh studied all of the major collections of ḥadīth with some of the leading scholars of his day. Ibn Ḥajar, in whose presence Taghrī Birmish read the *Sunan* of Abū Dā'ūd, referred to his Mamluk student as "our companion, the outstanding *muḥaddith*," using a technical term that indicated a transmitter of traditions of wide knowledge and prominent standing.[78]

The widespread interest of the Mamluks in the Prophetic traditions has great significance for the social and cultural history of medieval Cairo, and in particular has a direct bearing on the integration of the military elite into the cultural life of their Muslim subjects, despite the widely

[77] On Taghrī Birmish al-Faqīh, see Jonathan Berkey, " 'Silver Threads among the Coal': A Well-Educated Mamluk of the Ninth/Fifteenth Century," *Studia Islamica* 73 (1991).

[78] Al-Sakhāwī, *al-Ḍaw'*, 3:33–34; cf. Ibn Taghrī Birdī, *al-Manhal al-ṣāfī*, 4:68–74. See also al-Sakhāwī, *al-Ḍaw'*, 2:267, 3:177, 287. The *Maṣabīḥ* was compiled by Ḥusayn b. Masʿūd al-Farrā' al-Baghawī (d. 1122).

held prejudice that Mamluks were by nature and training unsuited to academic pursuits. Sometimes the transmission of ḥadīth forged tangible links between Mamluks and scholars, or brought them together in specialized, institutionalized settings. As we shall see, most of the schools established by Mamluks and others made provisions for the public recitation of particular collections of ḥadīth during Ramaḍān and the two months that preceded it; but some members of the military elite organized such sessions in their own homes. Thus during Rajab, Shaʿbān, and Ramaḍān, Bardbak al-Ashrafī, a Mamluk of Sultan Īnāl who amassed extraordinary wealth, would hold in his home sittings for the recitation of the *Ṣaḥīḥ* of al-Bukhārī "to which legal scholars, judges, and the like would hurry."[79] One historian even reports that at the end of the fourteenth century the Mamluk amirs "paid great attention to the ulama, and each amir had his own scholar of ḥadīth [*ʿālim bi'l-ḥadīth*] who would recite to the Mamluks [*al-nās*] and summon them to listen."[80] These "private scholars" or tutors were not necessarily men of minimal standing in the academic community, who gratefully accepted the direct patronage of amirs after failing to secure reputable positions in educational institutions. They might in fact be prominent ḥadīth transmitters: Zayn al-Dīn ʿAbd al-Raḥīm al-ʿIrāqī (d. 1404), who held positions as professor of ḥadīth in the mosque of Ibn Ṭūlūn, the *dār al-ḥadīth* al-Kāmiliyya, and the Qarāsunquriyya and Ẓāhiriyya madrasas, at different times had two leading Mamluks as "his amir."[81]

The recitation of ḥadīth was a common phenomenon even at the very heart of the Mamluk state. In the Citadel that towered above the city of Cairo, traditionists were routinely appointed to the position of "reader of ḥadīth" (*qāri' al-ḥadīth*). We do not know what stipend the appointment carried, but it was held by some of the leading scholars of Mamluk Cairo, including Shihāb al-Dīn Aḥmad Ibn Asad (d. 1468), a specialist in the Quran readings who also held teaching positions in the mosque of al-Mu'ayyad Shaykh and the Sābiqiyya and Ẓāhiriyya madrasas.[82] Ibn Asad's appointment to the position was made through the intervention of his pupil Yashbak al-Faqīh, an exceptionally well educated Mamluk.

At least some Mamluks also participated actively in the transmission of this particular field of Islamic learning. One mark of the exceptional quality of the learning of ʿAlam al-Dīn Sanjar, whom we encountered as the founder of the Jāwuliyya madrasa, is that, in addition to writing books or treatises and issuing fatwās, he transmitted ḥadīth to other students of

[79] Al-Sakhāwī, *al-Ḍaw'*, 3:4–5.

[80] Al-Sakhāwī, *al-Ḍaw'*, 4:177; al-Sakhāwī is apparently quoting the earlier historian Ibn Qāḍī Shuhba.

[81] Al-Sakhāwī, *al-Ḍaw'*, 4:177.

[82] Al-Sakhāwī, *al-Ḍaw'*, 1:229–30.

the subject.[83] Amir Āl Malik, who built a teaching mosque in the Ḥusayniyya district outside of Cairo, also recited the Prophetic traditions.[84] Mamluks were occasionally mentioned by prominent ḥadīth scholars in their *mashyakhas*, the book-length lists or biographical dictionaries of those on whose authority an individual transmitted the Prophetic traditions. Thus Aqṭuwān al-ʿIzzī, an otherwise obscure Mamluk of whose education we know almost nothing, was mentioned in the mashyakha of Abū Jaʿfar Ibn al-Kuwayk, a scholar who held the professorship in ḥadīth at the tomb attached to the madrasa of al-Ẓāhir Baybars in Cairo.[85] Ibn Ḥajar al-ʿAsqalānī himself, in his own account of those with whom he studied and on whose authority he recited ḥadīth, mentioned at least two Mamluks. One of them was Yalbughā al-Ẓāhirī (d. 1409), who heard ḥadīth in Ibn Ḥajar's company for a time. The other was Sultan al-Mu'ayyad Shaykh who, according to Ibn Ḥajar, "transmitted the *Ṣaḥīḥ* of al-Bukhārī on the authority of *shaykh al-islām* Sirāj al-Dīn [ʿUmar] al-Bulqīnī, with [his] *ijāza* [license to transmit]."[86] Admittedly, both received mention only in *al-ṭabaqa al-ṣughrā* of Ibn Ḥajar's list, that is, the "minor class" that included a wide variety of people, mostly nonspecialists or transmitters of only minimal repute. But the point is not that the Mamluks ever became a mainstay of preservation of and instruction in the Prophetic traditions. It is simply that they found it worthwhile to participate in the transmission of this culturally valuable body of knowledge, and that the ulama provided them with space in which to pursue their interest.

That they were able to do so was in part a function of the principles and values that governed the transmission of Muslim texts, and in particular the persistent priority given to personal oral contacts over institutional affiliations. From a comparatively early period, it was accepted that one could only transmit ḥadīth on the basis of a sound *isnād*, a chain of the names of those individuals who had personally "received" the ḥadīth from an earlier transmitter, ultimately linking the student through an unbroken succession to the Prophet himself or to one of his companions. This same principle was applied to virtually all texts and to the transmission of the later collections of ḥadīth. Consequently, it was imperative

[83] Thus, *samiʿa al-ḥadīth wa-rawāhu . . . wa-aftā wa-ṣannafa*. Ibn Ḥabīb, *Tadhkirat al-nabīh*, 3:75–76.

[84] Ibn Ḥabīb, *Tadhkirat al-nabīh*, 3:82–83.

[85] Ibn Ḥajar al-ʿAsqalānī, *al-Durar*, 1:422. The Abū Jaʿfar Ibn al-Kuwayk in whose mashyakha Aqṭuwān was mentioned was ʿIzz al-Dīn Abū Jaʿfar Muḥammad b. ʿAbd al-Laṭīf b. Aḥmad b. Maḥmūd Ibn al-Kuwayk, who died in Ramaḍān, 769 (May 1368); see ibid., 4:143.

[86] Ibn Ḥajar al-ʿAsqalānī, *al-Majmaʿ al-mu'assas bi'l-muʿjam al-mufahras*, Dār al-Kutub al-Miṣriyya, "Muṣṭalaḥ" No. 75, pp. 460–61, and idem, *Inbā' al-ghumr*, 6:133–35; Ibn Ḥajar, *al-Majmaʿ al-mu'assas*, 394–96.

that one who wished to transmit ḥadīth receive a personal authorization to do so from one who was himself (or herself) a recognized transmitter. The authorization could take one of several forms. In the most reliable and authoritative form of transmission, a student heard the transmitter himself recite a particular collection of ḥadīth (*samāʿ*, literally "hearing"). Marginally less reliable was the case in which the student read, or heard another read, ḥadīth to the transmitter (*qirā'a*, literally "reading"). But the personal connection between student and transmitter could be established even without an actual encounter; the student simply requested, perhaps in writing, a shaykh to issue to him an authorization (*ijāza*) to transmit a particular collection. The simple ijāza, however, was considerably less reliable or prestigious than one issued to a student who could claim to have personally heard the shaykh recite the ḥadīth, or at least to have himself recited them in the shaykh's presence.[87]

It was also important, however, to reduce to as low a number as possible the names in the isnād, on the theory that with fewer links in the chain, errors in transmission were less likely to occur. Consequently, transmitters of ḥadīth generally became more prominent as they aged. Mamluks, therefore, like anyone else, might distinguish themselves by transmitting ḥadīth on the authority of respected shaykhs who had died some time previously. The biographers note, for example, that several amirs heard the recitation of ḥadīth from "al-Ghumārī" in A.H. 802 (1399–1400), and that thereafter the amirs transmitted the ḥadīth they had heard. Most likely the shaykh in question was Muḥammad b. Muḥammad b. ʿAlī al-Ghumārī, a famous muḥaddith and grammarian who died in that same year. The amirs, in other words, became valued transmitters on the authority of al-Ghumārī because they were among the last to hear ḥadīth directly from the shaykh; they were even cited among those from whom the famous muḥaddith al-Baqāʿī transmitted traditions.[88] Similarly, Alṭunbughā al-Turkī (d. 1412–13) survived to become the last man to transmit ḥadīth on the authority of Abū 'l-ʿAbbās Aḥmad al-Ḥajjār (a woman who also transmitted on the authority of al-Ḥajjār outlived Alṭunbughā by a year, as we shall see). That he had studied with the master

[87] On ijāzas and the other forms of transmission of ḥadīth, see Chapter Two. Cf. *Encyclopedia of Islam*, 2nd edition, s.v. "*Ḥadīth*" (by J. Robson).

[88] See al-Sakhāwī's biographies of the amirs al-Sayfī Bakalmish and al-Sayfī Balāṭ, *al-Ḍaw'*, 3:17, 18, respectively. The identification of al-Ghumārī as the Muḥammad b. Muḥammad b. ʿAlī who bore that name is based on (a) the fact that he died in the year the two amirs are said to have heard his recitation of ḥadīth—and hence the detail's significance to the historian; and (b) the fact that Bakalmish is said to have transmitted "as a companion" of al-Sakhāwī's shaykh al-Zayn Riḍwān, who was also a student of al-Ghumārī's. For al-Ghumārī's biography, see ibid., 9:149–50. The al-Baqāʿī who listed both amirs among his shaykhs was probably Burhān al-Dīn Ibrāhīm b. ʿUmar b. Ḥasan al-Baqāʿī (d. 1480), whose obituary notice is given in Ibn Iyās, *Badā'iʿ al-zuhūr*, 3:169.

muḥaddith, however, did not become known until shortly before his death, at which point many sought from him an ijāza.[89] Al-Sayfī Taghrī Birdī al-Ẓāhirī (d. 1472) was not unusual for having studied ḥadīth, but he did distinguish himself as the last "of the sons of his race" (i.e., as the last Mamluk) to have studied with Ibn Ḥajar al-ʿAsqalānī.[90]

Here again, the persistent informality of Islamic education proved vitally significant, not simply to the academic world, but to its link to the broader society, of which, of course, the Mamluks formed a vital part. To be sure, we must not emphasize too strongly the role played by Mamluks in the transmission of ḥadīth. The Prophetic traditions that occupy such a noble place in the world of Islamic learning would have been passed on successfully to succeeding generations of Muslims without the direct participation of the military elite in their transmission. But the Mamluks' interest in ḥadīth was nonetheless important. Consider, for example, the case of Uzbak min Ṭuṭukh al-Ẓāhirī, whom we have already encountered as the founder of a teaching mosque. Brought to Egypt as a young boy in 1437–38, he was originally a Mamluk of Sultan Barsbāy. When Jaqmaq came to the throne the following year, he purchased the young Uzbak and eventually freed him, appointing him later to several important military positions and marrying him to one of his daughters. We know that at some point before 1448 he studied with Ibn Ḥajar. More importantly, in 1441–42, while still a young Mamluk in the barracks, he attended sessions for the recitation of ḥadīth in the Citadel arranged by the fortress's deputy at the time, Taghrī Birmish al-Faqīh. The three scholars presiding over the recitation—Zayn al-Dīn ʿAbd al-Raḥmān ibn al-Ṭaḥḥān, ʿAlāʾ al-Dīn ʿAlī ibn Birdis, and Shihāb al-Dīn Aḥmad ibn Nāẓir al-Ṣāḥiba—had been brought to Egypt from Syria by Taghrī Birmish especially for this occasion. From the accounts in al-Sakhāwī's and Ibn Taghrī Birdī's biograhical dictionaries, it would seem that Uzbak was not present for the entire series of sessions, in which those assembled heard recitations of and received ijāzas authorizing them to transmit various collections of ḥadīth, including several of the "canonical" compilations, such as the *Sunan* of Abū Dāʾūd, the *Musnad* of Aḥmad ibn Ḥanbal, and the *Jāmiʿ* of al-Tirmidhī, as well as al-Tirmidhī's shorter work *al-Shamāʾil al-muḥammadiyya*, a selection of 400 traditions recounting the attributes of the Prophet. Moreover, the comment of al-Taqī al-Qalqashandī, the official reader of ḥadīth at these sessions, casts doubt, to say the least, on Uzbak's ability at that time to understand all that he heard.[91]

[89] Ibn Ḥajar, *Inbāʾ al-ghumr*, 7:82.

[90] Al-Sakhāwī, *al-Ḍaw*', 3:28.

[91] Uzbak's biography is found in al-Sakhāwī, *al-Ḍaw*', 2:270–72. A fuller account of the sessions in the Citadel may be found in Ibn Taghrī Birdī's biographical notice of Taghrī Birmish, in *al-Manhal al-ṣāfī*, 4:72–73.

But the significance of the event lies elsewhere. It lies, above all, in the importance that was apparently attached to the attendance of young Mamluks from the royal barracks at sessions for the recitation of ḥadīth. Uzbak may not have attended all the sessions, and he may not have understood all that he heard; but more than half a century later, his biographer found the event significant enough, and found at his disposal sufficient materials, to tell us precisely which portions of the books Uzbak *did* hear recited. In other words, it mattered to Uzbak that he had attended the sessions, and that he had studied with the visiting shaykhs. In this event we may catch a glimpse of a world in which young Mamluks were introduced to the sciences of Islam and to the shaykhs who transmitted that knowledge, an acquaintance that in many engendered respect and a desire to "learn" (however thoroughly) more, and which no doubt contributed later in life to an inclination to establish and endow schools for the inculcation of those sciences.

Whether they heard the recitation of ḥadīth or plunged into the intricacies of jurisprudence, the Mamluks as a group and as individuals were continually exposed to Islamic higher education. Regardless of the success or lack thereof of their intellectual endeavors, the decision of individual Mamluks to endow institutions of learning must be seen against this background, as a gesture of an individual to an academic world in which, in some limited but meaningful way, he had shared.

VI

WOMEN AND EDUCATION

"THE SEEKING of knowledge is a duty of every Muslim," went a popular ḥadīth of the Prophet. The historian and traditionist al-Sakhāwī, in his compilation of well-known traditions, warned that a number of copyists had added to the end of the ḥadīth the words *wa-muslima*, so as to make the search for knowledge the "duty of every male and female Muslim." Accuracy in the transmission of the Prophet's words of course commanded a premium, and al-Sakhāwī felt constrained to warn his readers that the addition was not supported by the best authorities. It is nonetheless a matter of *historical* interest that the scribes who copied the books of traditions added, as a matter of course, two small extra words so as to make women, too, explicitly subject to the command of the Prophet. And in any case, as al-Sakhāwī noted, whatever Muḥammad's actual words, the *meaning* of the modified ḥadīth was nonetheless "correct."[1]

Given the extraordinary value that Muslim society placed on knowledge and its acquisition and transmission, it is hardly surprising that women, too, should be encouraged to seek out and treasure religious knowledge. After all, the lure and prestige of learning proved so compelling that it managed to draw into the cultural center a military elite otherwise alienated from many of the forms of Muslim cultural life. And of course most of the Muslim women of Cairo—native speakers of Arabic, born to the Muslim faith—suffered from none of the cultural handicaps that the Mamluks had to overcome. In another sense, however, women, like the Mamluks, formed a group of "outsiders." Even if not always confined strictly to the bounds of the *ḥarīm*, their lives were nonetheless circumscribed by a variety of legal and social restrictions, some of which bore directly on the availability of opportunities for their education.

This ambivalence carried over into attitudes regarding the very propriety of educating women. For example, a manual for market inspectors (*muḥtasibs*) dating from the Mamluk period cautioned against teaching women to write, citing a tradition of the Prophet to that effect. According to the manual, a woman might be safely instructed in certain passages of the Quran, in particular *Sūrat al-Nūr*, but "it is said that a woman who

[1] Shams al-Dīn Muḥammad al-Sakhāwī, *al-Maqāṣid al-ḥasana fī bayān kathīr min al-aḥādīth al-mushtahara ʿalā ʾl-alsina* (Cairo, 1956), 275–77.

learns [how to] write is like a snake given poison to drink."[2] Such an attitude may have reflected a certain "folk wisdom" among the general urban population, but was by no means universally shared, especially by the ulama. More representative of feeling among the learned elite, perhaps, was the opinion of a leading Shāfiʿī jurist of the thirteenth century who cited another tradition, this one from the *Ṣaḥīḥ* of al-Bukhārī: "How splendid were the women of the *anṣār*," the Medinese "helpers" of the Prophet. "Shame did not prevent them from becoming learned [*yatafaqqahna*] in the faith."[3]

Whatever the theoretical duty of Muslim women to seek knowledge, the practical obstacles facing those living in medieval Cairo were hardly insignificant. Their restricted role in society at large combined with the ambivalence of certain shapers of public opinion to make it difficult, although by no means impossible, for a woman to acquire a significant education in the religious sciences. The fact that many did nonetheless become learned, as we shall see, testifies both to their own perseverance and, once again, to the extraordinary power of attraction that knowledge wielded in this society, the respect accorded those who possessed it, and its capacity to overcome, if not flatten, many of the social and cultural barriers that cut across the medieval Islamic world.

The Place of Women in Educational Institutions

If the spread of institutions devoted to religious education over the later Middle Ages proved beneficial to the academic world generally, it was not necessarily so with regard to women inclined to intellectual pursuits. Here, as much as anywhere, the ambivalence in Islamic cultural attitudes toward the education of females had practical consequences. The ties between women and the world of formal academic institutions were complex and uneven. Muslim women could own, inherit, and dispose of property, and so it is only natural that women as well as men gave generously of their wealth to secure the transmission of Muslim religious knowledge. The administration of schools, no matter who their founder and benefactor, and of their endowments could also fall upon the shoulders of women. In matters relating more directly to instruction, however, institutions of learning accorded women a far more circumscribed role.

Muslim women were susceptible to the same feelings of practical concern for the community of Islam and pious consideration for the welfare of their souls that encouraged Muslim men to build and endow religious institutions. No woman ever established a mosque or school as presti-

[2] Muḥammad Ibn al-Ukhuwwa, *Maʿālim al-qurba fī aḥkām al-ḥisba*, ed. Reuben Levy, (London, 1938), 171–72.

[3] Cited in Abū Zakariyyā al-Nawawī, *al-Majmūʿ* (Cairo, n.d.), 1:29.

gious or wealthy as those of the sultans al-Nāṣir Ḥasan or al-Mu'ayyad Shaykh, but the size and type of institutions founded by women varied widely. They included mosques, *ribāṭs* (hospices) devoted specifically to women, and mausoleums, as well as explicitly educational institutions.[4] At least five schools owing their endowment to women were established in Cairo before or during the Mamluk period. The first, the ʿAshūriyya, devoted to students of the Ḥanafī rite and established by the wife of a powerful amir at least half a century before the Mamluk coup, and named for her, consisted of a house located in a predominantly Jewish neighborhood of the Zuwayla quarter of Cairo. The literary sources of the period preserve almost no information regarding this madrasa. By the early fifteenth century its fortunes had declined, and its door was usually kept locked.[5]

Not surprisingly, several schools were established by female members of royal families. One madrasa, al-Quṭbiyya, providing lessons in both Shāfiʿī and Ḥanafī jurisprudence, owed its creation to ʿIṣmat al-Dīn, daughter of the Ayyubid sultan al-Malik al-ʿĀdil, and sister of al-Malik al-Afḍal Quṭb al-Dīn Aḥmad, for whom it was named. ʿIṣmat al-Dīn, like other members of Saladin's family, was "intelligent and religious," having studied ḥadīth, and dispensed her wealth liberally in a variety of charitable endeavors, among them this madrasa, probably constructed just after her death toward the end of the thirteenth century.[6] A more significant institution was endowed by a daughter of Sultan al-Nāṣir Muḥammad who married a Mamluk amir named Baktimur al-Ḥijāzī, from whose *nisba* the madrasa took its name. Endowments at the Ḥijāziyya supported courses in Shāfiʿī and Mālikī law, as well as a Friday sermon; its first professor was no less a figure than Sirāj al-Dīn al-Bulqīnī. The founder of the Ḥijāziyya, like those of other schools, also constructed a neighboring *qubba* (domed chamber) for her own burial, since the souls of women, as well as men, might benefit from the *baraka* (blessing) associated with religious learning.[7] Perhaps the most famous madrasa endowed by a woman was that established by Barakāt, the mother of Sultan al-Ashraf Shaʿbān, in 1369–70. This madrasa, which became known as

[4] Aḥmad ʿAbd al-Rāziq, "Trois fondations féminines dans l'Égypte mamlouke," *Revue des études islamiques* 41 (1973), 96, lists a number of religious institutions endowed by women, as does Carl Petry, "A Paradox of Patronage," *The Muslim World* 73 (1983), 199–200.

[5] Taqī 'l-Dīn Aḥmad al-Maqrīzī, *al-Mawāʿiẓ wa'l-iʿtibār bi-dhikr al-khiṭaṭ wa'l-āthār* (Būlāq, A.H. 1270; reptd. Beirut, n.d.), 2:368.

[6] Ibid., 2:368, 391. Note that the date given by al-Maqrīzi for the school's endowment, A.H. 605, is certainly incorrect, as ʿIṣmat al-Dīn herself did not die until A.H. 693. Cf. Gary Leiser, "The Restoration of Sunnism in Egypt: Madrasas and Mudarrisūn, 495–697/1101–1249," dissertation, University of Pennsylvania (1976), 347–49.

[7] Al-Maqrīzī, *Khiṭaṭ*, 2:382–83.

"the madrasa of the mother of al-Ashraf Shaʿbān," sponsored classes in Shāfiʿī and Ḥanafī law. Inscriptions on the building suggest that it was in fact built by the sultan, her son, in honor of his mother, although al-Maqrīzī states unequivocally that it was Barakāt herself who built and endowed the school. According to Max van Berchem, this ascription was merely a popular fiction; if so, however, it was already current when al-Maqrīzī wrote, within two generations of the institution's foundation, and that it *could* be attributed to her is of course interesting in itself.[8] It is perhaps worth noting that each of these schools became known, not by the name of its founder, but by that of her brother, husband, or father.

At least one more school of higher religious education was endowed by a woman before the end of the Mamluk period. This institution, of which we know little except that it was known as the madrasa of Umm Khawand, was built by Fāṭima bint Qānibāy al-ʿUmarī al-Nāṣirī, the wife of the Mamluk soldier Taghrī Birdī al-Mu'adhdhī, at some point in the late fifteenth century.[9] Finally, at least one more was established within a decade of the Ottoman conquest, by a woman with the unusual name of Khadīja bint al-Dirham wa-Niṣf.[10]

If it was not the rule, therefore, neither was it unheard of for a woman to participate in a public act of religious charity by committing a significant portion of her wealth to the construction and endowment of a school of higher religious education. According to a sixteenth-century history of Damascene madrasas, the Syrian capital boasted even more such institutions.[11] Other women shared in the abiding interest felt by their families for schools established by some relative or ancestor, as when a female scion of the scholarly Bulqīnī family named Alif provided endowments to support Quran readers in her grandfather's madrasa. Two of her cousins, both of whom died during the last decades of the fifteenth century, at the end of their lives began to pass their time in the family school, and were eventually buried next to their scholarly relatives.[12] The Bulqīnī family was hardly unusual in this respect. Quite a few women—daughters and wives of Mamluk as well as scholarly families—were buried in tombs attached to schools founded by a husband, father, or grandfather.

It was also possible for a woman to be vested with a supervisory role

[8] Ibid., 2:399–400. Max van Berchem, *Matériaux pour un corpus inscriptionum arabicarum*, pt. 1 [= *Mémoires publiées par les membres de la mission archéologiques françaises au Caire*, vol. 19] (Paris, 1903), 278–79, 284 note 1.

[9] Shams al-Dīn Muḥammad al-Sakhāwī, *al-Ḍaw' al-lāmiʿ li-ahl al-qarn al-tāsiʿ* (Cairo, A.H. 1353; reptd. Beirut, n.d.), 12:98.

[10] Muḥammad ibn Aḥmad Ibn Iyās, *Badā'iʿ al-zuhūr fī waqā'iʿ al-duhūr* (Cairo, 1982–84), 5:336.

[11] ʿAbd al-Qādir al-Nuʿaymī, *al-Dāris fī tārīkh al-madāris* (Damascus, 1948).

[12] Al-Sakhāwī, *al-Ḍaw'*, 12:7–8, 41, 93–94.

in the administration of a school. Normally, the deeds that enunciated the terms by which the schools would be run placed financial and administrative control of the institutions and their endowments in the hands of the founders. When they died, or when they voluntarily surrendered their supervisory rights, the position of controller (*nāẓir*) normally passed to their children and descendants—usually specified as "the most rightly guided" (*al-arshad*) of the descendants—or to the founder's trusted retainers, to powerful amirs or leading judges, or some combination thereof. The "rightly guided" descendants of the founder might include women, of course. How often did such stipulations result in a woman assuming the controllership of an institution of higher education? One researcher who knows the documentary sources well has concluded that the practice was common.[13] Several deeds stipulated specifically that the female as well as the male descendants of the founder were to be eligible to serve as controller of endowments supporting their schools.[14] On the other hand, it lay within the founder's discretionary powers to exclude his daughters and female descendants from the controllership, and the sultans al-Ẓāhir Barqūq and al-Mu'ayyad Shaykh, among others, chose to make such a stipulation in establishing their madrasas.[15]

Thus the wives and daughters of the Mamluk and civilian elites were not entirely strangers to the world of institutionalized education, and several participated actively in the creation and administration of the endowments on which that world relied. As benefactors, several women invested substantial sums in the establishment of institutions of learning, like their male counterparts appropriating to themselves the baraka thought to be gained from supporting the pious activities of the schools. As administrators, they found themselves, at least in theory (for substitutes might always be appointed), actively managing a school's assets and appointing its professors and other functionaries.

The intellectual, as opposed to the purely administrative side of institutional education, however, presents an entirely different picture. Women played virtually no role, as either professor or student, in the formal education offered in schools of higher education and supported by their endowments. The chronicles and biographical dictionaries of the Mamluk period yield not a single instance of the appointment of a woman to a professorship or, indeed, to any post in an endowed institution of

[13] Petry, "Paradox," 199; on pp. 200–201 Petry lists a number of women who served various endowments as *nāẓirāt* ([female] controllers).

[14] See, for example, the following waqfiyyas: that of Mughulṭāy al-Jamālī, Wizārat al-Awqāf o.s. No. 1666; Zayn al-dīn Ṣidqa, Dār al-Wathā'iq No. 59; Sūdūn min Zāda, Dār al-Wathā'iq No. 58; and Jamāl al-Dīn al-Ustādār, Dār al-Wathā'iq No. 106.

[15] *Waqfiyyat* al-Ẓāhir Barqūq, Dār al-Wathā'iq No. 51, l. 1070; *Waqfiyyat* Sultan al-Mu'ayyad Shaykh, Wizārat al-Awqāf o.s. No. 938, ll. 740–49.

education, except that of controller. Nor did any woman, so far as we know, formally enroll as a student in an institution providing endowed student fellowships in jurisprudence, ḥadīth, Quranic exegesis, or any of their related subjects. In practical terms, there was, quite simply, no need for them to do so. Women were excluded, by law or by social convention, from active participation in those legal, religious, or bureaucratic occupations for which the systematic legal curriculum of the madrasa and its cognate institutions was designed to produce qualified candidates. The consensus of the jurists, for example, refused to admit the possibility that a woman might serve as a qāḍī, on the authority of the Quranic verse which declared that "men are the guardians of women, because God has set the one above the other."[16]

Another reason for the formal exclusion of women from those schools that provided organized and continual instruction was the intrinsic threat to sexual boundaries and taboos their presence was believed to represent in an institution housing any number of young male Muslims. Many felt that only a strict separation of men and women would prove conducive to instruction and study. Theorists on education routinely urged students to remain single, at least at the outset of their studies, so as to avoid being burdened by "the claims of a wife and the responsibility of earning a livelihood."[17] Such advice, generally following the admonition of the eleventh-century scholar al-Khaṭīb al-Baghdādī, was part of a broader call for scholars to deemphasize, if not altogether to ignore, the cares of the "world" (*al-dunyā*).[18] Feminine allures, in particular, posed a threat to the serious student. Women, wrote the fourteenth-century scholar Badr al-Dīn Ibn Jamāʿa in a treatise on the manners and methods of education, should not live in madrasas, or nearby where men and boys from the madrasa would pass by their doors, or even in buildings with windows overlooking the courtyards of the schools.[19]

Whatever the theory, of course, in practice madrasas were by no means monastic in character. Islam, by and large, had always rejected celibacy as a permanent lifestyle. Despite Ibn Jamāʿa's injunction, many people actually lived within the precincts of medieval schools, including married scholars with their families, as witnessed by the not infrequent reports in the chronicles that an individual was born in a madrasa or other

16 Quran 4: 34. Cf. Abū'l-Ḥasan ʿAlī al-Māwardī, *al-Aḥkām al-sulṭāniyya wa'l-wilāya al-dīniyya* (Beirut, 1985), 83.

17 Al-Nawawī, *al-Majmūʿ*, 1:35.

18 Badr al-Dīn Muḥammad Ibn Jamāʿa, *Tadhkirat al-sāmiʿ wa'l-mutakallim fī adab al-ʿālim wa'l-mutaʿallim* (Hyderabad, A.H. 1353), 71–72; Muḥammad b. ʿAbd al-Raḥmān al-ʿUthmānī, *Īḍāḥ al-taʿrīf bi-baʿḍ faḍāʾil al-ʿilm al-sharīf*, Princeton University Library, Yahuda Ms. 4293, fol. 63v, 71v.

19 Ibn Jamāʿa, *Tadhkirat al-sāmiʿ*, 87.

religious institution.[20] But the underlying suspicion that males should be educated in a sexually isolated environment remained. Several schools required that most of their students, or at least those who lived within the building, be unmarried.[21] At the Ẓāhiriyya madrasa of Sultan Barqūq, if one of the students housed within the madrasa wished to marry, he was to surrender his residence (*baytuhu*) to a bachelor "from among those who frequent the madrasa for the study of the holy sciences."[22] Such precautions aimed principally at encouraging students to focus their attentions on their studies, but also reflected a deeper concern to maintain the ritual purity of those engaged in the transmission of knowledge, which was, after all, a pious task. At the Jamāliyya khānqāh, all who lived inside, except the Shāfiʿī shaykh, were to be single, so that, as the deed of endowment put it, the institution would not be "contaminated" by menstruating women.[23]

The Education of Women

Yet the Islamic tradition, as understood in the later Middle Ages, was by no means uniformly hostile to the notion of educating women, of imparting to them at least some of the fundamentals of religious learning. As the sources attest, many medieval women were, in some sense, educated. For example, of the 1,075 biographies of women in al-Sakhāwī's *al-Ḍaw' al-lāmiʿ*, 411 can definitely be said to have received some degree of religious education: to have memorized the Quran, studied with a particular scholar, or received an *ijāza*. The biographies of the remaining women are not detailed enough to allow definite judgments as to the extent of their intellectual training, but given al-Sakhāwī's interests, it seems probable that they, too, were educated: the eleven volumes devoted to men consist largely of details of the lives and careers of the educated elite.[24] But if women were excluded from formal enrollment in the classes endowed in madrasas, mosques, and Sufi convents, what did they study, where, with whom, and why?

[20] Al-Sakhāwī, *al-Ḍaw'*, 1:210. A daughter of Ibn Ḥajar al-ʿAsqalānī was born in the "hall" (*qāʿa*) of the Baybarsiyya khānqāh, where her father was professor of ḥadīth; ibid., 12:3.

[21] Taqī 'l-Dīn Aḥmad al-Maqrīzī, *Kitāb al-sulūk li-maʿrifat duwal al-mulūk* (Cairo, 1934–73), 3:17.

[22] *Waqfiyyat* al-Ẓāhir Barqūq, Dār al-Wathā'iq No. 51, ll. 974–75.

[23] *Waqfiyyat* Jamāl al-Dīn al-Ustādār, Dār al-Wathā'iq No. 106, ll. 304–5.

[24] Cf. Carl Petry's comments on al-Sakhāwī's purposes in *The Civilian Elite of Cairo in the Later Middle Ages* (Princeton, 1980), 9. Ignaz Goldziher first suggested that medieval Muslim women were more highly educated than we would otherwise think, and in particular that they formed important links in the chains through which ḥadīth were transmitted. *Muslim Studies*, trans. C. R. Barber and S. M. Stern (London, 1971), 2: 276–77, 366–68.

Islamic education, of course, aims not only at producing a cadre of judges and scribes to regulate social intercourse, but also at inculcating the principles and practices that shape the character and behavior of a good Muslim—in other words, the individual soul and its fate, a concern in which men and women share equally. Obviously, not everyone possessed the means to become an *ʿālim*, a fully trained scholar, but all Muslims should obtain the degree of knowledge requisite for their station in life, according to an important treatise on knowledge and learning that circulated widely during the Mamluk period.[25] Everyone, for example, must know enough of the law to fulfill his or her duties to pray, fast, pay *zakāt* (the obligatory alms tax), and perform the pilgrimage, duties incumbent upon women as well as men. But *ʿilm*, the knowledge embodied in the law and ḥadīth, involved more than the minimum knowledge needed to fulfill one's religious obligations. The same text noted that "[knowledge has an important bearing] on all other qualities [of human character] such as generosity and avarice, cowardice and courage, arrogance and humility, chastity [and debauchery], prodigality and parsimony, and so on. For arrogance, avarice, cowardice and prodigality are illicit. Only through knowledge of them and their opposites is protection against them possible. Thus learning is prescribed for all of us."[26]

For all of us—including women. If women did not function in society as lawyers, judges, or bureaucrats in the various governmental offices, they had no less need of religious knowledge at the personal level than did men. Islamic lawyers busied themselves with prescribing rules for the regulation of women's personal and social affairs, and their ritual and hygienic behavior—one need only consider the extensive chapters in the law books on menstruation and other matters of ritual purity of special interest to women—and somehow their precepts and regulations had to be transmitted to those they most concerned. A problem that could be perplexing, however, was how: how was the knowledge they required to be transmitted to women and young girls? In particular, how could it be achieved when women were systematically excluded from formal participation in the intellectual life of educational institutions? The matter was a delicate one, for somehow it had to be accomplished without threatening the gender boundaries that cut across the medieval Islamic world and that the ulama, with their greater familiarity with the precepts of the law and their deeper concern with moral rectitude, perhaps took more seriously than others.

Much of the answer lies in the persistent informality of Islamic educa-

[25] Burhān al-Dīn al-Zarnūjī, *Taʿlīm al-mutaʿallim, ṭarīq al-taʿallum* (Cairo, 1977), 9, trans. G. E. von Grunebaum and Theodora M. Abel, *Instruction of the Student, the Method of Learning* (New York, 1947), 21.

[26] Al-Zarnūjī, *Taʿlīm*, 11, von Grunebaum and Abel, *Instruction*, 22.

tion. The remarkable growth in the number of madrasas notwithstanding, the institution never established a monopoly on the inculcation of the Islamic sciences. Lessons continued to be given to informal circles, in mosques and in private homes. Moreover, of course, even those institutions that made specific provisions for endowed courses, with precise stipulations as to which classes were to be held when and in which parts of the building, and who was to attend, were nevertheless public forums, and many came and went who were not formally enrolled. In such a system and in such venues, women might be found alongside men, receiving instruction, attending the recitation of ḥadīth, or, in some cases, reciting the traditions to others.

The transmission of knowledge in the later Middle Ages continued to depend far more upon the relationship between teacher and student than it did upon any institutional framework. Most educations began with the closest relationship of all, that of kinship. Very often, when listing those with whom a particular individual had studied, al-Sakhāwī and other biographers will begin with the subject's father, grandfather, or uncle, and only then move on to others; this seems to be especially true in his biographies of women. Given the jealousy with which Muslim families protected the privacy of their women, it was only natural that girls should turn first to their closest male relatives for instruction. The exception, as is so often the case, proves the rule. The mother of Umm al-Ḥusayn bint ʿAbd al-Raḥmān b. ʿAbd Allah (d. 1422) herself instructed her daughter in certain basics—writing, particular chapters of the Quran, and al-Nawawī's popular collection of forty ḥadīth, the *Arbaʿīn*—because her husband had divorced her before the birth of their daughter. The implication of the narrative, however, is clearly that, under more normal circumstances, this duty would have fallen to the husband and father.[27]

Zaynab al-Ṭukhiyya (d. 1388) provides a case in point. The daughter of ʿAlī ibn Muḥammad al-Dīrūtī al-Maḥallī, she received from family members a basic but substantial education typical of that given many girls. As a child in Maḥallat Rūḥ, a town in the Egyptian Delta, her father made her memorize the Quran and taught her to write, but also instructed her in a number of books that formed core elements in the advanced education of any late medieval Muslim of the Shāfiʿī rite. She studied several fundamental works of Shāfiʿī jurisprudence, including Najm al-Dīn ʿAbd al-Ghaffār al-Qazwīnī's *al-Ḥāwī al-ṣaghīr fīʾl-furūʿ*, the *Mukhtaṣar* (abridged treatise) of Abū Shajjāʿ Aḥmad al-Isfahānī, and a treatise in verse on Arabic grammar entitled *al-Mulḥa*, written by Abū Muḥammad Qāsim al-Ḥarīri.[28]

[27] Al-Sakhāwī, *al-Ḍawʾ*, 12:140.

[28] Al-Sakhāwī, of course, only refers to these works in a shorthand form—for example, as

Once a woman left the paternal household, her husband, no less than her father, grandfathers, or uncles, assumed a responsibility for the education of his wife. Thus, after her marriage, Zaynab al-Ṭukhiyya's husband undertook to continue her education, guiding her through the two principal collections of ḥadīth, the *Ṣaḥīḥ* of al-Bukhārī and that of Muslim ibn al-Ḥajjāj.[29] Writing in the twelfth century, the influential jurist Qāḍī Khān recognized very few situations in which women were permitted to leave their homes without their husband's permission, but among them was the case of a woman who wanted to attend an academic class (*majlis al-ʿilm*) and whose husband was not a *faqīh*—that is, was not himself qualified to instruct her. Clearly, the jurist understood that the primary responsibility for a woman's education lay with her husband.[30]

Families belonging to the scholarly elite took special care to educate their female offspring. The biographical dictionaries frequently comment that boys who were to become famous scholars began their education, and more specifically received ijāzas permitting them to transmit a certain book or collection of traditions, at extraordinarily young ages, at the instigation of their fathers or other close relatives. Their sisters, too, shared in this distinction. Zaynab, daughter of ʿAbd al-Raḥīm ibn al-Ḥasan al-ʿIrāqī al-Qāhirī (d. 1461), accompanied her brother to classes given by her father and other scholars before she had reached the age of five. Her older contemporary Zaynab bint ʿAbd Allah ibn Aḥmad, known as Ibnat al-ʿAryānī (d. 1452), was similarly brought before a scholar for the first time at the age of two. A prominent jurist and traditionist such as Ibn Ḥajar al-ʿAsqalānī brought along his daughter Zayn Khātūn, in the third year after her birth, to hear the recitation of a particular collection of ḥadīth. Sāra (d. 1403), the daughter of the scholar and judge Taqī 'l-Dīn ʿAlī al-Subkī, received licenses to transmit ḥadīth from some of the leading traditionists of both Cairo and Damascus before her fourth birthday. It was even possible for a girl to acquire an ijāza, and from a respectable scholar such as ʿIzz al-Dīn Ibn Jamāʿa, within a few months of her birth.[31]

Such exposure held value chiefly as a first step in a process of familiarizing young students with the academic world. The full significance of

---

al-Ḥāwī or *al-Mulḥa*. Their identification is based on other references in al-Sakhāwī's biographical dictionary, or in Ḥājjī Khalīfa's seventeenth-century encyclopedia of Muslim learning, *Kashf al-ẓunūn ʿan asāmī 'l-kutub wa'l-funūn* (Istanbul, 1941).

[29] Al-Sakhāwī, *al-Ḍaw'*, 12:45.

[30] Fakhr al-Dīn Qāḍī Khān, *Fatāwā* (Būlāq, 1865), 1:374.

[31] See, respectively, al-Sakhāwī, *al-Ḍaw'*, 12:41–42; Ibn Ḥajar al-ʿAsqalānī, *al-Majmaʿ al-mu'assas bi'l-muʿjam al-mufahras*, Dār al-Kutub al-Miṣriyya, "Muṣṭalaḥ al-Ḥadīth" Ms. 75, p. 296; ibid., 114–15, and al-Sakhāwī, *al-Ḍaw'*, 12:51–52; Ibn Ḥajar, *al-Majmaʿ al-mu'assas*, 384–85.

their attendance at lectures or their acquisition of ijāzas will become apparent soon. For the moment, however, it is important to recognize that girls as well as boys were consciously drawn into the process and that, at such ages, the initiative for educating them lay with their families, that is to say, with fathers or, possibly, older brothers. In *al-Majmaʿ al-muʾassas biʾl-muʿjam al-mufahras*, an account of his education and a list of his teachers covering more than 400 manuscript pages, Ibn Ḥajar al-ʿAsqalānī carefully indicated those shaykhs from whom he had secured ijāzas for his daughters. It should therefore come as no surprise that the scholarly Bulqīnī family produced many learned women whose biographies are found in al-Sakhāwī's collection. Indeed, so accepted was the education of women among families of learning that al-Sakhāwī was able to comment regarding one woman that, although he had no direct knowledge of her education, "I do not doubt that she had obtained ijāzas, as her family was well known [for its learning]."[32]

Alternative Venues for the Education of Women

Thus, although women never enrolled in formal classes, in the less formal venues in which instruction thrived—private teaching circles in madrasas, mosques, or homes—women might be found studying alongside men. That this occurred, there can be no doubt; how frequently, and how well it was accepted, is more problematic. Occasionally, the biographers mention that a particular individual "brought his daughter to the Ẓāhiriyya madrasa to hear the recitation of [the *Ṣaḥīḥ*] of al-Bukhārī."[33] Al-Sakhāwī, too, records that once, in Damascus, he heard a recitation, probably of traditions, from Sitt al-Quḍāt bint Abī Bakr Ibn Zurayq (d. 1459 or 1460), in the company of that woman's granddaughter and her brothers.[34] Moreover, according to the complaint of Ibn al-Ḥājj in his lengthy treatise describing practices of which he did not approve, the spontaneous lectures and classes that met in various religious institutions and other public spaces attracted women participants as well as men:

> [Consider] what some women do when people gather with a shaykh to hear [the recitation of] books. At that point women come, too, to hear the readings; the men sit in one place, the women facing them. It even happens at such times that some of the women are carried away by the situation; one

[32] Al-Sakhāwī, *al-Ḍawʾ*, 12:6.

[33] Al-Sakhāwī, *al-Ḍawʾ*, 12:31. A study of Ayyubid-period madrasas has suggested that the daughter of a prominent transmitter of ḥadīth, who herself became a renowned traditionist, may have studied in the madrasa in which her father taught. Leiser, "Restoration," 176–81.

[34] Al-Sakhāwī, *al-Ḍawʾ*, 12:3, 56–57.

> will stand up, and sit down, and shout in a loud voice. [Moreover,] private parts of her body will appear; in her house, their exposure would be forbidden—how can it be allowed in a mosque, in the presence of men?[35]

"Private parts of her body"—the term Ibn al-Ḥājj used was *ʿawrāt*, literally "that which it is indecent to reveal." In the case of women, that might include everything except the face and hands; some might not even be that permissive. It is perhaps safe to assume that what concerned Ibn al-Ḥājj was not explicit exhibitionism, but the threat to established sexual boundaries represented by the mixing of men and women in these informal lessons. Here again, as with Mamluks and others, the persistent informality of Islamic education, its reliance on models that privileged direct personal contact, and the open, public character of Cairo's schools, expanded the limits of learning and eased the way for the participation of those—such as women—who might otherwise have been formally excluded from the institutions.

In many cases, of course, women could be educated and sexual boundaries preserved by providing for instruction from family members: fathers, brothers, or husbands. Even so, many women studied with and received ijāzas from scholars outside the immediate family circle, and very often the scholars with whom they studied were themselves women. This is not to suggest that education took place exclusively in groups segregated by sex. On the contrary, many whose biographies were recorded in compilations such as al-Sakhāwī's dictionary of fifteenth-century luminaries, males as well as females, were instructed by and received ijāzas from learned women, a point to which we shall return. But a thorough perusal of the *Kitāb al-nisā'*, that volume of al-Sakhāwī's work that is devoted to women, leaves one with the impression that girls, more than boys, received their instruction from other women.[36] Some educated women shouldered the specific responsibility for "teaching women the Quran and instructing them in ʿilm and righteous deeds."[37] The Muslim women of Cairo also took advantage of the comparatively free atmosphere of the public religious festivals, such as the Prophet's *mawlid* (birthday), to gather with a woman who, they claimed, was a *shaykha*, and who in-

[35] Ibn al-Ḥājj, *Madkhal al-sharʿ al-sharīf* (Cairo, 1929, in 4 vols.; reptd. Beirut, 1981), 2:219.

[36] Huda Lutfi has explored the potential of volume 12 of this work, *al-Ḍaw' al-lāmiʿ li-ahl al-qarn al-tāsiʿ*, for the study of the history of women in the fifteenth century. See "Al-Sakhāwī's *Kitāb al-Nisā'* as a Source for the Social and Economic History of Muslim Women during the Fifteenth Century A.D.," in *The Muslim World* 71 (1981), 104–24. Other biographical dictionaries of earlier periods of Islamic history, such as those of Ibn Saʿd and Ibn ʿAsākir, also contained volumes devoted to women.

[37] Ibn Ḥajar al-ʿAsqalānī, *al-Durar al-kāmina fī aʿyān al-mi'a al-thāmina* (Cairo, 1966–67), 1:383; cf. ibid., 3:307–8.

terpreted to them the Quran, or read to them from the popular tales of the prophets. Ibn al-Ḥājj, of course, disapproved, although his censure derived as much from the dubious nature of the stories transmitted to them as from the doubtful qualifications of the female transmitters.[38] He could not, however, have condemned all of those learned women who sought to share their knowledge. A comment of al-Sakhāwī's offers an insight into a world in which learned women transmitted to other women the precepts of the law—that is to say, ʿilm—of special concern to them. A certain Khadīja, daughter of ʿAlī ibn ʿUmar al-Anṣārī, who died in 1469, "informed [other] women concerning the chapters [from the law books] on menstruation and like matters."[39] Women may not have explicitly formulated the law even as it regarded specifically feminine matters, but they did play an active role in transmitting its principles and regulations to each other.

It was not necessary to establish a completely separate structure for this purpose. As we have seen, even in Mamluk Cairo structure was very much a secondary element in the organization of education and the transmission of knowledge. Nonetheless, the need to preserve sexual boundaries did encourage the focusing of efforts to educate women on particular institutions and locations. The forums might well be found—a point worthy of special note—in private homes, such as that of one learned woman of the fifteenth century whose family seems to have devoted itself especially to the religious edification of women, for "her house was a gathering place for divorced and widowed women, devoted to the instruction of young girls."[40] True to form, Ibn al-Ḥājj expressed astonishment that a respected scholar had offered his home as a forum for the instruction of women by a shaykha.[41] Thus men, too, might take a special interest in the education of women, as did the professor and Ḥanbalī chief judge ʿIzz al-Dīn Aḥmad al-Kinānī (d. 1471), whose house was a "gathering spot" for "widows and the like."[42]

Mamluk Cairo did boast a few endowed institutions specifically devoted to housing women, which might provide their residents with instruction in the religious sciences. Generally, such establishments were known as *ribāṭs*, a term that usually referred to a hospice for Sufis. Little is known of these institutions, such as those established "for widows" by Khadīja (d. 1474), the daughter of Amir Ḥajj al-Baysarī, and Zaynab, the wife of Sultan Īnāl (reigned 1453–61).[43] At least two maintained some

[38] Ibn al-Ḥājj, *Madkhal*, 2:12–13.
[39] Al-Sakhāwī, *al-Ḍaw'*, 12:29.
[40] Al-Sakhāwī, *al-Ḍaw'*, 12:148.
[41] Ibn al-Ḥājj, *Madkhal*, 2:13.
[42] Al-Sakhāwī, *al-Ḍaw'*, 1:207.
[43] Al-Sakhāwī, *al-Ḍaw'*, 12:26, 45.

undefined connection with a neighboring madrasa. Shams al-Dīn Sunqur al-Saʿdī constructed "a ribāṭ for women" in the madrasa that he built in 1315–16, while the founder of the Bāsiṭiyya "built behind his madrasa a ribāṭ for foreign and poor women."[44] Apparently a total of at least five were established in Cairo over the course of the Mamluk period, in addition to a large number in the necropolis (*al-qarāfa al-kubrā*) outside the city.[45] Principally, they seem to have served as places of residence for elderly, divorced, or widowed women who had no other place of abode, until their death or remarriage.

In addition to providing shelter, however, at least some of these institutions were expected to satisfy the intellectual and spiritual needs of women left without family members capable of providing them with whatever education they might need. In particular this was true of the ribāṭ al-Baghdādiyya, established toward the end of the thirteenth century by a daughter of Sultan al-Ẓāhir Baybars. The shaykha who supervised this institution routinely preached to the female residents and instructed them in the science of Islamic jurisprudence, "until such time as they should remarry or return to their husbands."[46] Among the women who taught and administered this ribāṭ were some of the most accomplished female scholars of the period. Prominent among them was Fāṭima bint ʿAbbās al-Baghdādiyya (d. 1314–15), who apparently gave her name to (or took it from) the institution. According to her biographer, she was well versed in jurisprudence, to an extent that impressed even the strict Ḥanbalī scholar Ibn Taymiyya.[47] At an institution such as the ribāṭ al-Baghdādiyya, the instruction of women may have actually helped to protect and reaffirm those sexual boundaries that a divorced or widowed woman might threaten by her independent status.

The use of the term "ribāṭ" to describe these institutions suggests, too, that some women may have been drawn into the world of learning through Sufism. A number of women were clearly initiated into Sufi orders: one young fourteenth-century male even received from his grandmother a *khirqa*, the robe that a Sufi novice received from his master.[48] Of course, an introduction into Islamic mysticism was by no means synonymous with education in the religious and legal sciences, but neither

[44] Al-Maqrīzī, *Khiṭaṭ*, 2:397; Ibn Iyās, *Badāʾiʿ al-zuhūr*, 2:59.

[45] Aḥmad ʿAbd al-Rāziq, *La femme au temps des mamlouks en égytpe* (Cairo, 1973), 72–74, discusses the scattered references in the sources. On those in the Qarāfa, see al-Maqrīzī, *Khiṭaṭ*, 2:454.

[46] The ribāṭ, al-Maqrīzī wrote, *lahu dāʾiman shaykha taʿiẓu al-nisāʾ wa-tudhakkiruhunna wa-tufaqqihuhunna*. Al-Maqrīzī, *Khiṭaṭ*, 2:427–28.

[47] Al-Maqrīzī, *Khiṭaṭ*, 2:428; Ibn Ḥajar, *al-Durar al-kāmina*, 3:307–8. The printed text of *al-Durar* gives her name as Fāṭima bint ʿAyyāsh.

[48] Ibn Ḥajar, *al-Durar*, 1:320. For an example from the fifteenth century, see al-Sakhāwī, *al-Ḍawʾ*, 1:205.

were the two worlds entirely separate, and as we have seen both the institutions and the personalities involved in each sphere tended to overlap. The ribāṭ al-Baghdādiyya may be a case in point. What exactly its connections to the organized mystical orders were remains obscure, but at least one of its shaykhas was accomplished in Sufism.[49] Indeed, formal Sufism and the broader forms of Muslim mysticism may have been an important route by which learned women could acquire standing in the religio-academic world, since women, like men, were capable of accumulating those qualities—learning, piety, the ability to perform miracles—that conferred status and encouraged veneration. If women were never appointed to professorships, several seem to have become shaykhas of the Sufis established in several, albeit minor, mosques.[50]

Women and the Transmission of Ḥadīth

Fāṭima al-Baghdādiyya was, however, somewhat unusual in her acknowledged expertise in Islamic jurisprudence. Law and its related subjects were, to be sure, not entirely off-limits to women. Girls might receive instruction in the fundamentals of jurisprudence, as did Zaynab al-Ṭukhiyya. Many popular introductory texts formed part of the curriculum of the education of females, such as Ibn Mālik's versified introduction to Arabic grammar, the *Alfiyya*; al-Qāsim al-Shāṭibī's popular poem on the Quran; Sharaf al-Dīn al-Būsīrī's *qaṣīda* in praise of the Prophet; and the *ʿAqīda* of al-Ghazālī. A girl's education might even include basic textbooks in the precepts of the law, such as the abridged treatise (*Mukhtaṣar*) in Shāfiʿī law by al-Qudūrī.[51] On the other hand, the biographical dictionaries reveal the paucity of women who are said to have excelled in jurisprudence, *uṣūl* (the foundations of jurisprudence), *kalām* (theology), or any of those subjects in which male scholars are so often said to have been proficient. Relatively few women were referred to as *faqīhas* in contexts that specifically suggest an expertise in jurisprudence. Beyond the

[49] Thus Ḥujjāb bint ʿAbd Allāh (d. 1324 or 25), shaykha of the ribāṭ; Jamāl al-Dīn Yūsuf Ibn Taghrī Birdī, *al-Nujūm al-zāhira fī mulūk miṣr wa'l-qāhira* (Cairo, 1929–72), 9:266; cf. Ibn Ḥajar, *al-Durar*, 2:86.

[50] Zaynab, the daughter of Dāwūd Abū 'l-Jawad (d. 1459), apparently succeeded her father as shaykh of the Sufis at the mosque of ʿAlam Dār near the Bāb al-Barqiyya in Cairo, although al-Sakhāwī failed to give her a biographical entry of her own; see al-Sakhāwī, *al-Ḍaw'*, 3:211, 237. In 1486 a certain Qilij al-Rūmī al-Adhamī died, and his wife was appointed—the word used is *qurrirat*—to his position as "shaykh" of Sultan Qaytbāy's *zāwiya*. The significance of this event is not at all clear, although the chronicler does record his surprise at the occasion. Ibn Iyās, *Badāʾiʿ al-zuhūr*, 3:233; cf. ʿAbd al-Rāziq, *La femme*, 74.

[51] For example, al-Sakhāwī, *al-Ḍaw'*, 12:9, 15, 53.

elementary stages, a woman's education focused almost exclusively on ḥadīth, and in that field lay her surest path to prominence.

The public recitation of ḥadīth played a central role in the religious experience of the average Muslim, and the general Muslim population of medieval Cairo took a keen interest in their study. As we have seen, even the Mamluks found the study of traditions especially rewarding, so that ḥadīth provided the most popular channel for the integration of the military elite into the world of religious learning. But the role of women in the actual transmission of ḥadīth dwarfed that of the Mamluks. Well-known *muḥaddithūn* (those who had memorized and taught traditions) routinely compiled lists of those on whose authority they recited ḥadīth; in them, most important male scholars included significant numbers of women. Of the 172 names on his list, Tāj al-Dīn ʿAbd al-Wahhāb al-Subkī (d. 1370) included 19 women. Ibn Ḥajar al-ʿAsqalānī left us the names of 53 different women with whom, in one way or another, he studied ḥadīth. No less a scholar than Jalāl al-Dīn al-Suyūṭī (d. 1505) relied heavily on women as his sources for ḥadīth: of the 130 shaykhs of exceptional reliability on whose authority he transmitted, fully 33—more than a quarter of the total—were women.[52]

Ḥadīth, of course, could be transmitted in a number of ways. A student might actually read them or hear them read in the presence of the muḥaddith, or he or she might simply receive an ijāza authorizing their further transmission. Al-Sakhāwī himself, in his biographical dictionary, names sixty-eight women with whom he, in some fashion, studied; of these, forty-six issued to him ijāzas. Since it was possible, by the standards of the time, to receive an ijāza from a scholar without actually studying or reciting a work in his or her presence, women might participate in the transmission of ḥadīth without always encountering male students or teachers.[53] Malika al-Ṣāliḥiyya (d. 1400), for example, issued an ijāza to Ibn Ḥajar, but died in Damascus four months before he visited the city.[54] Here again, the family connection proved crucial. Consider, for example, the two sisters who apparently received ijāzas simply by virtue of their association with their scholarly brothers.[55] In an ijāza issued by al-Sakhāwī himself, the scholar authorized Abū Bakr ibn al-Hīshī and his

[52] Tāj al-Dīn ʿAbd al-Wahhāb al-Subkī, *Muʿjam shuyūkh al-Subkī*, Dār al-Kutub al-Miṣriyya, Aḥmad Tīmūr Pāshā Collection, "Tārīkh" Ms. 1446 [= Maʿhad Iḥyāʾ al-Makhṭūṭāt al-ʿArabiyya, "Tārīkh" Ms. 490]; Ibn Ḥajar, *al-Majmaʿ al-muʾassas*; Jalāl al-Dīn al-Suyūṭī, *al-Taḥadduth bi-niʿmat allāh*, ed. Elizabeth M. Sartain (Cambridge, 1975), 43–70. Also, six of thirty-one names in the *mashyakha* of ʿAbd al-Qādir al-Yūnīnī (d. 1346) belonged to women. Georges Vajda, "La mashyakha de ʿAbd al-Qādir al-Yūnīnī," *Journal asiatique* 259 (1971), 226–36.

[53] Goldziher, *Muslim Studies*, 2:176–78.

[54] Ibn Ḥajar, *al-Majmaʿ al-muʾassas*, 327–28.

[55] Al-Sakhāwī, *al-Ḍawʾ*, 12:120.

three sons, who had heard him recite the traditions in his *Kitāb al-buldāniyyāt*, to transmit the work; the same license was issued to Ibn al-Hīshī's younger daughter ʿĀ'isha, although there is nothing to suggest that she was actually present at the recitations.[56]

On the other hand, very often the transmission of ḥadīth represented a world in which gender barriers, if they did not actually dissolve, were at least permeable. We have already seen how al-Sakhāwī mentioned having heard ḥadīth read by an elderly woman in the presence of her granddaughter and grandsons. The terms that al-Sakhāwī and other biographers used—that an individual "heard" (*samiʿa*) the recitation from a transmitter, or "read [a work] in" his/her presence (*qara'a ʿalā*)—leave no doubt that males and females often interacted directly to secure the transmission of ḥadīth. Zaynab bint al-Kamāl heard recitations by scholars from all the major cities of Syria and Egypt—when she died she left behind a camel-load of ijāzas—and was herself such a popular transmitter that "students pressed about her and read to her the great books."[57]

The very nature of the culture of ḥadīth transmission ensured that women, no less than men, could become prized teachers. Clearly it was imperative that one study ḥadīth with a shaykh of wide knowledge and blameless reputation, not only to increase the number of traditions one knew and could transmit, but also to draw upon a shaykh's authority and so enhance one's own reputation as a muḥaddith. But the selection of a teacher of ḥadīth involved another criterion as well: reducing the number of transmitters in a given chain of authority (*isnād*). In other words, a man or woman might become a prized teacher of ḥadīth because he or she could claim to have studied directly with an especially revered transmitter of traditions. An inevitable consequence was the preference of young pupils for older teachers for, as they aged, these privileged students might become the sole surviving muḥaddith in a particular city or region to transmit ḥadīth on the direct authority of a prominent shaykh.

At this level women could compete directly with men, and in fact a number of women are noted for having distinguished themselves as the sole surviving transmitter of ḥadīth from prominent teachers. ʿĀ'isha, the daughter of Muḥammad ibn ʿAbd al-Hādī, achieved a position in the transmission of ḥadīth unequalled by many men, and in her life we may see a model for female transmitters. Born in Damascus in the early fourteenth century, in her fourth year she was brought before Abū 'l-ʿAbbās Aḥmad al-Ḥajjār, a famous muḥaddith who died in A.H. 730, from whom

[56] A. J. Arberry, *Sakhawiana* (London, 1951), 4–5. Arberry suggests that ʿĀ'isha may have "sometimes" attended the lessons with her father, but that hardly follows from the evidence of the ijāza itself: that the license was issued in her name does not guarantee that she was present.

[57] Ibn Ḥajar, *al-Durar*, 2:209–10.

she heard two small but popular collections of ḥadīth.[58] Later, she studied Muslim ibn al-Ḥajjāj's important compendium of traditions, the *Ṣaḥīḥ*, with a friend of her father's[59] and other scholars, and Ibn Hishām's *ṣīra* (biography) of the Prophet. During her lifetime she collected ijāzas from scholars in Aleppo, Hama, Nablus, and Hebron, and became herself one whom the *raḥḥāla*—those scholars and others who traveled the Islamic world in search of ḥadīth and of new and stronger authorities for their transmission—eagerly sought out. Her fame spread—as important a scholar as Ibn Ḥajar was proud to list her among his principal teachers—so that the seventeenth-century historian Ibn al-ʿImād gave her the epithet "muḥadditha of Damascus," and remarked that she was "the most supported [i.e., in the reliability of her transmissions] of the people of her time."

The critical factor in ʿĀ'isha's success lay in the unique circumstances in which, as an elderly woman, she found herself. She well deserved the great respect in which she was held, for she "aged until she stood alone [as a transmitter] from the majority of her shaykhs."[60] Thus the early education of girls (and boys), in which they were brought before prominent teachers and transmitters of ḥadīth at extraordinarily young ages, when (at least in the case of girls) they were not formally enrolled as students in an institution of instruction, played a critical role, and allowed women to establish independent reputations as valuable links in the chains of authority on which Muslim learning rested. ʿĀ'isha was 4 and al-Ḥajjār 103 (lunar) years old when she heard from the famous traditionist the *Ṣaḥīḥ* of al-Bukhārī, so that in her old age, as her student Ibn Ḥajar al-ʿAsqalānī announced proudly in his account of his education, "no one other than [ʿĀ'isha] remained on the earth who transmitted from al-Ḥajjār."[61]

ʿĀ'isha was an exceptional woman, but she by no means stood alone.

[58] Ibn Ḥajar al-ʿAsqalānī gives the date of her birth as A.H. 724; his student al-Sakhāwī, followed by the seventeenth-century historian Ibn al-ʿImād, altered the year of her birth to 723, which, on internal evidence, must be the correct date. The information for her life is drawn from the accounts of these three biographers: Ibn Ḥajar al-ʿAsqalānī, *Inbā' al-ghumr bi-abnā' al-ʿumr* (Hyderabad, 1967; reptd. Beirut, 1986), 7:132–33, and idem, *al-Majmaʿ al-mu'assas*, 240–43; al-Sakhāwī, *al-Ḍaw'*, 1281; ʿAbd al-Ḥayy Ibn al-ʿImād, *Shadharāt al-dhahab fī akhbār man dhahab* (Cairo, 1931; reptd. Beirut, 1979), 7:120–21. For al-Ḥajjār's biography, see Ibn Ḥajar, *al-Durar*, 1:152–53.

[59] This scholar is identified only as Sharaf al-Dīn ʿAbd Allāh ibn al-Ḥasan; probably the name refers to Sharaf al-Dīn ʿAbd Allāh ibn al-Ḥasan (not al-Ḥusayn) ibn ʿAbd Allāh al-Maqdasī al-Ḥanbalī (d. 1331–32), who, significantly, seems to have been a colleague of ʿĀ'isha's father Muḥammad. Ibn Ḥajar, *al-Durar*, 2:361–62.

[60] Al-Sakhāwī, *al-Ḍaw'*, 12:81.

[61] Ibn Ḥajar, *al-Majmaʿ al-mu'assas*, 240. Richard Bulliet, *The Patricians of Nishapur* (Cambridge, Mass., 1972), 57, 59–60, discusses similar examples in a very different Islamic society.

Other women achieved distinction as prominent transmitters of ḥadīth, among them Khadīja al-Dimashqiyya, who, by the time of her death at the age of almost 90 in 1400–1401, was the last to transmit ḥadīth on the authority of al-Qāsim b. Muẓaffar Ibn ʿAsākir, a prominent Syrian traditionist who died in 1323, *bi'l-samāʿ*—that is, having heard Ibn ʿAsākir himself read traditions.[62] Both Maryam bint Aḥmad ibn Ibrahīm (d. 1402–03) and Fāṭima bint Khalīl ibn Aḥmad (d. 1434) ended their lives as the sole authorities for the direct transmission of ḥadīth from a number of their shaykhs. Both, moreover, achieved the further distinction of having *mashyakhas* (lists of those on whose authority they transmitted ḥadīth) composed for them—in the case of Fāṭima, by Ibn Ḥajar himself—a further indication that women studied traditions not only as a pious activity, but so as to participate actively in the transmission of this important field of Muslim intellectual endeavor.[63]

That women frequently excelled in the transmission of ḥadīth, however, should not obscure from us the fundamental difference between the character of the education they received and that accorded men, a difference the most practical consequence of which—namely, the absence of women from endowed positions in schools of higher learning and from judicial posts—we have already noted. The gender barrier affected the core of the relationship between teacher and student as it was known in medieval Islam. Instruction, it may be argued, necessarily implies a power relationship between instructor and student. Certainly, as we have seen, Islamic pedagogical literature abounds with normative guidelines that reinforced the subservient role of the instructed. Frequently, the relationship between teacher and student is described with the metaphor of a father and his child. Inside a school, or in situations of special intimacy between instructor and instructed, a teacher's control over his pupils extended to a close supervision of their behavior and morals, as well as their educational progress. Consequently, a careful reader of the biographies of women in al-Sakhāwī's *al-Ḍaw' al-lāmiʿ* and other biographical dictionaries will note the virtual absence of terms such as *ṣāḥaba*, *lāzama*, and *ittabaʿa* that describe the intimate personal and intellectual relationship between gifted students and particular prominent teachers, and which occur with such frequency in the biographies of men. And, of course, few women indeed studied more than the funda-

[62] Ibn Ḥajar, *al-Majmaʿ al-mu'assas*, 104ff.; al-Sakhāwī, *al-Ḍaw'*, 12:24.

[63] On Maryam, see Ibn Ḥajar, *al-Majmaʿ al-mu'assas*, 322–27, and al-Sakhāwī, *al-Ḍaw'*, 12:124; on Fāṭima, see al-Sakhāwī, *al-Ḍaw'*, 12:91, and, on Fāṭima's mashyakha, Jacqueline Sublet, "Les Maîtres et les études de deux traditionnistes de l'époque mamelouke," *Bulletin d'études orientales* 20 (1967), 9–99. Other women, too, had mashyakhas compiled for them: Ibn Ḥajar, *al-Durar*, 2:205, and al-Sakhāwī, *al-Ḍaw'*, 12:6–7.

mentals of any subject besides ḥadīth, and in particular few became expert in jurisprudence.

To be sure, the study of ḥadīth formed a core element in the education of any medieval Muslim, including those such as merchant-scholars who, though not perhaps full-time academics, nonetheless devoted great time and energy to the pursuit of learning. Moreover, the ḥadīth themselves played a formative role in the shaping of Islamic thought and society. Not only did the Prophetic traditions constitute one of the bases—in many ways the most important basis—of Islamic law, but their public recital on feast days during the months of Rajab, Shaʿbān, and Ramaḍān, and on other special occasions, was a central feature of popular Muslim religious celebration.

But the culture of ḥadīth transmission in some respects differed sharply from the rigorous education offered in the formal classes of jurisprudence in the madrasas and other schools of medieval Cairo. In the first place, most women (and men, for that matter) would become prominent transmitters of ḥadīth only at a relatively advanced age, when the chains of authority on which their learning rested would be comparatively shorter; and to a system protective of its gender boundaries, an elderly woman transmitting a text or a body of traditions posed a less serious threat than one of a younger age.[64] Moreover, the most important quality of the muḥaddithūn was memory, the ability to remember and transmit accurately ḥadīth that they themselves had studied, as well as the chains of authorities on which their transmission rested. Such stress was laid on memory that medieval writers sometimes complained of traditionists who merely memorized and recited ḥadīth, without in fact understanding them.[65] Memorization, of course, played a critical instructional role in other fields as well, but the study of the law and related subjects revolved around *munāẓara*, the disciplined disputation of fine points of the law and the resolution of controversial questions.[66] That women played a critical role in the transmission of ḥadīth, and virtually none in higher legal training, may reflect this pedagogical difference. Women were systematically excluded from holding judicial posts that would position them to resolve disputes among men, or formal instructional positions that implied a personal, institutional, or metaphorical authority over young men. A similar concern may have lurked subconsciously behind their apparent exclusion from the intensive study of subjects such as jurisprudence, where the assertion of a woman's analytical and forensic skills could have threatened to place her—intellectually,

[64] Elizabeth Sartain makes this point in her outstanding study of Jalāl al-Dīn al-Suyūṭī, *Jalāl al-Dīn al-Suyūṭī*, vol. 1: *Biography and Background* (Cambridge, 1975), 127.

[65] On this point and on instruction in ḥadīth generally, see Makdisi, *Colleges*, 210–13.

[66] Ibid., 109–11; see also Chapter Two.

at least—in a position of authority over men. In the transmission of ḥadīth, of course, disputes might also arise, for example over the accuracy of a transmitter's memory, but such disputes could be resolved by reference to a text.

Such limitations, however, should not disguise the prominent role that women did play in the transmission of a critical field of traditional Muslim learning. The extent of their contribution is difficult to measure, obscured as it is by the indifference or embarrassment of sources written exclusively by men, and by the private venue in which much of their teaching would have taken place. But the fact remains that prominent ḥadīth scholars of the stature of Ibn Ḥajar and al-Suyūṭī openly relied on many women for secure and persuasive chains of authority. Their reliance suggests that active participation in the transmission of Muslim knowledge in the Middle Ages was by no means an exclusively male preserve, and—as with those Mamluks who took such interest in it—that the social horizons of Islamic education were very wide indeed.

VII

BEYOND THE ELITE

EDUCATION AND URBAN SOCIETY

IN A LONG passage in his treatise *Madkhal al-sharʿ al-sharīf*, Ibn al-Ḥājj (d. 1336) scathingly criticized the educated elite of Cairo of his day for their proclivity for dressing in ostentatious garments. "It is well known to those who are insightful," he wrote, that many scholars—literally, "those who are linked to [religious] knowledge"—ignore a warning of the Prophet and have tailored for themselves garments that are wasteful in their use of cloth, since "from them could be tailored an [entire] garment for another." Some went so far as to wear silk, a fabric denied to men by Islamic tradition, and indulged in showing off their sumptuous garments "as is the custom with women." God had made the mark of honor (*khilʿa*) of the ulama the "fear" or "reverence" (*khashya*) that their studies inspired in them; some of Ibn al-Ḥājj's educated contemporaries apparently made it the grandeur, beauty, and refinement of their clothing.[1] Scholars were identified primarily by the size and form of the turbans that they wore. Over the course of the Middle Ages, this headgear took on monumental proportions, until the turban protruding from a scholar's head began to resemble a small tower. Ibn Baṭṭūṭa noted the "extraordinary size" of the turban worn by the qāḍī of Alexandria. "Never either in the eastern nor in the western lands have I seen a more voluminous headgear than this," he remarked. When the qāḍī sat before a *miḥrāb* his turban obscured the prayer niche completely.[2] The experience of others confirmed Ibn al-Ḥājj's observations. In particular, the common people of Cairo seem to have sensed that clothing and fashion played a surprising role in marking out those individuals identified as learned men. Ibn al-Ḥājj recorded, for example, that street players (*al-mukhāyilīn min ahl al-lahw wa'l-laʿb*) would perform in the city's thoroughfares a popular game or skit that they called "The Manner of the Judge" (*bābat al-qāḍī*). In the game, the jurists of the holy law were lampooned by parading those who represented them in oversized turbans,

[1] Muḥammad Ibn al-Ḥājj, *Madkhal al-sharʿ al-sharīf* (Cairo, 1929; reptd. Beirut, 1981), 1:130, 145, 146, 139. Cf. Quran 35:28. L. A. Mayer, *Mamluk Costume* (Geneva, 1952), 62, gives an example of an important shaykh eagerly accepting a silken robe of honor.

[2] Ibn Baṭṭūṭa, *The Travels of Ibn Baṭṭūṭa*, trans. H. A. R. Gibb (Cambridge, 1958), 1:21. Cf. Mayer, *Mamluk Costume*, 49.

sleeves, and *ṭaylasāns* (a long scarf worn over the turban and neck, and falling around the shoulders).[3]

This obsession for fashion, for establishing their identity through garments and outerwear rather than through piety and learning, represented more than the mere arrogance of learned men. On one level, it was an unobjectionable phenomenon, natural in a society in which one's outward appearance was often taken as a mark of some inward characteristic: Jews, Christians, Samaritans, and, later, descendants of the Prophet were all identifiable (theoretically, at least) by the color of their clothing or turbans. Preachers in congregational mosques, for example, routinely dressed in black, the color of the ʿAbbasids, since the delivery of the Friday sermon was an official act that included an explicit acknowledgement of the nominal suzerainty of the ʿAbbasid caliph. Moreover, the ancient Near Eastern custom of bestowing robes of honor on officials and other notables, as both a measure of protection and a mark of favor, crystallized in the Mamluk period into a carefully graded system by which qāḍīs, preachers, and other prominent scholars, as well as Mamluks and government officials, received robes of honor from the sultan, their varying forms, colors, and materials reifying and confirming the hierarchies that the ulama themselves nurtured.[4]

It is difficult to know why exactly Ibn al-Ḥājj seized on the apparently superficial issue of the ulama's clothing. One strand of Muslim tradition had always looked askance upon scholars accepting appointments and honors from the government, and something of this suspicion may have lain at the root of Ibn al-Ḥājj's complaint. Moreover, Ibn al-Ḥājj himself was somewhat "puritanical"—his four-volume work is as much a list of practices of which he disapproved as anything else—and he may have looked with wistful fondness on those elements in Muslim tradition that urged scholars to shun the material pleasures of this world. But of even greater concern to him was, I think, the threat to the identity of the educated elite and their intellectual traditions that he perceived in the ulama's obsession for fashion. Christians might be required to wear blue turbans, Jews yellow ones, and the descendants of the Prophet might be permitted to wear green headgear, but such distinctions marked nothing more than qualities and characteristics acquired at birth. In the case of the ulama, however, the problem was that their distinguishing characteristic was, or should have been, not an inherited status, but something acquired through long years of training. One of the practical conse-

[3] Ibn al-Ḥājj, *Madkhal*, 1:146. On the ṭaylasān, see Mayer, *Mamluk Costume*, 52; on the clothing of the ulama generally, see ibid., 49–55.

[4] On robes of honor, see Mayer, *Mamluk Costume*, 56–64; Ibn Faḍl Allāh al-ʿUmarī, *Masālik al-abṣār fī mamālik al-amṣār* (Cairo, 1985), 72; *Encyclopedia of Islam*, 2nd edition, s.v. "Khilʿa."

quences of the ulama's sartorial pretensions, according to Ibn al-Ḥājj, was that some poor people might be denied access to religious knowledge. The writer claimed himself to have known of such a case. He knew, he said, a man who wished to educate his sons, but was unable to do so because he could not afford to buy them the clothing they were expected to wear to their lessons. Without such finery they were not able to attend a teaching circle, and therefore they abandoned their studies.[5]

But another, and deeper, fear also gripped Ibn al-Ḥājj, one that found a certain resonance in the opinions of other contemporary commentators on the condition of learning in the Mamluk state. If the ulama distinguished themselves by their clothing rather than by their learning and comportment, it would be possible for those "who have no knowledge and are immersed in ignorance" to parade themselves as learned men. The ulama by no means formed an impregnable caste, set apart by ethnicity or heredity, but by their training they did constitute one element of the *khāṣṣa*, the "special people," and were thereby defined in opposition to the comparably uneducated common people, the *ʿāmma* or *ʿawāmm*.[6] Indeed, it was the case that "a common man [*baʿḍ al-ʿawāmm*] will dress himself in the same clothing as a scholar so as to appropriate to himself a position [*manṣib*, i.e., educational or religious employment] that he does not deserve."[7]

This was a serious charge indeed. It was linked to more general complaints, not limited to Ibn al-Ḥājj, of a breakdown in the moral fiber, public behavior, and depth of learning of many members of the learned elite. In the words of Ibn al-Ḥājj, many did not practice what they preached: "rarely does one find the man who behaves according to the precepts he outlines with his tongue in his lessons." Other Mamluk writers also remarked on the blameworthy behavior of the ulama. Badr al-Dīn Ibn Jamāʿa, for example, after listing many of the vices and attitudes that a scholar of the religious sciences should avoid, complained that many in his day were known for the very characteristics they should have shunned. But the critical problem was to assure the integrity of the process of the transmission of knowledge. Tāj al-Dīn al-Subkī, like the others, complained of supposedly learned men who made light of minor sins, and who felt that "our knowledge will hide our disobedience." Such men could not, however, possess true knowledge (*ʿilm*), since true knowledge only highlights the importance of obedience to the precepts of the law.[8]

[5] Ibn al-Ḥājj, *Madkhal*, 1:154.

[6] *Encyclopedia of Islam*, 2nd edition, s.v. "Khāṣṣa."

[7] Ibn al-Ḥājj, *Madkhal*, 1:155.

[8] Ibid., 1:156; Ibn Jamāʿa, *Tadhkirat al-sāmiʿ waʾl-mutakallim fī adab al-ʿālim waʾl-*

Indeed, Mamluk-period scholars who wrote on matters pertaining to education frequently disparaged the intellectual qualities and sense of professional responsibility of those active in the transmission of Muslim learning. Because of the extraordinary importance of religious knowledge and its transmission in this society, any threat to the competence and integrity of those who shouldered primary responsibility for learning and education could generate almost apocalyptic fears. Jalāl al-Dīn al-Suyūṭī, a controversial scholar of the late fifteenth and early sixteenth centuries, became embroiled in a public dispute over his claim to be the *mujaddid al-ʿaṣr*, "the restorer of the age" who would revitalize religion and religious learning at the turn of the ninth *hijrī* century. A precondition to his claim was the assertion that ignorance had spread throughout the earth, and that men of true learning and scholarship had disappeared.[9] Other warnings were less alarmist, but also, for that very reason, perhaps more credible. More than a century before al-Suyūṭī staked his claim, Badr al-Dīn Ibn Jamāʿa had written a treatise on the prescribed etiquette and behavior of both students and teachers. That section of the treatise which presents guidelines for the student is concerned largely with how students should deal with incompetent teachers: shaykhs who repeat themselves, fall asleep in class, or who in their answers to questions are simply wrong.[10]

Tāj al-Dīn al-Subkī left more precise descriptions of those who claimed to be members of the learned elite, but whose training and understanding of their subjects were superficial and incomplete. Some, he said, mistakenly call themselves *faqīh*—learned, that is, in the science of Islamic jurisprudence—after studying only *al-Ḥāwī al-ṣaghīr* of Najm al-Dīn al-Qazwīnī (d. 1266). The *Ḥāwī* was indeed an important textbook of Shāfiʿī jurisprudence, but reading it did not make one a faqīh. Others studied the commentary on the Quran entitled *al-Kashshāf* by al-Zamakhsharī (d. 1144), and then claimed to be "expert and knowledgeable in the exegesis of the Book of God."[11] Despite certain reservations among the ulama about the orthodoxy of all of its contents, the book was an important work of Quranic exegesis and formed a part of the curriculum of many students of the later Middle Ages. At the mosque of al-Ashraf Barsbāy, for example, it was required that the man hired as professor of Ḥanafī law be able

---

mutaʿallim (Hyderabad, A.H. 1353), 24; Tāj al-Dīn ʿAbd al-Wahhāb al-Subkī, *Muʿīd al-niʿam wa-mubīd al-niqam*, ed. David Myhrman (London, 1908), 131.

[9] See Elizabeth M. Sartain, *Jalāl al-dīn al-Suyūṭī*, vol. 1: *Biography and Background* (Cambridge, 1975), 71 and passim.

[10] Ibn Jamāʿa, *Tadhkirat al-sāmiʿ*, passim, especially the section "fī ādāb al-mutaʿallim maʿa shaykhihi."

[11] Al-Subkī, *Muʿīd al-niʿam*, 114–15, 116–17.

to deliver lectures on al-Zamakhsharī's work.[12] But again, reading it alone did not make one a scholar.

Those who claimed to be *muḥaddithūn*, prominent transmitters of ḥadīth, al-Subkī submitted to special scrutiny. The term muḥaddith, when used in its technical sense to refer to an individual ḥadīth scholar, indicated a transmitter of a significant level of accomplishment. The scholars who defined and regulated the transmission of ḥadīth did not always agree on the precise qualifications of those who might legitimately claim the title muḥaddith, but they did universally understand it to refer to one thoroughly trained in the study of the Prophetic traditions.[13] Al-Subkī spelled out precisely what the term meant to him. It indicated one who knew the names of the men and women in the chains of authority (*isnāds*) on which the recitation of the traditions rested, who knew which links in the chain were strong and which weak, who had memorized "a large quantity of ḥadīth texts," and who had heard recited the six "canonical" collections of ḥadīth, three others popular throughout the Middle Ages, and one thousand individual "volumes" (*juz' min al-ajzā'*—perhaps signifying simply a sizeable number) of the Prophetic traditions.[14]

[12] *Waqfiyyat* al-Ashraf Barsbāy, Dār al-Wathā'iq No. 173, fol. 116r. Al-Zamakhsharī belonged to the Muʿtazila, an early Islamic sect placing emphasis on the application of reason to theology. See *Encyclopedia of Islam*, 1st edition, s.v. "al-Zamakhsharī" (by C. Brockelmann). Al-Subkī considered the author of *al-Kashshāf* to be an "innovator" (*mubtadiʿ*) in certain respects, and recommended that the work be read only by those who adhere to the opinions of the orthodox community and are immune to the lures of the "Qadariyya." (The Qadariyya were an Islamic sect espousing a theology insisting on the radical free-will of human actors; by it, al-Subkī may simply have signified the Muʿtazila. Cf. *Encyclopedia of Islam*, 2nd edition, s.v. "Ḳadariyya" [by J. van Ess)]. He did acknowledge, however, that it was "a great book in its field, and its author a leader in his science." *Muʿīd al-niʿam*, 114.

[13] Precise definitions might vary, but in general it can be said that a muḥaddith ranked above a *musnid*, who merely recited traditions without necessarily knowing more about which were authentic and which were not, which transmitters were reputable and which were not, etc., and below a *ḥāfiẓ*, a transmitter of extraordinary accomplishments, who according to some authorities had memorized 100,000 ḥadīth or more. See Ṣubḥī al-Ṣāliḥ, *ʿUlūm al-ḥadīth wa-muṣṭalaḥuhu*, 3rd edition, (Beirut, 1965), 75–80; cf. Ẓafar Aḥmad al-Tahānawī, *Qawāʿid fī ʿulūm al-ḥadīth* (Beirut, 1971), 27–30. Jalāl al-Dīn al-Suyūṭī, in *Tadrīb al-rāwī fī sharḥ taqrīb al-nawāwī*, 2nd. edition (Cairo, 1966), 1:43–52, gives a survey of medieval definitions of the terms; among those he cites are those of al-Subkī from *Muʿīd al-niʿam*.

[14] Al-Subkī, *Muʿīd al-niʿam*, 116. The six "canonical" collections were the *Ṣaḥīḥ* of al-Bukhārī (d. 870), the *Ṣaḥīḥ* of Muslim b. al-Ḥajjāj (d. 875), the *Sunan* of Abū Dā'ūd (d. 888–89), the *Jāmiʿ* of al-Tirmidhī (d. 892–93), the *Sunan* of al-Nasā'ī (d. 915–16), and the *Sunan* of Ibn Māja (d. 896/97). The other three were: the *Musnad* of Aḥmad ibn Ḥanbal (d. 855); the *Sunan* of Aḥmad b. al-Ḥusayn al-Bayhaqī (d. 1066); and the *Muʿjam* of Sulaymān b. Aḥmad al-Tabarānī (d. 971). On these books and on the collection of traditions generally, see Ignaz Goldziher, *Muslim Studies*, trans. C. R. Barber and S. M. Stern (London, 1971), 2:216–44. A "juz' " was a collection of ḥadīth of variable size recited from one authority, or on a particular subject. See al-Ṣāliḥ, *ʿUlūm al-ḥadīth*, 125.

Yet as al-Subkī pointed out, by his day the title had undergone a certain debasement of value. With apparent success, many claimed to be muḥaddithūn who did not, by the strictest standards, so qualify. "At the most," he said, referring to several minor ḥadīth collections, "they look at *Mashāriq al-anwār* of al-Ṣaghānī, and if they get as far as the *Maṣābīḥ* of al-Baghawī they think they have reached the level of the muḥaddithūn." If they study a few more texts, such as Ibn al-Athīr's large compilation *Jāmiʿ al-uṣūl* and Ibn al-Ṣalāḥ's popular work on the science of the traditions *ʿUlūm al-ḥadīth*, or its abridgement by al-Nawawī, they call themselves, al-Subkī sarcastically noted, "the muḥaddith of the muḥaddithūn" and, referring to the great ninth-century compiler of traditions, Muḥammad b. Ismāʿīl al-Bukhārī, "the Bukhārī of the age." To make matters worse, he testified, many of those who study the traditions and transmit them are satisfied with learning the names in the chains of authority and the words of the texts, and with hearing many recitations, but do not understand what they have heard.[15]

These complaints about the intellectual quality and depth of learning of those who claimed to be scholars related to a more practical problem plaguing instruction in the Islamic sciences, one that reinforced Ibn al-Ḥājj's fear that unqualified common people were garnering to themselves teaching positions that should be held only by legitimate ulama. Al-Subkī was conscious of a tendency among some who called themselves professors and held paid teaching posts to come to their lessons unprepared, or to deliver their lectures improperly.[16] A professor, for instance, might "memorize two or three lines from a book, sit and deliver them in lecture, and then hurry away." In some cases, such laxity resulted from simple laziness on the part of professors who were capable of more; but in others, teaching posts were improperly held by men who were fundamentally incompetent.

The real danger in all this was that it led unqualified common people to seek teaching posts; after all, al-Subkī noted, it is a rare man who cannot memorize two lines. A good professor should give to his lessons all the time and effort that they required, and deliver stunning lectures, and satisfactorily answer all questions put to him, so that if an unlearned man or a beginning or intermediate student should attend the lesson, he will appreciate his own inability to teach properly the subject at hand. As

[15] Al-Subkī, *Muʿīd al-niʿam*, 115–16, 125. The references here are to: al-Ḥasan b. Muḥammad al-Ṣaghānī (d. 1252), *Mashāriq al-anwār*; al-Ḥusayn b. Masʿūd al-Baghawī (d. 1122), *Maṣābīḥ al-sunna*, a popular collection of ḥadīth dispensing with isnāds and arranged according to subject; Majd al-Dīn Ibn al-Athīr (d. 1209), *Jāmiʿ al-uṣūl fī aḥādīth al-rasūl*; ʿUthmān b. ʿAbd al-Raḥmān Ibn al-Ṣalāḥ (d. 1245), *ʿUlūm al-ḥadīth*; and Abū Zakariyyā al-Nawawī (d. 1277), *al-Taqrīb*.

[16] The following remarks are drawn from a passage in *Muʿīd al-niʿam*, 151–53.

things stood, however, the ulama "take liberties in their lessons, and do not give them their due, and waste so many working [i.e., teaching] days, and, if they do attend [their classes], give only brief replies to one or two questions." It was no surprise, therefore, that the ulama "are alarmed at the control over teaching positions of those who are not qualified [for them]." To their expressed anxieties, however, al-Subkī angrily replied: "You are the cause of this, in what you have done, and the offense is yours."

It is difficult to judge with certainty the extent to which the analysis of these men reflected accurately the state of learning and pattern of teaching appointments in late medieval Cairo. Ibn al-Ḥājj was an inveterate complainer, and of course al-Suyūṭī's allegations were designed, at least in part, as a weapon in his intense and personal rivalry with other scholars of the day. On the other hand, cumulatively they carry more weight. In particular, the specificity of al-Subkī's charges, and the fact that they paralleled in some way the accusations of other writers, may lend credence to them. Through them all runs a common thread. These writers feared a blurring of the *identity* of the educated elite. They feared that the "democratization" of education, the participation of the common people in the transmission of knowledge, might reduce standards. In a certain sense, such fears were not entirely misplaced. Despite the largely successful efforts of the ulama to ensure that their paid teaching positions were passed on to their sons or favorite students, the broader world of learning and of the transmission of knowledge remained largely open, even capable, as we have seen, of creating space within its boundaries for Mamluks and women. Similarly, through a number of important channels the broad Muslim population of Cairo—the ʿawāmm—was drawn intimately into the world of education and the life of the institutions that supported it.

The Schools in the Life of the Town: Nonacademic Functions

For the general Muslim population of Cairo, the presence of schools and the academic population who studied and taught in them were a dominant feature of urban life. Large schools, such as the madrasa of Sultan Ḥasan, dominated the physical landscape of the town. Schools tended to cluster together in groups, such as that along Bayn al-Qaṣrayn in the heart of the city—the Zimāmiyya madrasa was so close to the Ṣāḥibiyya that anyone praying in one school could clearly hear the worshippers in the other[17]—but no quarter was more than a brief walk from some center

[17] Taqī 'l-Dīn Aḥmad al-Maqrīzī, *al-Mawāʿiẓ wa'l-iʿtibār bi-dhikr al-khiṭaṭ wa'l-āthār* (Būlāq, A.H. 1270), 2:394.

of education. Men and women who had nothing directly to do with their affairs passed by the schools every day, or conducted business in the shops and stalls that frequently lined their exterior walls. The lives of academics and nonacademics were symbiotic. The contemporary sources leave little trace of any of that structural antagonism that set "town" against "gown" in late medieval Europe. It is true that, as Carl Petry has shown, particular schools were associated primarily with "foreign" groups, such as the Shāfiʿī and especially Ḥanafī scholars from Syria, Iran, and Anatolia who figured prominently in the major academic institutions of Cairo, and who provided the intellectual networks with much of their cosmopolitan air.[18] But their position was hardly exclusive, and most scholars and students were Cairene by birth or domicile. The life of the academic world blended thoroughly into that of the urban metropolis around it.

Over the course of the Mamluk period, those institutions housing lessons in the Islamic religious and legal sciences grew progressively more intertwined with the life of the neighborhoods surrounding them. The broader urban society sometimes made its presence felt within madrasas and other institutions in ways wholly unrelated to their academic and devotional functions. For example, until the year 1388, postal couriers arriving from Syria and elsewhere stayed exclusively at the Qarāsunquriyya madrasa, established at the beginning of the century.[19] When Jamāl al-Dīn Yūsuf al-Bahāsī was appointed to the high office of *ustādār*[20] under Sultan al-Nāṣir Faraj ibn Barqūq (reigned 1399–1412), he began to use the Ḥijāziyya madrasa as a prison, a practice continued by his successors. Despite this, al-Maqrīzī tells us, the madrasa remained among the most splendid in Cairo, and Shāfiʿī and Mālikī jurists continued to teach there and receive salaries through the end of the Mamluk period.[21]

More commonly, however, educational institutions provided a focal point for the prayer, worship, and other pious deeds of many besides those directly involved in teaching or attending classes. Some reflection of this may be seen in the architecture of the buildings themselves. A number of schools, of course, were located in the large, open communal mosques designed for use by a large and diverse public. Moreover, in

[18] Carl Petry, *The Civilian Elite of Cairo in the Later Middle Ages* (Princeton, 1981), 143–99.

[19] Al-Maqrīzī, *Khiṭaṭ*, 2:388.

[20] The official primarily responsible for the payment of their monthly salary to the royal Mamluks. On this office, see David Ayalon, "Studies in the Structure of the Mamluk Army —III," *Bulletin of the School of Oriental and African Studies* 16 (1954), 61–62.

[21] Al-Maqrīzī, *Khiṭaṭ*, 2:383. The post of Shāfiʿī professor at the Ḥijāziyya was held repeatedly in the fourteenth and fifteenth centuries by members of the famous al-Bulqīnī family, including Sirāj al-Dīn ʿUmar (d. 1403), Jalāl al-Dīn ʿAbd al-Raḥmān (d. 1421), and Walī ʾl-Dīn Aḥmad (d. 1461). Ibid., 2:382; al-Sakhāwī, *al-Ḍawʾ*, 2:189, 4:106–13.

those enclosed buildings more typical of some of the smaller madrasas, there was, over the course of the fourteenth century, a tendency toward removing the living accommodations set aside for students from the more "public" areas of the schools, so that windows, for example, overlooked interior openings or the outside street or alley, rather than the inner courtyard and arched recesses in which lessons, prayers, and other communal activities would take place.[22] The schools, in other words, were becoming more public spaces, so that a level of privacy and quietude had to be established for the students.

Here again, however, form may have followed function, since madrasas and cognate institutions of learning had begun to serve as public forums before the perceived architectural shift. The Ḥasaniyya madrasa (built 1356–62), as an institution that combined systematic education with all the functions of a congregational mosque, pointedly included living cells that were withdrawn from the central, open areas of the institution. Other, slightly later madrasas may have further separated living accommodations from the main structures of the schools.[23] But we know that functions such as daily prayers for the community at large and the Friday congregational prayers had been attached to educational institutions several decades earlier. Friday prayers had been instituted at the Ṣāliḥiyya madrasa as early as 1329–30, and other prominent schools had been established at large congregational mosques such as those of Ibn Ṭūlūn and al-Ḥākim.

Already at the end of the thirteenth or the beginning of the fourteenth century, Badr al-Dīn Ibn Jamāʿa had expressed concern about students in madrasas meeting and mixing with the general, nonacademic population during prayers.[24] Such encounters must have become routine, however. Sultan al-Nāṣir Muḥammad established his madrasa (1303–04), on Bayn al-Qaṣrayn in the heart of the city, specifically for the professors, teaching assistants, and students who lived and studied there. Their claims to the building were not, however, exclusive. On the contrary, it was also established "for those who frequent this madrasa and for those who gather [in it] for prayers and the performance of obligatory religious duties. And may it be left open to the Muslims in a legal fashion [*wa khallā bayn al-muslimīn wa-baynahā takhliya sharʿiyya*], so that it is permitted to them to pray in it, and may its administration be [like] that which is usual in madrasas."[25] After all, the Nāṣiriyya's stipendiaries in-

[22] Doris Behrens-Abouseif, "Change in Form and Function of Mamluk Religious Institutions," *Annales islamologiques* 21 (1985), 78 and passim.

[23] Ibid. Besides the Ḥasaniyya, the other madrasas that Behrens-Abouseif cites to define the shift are those of Umm al-Ashraf Shaʿbān (1368) and Aljāy al-Yūsufī (1373).

[24] Ibn Jamāʿa, *Tadhkirat al-sāmiʿ*, 232.

[25] From the summary of the Nāṣiriyya's endowment deed as provided by al-Nuwayrī in

cluded an imām and eight muezzins, to call the faithful to assemble and lead them in the five daily prayers. Similarly, the endowment deed of Mughulṭāy al-Jamālī expressed an intention that the khānqāh he established be used by the Sufi students and their shaykh who lived and studied in it, but also by "those who would routinely visit them."[26] Consequently, as at the Jamāliyya khānqāh, it became the duty of a school's gatekeeper to exclude from the premises, not the general public, but only those "dressed in filthy garments, and those of base professions, and those who by entering the place would harm it, and also those of doubtful [character] and of wickedness who would enter the khānqāh, and those who would enter for a reason harmful to the holy law."[27]

Schools of higher education thus provided focal points for the corporate religious life of the broader Muslim community. But the schools might be intimately tied to the surrounding neighborhoods in other ways as well. The contemporary chronicles, for example, mention the Ṣāliḥiyya madrasa on Bayn al-Qaṣrayn frequently as a site in which the chief judges met to hear pleas and render judgments, while other madrasas might provide the venue for settling marriage contracts.[28] More significantly, a school might have been conceived and fashioned by its founder not simply as an institution for the inculcation of the holy sciences, but also as the focus of neighborhood charity. After all, the endowment of a school was a self-consciously pious deed. The terms by which they were established often made provisions for the expenditure of residual income on the poor of Mecca and Medina, the twin holy cities of Arabia. Charity, however, begins at home, and a number of endowments supporting schools also provided food or income for the city's needy. For example, the endowment deed for the madrasa of Qalamṭāy stipulated that the controller of the institution distribute, every Friday, twenty dirhams' worth of bread to the neighborhood poor (*al-fuqarā' wa'l-masākīn*) from the doorway of the madrasa, as if to draw particular attention to the piety and charity of the munificent amir whose name the school bore. The mosque of Ibn Ṭūlūn, as restored by Sultan Lājīn, not only housed several important teaching circles, but also provided both bread and minor employment (for example, as water carriers) to the poor "from among the people of the street next to the mosque." Khushqadam al-Zimām endowed lessons in both Shāfiʿī and Ḥanafī jurisprudence, lessons that met

Nihāyat al-arab fī funūn al-adab, published as an appendix to Taqī 'l-Dīn Aḥmad al-Maqrīzī, *al-Sulūk li-maʿrifat duwal al-mulūk* (Cairo, 1934–73), 1:1045.

[26] *Waqfiyyat* Mughulṭāy al-Jamālī, Wizārat al-Awqāf, o.s. No. 1666, ll. 322ff.

[27] *Waqfiyyat* Jamāl al-Dīn al-Ustādār, Dār al-Wathā'iq No. 106, ll. 158–60.

[28] Petry, *Civilian Elite*, 153, 331; Gary Leiser, "The Restoration of Sunnism in Egypt: Madrasas and Mudarrisūn, 495–647/1101–1249," dissertation, University of Pennsylvania (1976), 426–27.

in al-Azhar until the separate mosque that was to house them had been completed; the endowment also specified that alms and clothing be distributed to the poor during the month of Ramaḍān.[29] Increasingly over the Mamluk period, school complexes included large cisterns to provide water to a thirsty public.

Unusual circumstances at the madrasa of Jawhar al-Lālā highlight the extent to which schools could become centers for thoroughly nonacademic activities. This madrasa had been built in southern Cairo on the hill between the Ḥasaniyya and the Citadel in 1430–31. Several years after its opening, the school's founder appended to its deed of endowment a stipulation regarding a white pearl that was to be housed inside the madrasa. The condition of the document leaves much to be desired, and parts of it are illegible. Enough can be read, however, to ascertain that the pearl and an accompanying copper pot, inscribed with appropriate Quranic verses, were believed to provide an effective cure for certain diseases of the urinary tract. One complaining of such an ailment was to place the pearl in the pot with a quantity of water, and then, after the water had absorbed the healing power of the pearl, drink the liquid. Leaving aside questions about the efficacy of the cure, what interests us is that Jawhar al-Lālā saw fit "to establish a place [for the healing pearl] in his madrasa" so that the "whole [community] of Muslims" (*sā'ir al-muslimīn*) could benefit from it.[30]

All this reflected the essentially public character of Islamic piety and charity. The benefactors who built and endowed schools did not, for the most part, tuck them away in isolated and unpopulated corners, but set them down in the busiest quarters of the city.[31] While a madrasa, mosque, or khānqāh might be designed principally to facilitate instruction in the Islamic legal and religious sciences, such a purpose was in no way incompatible with other charitable endeavors. Hence a secondary activity associated with virtually every school of higher education, and one from which any Muslim inhabitant of Cairo might derive benefit: the organized recitation of the Quran. Most schools included among their stipendiaries men whose duty it was to recite the Quran in small groups,

[29] *Waqfiyyat* Qalamṭāy, Dār al-Wathā'iq No. 68, ll. 300–302; *Waqfiyyat* al-Manṣūr Lājīn, Dār al-Wathā'iq No. 17, ll. 382ff.; *Waqfiyyat* Khushqadam al-Zimām, Wizārat al-Awqāf n.s. No. 188.

[30] *Waqfiyyat* Jawhar al-Lālā, Dār al-Wathā'iq No. 86. The particular document in question is the sixth on the scroll, dated 26 Rabī' al-Awwal, A.H. 840 (1446). Such vessels, inscribed with appropriate Quranic verses and, possibly, symbols and phrases endowed with magical properties efficacious in healing various ailments, appear to have been common in the medieval Islamic world. See H. Henry Spoer, "Arab Magic Medicinal Bowls," *Journal of the American Oriental Society* 55 (1935), 237–56, and Annette Ittig, "A Talismanic Bowl," *Annales islamologiques* 18 (1982), 79–94.

[31] Cf. Petry, *Civilian Elite*, esp. chap. 3.

often spaced over twenty-four hours so that the recitation would continue around the clock. This activity commonly occurred in the tombs attached to the schools, or in windows overlooking them, and thus was meant to bestow *baraka* (blessing) on the founder and any others that might be buried there. As at the madrasa of Qānī Bāy Qarā, however, it was also meant to instill "rapture and humility [*khushūʿ*] in the listeners, both those passing in the street and those living in the mosque."[32]

Education and the Noninstructional Staff of the Schools

The prominence of organized groups of Quran readers at virtually every school may suggest that one of the principal reasons why the academic and nonacademic spheres mixed so harmoniously was that these were more than mere institutions of education. They were also centers of public worship. This involved far more than the simple participation of the general population in prayer and ritual in those institutions. Larger schools hired substantial numbers of men to fill nonacademic positions deemed necessary to the proper functioning of an educational institution, individuals of varying degrees of academic attainment drawn principally from among the local population. An institution the size of the mosque of al-Mu'ayyad Shaykh, just inside the southern gate of the city of Cairo, could afford extensive specialization of function among those it hired. The Mu'ayyadiyya employed more than 150 men in occupations that had nothing directly to do with education, including 4 imāms, 17 muezzins, and a total of 59 Quran readers. The immense madrasa of Sultan Ḥasan was even more lavish, employing 6 imāms, 51 muezzins, and more than 120 Quran readers.[33]

But all medieval schools devoted sizeable portions of their expenditures to paying the salaries of functionaries whose duties were not directly instructional. Even late Mamluk madrasas that made no provisions at all for the direct financing of professors or students, such as those of Qānī Bāy Qarā, al-Sayfī Baybars, or Sultan al-Ghawrī, nonetheless hired a full complement of religious, service, and administrative functionaries. Some services could not be dispensed with by even the smallest schools. The madrasa of Qalamṭāy, for example, supported only five Ḥanafī students and their shaykh, but also employed an imām, three muezzins, a Quran reader, and a *bawwāb* (gatekeeper).[34]

[32] *Waqfiyyat* Qānī Bāy Qarā, Wizārat al-Awqāf o.s. No. 1019, ll. 303–4.

[33] *Waqfiyyat* al-Mu'ayyad Shaykh, Wizārat al-Awqāf o.s. No. 938.; *Waqfiyyat* al-Nāṣir Ḥasan, Dār al-Wathā'iq No. 40 and Wizārat al-Awqāf o.s. No. 881, published by Muḥammad M. Amīn as an appendix to al-Ḥasan b. ʿUmar Ibn Ḥabīb, *Tadhkirat al-nabīh fī ayyām al-manṣūr wa-banīh* (Cairo, 1986), 3:339–449.

[34] *Waqfiyyat* Qānī Bāy Qarā, Wizārat al-Awqāf o.s. No. 1019; *Waqfiyyat* al-Sayfī Baybars,

Leaving aside those involved in the administration of the properties that comprised the schools' endowments, the nonacademic functionaries of educational institutions executed a variety of responsibilities that demanded varying levels of academic accomplishment. The most prestigious positions in most institutions were those of the imām and the khaṭīb, who delivered the Friday sermon; at those late-Mamluk madrasas that hired no teachers or students, the imām and the khaṭīb led the list of the institutions' stipendiaries and received higher monthly salaries than other appointees.[35] Virtually every school hired at least one imām, and perhaps half hired khaṭībs as well. Most of these prayer leaders and preachers received a stipend between one-fifth and one-half that paid to professors of jurisprudence, but noticeably above that given to students.[36] Variations were possible, however. At the khānqāh of Jamāl al-Dīn al-Ustādār, for example, the position of imām was to be filled simply by one of the institution's Sufi students, who received a modest supplement to his normal stipend, while at other schools the imām was actually paid more than the professors.[37]

Dār al-Wathā'iq No. 313; *Waqfiyyat* Qānṣūh al-Ghawrī, Wizārat al-Awqāf o.s. No. 882.; *Waqfiyyat* Qalamṭāy, Dār al-Wathā'iq No. 68.

[35] *Waqfiyyat* Qānī Bāy Qarā, Wizārat al-Awqāf o.s. No. 1019, at whose madrasa the imām received 50 and the khaṭīb 33 1/3 dirhams niṣf, considerably more than any other stipendiary; *Waqfiyyat* al-Sayfī Baybars, Dār al-Wathā'iq No. 313, where the corresponding figures were 33 and 25, also the institution's highest; and *Waqfiyyat* Qānṣūh al-Ghawrī, Wizārat al-Awqāf o.s. No. 882, at whose madrasa the imām received 1,200 copper dirhams and the khaṭīb 800.

[36] Compare, for example, the stipends paid at the following institutions: at the madrasa of Jawhar al-Lālā, 500 copper dirhams for the Sufi shaykh/Ḥanafī professor, 300 for the imām, and 200 each for the Sufi students, *Waqfiyyat* Jawhar al-Lālā, Dār al-Wathā'iq No. 86; at the mosque of Sūdūn min Zāda, 250 dirhams for the Ḥanafī and Shāfiʿī professors, 100 each for the khaṭīb and the imām, and 30 dirhams for the students, *Waqfiyyat* Sūdūn min Zāda, Dār al-Wathā'iq No. 58; at the Ṣarghitmishiyya, 300 dirhams for the Ḥanafī professor, 70 for the imām, and 55 for the students of jurisprudence, *Waqfiyyat* Ṣarghitmish, Wizārat al-Awqāf o.s. No. 3195; at the Ashrafiyya (Barsbāy), 3,000 copper dirhams for the Sufi shaykh/Ḥanafī professor, 1,000 for the imām, 500 for the khaṭīb, and 300 for the students, *Waqfiyyat* al-Ashraf Barsbāy, Dār al-Wathā'iq No. 173. Since these represent institutions of differing size and wealth, founded at different times, the value of the currencies of account vary; comparisons are meant to be drawn only between employees of the same institution, to illustrate the level of the remuneration of the imāms and the khaṭībs relative to other stipendiaries.

[37] *Waqfiyyat* Jamāl al-Dīn al-Ustādār, Dār al-Wathā'iq No. 106; cf. the situation at the Ẓāhiriyya madrasa, *Waqfiyyat* al-Ẓāhir Barqūq, Dār al-Wathā'iq No. 51. At the mosque of al-Shiblī Kāfūr, the imām received 70 dirhams per month to 60 for the Shāfiʿī shaykh; *Waqfiyyat* al-Shiblī Kāfūr, Dār al-Wathā'iq No. 76. The endowment deed of Khushqadam al-Zimām stipulated that the imām was to have been paid as much as the Shāfiʿī and Ḥanafī professors combined; *Waqfiyyat* Khushqadam al-Zimām, Wizārat al-Awqāf n.s. No. 188. At the madrasa of Qalamṭāy, the imām and the Ḥanafī shaykh both received 100 dirhams per month; *Waqfiyyat* Qalamṭāy, Dār al-Wathā'iq No. 68.

Clearly those appointed as imām or khaṭīb had attained some level of academic accomplishment in the Islamic religious sciences. At some smaller schools, such as the khānqāh of Zayn al-Dīn Ṣidqa, the same man was to function as imām and Sufi shaykh and, if possible, as Shāfiʿī professor.[38] Several schools required that the imām and/or the khaṭīb be either Shāfiʿī or Ḥanafī, which may suggest that these appointees were assumed to have had at least a basic training in the jurisprudence of their rite.[39] Others made that assumption more explicit: Sultan Lājīn, for example, required that the imām at the mosque of Ibn Ṭūlūn, as well as its khaṭīb, be a "Shāfiʿī faqīh," that is, one who had studied jurisprudence according to the Shāfiʿī rite.[40] Similarly, the imām at the Jamāliyya khānqāh was to be a Sufi, a Shāfiʿī, and "a student of the noble sciences."[41] Moreover, since leading prayers or preaching the Friday sermon was, at least in the larger institutions, a prominent public activity, some of the most important jurists and religious scholars of the Mamluk period occasionally delivered the Friday sermon at different mosques and madrasas, especially the better-known Cairene institutions. Ibn Ḥajar al-ʿAsqalānī, for example, was successively khaṭīb at the famous al-Azhar and at the mosque of ʿAmr in al-Fusṭāṭ.[42]

But very often the positions of imām and khaṭīb, the remuneration for which was generally inferior to that available to a successful teacher, attracted men of only secondary academic accomplishments. While such prominent scholars as Burhān al-Dīn Ibn Khiḍr (d. 1448), ʿIzz al-Dīn ʿAbd al-Salām al-Baghdādī (d. 1455), and Taqī ʾl-Dīn al-Qalqashandī (d.

[38] *Waqfiyyat* Zayn al-Dīn Ṣidqa, Dār al-Wathāʾiq No. 59.

[39] At the Ashrafiyya (Barsbāy), the Ṣarghitmishiyya, and the mosque of Sūdūn min Zāda, the imāms were required to be Ḥanafīs, as was the khaṭīb at the mosque of Sūdūn (but this was apparently *not* required of the khaṭīb at the Ashrafiyya); *Waqfiyyat* al-Ashraf Barsbāy, Dār al-Wathāʾiq No. 173, fol. 134r; *Waqfiyyat* Ṣarghitmish, Wizārat al-Awqāf o.s. No. 3195, p. 29; and *Waqfiyyat* Sūdūn min Zāda, Dār al-Wathāʾiq No. 58, ll. 259–62. At the mosques of Zayn al-Dīn al-Ustādār and Ibn Ṭūlūn, and the khānqāh of Jamāl al-Dīn al-Ustādār, the imāms were to be Shāfiʿīs (including the khaṭīb at Ibn Ṭūlūn, but *not* his counterpart at Zayn al-Dīn al-Ustādār); *Waqfiyyat* Zayn al-Dīn al-Ustādār, Dār al-Wathāʾiq No. 110, ll. 1201–6; *Waqfiyyat* al-Manṣūr Lājīn, Dār al-Wathāʾiq No. 17, ll. 262–72; and *Waqfiyyat* Jamāl al-Dīn al-Ustādār, Dār al-Wathāʾiq No. 106, ll. 165–71.

[40] *Waqfiyyat* al-Manṣūr Lājīn, Dār al-Wathāʾiq No. 17, ll. 262–72.

[41] *Waqfiyyat* Jamāl al-Dīn al-Ustādār, Dār al-Wathāʾiq No. 106, ll. 165–66.

[42] Shams al-Dīn Muḥammad al-Sakhāwī, *al-Ḍawʾ al-lāmiʿ li-ahl al-qarn al-tāsiʿ* (Cairo, 1934; reptd. Beirut, n.d.), 2:39. Cf. Petry, *Civilian Elite*, 260. Note also the list of those occupational positions held by professors in List 16 of Appendix 2 in Petry's book, pp. 374–75. Of 496 professors identified, 28 were also at some stage of their careers imāms, and 51 were khaṭībs. While the results of Petry's survey certainly prove that some trained in the religious and legal sciences held appointments as imāms or khaṭībs, their relatively small proportion in relation to the larger group of professors may confirm that, as suggested below, the level of academic accomplishment of imāms and khaṭībs was generally lower than that of professors.

1467) taught jurisprudence at the Mankūtimuriyya madrasa, the post of the imām there was held by men of distinctly lesser repute, such as Burhān al-Dīn Ibrāhīm Ibn Sābiq (d. 1477), a minor scholar who was also a Sufi at several Cairene khānqāhs. Ibn Sābiq was succeeded as imām at the Mankūtimuriyya by his son, also named Ibrāhīm, an equally unprepossessing scholar who memorized the Quran and "read a little of the *Minhāj*" (a basic textbook in Shāfiʿī law), who had been muezzin at the Mankūtimuriyya before his appointment as imām, and who may have supplemented his income by working as a tailor.[43] A similar pattern prevailed at other institutions. ʿIzz al-Dīn al-Baghdādī studied jurisprudence and its foundations, ḥadīth, and a variety of other subjects in Baghdad, Aleppo, Damascus, and Jerusalem before coming to Cairo to complete his education. In the Egyptian capital, he built for himself an impressive teaching career, counting Taqī 'l-Dīn al-Qalqashandī, the historian al-Sakhāwī, and others among his students. In his academic career and the extent of his preparation, he typified those who held the teaching post (*taṣdīr*) at the Bāsiṭiyya madrasa. By contrast, the imāms and khaṭībs of that institution, judging from the biographical record, seem to have been scholars of markedly lesser academic accomplishments.[44]

A similar pattern emerges for those who held the post of librarian (*khāzin al-kutub*) in the various schools of Mamluk Cairo. Since hand-copied books were expensive, beyond the financial means of many scholars and most students, schools routinely provided for the purchase and maintenance of collections of books in the religious and legal sciences. Consequently, as the endowment deeds testify, many schools employed separate librarians. At several places the post was to be held by one of the institution's enrolled students, for which he received a supplement to his stipend.[45] The deed to the Jawhariyya madrasa required that, if possible,

[43] Al-Sakhāwī, *al-Ḍaw'*, 1:8, 151–52. On al-Baghdādī, Ibn Khiḍr, and al-Qalqashandī, scholars of considerably greater reputation, see ibid., 1:43–47, 4:46–48, 198–203. The *Minhāj* referred to here is presumably the *Minhāj al-ṭālibīn*, a popular basic textbook in Shāfiʿī law written by Abū Zakariyyā al-Nawawī in the thirteenth century.

[44] For example, ʿAbd al-Qādir b. Aḥmad b. Ismāʿīl (d. ?), its imām at some point during the fifteenth century, who studied jurisprudence, ḥadīth, grammar, logic, and other subjects both in Cairo and in Damascus, and was tutor to the children of the Ibn al-Shiḥna family and those of the Bāsiṭiyya's founder (*aqra'a banī ibn al-shiḥna thumma ibn ʿabd al-bāsiṭ*), but who, as far as we know, never held a teaching post; al-Sakhāwī, *al-Ḍaw'*, 4:261–62. Cf. Shihāb al-Dīn Aḥmad al-Azharī (d. 1477), khaṭīb at the Bāsiṭiyya, whose apparently meager education merited no details in his biography; ibid., 2:131.

[45] *Waqfiyyat* Jamāl al-Dīn al-Ustādār, Dār al-Wathā'iq No. 106, ll. 129–41; cf. *Waqfiyyat* al-Ẓāhir Barqūq, Dār al-Wathā'iq No. 51, ll. 865–68, which stipulates that the librarian is to be one of the madrasa's Sufis (who in this case, it will be remembered, formed a separate group from the school's students). *Waqfiyyat* Sūdūn min Zāda, Dār al-Wathā'iq No. 58, ll. 283–85, requires the mosque's librarian to be "from among the students of the holy sci-

the imām should supervise the library.[46] Wherever a librarian was employed, however, his salary was considerably below even that of the imām and the khaṭīb, ranking among the least remunerative and prestigious posts of the institution.[47] In some, he was even required to undertake certain menial tasks: at the Ẓāhiriyya, to care for the institution's "mats, carpets, and candles," as well as its books; and at the library of the Ghawriyya madrasa, to be not only librarian, but also *farrāsh*, a sort of factotum primarily responsible for housekeeping duties.[48]

Again, holding the post of librarian clearly required a certain level of academic accomplishment: he must be able to read, and should have some knowledge of the works with whose care he was charged. Some librarians were very successful scholars indeed. At the Maḥmūdiyya madrasa, whose extensive library knew no equal in either Egypt or Syria, according to al-Maqrīzī, librarians included scholars of the stature of Ibn Ḥajar al-ʿAsqalānī.[49] ʿAlāʾ al-Dīn al-Qalqashandī (d. 1452), a scion of a prominent Cairene ulama family and brother to Taqī ʾl-Dīn al-Qalqashandī, who studied with the leading Shāfiʿī jurists and ḥadīth scholars of the Egyptian capital and who held several prestigious teaching posts, at some point in his career was also librarian at the Ashrafiyya; he was followed in the post by his son Jamāl al-Dīn Ibrāhīm.[50] But the biographical sources themselves rarely list employment as a librarian among the activities of those whose life stories they record.[51] This lacuna does not

ences," without specifying that the officeholder be an enrolled student in that particular institution.

[46] *Waqfiyyat* Jawhar al-Lālā, Dār al-Wathāʾiq No. 86, ll. 315–19.

[47] At the mosques of al-Ashraf Barsbāy and al-Muʾayyad Shaykh, the librarian received the same stipend as a student; *Waqfiyyat* al-Muʾayyad Shaykh, Wizārat al-Awqāf o.s. No. 938; *Waqfiyyat* al-Ashraf Barsbāy, Dār al-Wathāʾiq No. 173, f. 123v-124r. He received the same salary as the bawwāb at the Nāṣiriyya madrasa on Bayn al-Qaṣrayn, and less than the bawwāb at the madrasas of al-Sayfī Baybars and Qānī Bāy Qarā; *Waqfiyyat* al-Nāṣir Muḥammad, as summarized by al-Nuwayrī in *Nihāyat al-arab*, published in al-Maqrīzī, *al-Sulūk*, 1:1047; *Waqfiyyat* al-Sayfī Baybars, Dār al-Wathāʾiq No. 313, ll. 160–62; *Waqfiyyat* Qānī Bāy Qarā, Wizārat al-Awqāf o.s. No. 1019. There were exceptions to this rule, of course. We do not know what the stipend was for the librarian at the Maḥmūdiyya madrasa, but the importance of that library and the prestige of at least some of its librarians may suggest that his salary was higher than most; see below.

[48] *Waqfiyyat* al-Ẓāhir Barqūq, Dār al-Wathāʾiq No. 51, ll. 865–68; *Waqfiyyat* Qānṣūh al-Ghawrī, Wizārat al-Awqāf o.s. No. 882, pp. 188–89. At the Ghawriyya, while the librarian received a stipend of 1,500 dirhams "for the two waẓīfas" (i.e., for supervising the library and for underaking the *firāsha*), it is clear that he could hire another to be farrāsh, and pay him "what he wishes."

[49] On the Maḥmūdiyya library, see al-Maqrīzī, *Khiṭaṭ*, 2:395; al-Sakhāwī, *al-Ḍawʾ*, 2:39, mentions that Ibn Ḥajar held the post of librarian there.

[50] On ʿAlāʾ al-Dīn, see al-Sakhāwī, *al-Ḍawʾ*, 5:161–63; on Jamāl al-Dīn, see ibid., 1:77–78.

[51] Petry, *Civilian Elite*, 253–54, 376–77. Petry's survey of the educated elite in fifteenth-century Cairo revealed the names of only thirty-eight men who held the post of librarian.

imply that few were actually hired as librarians in the schools of medieval Cairo. On the contrary, the endowment deeds suggest that most institutions did employ someone to supervise their collections of books.[52] Rather, it probably indicates that the post was simply not that important, and that those who held it were generally minor scholars of insignificant academic accomplishment, who merited little or no mention in biographical compilations.

Moving down the list of those religious but nonacademic functionaries hired by most Cairene schools (who received, generally, progressively lower stipends), the level of their expected educational attainment also declined. The list of the functionaries at an institution the size of the Mu'ayyadiyya reads like a list of employment opportunities for unassuming and only partially educated ulama: muezzins, assistants to the khaṭīb, a *mādiḥ* to read poems in praise of the Prophet, a primary school teacher (*mu'addib*) and his assistant (*ʿarīf*), scribes to record the names of Sufis missing from their religious exercises, and of course any number of Quran readers. To be sure, most lower-level religious functionaries attached to madrasas, khānqāhs, or teaching mosques need not have received substantial higher instruction in jurisprudence or other Islamic sciences. A *muqri'* (Quran reader), for instance, need not have accomplished anything more than memorizing the Quran.[53]

But two things are important to note. The first is the sheer number of men in late medieval Cairo who participated directly in the functions of academic institutions, even if their duties were not strictly related to education. Nothing approaching a precise figure can be given, partly because the surviving deeds of endowment are so few in comparison to the total number of schools, and partly because many individuals might have concurrently held appointments in more than one institution. Moreover, references in the biographical dictionaries to these lower-level functionaries are relatively rare, since the comparative lack of prestige associated with their positions did not often excite the interest of the biographers and historians.[54] But it must have been a sizeable group. As we have

[52] Contra Petry, *Civilian Elite*, 253, who concluded that the lack of references to librarians in the biographical literature suggested that the post was not common in religio-academic institutions. When he wrote the book, however, Petry could not have known of the frequency with which the position appeared in the deeds of endowment of Cairene schools: more than half of those surveyed during the course of the present research provided for the hiring of librarians.

[53] Hence the standard requirement made by the terms of the institutions' endowments that the Quran readers (*muqri'ūn* or *qurrā'*) have memorized the Quran—*al-qurrā' al-muḥāfiẓīn bi-kitāb allāh*. This phrase is drawn from the *Waqfiyya* of Sultan Barqūq, Dār al-Wathā'iq No. 51, l. 944, but similar expressions are found in virtually every deed of endowment. Cf. Petry, *Civilian Elite*, 263.

[54] Petry's survey of the fifteenth-century Cairene elite, for example, identified only 187

seen, virtually every school hired several muezzins, Quran readers, and men in a variety of service positions—gatekeepers to guard the doors, farrāshes to clean the buildings, *waqqāds* to "wash the candles and clean them, to fill and hang them, to light and extinguish them," *mubakhkhirs* to "spread incense during gatherings in the aforementioned places [in the madrasa] and [during] Friday prayers, the two Feasts, and the *tarāwīh* [the nightly prayers during the month of Ramaḍān]."[55] Even if most schools hired considerably fewer men than the Mu'ayyadiyya or the Ḥasaniyya, the total number of Cairenes directly employed by academic institutions—dependent, that is, for at least a portion of their livelihood on the world of education—must have reached several thousands at any given point in time.

More importantly, however, it was possible, and probably not that uncommon, for these lower-level functionaries to attend and to participate directly in classes in the higher Islamic sciences. To be sure, the deeds of endowment for several schools specified that their own students were to hold these posts—to act as gatekeeper, or as Quran readers, or even as imām—in addition to fulfilling their academic and devotional responsibilities; this was especially true in institutions whose students were also required to be Sufis.[56] The Ghawriyya madrasa, although it provided no stipends for students, nonetheless required that some of its functionaries, for example the three Quran readers in the *qubba* (domed burial chamber), be drawn from among "the students of the holy sciences," perhaps those who frequented the school.[57] The biographical dictionaries, too, indicate that many of the lower-level religious functionaries of the schools, and even those who held service positions in them, were local men sometimes educated in the very subjects those schools taught.

---

professional Quran readers, compared to 238 imāms, 279 khaṭībs, and 496 professors—despite the fact that Quran readers hired by academic institutions often outnumbered professors in those schools by a factor of five, six, or more. Petry, *Civilian Elite*, 375, 379, 381, 383.

[55] *Waqfiyyat* Jamāl al-Dīn al-Ustādār, Dār al-Wathā'iq No. 106, ll. 203–4; *Waqfiyyat* al-Nāṣir Ḥasan, Wizārat al-Awqāf o.s. No. 881, p. 452.

[56] The Jamāliyya reserved a number of minor positions for its Sufi students, including those of mādiḥ, librarian, teacher for the institution's primary school, and imām, six muezzins, seven to act as farrāshes and waqqāds, and others. *Waqfiyyat* Jamāl al-Dīn al-Ustādār, Dār al-Wathā'iq No. 106. The Sufi students at the khānqāh of Zayn al-Dīn Ṣidqa doubled as primary school teacher, muezzin, and gatekeeper, among other occupations. *Waqfiyyat* Zayn al-Dīn Ṣidqa, Dār al-Wathā'iq No. 59. At another mosque, a Shāfi'ī student was librarian, while at a khānqāh, a Ḥanafī student was *qāri' al-mī'ād* (on which position see below); *Waqfiyyat* Zayn al-Dīn al-Ustādār, Dār al-Wathā'iq No. 110; *Waqfiyyat* Mughulṭāy al-Jamālī, Wizārat al-Awqāf o.s. No. 1666.

[57] *Waqfiyyat* Qānṣūh al-Ghawrī, Wizārat al-Awqāf o.s. No. 882, pp. 193–94. The fact that this particular phrase was not used regarding the imām, the muezzins, and other functionaries, of course, does not necessarily imply that these men were not themselves students.

Consider, for example, two muezzins. Badr al-Dīn Ḥasan al-Qaymarī al-Shāfiʿī (d. 1480) studied a number of subjects, including jurisprudence and grammar, but especially *farāʾiḍ*, that is, the science of apportioning inheritances according to the strict rules of Islamic law; eventually he succeeded his teacher Abū ʾl-Jawād al-Mālikī as professor of the subject at a small madrasa outside Cairo. But before that, he had been muezzin in several institutions, including the madrasa of Sultan Ḥasan.[58] Shihāb al-Dīn Aḥmad Ibn Sukkur (d. 1404) was muezzin in the Manṣūriyya madrasa and the Ḥākimī mosque, near which he also had a shop in which he sold pottery. Ibn Sukkur, in contrast to al-Qaymarī, devoted most of his education to ḥadīth: not only did he hear ḥadīth read by a number of transmitters and receive from them ijāzas, but he transmitted much of what he heard. The historian al-Maqrīzī was one of his students, as was Ibn Ḥajar al-ʿAsqalānī, who accorded him an entry in his biographical account of those with whom he had studied.[59] This is not to suggest that muezzins and other lower-level religious functionaries were frequently well-educated or became prominent teachers.[60] On the other hand, it is clear that they might partake in the education that made a full-fledged scholar, that they occasionally transmitted what they themselves had learned and received, and that their company included ulama of the highest stature.

What the network of schools provided, therefore, was an institutional structure that allowed many men who were not, strictly speaking, scholars, nonetheless to live on the periphery of the world of higher Islamic education. Many of the lower-ranking functionaries of these institutions, like the muezzin Ibn Sukkur, no doubt found it impossible to live exclusively on their meager stipends and supplemented their incomes with outside employment.[61] The important point, however, is that they were drawn into the academic world, and in the fluid situation in most madrasas and teaching mosques, in which students and even teachers might come and go with a fair degree of freedom, they had an opportunity to study or even teach. A gatekeeper at the Muʾayyadiyya might have studied the classical Arabic language, while a simple Quran reader could study ḥadīth and issue an ijāza to a scholar of the stature of the historian

[58] Al-Sakhāwī, *al-Ḍawʾ*, 3:119.

[59] Al-Sakhāwī, *al-Ḍawʾ*, 2:33–34; Ibn Ḥajar al-ʿAsqalānī, *al-Majmaʿ al-muʾassas biʾl-muʿjam al-mufahras*, Dār al-Kutub al-Miṣriyya, "Muṣṭalaḥ" No. 75, pp. 69–70. Among the works of ḥadīth which Ibn Ḥajar reports that Ibn Sukkur transmitted are: the *Ṣaḥīḥ* of Muslim ibn al-Ḥajjāj, the *ʿUmdat al-aḥkam*, and the *Kitāb al-shifā* (on which works, see below).

[60] Petry's survey apparently revealed no professors who were also muezzins; *Civilian Elite*, 375. Presumably his pool of professors did not include those who, like al-Qaymarī, were professors of farāʾiḍ.

[61] Ira Lapidus, *Muslim Cities in the Later Middle Ages* (Cambridge, Mass., 1967), 139.

al-Sakhāwī.[62] A gatekeeper and Quran reader of the first half of the fifteenth century "studied a little jurisprudence and Arabic" and heard Ibn Ḥajar, Walī 'l-Dīn al-ʿIrāqī, and other prominent scholars recite ḥadīth, and eventually himself read traditions to the common people at al-Azhar and elsewhere.[63] Even a *muzammalātī*, charged with supplying water to a khānqāh, studied both law and ḥadīth, memorized basic works on traditions and Shāfiʿi law, heard the recitation of ḥadīth by some of the most respected transmitters of his day, and himself issued an ijāza to al-Sakhāwī.[64] In men such as these, the boundaries between the ulama and the common people became blurred and indistinct. They belonged to the world of education just as legitimately, if not as exclusively, as those whose lives were devoted to scholarship and teaching. Through them, the process of transmitting Islamic religious knowledge reached ever more deeply into the fabric of urban Muslim life.

Madrasas and Mosques as Centers of Public Instruction

The social networks through which knowledge was transmitted also included large numbers of urban Muslims who had no formal ties at all to the world of institutional education, who relied not at all upon employment in those institutions, and who held no promise for any career in education. It included, in other words, the common people of the city. As we saw above, instruction in madrasas, teaching mosques, and khānqāhs was by no means limited to those actually resident in the institutions. Well over half of those receiving stipends from a school's endowments might actually reside somewhere other than the school, as at the khānqāh of Jamāl al-Dīn al-Ustādār, where only 20 of the school's 113 Sufi students lived on the premises. But more importantly, there was nothing to prevent many from attending an institution's teaching circles who did not even receive a stipend from the school's endowments. In this fluid

[62] For example, ʿAbd al-Qādir b. Abī Bakr al-Shāfiʿī, who "studied a little and read in [the subject of] Arabic" (*ishtaghala yasīran wa-qara'a fī'l-ʿarabiyya*), but who became best known for his poetry; and Ibrāhīm b. Aḥmad al-Muqri', who issued an ijāza to al-Sakhāwī; see, respectively, al-Sakhāwī, *al-Ḍaw'*, 4:264–65, 1:30.

[63] Shams al-Dīn Muḥammad Ibn al-Shaykh ʿAlī al-Makhbazī; see al-Sakhāwī, *al-Ḍaw'*, 8:195–96; cf. Petry, *Civilian Elite*, 264.

[64] Shihāb al-Dīn Aḥmad al-Shāfiʿī al-Muzammalātī; see al-Sakhāwī, *al-Ḍaw'*, 2:99. His biographer referred to the works that he memorized simply as *al-ʿUmda* and *al-Tanbīh*. The former is probably a reference to Taqī 'l-Dīn ʿAbd al-Ghanī al-Jammāʿīlī's (d. 1203) collection of traditions about the Prophet, *ʿUmdat al-aḥkām ʿan sayyid al-anām*; cf. Ḥājjī Khalīfa, *Kashf al-ẓunūn ʿan asāmī 'l-kutub wa'l-funūn* (Istanbul, 1941–43), 2:1164–65. The latter may refer to Ibrāhīm b. ʿAlī al-Shīrāzī (d. 1083), *al-Tanbīh fī furūʿ al-shāfiʿiyya*, a popular compendium of Shāfiʿī law; cf. ibid., 1:489–93, and *Encyclopedia of Islam*, 1st edition, s.v."al-Shīrāzī."

situation, with many from the surrounding community coming to the schools for prayers, sermons, or even medicinal cures, professors might find themselves instructing many besides those young students formally "enrolled" and planning an academic or juristic career: other scholars, part-time students, or members of the local community simply pursuing a pious interest in the Islamic sciences.

The fact is that madrasas, khānqāhs, and teaching mosques, while training a group of students who would go on to form the academic and judicial elite, fulfilled a secondary educational function of providing instruction at a variety of levels to the broader Muslim community. Consider, for example, the following passage from Ibn al-Ḥājj's (d. 1336–37) treatise *al-Madkhal*:

> It is desirable [that the scholar] in a madrasa, as has been described in a mosque, be humble and approachable to any student or any other who attends him, and that he forbid no one from among the common people [to approach him], because if religious knowledge is forbidden to the common people, the elite [*al-khāṣṣa*, i.e., the ulama] will not benefit from it either, as has been explained. To lock the door of a madrasa is to shut out the masses and prevent them from hearing the [recitation of] knowledge [*al-istimāʿ li'l-ʿilm*] and being blessed by it and by its people [i.e., the ulama]. The doorkeeper, too, [should exclude no one], since to do so is a barrier to knowledge and a restriction of it, as has been explained. On the contrary, let the door be opened and forbid no one of God's creatures to enter, just as if it were a mosque.[65]

The thrust of Ibn al-Ḥājj's remarks, both in this passage and elsewhere in his treatise, is that nothing and no one should prevent the broad Muslim populace from attending lessons and teaching circles, whether in madrasas, mosques, or other venues. Of course, the very fact that Ibn al-Ḥājj condemned efforts to exclude the common people from participating in, or at least attending, teaching circles suggests that some scholars did precisely that. On this point, however, Ibn al-Ḥājj's views were by no means extreme, and corresponded to the best opinion of mainstream Muslim scholars, jurists, and educators. Two years after Ibn al-Ḥājj's death, the prominent Shāfiʿī jurist Taqī 'l-Dīn al-Subkī issued a *fatwā* (legal opinion) in which he forbade a scholar who held an endowed teaching post in one mosque to move his teaching circle to the larger mosque of ʿAmr ibn al-ʿĀṣ in al-Fusṭāṭ. In doing so, al-Subkī stressed the right of the people of a particular location to the benefits of a lesson endowed in their neighborhood:

[65] Ibn al-Ḥājj, *Madkhal*, 2:104.

> It is required of a teaching position [*tadrīs al-ʿilm*] [established] in a particular place that it propagate knowledge in that place and spread it among the people [of that place], for there may be among them one who cannot attend [a lesson] in another spot. . . . Whether a teaching position is [established] in a mosque or madrasa or other [institution], the people of that locale have a right to it, and when it is transported and moved to another place, their right is transgressed.[66]

Instructing the general Muslim population in the fundamentals of their religion formed, at least in theory, one of the primary duties of the educated class. Much of the substantive content of that knowledge which was transmitted—knowledge embedded in the ḥadīth and in legal textbooks—was of direct service to each and every Muslim in setting the course of his or her life and in establishing guidelines for his or her relationships with God and with fellow Muslims. A Mamluk-period treatise on education compared the scholar to "a skillful doctor who employs serious medicine, applying it only where necessary and to the extent necessary, . . . so as to resist the corruption of the beliefs of the common people."[67] Consequently, an important fifteenth-century scholar could comment of another who "sat with the common people and elucidated to them many things of importance to religion" that "you have relieved us of a duty incumbent on the Muslim community [*farḍ kifāya*]."[68]

Schools in fact provided a wide range of educational services to the surrounding community. Several schools of the Mamluk period hired men to instruct others in the Quran or how to write Arabic. The mosque of Ibn Ṭūlūn, for example, employed a *ḥāfiẓ*—one who knew the Quran by heart—to "teach the book of God to whoever desires it." A document appended to the endowment deed of the madrasa of Sultan Barqūq directed the controller of the institution to appoint one "knowledgeable in the rules of writing Arabic script" who was to sit in the madrasa every day and assist whoever asked for instruction in learning how to write.[69] The student stipendiaries of Ibn Ṭūlūn and the Ẓāhiriyya would presumably have learned both the Quran and how to write well before beginning their advanced studies, and both institutions contained separate *maktabs* (primary schools) for the instruction of younger pupils. It seems likely,

[66] Taqī ʾl-Dīn ʿAlī al-Subkī, *Fatāwā ʾl-Subkī* (Cairo, A.H. 1356; reptd. Beirut, n.d.), 1:480.

[67] Muḥammad b. ʿAbd al-Raḥmān al-ʿUthmānī, *Īḍāḥ al-taʿrīf bi-baʿḍ faḍāʾil al-ʿilm al-sharīf*, Princeton University Library, Yahuda Ms. No. 4293, fol. 20r.

[68] Al-Sakhāwī, *al-Ḍawʾ*, 2:204–5.

[69] *Waqfiyyat* al-Manṣūr Lājīn, Dār al-Wathāʾiq No. 17, ll. 320–22; *Waqfiyyat* al-Ẓāhir Barqūq, Dār al-Wathāʾiq No. 51. The document in question, coming at the end of the scroll, is incomplete, and no date for it survives; however, it immediately follows one dated 3 Shaʿbān, A.H. 797.

therefore, that many of those availing themselves of this instruction would have been residents of the quarters in which these schools were found. At the madrasa complex of Sultan al-Ghawrī, the man hired to teach writing (*waẓīfat al-taktīb*) was explicitly instructed to direct his efforts to *al-nās*, a term that here seems to refer to the general population.[70] Similarly, the primary school teacher attached to the madrasa of Jawhar al-Lālā was required, in addition to his normal duties in the school's maktab, to instruct Sufis "and others" in the art of writing.[71]

The biographical dictionaries tell us little about the individuals who earned a living teaching the art of writing and calligraphy. Of Khaṭṭāb b. ʿUmar al-Mukattib (d. 1486), for example, we know only that he studied the Quran, ḥadīth, and the Arabic language, and that his education sufficed to qualify him to hold minor religious positions, such as Quran reader in the mosque of Uzbak al-Ẓāhirī, as well as "the post for teaching writing" (*al-taṣaddur li'l-taktīb*) at that institution. Another instructor in writing, Aybak b. ʿAbd Allāh al-Turkī (d. 1374–75), was, judging by his name, a member of the Mamluk military caste rather than the educated civilian elite. We know only that he studied the art of writing from Fakhr al-Dīn al-Sinbāṭī, and that he so excelled in the field that "he was appointed to the madrasa of Umm al-Sultān, there to teach calligraphy [*al-khaṭṭ*] to the people."[72] The very fact, however, that Ibn Ḥajar al-ʿAsqalānī, al-Sakhāwī, and the other biographers record little or no information about the education and careers of such men suggests that they belonged, if at all, to the lowest ranks of the educated class.

At a slightly more sophisticated level, there existed a cadre of minor scholars who supported themselves, in whole or in part, by delivering simple lessons to the masses of the Muslim population who were not full-time students, or by reading to them from introductory religious and legal texts. The sources refer to such individuals as the *quṣṣāṣ* (sing. *qāṣṣ*), "narrators" or "storytellers" who sat or stood in the streets of the city, reciting from memory verses of the Quran, or traditions of the Prophet, or stories of the pious early Muslims.[73] The quṣṣāṣ, of course, had been active in Muslim societies for centuries, and not always with blameless reputations. Drawing on both ḥadīth and popular anecdotes and catering

[70] *Waqfiyyat* Qānṣūh al-Ghawrī, Wizārat al-Awqāf o.s. No. 882, pp. 202–3. In the context, it seems likely that the term *al-nās* refers simply to the people, rather than to the Mamluks, whom it often signified in medieval literature.

[71] *Waqfiyyat* Jawhar al-Lālā, Dār al-Wathā'iq No. 86, document dated 10 Jumādā al-Thānī, A.H. 836, l. 85.

[72] Al-Sakhāwī, *al-Ḍaw'*, 3:181; Ibn Ḥajar, *al-Durar*, 1:450.

[73] Al-Subkī, *Muʿīd al-niʿam*, 162; cf. Makdisi, *Colleges*, 218. On the earlier history of the quṣṣāṣ, see Ignaz Goldziher, *Muslim Studies*, trans. C. R. Barber and S. M. Stern (London, 1971), 2:152ff.

to a wide audience, their recitations tended to the outlandish and the bizarre, and sometimes incurred the disapprobation of more rigorous and staid theologians and scholars. But the quṣṣāṣ also responded to a genuine if not altogether discriminating demand among the populace for knowledge and information of a religious character. In the Mamluk period, lessons delivered by the quṣṣāṣ resembled exhortatory sermons (*waʿẓ, khuṭba*) more closely than they did formal instruction in jurisprudence or another religious science, so that they were urged not to recite to the common people material that they would not understand, such as complicated questions of theology, but to concentrate on simple matters such as fasting, prayer, and the alms tax.

More rigorous still, and more closely tied to the various textual traditions of the scholarly community and to institutions of education, was the instruction offered by the *qāriʾ al-kursī*, literally "the reader of the chair." This figure sat in mosques, madrasas, or khānqāhs, and read (as opposed to the qāṣṣ, who recited from memory) from various books of the religious sciences: ḥadīth, Quranic commentaries, and traditions describing exemplary Muslim behavior (*kutub al-raqāʾiq*). Here again, his audience consisted chiefly of common people not connected formally to institutions of learning. Like the qāṣṣ, he was enjoined to read from books that his listeners would understand easily, and that would not frighten them. Tāj al-Dīn al-Subkī (d. 1370), for example, in his work *Muʿīd al-niʿam wa-mubīd al-niqam* ("The Restorer of Blessings and Destroyer of Misfortunes"), gave a list of works from which he felt the qāriʾ al-kursī could appropriately read; they included collections of sermons (*kutub al-waʿẓ*) and al-Nawawī's popular compendium of ḥadīth, the *Riyāḍ al-ṣāliḥīn*, but also al-Ghazālī's famous work of religious exposition, *Iḥyāʾ ʿulūm al-dīn.*[74]

Although they are not always referred to as qāriʾ al-kursī, quite a few Muslims in the Mamluk period spent their time teaching or "reading to the common people" from basic books of ḥadīth, exegesis, etc. Karīm al-Dīn ʿAbd al-Karīm al-Shāfiʿī (d. 1474), for example, "read from *al-Targhīb waʾl-tarhīb* and *al-Tadhkira* and the like to the common people in the mosque of the Moroccans, and perhaps," al-Sakhāwī adds, "he delivered the Friday sermon there."[75] It was possible to earn a living at least

[74] Al-Subkī, *Muʿīd al-niʿam*, 162–63; Makdisi, *Colleges*, 218.

[75] Al-Sakhāwī, *al-Ḍawʾ*, 4:318. *Al-Targhīb* refers to Zakī ʾl-Dīn ʿAbd al-ʿAzīz al-Mundhirī's (d. 1250) collection of ḥadīth of a primarily ethical nature, drawn from the larger compendia, entitled *al-Targhīb waʾl-tarhīb min al-ḥadīth al-sharīf*. See Ḥājjī Khalīfa, *Kashf al-ẓunūn*, 1:400; cf. Goldziher, *Muslim Studies*, 2:248. Identifying *al-Tadhkira* is more problematic. Clearly it was a popular work; al-Sakhāwī felt that the abbreviated reference he gave would suffice to identify the work in the minds of his readers. Ḥājjī Khalīfa, *Kashf al-ẓunūn*, 1:383–93, lists eighty-nine works whose titles begin with the word *tadhkira*. Of

partially through this activity, presumably through fees charged to or voluntary donations from those attending the recitations. Aḥmad b. Mūsā al-Matbūlī, for example, whose wide-ranging education embraced the subjects of jurisprudence, exegesis, the foundations of jurisprudence, ḥadīth, rhetoric, and the Arabic language, earned a living "reading to the common people," as well as by delivering the Friday sermon and as a *shāhid*, a notary who transacted minor legal affairs. But some scholars who held endowed teaching posts in prestigious schools also devoted their free time to the informal instruction of the Muslim masses, as did Aḥmad b. ʿAlī b. Aḥmad al-Maydāwī, who held the professorship in Ḥanbalī law at the Ashrafiyya madrasa, but who was also popular among the citizens of Cairo for reading to them from works of ḥadīth and exegesis.[76]

It is the qāri' al-kursī who mosts interests us, since he was specifically a figure who operated in institutions of learning in Mamluk Cairo. Clearly his activities, directed at the general Muslim population, had an exhortatory purpose; one modern scholar has even labeled him a "preacher."[77] But what this shows us more than anything else is how, as education became less rigorous and more accessible to a wider audience, the boundaries between it and the parallel Muslim tradition of preaching and exhortation blurred.

The terms were never, to my knowledge, equated in the contemporary sources, but in fact the qāri' al-kursī's function, as described by al-Subkī, was replicated in the post known as the *mīʿād* (literally, "appointment" or "appointed time"), as it was established in a number of schools. The mīʿād could be held simply by a reader (qāri'), who would read his texts aloud, or jointly by a reader and a shaykh who would listen, approve, and explain. At the khānqāh of Mughulṭāy al-Jamālī, for example, the Ḥanafī shaykh was required, following afternoon prayers on Friday, to undertake the position of:

> teacher [*mutaṣaddir*] of general instruction [*mīʿād ʿāmm*] in the large recessed hall [facing Mecca]. A reader of good voice, from among the twenty

---

these, a number can be discarded immediately as belonging to the post-Mamluk period, or because they were written in Turkish or Persian. Of the remainder, three seem to be the most likely candidates to be that which Karīm al-Dīn read to the common people of Cairo. They are: Sirāj al-Dīn ʿUmar Ibn al-Mulaqqin (d. 1401), a prominent Egyptian Shāfiʿī scholar, *al-Tadhkira fī ʿulūm al-ḥadīth*, on the science of the traditions; or idem, *al-Tadhkira fī 'l-furūʿ ʿalā madhhab al-shāfiʿī*, a textbook of Shāfiʿī law; or Shams al-Dīn Muḥammad al-Qurṭubī (d. 1272), *al-Tadhkira bi-umūr al-ākhira*, a collection of traditions relating to heaven, hell, the day of judgment, and the coming of the *Mahdī* (see *Encyclopedia of Islam*, 2nd edition, s.v. "al-Ḳurṭubī" and "al-Mahdī").

76 Al-Sakhāwī, *al-Ḍaw'*, 2:9–11, 228.

77 Makdisi, *Colleges*, 218.

Sufis of the khānqāh, shall be appointed with him, and he shall read, in the presence of the shaykh and whoever might attend from among the general Muslim populace, what seems appropriate to him from books of Quranic exegesis, from books of reliable and well-known ḥadīth, and from books of traditions of an exhortatory purpose [*kutub al-raqā'iq wa'l-adhkār*].[78]

This stipulation from the khānqāh's deed of endowment highlights two important points: first, that many besides those formally enrolled in the classes, and implicitly many who were not full-time students, attended the mīʿād sessions; and second, that the transmission and explication of at least basic works of scholarship formed the core element of this popular Muslim religious experience.

What, exactly, did the mīʿād represent? A precise definition is elusive, and it may be that the sessions varied significantly from one institution to another, but certain common features can be identified. Fundamentally, it provided a more or less structured opportunity for the transmission of some of the basic texts of Muslim learning to the common people of Cairo. Naturally, ḥadīth formed one important element in the materials available and appropriate to the shaykh al-mīʿād, and the popularity of the Prophetic traditions both as a source for practical normative guidelines and as texts for pious recitation gave them a special weight. Mīʿād sessions, however, provided scope for the introduction of materials from other fields of learning as well, and the texts recited and commented upon were not limited to ḥadīth.[79] At the Ẓāhiriyya madrasa of Sultan Barqūq, for example, it was the professor of Quranic exegesis who also functioned as the shaykh al-mīʿād, and not the professor of ḥadīth.[80]

Eventually the post became one of the most common features of Mamluk schools. Every Tuesday from noon until the call to afternoon prayers at the madrasa of Zayn al-Dīn al-Ustādār, the qāri' al-mīʿād was to read from and discuss books of Quranic exegesis, ḥadīth, and the accounts of pious early Muslims (*akhbār al-ṣāliḥīn*). The qāri' al-mīʿād at the mosque of Sūdūn min Zāda undertook similar responsibilities, although he held his sessions after congregational prayers on Friday. Friday afternoons were also set aside at the Ẓāhiriyya madrasa for the mīʿād session. There, after the qāri' had read aloud certain chapters of the Quran and appropriate passages from exegetical works and the collections of ḥadīth, the shaykh al-mīʿād discoursed on and explained what those assembled had heard. The madrasa of Sultan Ḥasan, like the Ẓāhiriyya and the khānqāh

[78] *Waqfiyyat* Mughulṭāy al-Jamālī, Wizārat al-Awqāf o.s. No. 1666, ll. 381–89.

[79] Compare Makdisi, *Colleges*, 213, where he links the mīʿād sessions closely to the transmission of ḥadīth.

[80] *Waqfiyyat* al-Ẓāhir Barqūq, Dār al-Wathā'iq No. 51, the second document on the scroll, dated 6 Dhū'l-Qaʿda, A.H. 788.

of Mughulṭāy al-Jamālī, employed both a qāri' who read and a shaykh who expounded on the Quran, ḥadīth, exegetical works, and exhortatory traditions. In this more august institution, however, the mīʿād met four times a week, including a session after Friday congregational prayers. Even institutions that did not specifically appoint a "shaykh al-mīʿād" hired functionaries who effectively discharged the same duties. At the zāwiya of Zayn al-Dīn Ṣidqa, the professor was required to hold twice-weekly sessions that, although not referred to as mīʿād in the deed of endowment, effectively functioned as appointments for public instruction: in addition to the four days on which he gave formal lessons, the professor was to sit and read to those assembled from books of exegesis, ḥadīth, and accounts of pious Muslims. At the great teaching mosque of Ibn Ṭūlūn, a Shāfiʿī scholar (*faqīh*) was appointed, along with a reader, to hold special sessions on three days (Fridays, Sundays, and Wednesdays) each week, in which they would read aloud from books of exegesis, ḥadīth, and stories of the pious.[81]

It appears, then, that the post of mīʿād in institutions of learning in the Mamluk period conflated with the less formal responsibilities of the qāri' al-kursī. Both directed their attention broadly to the entire Muslim population, and both used basic books of ḥadīth, Quranic exegesis, sermons, and the like to instruct their audience as well as exhort them to a more pious life. Al-Subkī, in his *Muʿīd al-niʿam*, failed to mention the post of shaykh (or qāri') al-mīʿād; his omission is surprising because virtually every other educational, religious, and administrative post connected with institutions of learning received his critical attention. If the shaykh al-mīʿād performed essentially the same functions as the qāri' al-kursī, as the deeds of endowment for various madrasas and mosques suggest, the absence of the former from al-Subkī's work appears less puzzling.

From the middle of the fourteenth century, exactly the time in which al-Subkī wrote his treatise, the mīʿād appeared with increasing frequency in a number of Cairene schools as an endowed post. In addition to the institutions in the foregoing discussion, we know that scholars received appointments as shaykhs of the mīʿād at the Aljayhiyya, Baqariyya, Ḥijāziyya, and Sābiqiyya madrasas, and at the Ḥākimī mosque and

81 *Waqfiyyat* Zayn al-Dīn al-Ustādār, Dār al-Wathā'iq No. 110, ll. 1251–56; *Waqfiyyat* Sūdūn min Zāda, Dār al-Wathā'iq No. 58, ll. 268–70; *Waqfiyyat* al-Ẓāhir Barqūq, Dār al-Wathā'iq No. 51, the second document on the scroll (dated 6 Dhū 'l-Qaʿda, A.H. 788), ll. 74–78; *Waqfiyyat* al-Nāṣir Ḥasan, Wizārat al-Awqāf o.s. No. 881, pp. 443–44; cf. Amīn's edition, in Ibn Ḥabīb, *Tadhkirat al-nabīh*, 3:400; *Waqfiyyat* Zayn al-Dīn Ṣidqa, Dār al-Wathā'iq No. 59, ll. 121–25; Waqfiyyat al-Manṣūr Lājīn, Dār al-Wathā'iq No. 17, ll. 350–59.

that of al-Ẓāhir Baybars in the Ḥusayniyya district north of Cairo.[82] A full *mashyakhat al-mīʿād* (the post the shaykh held) was an important and lucrative position, usually paying more than that of the qāriʾ who, in general, simply read the texts without commenting on them. At the Ḥasaniyya, as at other schools, he received the same monthly salary (300 dirhams) as the professors of jurisprudence, ḥadīth, and exegesis; the qāriʾ, by contrast, received only 40 dirhams per month.[83]

Not surprisingly, becoming a shaykh al-mīʿād required considerable training, as did any other educational post. A student might request the "permission" of a well-known scholar to function as a shaykh al-mīʿād, as he did to secure authority to hold a regular teaching post. Ibn Ḥajar al-ʿAsqalānī, for example, issued an ijāza to ʿAbd al-Raḥmān b. ʿAlī al-Qāhirī (d. 1457) and "granted him permission, according to his request, to undertake the mīʿād."[84] The deed of the Ḥasaniyya madrasa required that the institution's shaykh al-mīʿād be a recognized teacher (*mutaṣaddir*) and *muftī*, (i.e., a jurisconsult authorized to issue legal opinions).[85] Shaykhs who held the mīʿād at Cairene schools included several of the more important Muslim educators of the Mamluk capital. At the Ẓāhiriyya, where the professor of Quranic exegesis functioned also as shaykh al-mīʿād, the joint appointment was held throughout much of the late fourteenth and early fifteenth centuries by successive members of the Bulqīnī family, including Sirāj al-Dīn ʿUmar, arguably the most prominent scholar of his generation, and his sons Jalāl al-Dīn ʿAbd al-Raḥmān and ʿAlam al-Dīn Ṣāliḥ; the latter also was shaykh al-mīʿād at the madrasa of Sultan Ḥasan.[86] The family of Sirāj al-Dīn ʿUmar Ibn al-Mulaqqin, too, held a monopoly on the mīʿād at the Sābiqiyya madrasa for almost a century from its foundation in the 1370s. ʿUmar, a leading scholar of jurisprudence and ḥadīth, was shaykh al-mīʿād and professor of Shāfiʿī law at the Sābiqiyya until his death in 1401. His son, Nūr al-Dīn ʿAlī, followed ʿUmar in both positions, even though he was not, in the words of one contemporary scholar, "his father's equal." ʿAlī died in 1405, and his more accomplished son Jalāl al-Dīn ʿAbd al-Raḥmān succeeded to

[82] Examples of those who held the post of mīʿād at these institutions can be found in al-Maqrīzī, *Khiṭaṭ*, 2:278, 391, and al-Sakhāwī, *al-Ḍawʾ*, 1:162, 2:189, 3:234–38, 4:101–02, 106–13, 246–47.

[83] *Waqfiyyat* al-Nāṣir Ḥasan, Wizārat al-Awqāf, o.s. No. 881, pp. 443–44; in Amīn's edition, in Ibn Ḥabīb, *Tadhkirat al-nabīh*, 3:400.

[84] Al-Sakhāwī, *al-Ḍawʾ*, 4:97. The phrase (*adhina lahu . . . fī ʿamal al-mīʿād*) parallels exactly that often used for the action of granting a student permission to teach (*adhina lahu fīʾl-tadrīs*).

[85] *Waqfiyyat* al-Nāṣir Ḥasan, Wizārat al-Awqāf o.s. No. 881, p. 444; in Amīn's edition, in Ibn Ḥabīb, *Tadhkirat al-nabīh*, 3:400.

[86] Al-Sakhāwī, *al-Ḍawʾ*, 3:313, 4:106–13, 6:85–90; al-Maqrīzī, *al-Sulūk*, 3:814.

both the professorship and the mīʿād, holding them until his own death in 1466.[87]

The chronicles and biographical dictionaries of the period offer more examples of prominent scholars and educators who held posts as shaykhs of the mīʿād. The point, however, is to demonstrate that, through this institution, pious and interested Muslims who had not devoted their lives solely to the study of the holy law and the religious sciences nonetheless had contact of an instructional nature with the leading scholars and educators of the day. This is not to say that the objectives and methods of the mīʿād necessarily mirrored the more rigorous instruction received by full-time students: the purpose of the mīʿād, after all, was as much exhortatory as anything else. But neither were they entirely dissimilar. The books of ḥadīth and exegesis that were read and expounded upon in the mīʿād also formed part of the curriculum of a full-time student of the Islamic sciences. Organized lessons met less frequently at several schools than did the mīʿād at the madrasa of Sultan Ḥasan, although, admittedly, no one was required to attend the more "public" sessions of the mīʿād. Judging by the guidelines laid down in their deeds of endowment, classes at a number of the smaller and less well-endowed schools of Mamluk Cairo were hardly more rigorous than were many mīʿād sessions. The mīʿād, in fact, represented one end of a broad instructional spectrum, through which many nonscholars could enter the arena of and take part in Islamic education.

The Transmission of Ḥadīth as a Community Activity

In no field of intellectual endeavor did the general Muslim population participate more actively than in the transmission of ḥadīth. The Prophetic traditions formed one of the bases, and in many ways the most critical one, of Islamic law. At this level, the serious study of ḥadīth constituted an important element in any jurist's or scholar's education. One might specialize in ḥadīth as a distinct subject of study, as did no small number of prominent and accomplished scholars of the Mamluk period—Ibn Ḥajar al-ʿAsqalānī and Sirāj al-Dīn ʿUmar al-Bulqīnī, for example, to recall two whom we have already had occasion to mention. As we have seen, a number of prominent Cairene schools provided separate endowed professorships for instruction in ḥadīth, as well as stipends for students to attend the classes. In other, smaller and less rigorous schools,

[87] Al-Sakhāwī, *al-Ḍaw'*, 4:101–2, 5:267–68, 6:100–105. The negative assessment of ʿAlī's abilities belonged to Badr al-Dīn al-ʿAynī; it is possible, of course, that his judgment was clouded by ʿAlī's close friendship with the jurist and historian al-Maqrīzī, with whom al-ʿAynī conducted a well-publicized feud.

ḥadīth was counted among the subjects taught in a more general curriculum.

But the recitation of ḥadīth, legal, moral, and exhortatory, traced through chains of authorities to the Prophet or his Companions, also formed an important element in the broader forum of Muslim piety and worship. The act of publicly and piously pronouncing the recorded words of Muḥammad possessed, in the popular eye, extraordinary efficacy and power. Once, according to al-Sakhāwī, the historian of fifteenth-century scholars, jurists, and other luminaries,

> it happened that Aleppo was besieged. One of its inhabitants saw al-Sirāj al-Bulqīnī in a dream, and [the famous traditionist] said to him: "Let not the people of Aleppo fear. Rather, go to the servant of the *sunna* [the customs and traditions of the Prophet and of his community] Ibrāhīm [Sibt Ibn al-ʿAjamī] the *muḥaddith*, and tell him to read customs and *ʿUmdat al-Aḥkām* [a popular collection of ḥadīth] so that God might liberate the Muslims." The man awoke and informed the shaykh [Ibrāhīm], who hurried to read the prescribed book to a group of students and others in the Sharafiyya madrasa on Friday morning, after which he prayed for the safe release of the Muslims. And it so happened that at the end of that day, God gave victory to the people of Aleppo.[88]

Similarly, when a plague struck the city of Cairo in 1388, the Shāfiʿī chief qāḍī called together a group of men to al-Azhar to read the *Ṣaḥīḥ* of al-Bukhārī and pray for deliverance. After two weeks, al-Bukhārī's collection of traditions was read for a second time, in the Ḥākimī mosque, and again three days later in al-Azhar with, interestingly enough, a group of children and orphans.[89] Even under less unusual circumstances, the recitation of ḥadīth served as the centerpiece of public celebration, for example at ceremonies marking the dedication of a new educational or religious institution. Thus on the occasion of the opening of Sultan al-Nāṣir Muḥammad's khānqāh at Siryāqūs north of Cairo, Badr al-Dīn Muḥammad Ibn Jamāʿa presided over a session in which his son, ʿIzz al-Dīn ʿAbd al-ʿAzīz, recited twenty traditions. The sultan and those assembled listened to the recitation, at the end of which Ibn Jamāʿa issued ijāzas to all those present.[90]

That the scholars reciting traditions at such sessions, or supervising their recitation by others, issued ijāzas to those present, testifies to the

[88] Al-Sakhāwī, *al-Ḍaw'*, 1:142. The collection of ḥadīth referred to is probably *ʿUmdat al-aḥkām min kalām khayr al-anām*, by Taqī 'l-Dīn ʿAbd al-Ghanī al-Maqdisī al-Jammāʿīlī (d. 1203); cf. Brockelmann, *Geschichte der Arabischen Litteratur* (Leiden, 1937–49), 1:356, Suppl. I, 605.

[89] Al-Maqrīzī, *al-Sulūk*, 3:577.

[90] Al-Maqrīzī, *Khiṭaṭ*, 2:422.

seriousness with which participants approached the occasions. Such sessions may have been primarily devotional, and did not, perhaps, provide the setting for rigorous instruction found in madrasas and mosques that offered organized classes in ḥadīth. At the mosque of Ibn Ṭūlūn, for example, a more gradual and methodical approach was taken, and the institution's students of ḥadīth were required to memorize at least one tradition per day.[91] The occasional public recitation of ḥadīth did provide, however, a forum in which large and varied segments of the community would gather to display their piety and demonstrate their interest in this particular form of Islamic learning.

No doubt the vast majority of Muslims heard the recitation of ḥadīth, if at all, from men and women of relatively inferior education and transmitters of no special reputation. Shihāb al-Dīn Aḥmad al-Nāsikh (d. 1479) was perhaps typical of such transmitters. Having received a basic education in the religious sciences he became a scribe, known for the speed rather than the accuracy of his writing. At other stages of his career he led prayers and delivered Friday sermons at several Cairene mosques, and also acted as a legal notary. But most importantly for our purposes, this Shihāb al-Dīn regularly "read ḥadīth to the common people in one [or several] of the mosques" (*qara'a al-ḥadīth ʿalā 'l-ʿāmma bi-baʿḍ al-jawāmiʿ*). The biographical dictionaries contain frequent references to such minor ulama, the extent of whose education was not wide, and who may or may not have held minor religious, legal, or instructional posts, but who informally read or recited ḥadīth to the general Muslim population.[92]

On the other hand, a budding young scholar, early in his career, might read ḥadīth to the common people before his appointment to permanent and more lucrative educational or legal posts. Shihāb al-Dīn Aḥmad Ibn Asad (d. 1468), for example, eventually became a prominent muḥaddith and later held teaching positions in prestigious schools such as the madrasa of al-Ẓāhir Barqūq and the mosque of al-Mu'ayyad Shaykh, as well as the post of official reader of ḥadīth in the Citadel. At the outset of his career, however, while he was still earning a living instructing children in the Quran and functioning as a legal notary, he "read [in the mosque of al-Ḥākim] the *Ṣaḥīḥ* and the *Targhīb* and other [books of ḥadīth] to the common people."[93]

The various schools of Mamluk Cairo responded to this pervasive interest in ḥadīth shared by all Muslim inhabitants of the city, both scholars

[91] *Waqfiyyat* al-Manṣūr Lājīn, Dār al-Wathā'iq No. 17, ll. 327–32.

[92] Al-Sakhāwī, *al-Ḍaw'*, 2:20. For other examples, see ibid., 1:83–84, 2:303, 3:144–45.

[93] Ibid., 1:229. On the *Targhīb*, see above, note 75.

and laypersons. Madrasas, mosques, and khānqāhs routinely employed men knowledgeable in the subject to recite various collections of ḥadīth in organized public sessions separate from any formal classes. These recitations became a distinctive feature of religious celebration, especially during the months of Rajab, Shaʿbān, and Ramaḍān, and drew many members of the urban community into the corporate life of the schools. At the Ẓāhiriyya madrasa founded by Sultan Barqūq, for example, a qāriʾ was hired at 50 dirhams per year to recite the two principal collections of ḥadīth, the *Ṣaḥīḥ* of al-Bukhārī (d. 870) and that of Muslim ibn al-Ḥajjāj (d. 875), during Shaʿbān and Ramaḍān. In addition, an annual payment of 100 dirhams went to a *shaykh musammiʿ*, whose responsibility it was to attend and supervise the sessions at which the qāriʾ read the *Ṣaḥīḥs*. The school's deed of endowment therefore required that the shaykh be authorized to transmit the works through a strong chain of authorities (*sanad, isnād*). Two others were employed for similar purposes at the teaching mosque of Sūdūn min Zāda; their combined emolument totaled 300 dirhams per year, and their recitation was to spread itself across the three months of Rajab, Shaʿbān, and Ramaḍān.[94]

The deed of endowment for the teaching khānqāh of Jamāl al-Dīn al-Ustādār is especially instructive. Ḥadīth formed an important part of the school's curriculum, and the professorship was held at various times in the fifteenth century by such prominent transmitters as Ibn Ḥajar al-ʿAsqalānī, al-Taqī ʾl-Qalqashandī (d. 1466–67), and ʿAbd al-Barr Ibn al-Shiḥna (d. 1515–16).[95] There, the primary responsibility of the professor of ḥadīth was to instruct ten students in the subject. But during the months of Rajab, Shaʿbān, and Ramaḍān, he was also to

> supervise the reading [to] the students and whoever attends from among the Muslims of one of the [six] authoritative books of traditions [*al-kutub al-ṣiḥāḥ al-sanad*], except for the *Ṣaḥīḥ* of al-Bukhārī. From the beginning of the month of Rajab until the last day of Shaʿbān, one of the five books is to be read in his presence; in the month of Ramaḍān, the *Ṣaḥīḥ* of al-Bukhārī is to be read. For that [purpose], a qāriʾ is to be appointed who has experience and knowledge in reading ḥadīth, and he is to read them in order to the shaykh from a raised platform so that all who are present, those far and near, can hear [the recitation].[96]

[94] *Waqfiyyat* al-Ẓāhir Barqūq, Dār al-Wathāʾiq No. 51, ll. 1012–16; *Waqfiyyat* Sūdūn min Zāda, Dār al-Wathāʾiq No. 58, ll. 270–72.

[95] Al-Maqrīzī, *Khiṭaṭ*, 2:401–2; al-Sakhāwī, *al-Ḍawʾ*, 2:36–40, 4:33–35, 46–48.

[96] *Waqfiyyat* Jamāl al-Dīn al-Ustādār, Dār al-Wathāʾiq No. 106, ll. 87–91. The six authoritative collections included the *Ṣaḥīḥ* of al-Bukhārī and that of Muslim b. al-Ḥajjāj, the *Sunan* of Abū Dāʾūd (d. 888–89), the *Jāmiʿ* of al-Tirmidhī (d. 892–93), the *Sunan* of al-Nasāʾī (d. 915–16), and the *Sunan* of Ibn Māja (d. 896–97).

Such recitations became a standard feature of schools of higher education during the Mamluk period. Most commonly, the principal work recited was the *Ṣaḥīḥ* of al-Bukhārī, not infrequently supplemented by the *Ṣaḥīḥ* of Muslim; in at least one madrasa, however, the reciter of ḥadīth was also to read aloud another collection, *al-Shifā*.[97] In general, the recitations were spread out over the three months, culminating during the month-long fast of Ramaḍān, although they might, as at the madrasa of Barqūq, be limited to Shaʿbān and Ramaḍān.[98] Less frequently, a school's endowment might make provisions for the continual public recitation of the *Ṣaḥīḥ* of al-Bukhārī over the course of the entire year, as did Sultan Lājīn's for the mosque of Ibn Ṭūlūn.[99]

Several points need to be stressed. These recitations, whether lasting for two months or three, were clearly associated with the public religious celebration of the holy month of Ramaḍān, and were not necessarily a substitute for formal instruction in ḥadīth, at least in those schools that offered separate endowed courses in that subject. The daily recitation of the *Ṣaḥīḥ* of al-Bukhārī at Ibn Ṭūlūn, for example, in no way displaced the morning lesson in ḥadīth that a shaykh and his assistant delivered to twenty registered students.[100] Similarly, at the madrasa of Sultan al-Ẓāhir Barqūq, the endowment provided for a separate course in ḥadīth for fifteen students and their teacher. Yet the public recitation there during Shaʿbān and Ramaḍān of the *Ṣaḥīḥs* of al-Bukhārī and Muslim ibn al-Ḥajjāj was extraordinarily popular, and was attended by many of the citizens of Cairo.[101] Here, too, we may see a blurring of the boundaries between rigorous education and popular devotional activities.

Such public recitations may have been distinct from organized and endowed classes in ḥadīth, and were certainly attended by a larger and more varied assortment of people. But it was precisely on such public gatherings that many medieval Muslims relied for acquiring the "chains of authorities" (isnāds) that might make them prominent and sought-after transmitters of ḥadīth. That these sessions, even those which met only during the three months of Rajab, Shaʿbān, and Ramaḍān, were instituted for *both* instructional and devotional purposes is clear even from the terminology employed by several of the deeds of endowment, in

[97] ʿIyād b. Mūsā al-Yahsūbī (d. 1149), *al-Shifā bi-taʿrīf ḥuqūq al-muṣṭafā*; cf. Ḥājjī Khalīfa, *Kashf al-ẓunūn*, 2:1052–55. The madrasa in question was the Jawhariyya; *Waqfiyyat* Jawhar al-Lālā, Dār al-Wathā'iq No. 86, ll. 301–6.

[98] Cf. the khānqāh of Zayn al-Dīn Ṣidqa, *Waqfiyyat* Zayn al-Dīn Ṣidqa, Dār al-Wathā'iq No. 59, the second document on the scroll, dated 3 Muḥarram, A.H. 803, ll. 22ff.

[99] *Waqfiyyat* al-Manṣūr Lājīn, Dār al-Wathā'iq No. 17, ll. 365–71.

[100] *Waqfiyyat* al-Manṣūr Lājīn, Dār al-Wathā'iq No. 17, ll. 327–32.

[101] Al-Sakhāwī's biographical dictionary of fifteenth-century luminaries, *al-Ḍaw' al-lāmiʿ*, is full of references to those, many of them by no means well-educated, who "heard [the recitation of the *Ṣaḥīḥ* of] al-Bukhārī at the Ẓāhiriyya."

which the shaykh presiding over the session is called a *mutaṣaddir*, a teacher.[102] They are virtually indistinguishable from the sessions described by the Syrian scholar and historian Ibn Ḥabīb. He recorded that he attended in Aleppo a series of public sessions in which the traditionist Shams al-Dīn Muḥammad Ibn al-Naqīb (d. 1344–45) transmitted an important collection of ḥadīth to a group of Muslims from that city:

> I, along with a group of Aleppans, heard [from Ibn al-Naqīb] the entire *Sunan* of Abī Dā'ūd, on the authority of his *samāʿ* [the certificate that he had heard the book] from Jamāl al-Dīn Abī 'l-Ḥasan [in the presence of the famous traditionist] Ibn al-Bukhārī, in sixteen sessions, the last of which was on the second day of Muḥarram, in the year A.H. 731 [1330], in the ʿAṣrūniyya madrasa in Aleppo.

Most importantly, Ibn Ḥabīb noted, Ibn al-Naqīb "issued to us ijāzas for all that had been recited."[103]

Public sessions in madrasas and mosques, delivered during periods of religious festivity or at other times, while aiming at a larger audience and with partially devotional purposes, thus provided an opportunity for men and women[104] to acquire certificates testifying to their having heard a given collection of ḥadīth from a recognized transmitter, thereby earning for themselves a role in the transmission of this body of religious knowledge. The Ẓāhiriyya madrasa, for example, specifically provided for the employment of a *kātib ṭabaqāt al-muḥaddithīn* to record the names of those present at the public sessions, and what portions of the ḥadīth collections they had actually heard, proving conclusively that many attended these sessions to acquire certificates of audition (*samāʿs* or *ijāzāt al-samāʿ*) authorizing them to transmit what they had heard.[105] These sessions brought together scholars of varying credentials and broad segments of the urban Muslim population. The point is not to insist that the ʿāmma, the Muslim masses, were instrumental in the teaching of the traditions or were extensively educated. It is clear, however, that the transmission of this important field of Muslim learning took place in a very open world, one that drew no distinct boundaries between instruc-

[102] For example, *Waqfiyyat* Jamāl al-Dīn al-Ustādār, Dār al-Wathā'iq No. 106, l. 87; *Waqfiyyat* Zayn al-Dīn al-Ustādār, Dār al-Wathā'iq No. 110, ll. 1219–32.

[103] Ibn Ḥabīb, *Tadhkirat al-nabīh*, 3:67.

[104] Khadīja and Zaynab, daughters of Muḥibb al-Dīn Muḥammad al-Qādirī, were both brought by their father to hear the recitation of the *Ṣaḥīḥ* of al-Bukhārī in the Ẓāhiriyya; al-Sakhāwī, *al-Ḍaw'*, 12:31, 47. On the larger role of women in the transmission of ḥadīth, see Chapter Six.

[105] *Waqfiyyat* al-Ẓāhir Barqūq, Dār al-Wathā'iq No. 51, l. 1015. On the duties of the kātib ṭabaqāt al-muḥaddithīn, see Makdisi, *Colleges*, 141.

tion and devotion, and in which large and disparate groups of Muslims could and did participate.

The Transmission of Knowledge in a Diverse and Inclusive World

This book began by taking note of an extraordinary story about Imām al-Shāfiʿī and his intense devotion to learning and scholarship. It may be doubted whether all medieval Muslims felt the same attraction to knowledge and learning that led him to scorn a beautiful slave-girl in favor of long nights of reading and study. Few in any society, no doubt, are capable of such discipline. But this and all Islamic societies have always placed a supreme value on religious knowledge and its transmission, and as a result they have always exerted a powerful pull, in one form or another, on virtually every Muslim.

The inclusion of the broad spectrum of the Muslim population in the transmission of knowledge was perhaps an inevitable consequence of the very methods and system of education. For centuries in the medieval West, higher education, often even literacy itself, was the almost exclusive prerogative of a clerical elite consecrated to the service of an established Church. Islam, of course, has neither a church nor a clergy, and therefore lacks two fundamental impediments to broad social interest and participation in education. But that participation was secured even more firmly by the most basic values that guided the transmission of religious knowledge. In particular, the emphasis on personal as opposed to institutional contacts and relationships, and the unquestioned superiority of the spoken as opposed to the written word guaranteed the persistent openness and informality of the system of education.

This is not to say, of course, that there were no hierarchies or barriers that worked to limit access to knowledge, or at least to bar full participation in recognized channels of its transmission. Some of them perhaps grew out of the very importance attached to knowledge and, consequently, those most deeply engaged in its preservation and transmission: the complaint of Ibn al-Ḥājj that opened this chapter, about the ostentation and waste of the ulama's clothing, which effectively barred educational opportunities to the poor, provides a case in point. But the system of education itself, which developed over the Mamluk period into an awesome and wealthy network of schools and other institutions, threw up barriers of its own. In particular, the ability of the ulama to privilege their own sons, and later almost to guarantee their succession to their fathers' teaching positions, must have acted to set the learned apart as a formidable, if not entirely impenetrable, elite.

Such tendencies were countered, however, by a number of factors, not least of which was the extraordinary diversity of the schools themselves.

The vast range in the size, wealth, and quality of the schools, from immense and well-endowed madrasas such as that of Sultan Ḥasan to the tiny institutions that supported only a few students with their teacher, provided scope for the incorporation into the educational system of a large and diverse group of men. Each school hired any number of men trained to varying degrees in the religious sciences, and responsible for some activity deemed indispensable to an educational institution. Through such channels, not only full professors, but prayer leaders, preachers, librarians, Quran readers, gatekeepers, and others tied their fortunes directly to the institutional structure of education, and seized the opportunity in some way to participate in the transmission of knowledge. Moreover, the schools as public spaces provided forums for prayer and worship by members of the community at large; the distinction between learning and simple worship, already weakened by the values of Islamic religion, was blurred even further.

The active participation of the common people of Cairo in the transmission of knowledge, if a distinct phenomenon, nonetheless parallels the ability of Mamluks and women, comparative outsiders, to acquire for themselves a niche within the educational system. What all this suggests is that Muslim society in the later Middle Ages was far less segmented and divided than we might otherwise have thought. To be sure, linguistic and cultural barriers separated the Mamluks from local Cairenes; legal and social restrictions imposed upon Muslim women set them apart from their fathers, brothers, and husbands; efforts to secure the inheritance of teaching posts by the sons of their incumbents reinforced the collective identity of the educated elite. But education, if it did not obliterate those boundaries, at least rendered them porous and permeable. In a very real sense, education acted as a leveler. It did not transform a Mamluk into a native member of Cairene society, nor a woman into a man. But it did bring together in the public sphere groups that might otherwise have remained separated in their private worlds.

What made this possible was, above all, the personal and *oral* nature of the transmission of knowledge. Education in the medieval period was never framed by any system of institutional degrees. Despite the proliferation of schools devoted to the religious sciences, instruction was never limited to particular institutions: it could go on wherever a scholar sat down, and could be shared by all those to whom he chose to speak. It was its personal and oral character that, in some form, made education accessible to all.

But just as important was the very frame of mind in which this society approached its religious texts. Learning constituted the highest form of worship recognized by Muslim civilization. If one studied ḥadīth, for example (and it was ḥadīth that provided entry into the world of learning for many Mamluks, women, and others), one did so not only because they formed the most important basis of Islamic law. One studied these texts because to do so was itself a pious deed. Classes in any of the religious subjects routinely began with a long series of prayers, and could not be commenced unless all participating were in a state of ritual purity. One studied these texts because their very pronunciation contained a reservoir of enormous power, capable, as we have seen, of defeating Mongol armies and warding off the dreaded plague. One studied these texts because they provided a convenient and recognized model on which to pattern one's own life. To transmit them to others, to Mamluks, women, and common people, as well as to full-time students, was to transmit a body of information valuable to each and every Muslim.

It was factors such as these that encouraged every Muslim to seek out, to *hear* books and traditions recited. Mamluks, common people, and women, as well as the academic elite, all participated, on some level, in the transmission of the texts that embodied Muslim learning. This world of education, broadly conceived, possessed an extraordinary diversity. This very diversity may have bothered some, who felt that broad participation would threaten the integrity of Muslim learning. But from another perspective, that diversity stands as one of the monumental achievements of this medieval civilization.

BIBLIOGRAPHY

WAQFIYYAS

The *waqfiyyas* (deeds of endowment) on which much of this study was based are housed in three Cairene archives: (1) Dār al-Wathā'iq al-Qawmiyya (the National Documents Archive), specifically the collection belonging to the Maḥkama Shar'iyya, until recently housed in the Citadel; (2) the archives of the Wizārat al-Awqāf (the Waqf Ministry), sometimes referred to as the Daftarkhāna; and (3) Dār al-Kutub al-Miṣriyya (the Egyptian National Library). For those from Dār al-Wathā'iq, the numbers given below (and in footnotes) correspond to the numbers in the Maḥkama's *sijill* (register). Documents from the Wizārat al-Awqāf are, in the Ministry's register, followed by the Arabic letter *qāf* or *jīm*, abbreviations for the words *qadīm* (old) or *jadīd* (new), according to whether the document belongs to the Ministry's old collection or to that series of documents discovered since 1967. For the sake of convenience, I have substituted the usual English abbreviation "o.s." (for "old series") and "n.s." (for "new series") in referring to the Ministry's waqfiyyas. Most of these deeds are on long scrolls, and contain several related documents. The date (according to the Muslim calendar) given after the waqfiyya's register number is that of the first document on the scroll. Where the document in question has been published, I have also given the appropriate bibliographic references, although the editions of some waqfiyyas are far better than those of others.

An essential tool for researchers using these documents is the catalog published by Muḥammad M. Amīn, *Fihrist wathā'iq al-qāhira hattā nihāyat 'aṣr salāṭīn al-mamālīk* (Cairo, 1981).

Waqfiyyat al-Ashraf Barsbāy, Dār al-Wathā'iq No. 173, 16 Jumādā al-Ākhira, A.H. 827.

Waqfiyyat al-Ashraf Barsbāy, Dār al-Kutub al-Miṣriyya, Ms. "Tārīkh" No. 3390, 15 Jumādā al-Ākhira, A.H. 827 [Published by Ahmad Darrag, *L'Acte de Waqf de Barsbay* (Cairo, 1963)].

Waqfiyyat al-Ashraf Qayt Bāy, Wizārat al-Awqāf o.s. No. 886, 24 Jumādā al-Ākhira, A.H. 879.

Waqfiyyat Baybars al-Jāshnakīr, Dār al-Wathā'iq No. 22, 26 Shawwāl, A.H. 707.

Waqfiyyat al-Fakhrī 'Abd al-Ghanī, Dār al-Wathā'iq No. 72, 18 Ramaḍān, A.H. 820.

Waqfiyyat Ibn Badīr al-'Abbāsī, Dār al-Wathā'iq No. 43, 25 Jumādā al-Ākhira, A.H. 765.

Waqfiyyat Jamāl al-Dīn Yūsuf al-Ustādār, Dār al-Wathā'iq No. 106, 16 Jumādā al-Ūlā, A.H. 852 [Published by Muḥammad ʿAbd al-Sattār ʿUthmān, *Wathīqat waqf jamāl al-dīn yūsuf al-ustādār* (Cairo, 1983)].
Waqfiyyat Jawhar al-Lālā, Dār al-Wathā'iq No. 86, 23 Ramaḍān, A.H. 834.
Waqfiyyat Jawhar al-Lālā and Jawhar al-Qunuqbā'ī, Dār al-Wathā'iq No. 89, 18 Jumādā al-Ākhira, A.H. 834.
Waqfiyyat Khushqadam al-Zimām, Wizārat al-Awqāf n.s. No. 188, 15 Jumādā al-Ākhira, A.H. 833.
Waqfiyyat al-Manṣūr Lājīn, Dār al-Wathā'iq No. 17, 21 Rabīʿ al-Thānī, A.H. 697.
Waqfiyyat al-Manṣūr Qalāwūn, Wizārat al-Awqāf n.s. No. 706, 23 Dhū 'l-Ḥijja, A.H. 684.
Waqfiyyat al-Mu'ayyad Shaykh, Wizārat al-Awqāf o.s. No. 938, 4 Jumādā al-Ākhira, A.H. 823.
Waqfiyyat Mughulṭāy al-Jamālī, Wizārat al-Awqāf o.s. No. 1666, 29 Rabīʿ al-Thānī, A.H. 729 [The original document has been moved to Dār al-Wathā'iq].
Waqfiyyat al-Nāṣir Ḥasan, Dār al-Wathā'iq No. 40, 6 Rajab, A.H. 760 [Published by Muḥammad M. Amīn, in al-Ḥasan ibn ʿUmar Ibn Ḥabīb, *Tadhkirat al-nabīh fī ayyām al-manṣūr wa banīh* (Cairo, 1986), 3:339–449].
Waqfiyyat al-Nāṣir Ḥasan, Wizārat al-Awqāf o.s. No. 881, 6 Rajab, A.H. 760 [Also published by Muḥammad Amīn, in Ibn Ḥabīb, *Tadhkirat al-nabīh*].
Waqfiyyat al-Nāṣir Muḥammad ibn Qalāwūn, as summarized by Shihāb al-Dīn Aḥmad al-Nuwayrī in *Nihāyat al-arab fī funūn al-adab*, and published as an appendix to Taqī 'l-Dīn Aḥmad al-Maqrīzī, *al-Sulūk li-maʿrifat duwal al-mulūk* (Cairo, 1934–73), 1:1040ff.
Waqfiyyat Qalamṭāy, Dār al-Wathā'iq No. 68, 28 Jumādā al-Ākhira, A.H. 813.
Waqfiyyat Qānī Bāy Qarā, Wizārat al-Awqāf o.s. No. 1019, 10 Ramaḍān, A.H. 908.
Waqfiyyat Qānṣūh al-Ghawrī, Wizārat al-Awqāf o.s. No. 882, 26 Muḥarram, A.H. 909.
Waqfiyyat Ṣarghitmish, Wizārat al-Awqāf o.s. No. 3195, 27 Ramaḍān, A.H. 757 [Published by ʿAbd al-Laṭīf Ibrāhīm ʿAlī, "Naṣṣān jadīrān min wathīqat al-amīr ṣarghitmish," pts. 1 and 2, *Jāmiʿat al-qāhira. Majallat kulliyat al-ādāb* 27 (1965), 121–58, and 28 (1966), 143–200].
Waqfiyyat al-Sayfī Baybars, Dār al-Wathā'iq No. 313, 29 Jumādā al-Ūlā, A.H. 916.
Waqfiyyat al-Shiblī āfūr, Dār al-Wathā'iq No. 76, 12 Jumādā al-Ākhira, A.H. 814.
Waqfiyyat Sūdūn min Zāda, Dār al-Wathā'iq No. 58, Ramaḍān, A.H. 804 [Published by Ḥuṣnī Nuwayṣar, *Madrasa jarkasiyya ʿalā namaṭ al-masājid al-jāmiʿ: madrasat al-amīr sūdūn min zāda bi-sūq al-silāḥ* (Cairo, 1985)].
Waqfiyyat al-Ẓāhir Barqūq, Dār al-Wathā'iq No. 51, 6 Shaʿbān, A.H. 788.
Waqfiyyat al-Ẓāhir Khushqadam, Wizārat al-Awqāf o.s. No. 809, 25 Dhū 'l-Qaʿda, A.H. 868.
Waqfiyyat Zayn al-Dīn ʿAbd al-Bāsiṭ, Wizārat al-Awqāf n.s. No. 189, 21 Muḥarram, A.H. 829.
Waqfiyyat Zayn al-Dīn Ṣidqa, Dār al-Wathā'iq No. 59, 3 Muḥarram, A.H. 803.
Waqfiyyat Zayn al-Dīn al-Ustādār, Dār al-Wathā'iq No. 110, 6 Ṣafar, A.H. 855.

OTHER PRIMARY SOURCES

Al-Ajhūrī, Nūr al-Dīn ʿAlī, *Risāla fī faḍl inshā' al-masājid wa-ʿimāratihā*, 2nd edition (Cairo, 1981).

Amīn, Aḥmad, *My Life*, trans. Issa J. Boullata (Leiden, 1978).

Al-Anṣārī, Abū Yaḥyā Zakariyyā, *al-Lu'lu' al-naẓīm fī rawm al-taʿallum wa'l-taʿlīm* (Cairo, A.H. 1319).

Al-ʿAskarī, Abū 'l-Hilāl al-Ḥasan b. ʿAbd Allāh, *al-Ḥathth ʿalā ṭalab al-ʿilm*, Hamidiye (Istanbul), Ms. 1464/3 [= Maʿhad Iḥyā' al-Makhṭūṭāt al-ʿArabiyya, Ms. "Taṣawwuf" 124].

Ḥājjī Khalīfa (= Kātib Çelebi), *Kashf al-ẓunūn ʿan asāmī 'l-kutub wa'l-funūn* (Istanbul, 1941–43).

Ibn ʿAbd Allāh al-Ẓāhirī, Jamāl al-Dīn Abū 'l-ʿAbbās Aḥmad b. Muḥammad, *Mashyakhat ibn al-bukhārī*, Aḥmadiyya (Aleppo) Ms. No. 261 [= Maʿhad Iḥyā' al-Makhṭūṭāt al-ʿArabiyya, Ms. "Tārīkh" No. 800].

Ibn Aybak al-Dawādārī, Abū Bakr b. ʿAbd Allāh, *Kanz al-durar wa-jāmiʿ al-ghurar*, vol. 8: *al-Durra al-zakiyya fī akhbār al-dawla al-turkiyya*, ed. Ulrich Haarmann (Freiburg and Cairo, 1971).

Ibn Baṭṭūṭa, *The Travels of Ibn Baṭṭūṭa*, trans. H. A. R. Gibb (Cambridge, 1958).

Ibn Duqmāq, Ibrāhīm b. Muḥammad, *al-Intiṣār li-wasiṭat ʿiqd al-amṣār* (Paris, 1893; reptd. Beirut, 1966).

Ibn Faḍl Allāh al-ʿUmarī, *Masālik al-abṣār fī mamālik al-amṣār* (Cairo, 1985).

Ibn Ḥabīb, al-Ḥasan b. ʿUmar, *Tadhkirat al-nabīh fī ayyām al-manṣūr wa-banīh*, ed. Muḥammad M. Amīn (Cairo, 1976–86).

Ibn Ḥajar al-ʿAsqalānī, Shihāb al-Dīn Aḥmad, *al-Durar al-kāmina fī aʿyān al-mi'a al-thāmina* (Cairo, 1966–67).

———, *Inbā' al-ghumr bi-abnā' al-ʿumr* (Hyderabad, 1975; reptd. Beirut, 1986).

———, *al-Majmaʿ al-mu'assas bi'l-muʿjam al-mufahras*, Dār al-Kutub al-Miṣriyya, "Muṣṭalaḥ" Ms. No. 75.

———, *al-Muʿjam al-mufahras*, Dār al-Kutub al-Miṣriyya, "Muṣṭalaḥ" Ms. No. 82.

Ibn al-Ḥājj, Muḥammad b. Muḥammad, *Madkhal al-sharʿ al-sharīf* (Cairo, 1929; reptd. Beirut, 1981).

Ibn al-ʿImād, ʿAbd al-Ḥayy, *Shadharāt al-dhahab fī akhbār man dhahab* (Cairo, A.H. 1350; reptd. Beirut, 1979).

Ibn Iyās, Muḥammad b. Aḥmad, *Badā'iʿ al-zuhūr fī waqā'iʿ al-duhūr*, ed. Muhammad Mustafa (Cairo, 1982–84).

Ibn Jamāʿa, Badr al-Dīn Muḥammad, *Tadhkirat al-sāmiʿ wa'l-mutakallim fī adab al-ʿālim wa'l-mutaʿallim* (Hyderabad, A.H. 1353).

Ibn Khaldūn, ʿAbd al-Raḥmān b. Muḥammad, *The Muqaddimah*, trans. Franz Rosenthal, 2nd edition (New York, 1967).

Ibn Taghrī Birdī, Jamāl al-Dīn Yūsuf, *al-Manhal al-ṣāfī wa'l-mustawfī baʿd al-wāfī*, ed. Muḥammad M. Amīn (Cairo, 1984–).

———, *al-Nujūm al-zāhira fī mulūk miṣr wa'l-qāhira* (Cairo, 1929–1972).

Ibn al-Ukhuwwā, Ḍiyā' al-Dīn Muḥammad, *Maʿālim al-qurba fī aḥkām al-ḥisba*, ed. Reuben Levy (London, 1938).

Ibn Zurayq, Muḥammad b. Abī Bakr, *Mashyakha*, British Museum Ms. Or. 9792.

Al-Maqrīzī, Taqī 'l-Dīn Aḥmad, *al-Mawāʿiẓ wa'l-iʿtibār bi-dhikr al-khiṭaṭ wa'l-āthār* (Būlāq, 1853–54; reptd. Beirut, n.d.).

———, *Kitāb al-sulūk li-maʿrifat duwal al-mulūk*, ed. Muḥammad Muṣṭfā Ziyāda and Saʿīd ʿAbd al-Fattāḥ ʿAshūr (Cairo, 1934–73).

Al-Māwardī, Abū 'l-Ḥasan ʿAlī, *al-Aḥkām al-sulṭāniyya wa'l-wilāya al-dīniyya* (Beirut, 1985).

Mubārak, ʿAlī Pāshā, *al-Khiṭaṭ al-tawfiqiyya al-jadīda li-miṣr al-qāhira* (Būlāq, A.H. 1305).

Al-Nawawī, Abū Zakariyyā Muḥyī al-Dīn, *al-Majmūʿ* (Cairo, n.d.).

Al-Nuʿaymī, ʿAbd al-Qādir b. Muḥammad, *al-Dāris fī tārīkh al-madāris* (Damascus, 1948).

Al-Nuwayrī, Shihāb al-Dīn Aḥmad, *Nihāyat al-arab fī funūn al-adab* (Cairo, 1929–).

Al-Qalqashandī, Aḥmad b. ʿAlī, *Ṣubḥ al-aʿshā fī sināʿat al-inshā'* (Cairo, 1914–28).

Al-Ṣafadī, Khalīl b. Aybak, *al-Wāfī bi'l-wafayāt*, ed. H. Ritter et al. (Wiesbaden and Istanbul, 1931–).

Al-Sakhāwī, Shams al-Dīn Muḥammad, *al-Ḍaw' al-lāmiʿ li-ahl al-qarn al-tāsiʿ* (Cairo, 1934; reptd. Beirut, n.d.).

———, *al-Iʿlān bi'l-tawbīkh li-man dhamma ahl al-tārīkh* (Damascus, A.H. 1349).

———, *al-Jawāhir wa'l-durar fī tarjamat shaykh al-islām Ibn Ḥajar*, vol. 1 (Cairo, 1986).

———, *al-Maqāṣid al-ḥasana fī bayān kathīr min al-aḥādīth al-mushtahara ʿalā 'l-alsina* (Cairo, 1956).

Al-Samʿānī, ʿAbd al-Karīm ibn Muḥammad, *Kitāb adab al-imlā' wa'l-istimlā'*, ed. Max Weisweiler (Leiden, 1952).

Al-Subkī, Tāj al-Dīn ʿAbd al-Wahhāb, *Muʿīd al-niʿam wa-mubīd al-niqam*, ed. David Myhrman (London, 1908).

———, *Muʿjam*, Dār al-Kutub al-Miṣriyya, Aḥmad Tīmūr Pāshā Collection, "Tārīkh" Ms. 1446 [= Maʿhad Iḥyā' al-Makhṭūṭāt al-ʿArabiyya, "Tārīkh" Ms. 490].

Al-Subkī, Taqī 'l-Dīn ʿAlī, *Fatāwā 'l-subkī* (Cairo, A.H. 1356; reptd. Beirut, n.d.).

Al-Suyūṭī, Jalāl al-Dīn ʿAbd al-Raḥmān, *Ḥusn al-muḥāḍara fī tārīkh miṣr wa'l-qāhira* (Cairo, 1967).

———, *Tadrīb al-rāwī fī sharḥ taqrīb al-nawāwī*, 2nd edition (Cairo, 1966).

———, *al-Taḥadduth bi-niʿmat allāh*, ed. Elizabeth M. Sartain (Cambridge, 1975).

———, *Tārīkh al-khulafā'*, 3rd edition (Cairo, 1964).

Al-Ṭūsī, Naṣīr al-Dīn Muḥammad, *Risāla fī faḍl al-ʿilm wa-ādāb al-mutaʿallim*, Dār al-Kutub al-Miṣriyya Ms. 19113b, fol. 15v–24v.

Al-Udfuwī, Kamāl al-Dīn Jaʿfar, *al-Tāliʿ al-saʿīd, al-jāmiʿ asmā' nujabā' al-ṣaʿīd* (Cairo, 1966).

Al-ʿUthmānī, Muḥammad b. ʿAbd al-Raḥmān, *Īḍāḥ al-taʿrīf bi-baʿḍ faḍāʾil al-ʿilm al-sharīf*, Princeton University Library, Yahuda Ms. 4293.

Al-Zarnūjī, Burhān al-Dīn, *Taʿlīm al-mutaʿallim, ṭarīq al-taʿallum* (Cairo, 1977), trans. G. E. von Grunebaum and Theodora M. Abel, *Instruction of the Student, The Method of Learning* (New York, 1947).

SECONDARY WORKS

ʿAbd al-ʿĀṭī, ʿAbd al-Ghanī Maḥmūd, *al-Taʿlīm fī miṣr zaman al-ayyūbiyyīn wa'l-mamālīk* (Cairo, 1984).

ʿAbd al-Rāziq, Aḥmad, *al-Badhl wa'l-barṭala zaman salaṭīn al-mamālīk* (Cairo, 1979).

———, *La femme aux temps des Mamelouks en Égypte* (Cairo, 1973).

———, "Trois fondations féminines dans l'Égypte mamlouke," *Revue des études islamiques* 41 (1973), 95–126.

ʿAlī, ʿAbd al-Laṭīf Ibrāhīm, "Naṣṣān jadīrān min wathīqat al-amīr ṣarghitmish," pts. 1 and 2, *Jāmiʿat al-qāhira. Majjalat kuliyyat al-ādāb* 27 (1965), 121–58, and 28 (1966), 143–200.

———, "al-Tawthīqāt al-sharʿiyya wa'l-ishhādāt fī ẓahr wathīqat al-ghawrī," *Jāmiʿat al-qāhira. Majjalat kuliyyat al-ādāb* 19 (1957), 293–420.

Amīn, Muḥammad M., *al-Awqāf wa'l-ḥayāt al-ijtimāʿiyya fī miṣr* (Cairo, 1980).

———, *Fihrist wathāʾiq al-qāhira hattā nihāyat ʿaṣr salāṭīn al-mamālīk* (Cairo, 1981).

Arberry, A. J., *Sakhawiana* (London, 1951).

———, *A Twelfth-century Reading List* (London, 1951).

Ashtor, Eliyahu, *Histoire des prix et des salaires dans l'orient médiéval* (Paris, 1969).

ʿĀṣim, Muḥammad Rizq, "Madrasat al-qāḍī abū bakr mazhar bi'l-qāhira, 884–885/1479–1480," *Dirāsāt āthāriyya islāmiyya* 2 (1980), 69–91.

Ayalon, David, *The Mamlūk Military Society* (London, 1979).

———, "Notes on the *Furūsiyya* Exercises and Games in the Mamluk Sultanate," *Scripta Hierosolymitana* 9 (1961), 31–62.

———, *Outsiders in the Lands of Islam* (London, 1988).

———, *Studies on the Mamlūks of Egypt (1250–1517)* (London, 1977).

———, "Studies on the Structure of the Mamlūk Army—II," *Bulletin of the School of Oriental and African Studies* 15 (1953), 467–69.

———, "Studies on the Structure of the Mamlūk Army—III," *Bulletin of the School of Oriental and African Studies* 16 (1954), 57–58.

Balog, Paul, *The Coinage of the Mamlūk Sultans of Egypt and Syria* (New York, 1964).

———, "History of the Dirhem in Egypt from the Fāṭimid Conquest until the Collapse of the Mamlūk Empire," *Revue numismatique*, 6th series, 3 (1961), 109–46.

El-Beheiry, Salah, "Le décret de nomination de l'historien Ibn Wāṣil au poste de professeur de la mosquée al-Aqmar," *Annales islamologiques* 12 (1974), 85–94.

Behrens-Abouseif, Doris, *Azbakiyya and Its Environs from Azbak to Ismāʿīl, 1476–1879* (Cairo, 1985).

Behrens-Abouseif, Doris, "Change in Function and Form of Mamluk Religious Institutions," *Annales islamologiques* 21 (1985), 73–93.

Berchem, Max van, *Matériaux pour un corpus inscriptionum arabicarum*, pt. 1 [= *Mémoires publiées par les membres de la mission archéologiques françaises au Caire*, vol. 19] (Paris, 1903).

Bloom, Jonathan, "The Mosque of Baybars al-Bunduqdārī in Cairo," *Annales islamologiques* 18 (1982), 45–78.

Brinner, William M., "The Banū Ṣaṣrā: A Study in the Transmission of a Scholarly Tradition," *Arabica* 7 (1960), 167–95.

Brockelmann, C., *Geschichte der Arabischen Litteratur*, 2nd edition (Leiden, 1937–49).

Bulliet, Richard, *The Patricians of Nishapur: A Study in Medieval Islamic Social History* (Cambridge, Mass., 1972).

Comité de Conservation des Monuments de l'Art Arabe, *Rapport de la deuxième commission. Exercices*, various dates.

Crecelius, Daniel "The Organization of Waqf Documents in Cairo," *International Journal of Middle East Studies* 2 (1971), 266–77.

Creswell, K. A. C., *The Muslim Architecture of Egypt* (Oxford, 1959).

——— et. al. *A Bibliography of the Architecture, Arts and Crafts of Islam* (Cairo, 1961), suppls. (Cairo, 1973 and 1984).

Darraj, Ahmad, *L'Egypte sous la règne de Barsbay, 825–841/1422–1438* (Damascus, 1961).

———, "La vie d'Abū 'l-Mahāsin Ibn Taghrī Birdī et son oeuvre," *Annales islamologiques* 11 (1972), 163–81.

Dodge, Bayard, *Al-Azhar: A Millenium of Muslim Learning* (Washington, D.C., 1961).

Dols, Michael, *The Black Death in the Middle East* (Princeton, 1976).

Donaldson, Dwight M., "The Shrine Colleges of Meshed," *Moslem World* 16 (1926), 72–78.

Egypt. Ministry of Waqfs, *Masājid miṣr min 21–1365/641–1946* (Cairo, 1948).

Eickelmann Dale, "The Art of Memory: Islamic Education and Its Social Reproduction," *Comparative Studies in Society and History* 20 (1978), 485–516.

———, *Knowledge and Power in Morocco: The Education of a Twentieth-Century Notable* (Princeton, 1985).

Escovitz, Joseph H., *The Office of the Qāḍī al-Quḍāt in Cairo Under the Baḥrī Mamlūks* (Berlin, 1984).

Fakhry, Majid, "The Liberal Arts in the Medieval Arabic Tradition from the Seventh to the Twelfth Centuries," in *Arts libéraux et philosophie au moyen âge. Actes du quatrième congrès international de philosophie médiévale* (Montreal, 1969), 91–97.

Fernandes, Leonor, *The Evolution of a Sufi Institution in Mamluk Egypt: The Khanqah* (Berlin, 1988).

———, "Mamluk Politics and Education: The Evidence from Two Fourteenth Century Waqfiyya," *Annales islamologiques* 23 (1987), 87–98.

———, "Some Aspects of the *Zāwiya* in Egypt at the Eve of the Ottoman Conquest," *Annales islamologiques* 19 (1983), 9–17.

———, "Three Sufi Foundations in a Fifteenth Century Waqfiyya," *Annales islamologiques* 17 (1981), 141–56.

———, "Two Variations of the Same Theme: The *Zāwiya* of Ḥasan al-Rūmī, the *Takiyya* of Ibrāhīm al-Gulshāwī," *Annales islamologiques* 21 (1985), 95–111.

Flemming, Barbara, "Literary Activities in Mamluk Halls and Barracks," in *Studies in Memory of Gaston Wiet*, ed. Myriam Rosen-Ayalon (Jerusalem, 1977), 249–60.

Garcin, Jean-Claude, *Un Centre musulman de la haute Égypte médiévale: Qūṣ* (Cairo, 1976).

———, "Histoire, opposition politique et piétisme traditioniste dans la Ḥusn al-Muḥādarat de Suyūṭī," *Annales islamologiques* 7 (1967), 33–88.

Goitein, S. D., *A Mediterranean Society: The Jewish Communities of the Arab World as Portrayed in the Documents of the Cairo Geniza* (Berkeley, 1967–88).

Goldziher, Ignaz, *Muslim Studies*, trans. C. R. Barber and S. M. Stern (London, 1971).

Grabar, Oleg, "The Architecture of the Middle Eastern City from Past to Present: The Case of the Mosque," in *Middle Eastern Cities*, ed. Ira M. Lapidus (Berkeley, 1969), 26–46.

Guest, A. H., "A List of the Writers, Books, and Other Authorities Mentioned by El Maqrīzī in His Khiṭaṭ," *Journal of the Royal Asiatic Society* (1902), 103–25.

Haarmann, Ulrich, "Arabic in Speech, Turkish in Lineage: Mamluks and Their Sons in the Intellectual Life of Fourteenth-Century Egypt and Syria," *Journal of Semitic Studies* 33 (1988), 81–114.

———, "Ideology and History, Identity and Alterity: The Arab Image of the Turk from the ʿAbbasids to Modern Egypt," *International Journal of Middle East Studies* 20 (1988), 175–96.

———, "Mamluk Endowment Deeds as a Source for the History of Education in Late Medieval Egypt," *Al-Abḥāth* 28 (1980), 31–47.

———, "Rather the Injustice of the Turks than the Righteousness of the Arabs—Changing ʿUlamāʾ Attitudes Towards Mamluk Rule in the Late Fifteenth Century," *Studia Islamica* 68 (1988).

Hautecoeur, Louis, and Wiet, Gaston, *Les mosquées du Caire* (Paris, 1932).

Heyworth-Dunne, James, *An Introduction to the History of Education in Modern Egypt* (London, 1939).

Holt, P. M., *The Age of the Crusades: The Near East from the Eleventh Century to 1517* (London, 1986).

———, "Some Observations on the Abbasid Caliphate of Cairo," *Bulletin of the School of Oriental and African Studies* 47 (1984), 501–507.

———, "The Sultanate of al-Manṣūr Lāchīn (696–8/1296–9)," *Bulletin of the School of Oriental and African Studies* 36 (1973), 521–32.

Humphreys, R. Stephen, "The Expressive Intent of Mamluk Architecture in Cairo," *Studia Islamica* 35 (1972), 69–119.

Irwin, Robert, *The Middle East in the Middle Ages: The Early Mamluk Sultanate, 1250–1382* (Carbondale and Edwardsville, Illinois, 1986).

Ittig, Annette, "A Talismanic Bowl," *Annales islamologiques* 18 (1982), 79–94.

Kawash, Sabri K., "Ibn Ḥajar al-ʿAsqalānī (1372–1449 A.D.): A Study of the Background, Education, and Career of a ʿĀlim in Egypt," dissertation, Princeton University, 1969.

Khan, M. Abdul Muʿid, "The Muslim Theories of Education during the Middle Ages," *Islamic Culture* 18 (1944), 418–33.

Lapidus, Ira M., "Knowledge, Virtue, Action: The Classical Muslim Conception of *Adab* and the Nature of Fulfillment in Islam," in *Moral Conduct and Authority*, ed. Barbara Daly Metcalf (Berkeley, 1984), 38–61.

———, *Muslim Cities in the Later Middle Ages* (Cambridge, Mass., 1967).

Leiser, Gary, "The Endowment of the al-Zahiriyya in Damascus," *Journal of the Economic and Social History of the Orient* 27 (1984), 33–55.

———, "The *Madrasa* and the Islamization of the Middle East: The Case of Egypt," *Journal of the American Research Center in Egypt* 22 (1985), 29–47.

———, "Notes on the Madrasa in Medieval Islamic Society," *The Muslim World* 76 (1986), 16–23.

———, "The Restoration of Sunnism in Egypt: Madrasas and Mudarrisūn, 495–647/1101–1249," Ph.D. dissertation, University of Pennsylvania, 1976.

Little, Donald, *History and Historiography of the Mamluks* (London, 1986).

———, *An Introduction to Mamlūk Historiography* (Wiesbaden, 1970).

———, "Religion under the Mamluks," *The Muslim World* 73 (1983), 165–181.

Lutfi, Hoda, *Al-Quds al-Mamlūkiyya: A History of Mamlūk Jerusalem Based on the Ḥaram Documents* (Berlin, 1985).

———, "Al-Sakhāwī's *Kitāb al-Nisā'* as a Source for the Social and Economic History of Muslim Women during the Fifteenth Century A.D.," *The Muslim World* 71 (1981), 104–24.

Mahdi, Muhsin, "The Book and the Master as Poles of Cultural Change in Islam," in *Islam and Cultural Change in the Middle Ages*, ed. Speros Vryonis (Wiesbaden, 1975).

Makdisi, George, "Muslim Institutions of Learning in Eleventh-Century Baghdad," *Bulletin of the School of Oriental and African Studies* 24 (1961), 1–56.

———, *The Rise of Colleges: Institutions of Learning in Islam and the West* (Edinburgh, 1981).

———, "The Scholastic Method in Medieval Education: An Inquiry into Its Origins in Law and Theology," *Speculum* 49 (1974), 640–61.

———, "*Ṣuḥba* et *riyāsa* dans l'enseignement médiévale," in *Recherches d'islamologie. Recueil d'articles offert à Georges C. Anawati et Louis Gardet par leurs collègues et amis* (Louvain, 1977), 207–21.

Marrou, Henri, *A History of Education in Antiquity*, trans. George Lamb (London, 1956).

Mayer, L. A., *The Buildings of Qaytbay* (London, 1938).

———, *Mamluk Costume* (Geneva, 1952).

Meineke, Michael, *Die Restaurierung der Madrasa des Amirs Sabiq ad-Din Mitqal al-Anuki und die Sanierung des Darb Qirmiz in Kairo* (Mainz, 1980).

Memon, Muhammad Umar, *Ibn Taimiya's Struggle against Popular Religion* (The Hague, 1976).

Mostafa, Saleh Lamei, *Kloster und Mausoleum des Farağ ibn Barqūq in Kairo* [= Abhandlungen des Deutschen Archäologischen Instituts. Islamische Reihe, Band 2] (Glückstadt, 1968).

———, *Madrasa, Hanqah und Mausoleum des Barquq in Kairo* [= Abhandlungen des Deutschen Archäologischen Instituts. Islamische Reihe, Band 4] (Glückstadt, 1982).

———, *Moschee des Farağ ibn Baqūq in Kairo* [= Abhandlungen des Deutschen Archäologischen Instituts. Islamische Reihe, Band 3] (Glückstadt, 1972).

Mottahedeh, Roy, *Loyalty and Leadership in an Early Islamic Society* (Princeton, 1980).

———, *The Mantle of the Prophet: Religion and Politics in Iran* (New York, 1985).

Nuwayṣar, Ḥuṣnī, *Madrasa jarkasiyya ʿalā namaṭ al-masājid al-jāmiʿ: madrasat al-amīr sūdūn min zāda bi-sūq al-silāḥ* (Cairo, 1985).

Pedersen, Johannes, *The Arabic Book*, trans. Geoffrey French (Princeton, 1984).

———, "Some Aspects of the History of the Madrasa," *Islamic Culture* 3 (1929), 527–37.

Petry, Carl, *The Civilian Elite of Cairo in the Later Middle Ages* (Princeton, 1981).

———, "A Paradox of Patronage," *The Muslim World* 73 (1983), 182–207.

Pipes, Daniel, *Slave Soldiers and Islam* (New Haven, 1981).

Rabie, Hassanein, *The Financial System of Egypt, A.H. 564–741/A.D. 1169–1341* (Oxford, 1972).

Rosenthal, Franz, *A History of Muslim Historiography* (Leiden, 1952).

———, *Knowledge Triumphant* (Leiden, 1970).

———, *The Technique and Approach of Muslim Scholarship*, in *Analecta Orientalia* 24 (Rome, 1947).

Rostem, Osman R., *The Architecture of the Mosque of Sultan Hasan* (Beirut, 1970).

Salama, Ibrahim, *L'Ensiegnement islamique en égypte* (Cairo, 1938).

Salibi, Kamal S., "The Banū Jamāʿa: A Dynasty of Shāfiʿite Jurists," *Studia Islamica* 9 (1958), 97–109.

———, "Listes chronologiques des grands cadis de l'Égypte sous les mameloukes," *Revue des études islamiques* 25 (1957), 81–125.

Al-Ṣāliḥ, Ṣubḥī, *ʿUlūm al-ḥadīth wa-muṣṭalahuhu*, 3rd edition (Beirut, 1965).

Sartain, Elizabeth, *Jalāl al-Dīn al-Suyūṭī: Biography and Background* (Cambridge, 1975).

Schacht, Joseph, *Aus Kairiner Bibliotheken*, part 2, in *Abhandlungen der Preussischen Akademie des Wissenschaften*, 1929 (Berlin, 1930).

Schimmel, Anne-Marie, "Some Glimpses of the Religious Life in Egypt During the Mamlūk Period," *Islamic Studies* 4 (1965), 353–92.

Shalaby, Ahmad, *History of Muslim Education* (Beirut, 1954).

Sourdel, Dominique, "Réflexions sur la diffusion de la madrasa en orient du xie au xiiie siècle," *Revue des études islamiques* 44 (1976), 165–84.

Sourdel-Thomine, Janine, "Locaux d'enseignements et madrasas dans l'islam médiéval," *Revue des études islamiques* 44 (1976), 185–97.

Spoer, H. Henry, "Arab Magic Medicinal Bowls," *Journal of the American Oriental Society* 55 (1935), 237–56.

Sublet, Jacqueline, "Les Maîtres et les études de deux traditionnistes de l'époque mamelouke," *Bulletin d'études orientales* 20 (1967), 9–99.

Al-Tahānawī, Ẓafar Aḥmad al-ʿUthmānī, *Qawā'id fī ʿulūm al-ḥadīth*, 3rd edition (Beirut, 1971).

Tibawi, A. L., "Muslim Education in the Golden Age of the Caliphate," *Islamic Culture* 28 (1954), 418–38.

———, "Origin and Character of *Al-Madrasah*," *Bulletin of the School of Oriental and African Studies* 25 (1962), 225–38.

Tritton, A. S., *Materials on Muslim Education in the Middle Ages* (London, 1957).

Tyan, Emile, *Histoire de l'organization judiciare en pays d'islam*, 2nd edition (Leiden, 1960).

Udovitch, A. L., et al., "England to Egypt, 1350–1500: Long-term Trends and Long-distance Trade," in *Studies in the Economic History of the Middle East*, ed. Michael Cook (Oxford, 1970), 115–28.

Vajda, Georges, "De la transmission orale du savoir dans l'Islam traditionnel," *L'Arabisant* 4 (1975), 2–8.

———, *Le dictionnaire des autorités (muʿǧam as-šuyūkh) de ʿAbd al-Mu'min ad- Dimyāṭī* (Paris, 1962).

———, "La liste d'autorités de Manṣūr Ibn Salīm Waǧīh al-Dīn al-Hamdānī," *Journal asiatique*, 253 (1965), 341–406.

———, "La mašyakha de ʿAbd al-Qādir al-Yūnīnī," *Journal asiatique* 259 (1971), 223–46.

———, "La mašyakha d'Ibn al-Hattāb al-Rāzī. Contribution à l'histoire de sunnisme en Égypte fāṭimide," *Bulletin des études orientales* 23 (1970), 21–99.

———, *La transmission du savoir en Islam (viie-xviiie siècles)*, ed. Nicole Cottart (London, 1983).

Williams, John A., "The Khanqah of Siryaqus: A Mamluk Royal Religious Foundation," in *In Quest of an Islamic Humanism: Arabic and Islamic Studies in Memory of Mohamad al-Nowaihi*, ed. A. H. Green (Cairo, 1986).

———, "Urbanization and Monument Construction in Mamluk Cairo," *Muqarnas* 2 (1984), 33–45.

Winter, Michael, *Society and Religion in Early Ottoman Egypt* (New Brunswick, 1982).

INDEX

ʿAbbasids, 10, 183
ʿAbd al-Bāsiṭ, Zayn al-Dīn, 99
ʿAbd al-Ghanī, Fakhr al-Dīn, 49, 107
ʿAbd al-Qādir b. ʿAbd al-Ghanī, Zayn al-Dīn, 107–8
al-Abnāsī, ʿAbd al-Raḥīm, 117, 123n
al-Abnāsī, Burhān al-Dīn Ibrāhīm, 120, 123, 123n
Abū Dā'ūd, 155, 159, 186n, 215
Abū Yūsuf, 119
al-Abyārī, Nūr al-Dīn, 109n
accommodations, in schools, 7, 44, 47, 62, 67, 72, 74, 90–94, 145, 166–67, 190
al-Adhrāʿī, Shihāb al-Dīn Aḥmad, 99n
Aḥmad b. Aqqūsh al-Mihmandār, 49n
ʿĀ'isha bint Ibn al-Hishī, 177
ʿĀ'isha bint Muḥammad ibn ʿAbd al-Hādī, 177–78
al-ʿAjamī, al-Shaykh Zāda, 124
al-ʿAjamī, Badr al-Dīn Maḥmūd ibn Zāda, 101n, 124
Aleppo, 9, 131, 178, 196, 211, 215
Alexandria, 8, 9, 131, 139, 140
Aljāy al-Yūsufī, Sayf al-Dīn, 139–40
Āl Malik, Sayf al-Dīn, 148, 157
Almās al-Ashrafī, 144n
Almohads, 21
Alṭunbughā al-Turkī, 158–59
ʿāmil, 65
Amīn, Aḥmad, 4
amīr ākhūr, 66n
amīr al-ḥajj, 141
amīr jandār, 139
amīr majlis, 66n
amīr tablakhāna, 140
ʿāmma, *ʿawāmm*, 184, 188; and education, 201–16; and transmission of *ḥadīth*, 210–16
Anas, father of Barqūq, 145–46
Anatolia, 189
Andalusia, 26
anṣār, 162
al-Anṣārī, Zayn al-Dīn ʿUbāda, 99
Āqbughā al-Ustādār, ʿAlā' al-Dīn, 148
al-Aqṣarā'ī, Amīn al-Dīn, 42, 100–101, 135, 153–54
al-Aqṣarā'ī, Muḥibb al-Dīn, 104
Āq Sunqur al-Salārī, 53
Aqṭūh, Sayf al-Dīn, 151
Aqṭuwān al-ʿIzzī, 157
Arabic language, 11, 27–28, 76, 88, 90, 147, 200–201, 203–4, 206. *See also* linguistic sciences
Arghūn al-Nāṣirī, 150, 152–53, 154
ʿarīf, 198
al-ʿAsjadī, Shihāb al-Dīn Aḥmad, 106
Aṣlam al-Nāṣirī, 49, 53
al-ʿAsqalānī, ʿIzz al-Dīn Aḥmad, 113, 117
Asundumur, 139–40
atābak, 139–40
ʿatīq. See *ʿutaqā'*
Aybak, al-Muʿizz, 12, 61
Aybak al-Turkī, 204
Aydakīn al-Bunduqdārī, ʿAlā' al-Dīn, 137
al-ʿAynī, Badr al-Dīn Maḥmūd, 45, 100, 142, 153, 210n
Ayyubids, 8, 9, 46, 48, 51, 52, 112, 131–32, 137
Azdumur al-Ṭawīl, 152
al-Azharī, Sulaymān b. Shuʿayb, 117
al-Azharī, Zayn al-Dīn Khālid, 90

Bāb Zuwayla, 53, 63, 70, 78n, 80, 163
Baghdad, 7, 8, 9, 10, 47, 196
al-Baghdādī, ʿIzz al-Dīn ʿAbd al-Salām, 42, 89, 105, 195–96
al-Baghawī, al-Ḥusayn b. Masʿūd, 187
al-Bahnasī, Majd al-Dīn al-Ḥārith, 52
Bakalmish al-ʿAlā'ī, 150
Baktimur al-Ḥijāzī, 163
al-Baqā'ī, Burhān al-Dīn Ibrāhīm, 158
baraka, 144, 163, 193
Barakāt, Umm al-Ashraf Shaʿbān, 163
bardadār, 65
Bardbak al-Ashrafī, 156
Barqūq, al-Ẓāhir, 61, 66, 104, 104n, 129, 140–41, 144, 145, 165
Barsbāy, al-Ashraf, 47, 70, 99–100, 104–5, 153, 159
al-Basāṭī, Shams al-Dīn Muḥammad, 23n
Bashīr al-Nāṣirī, Saʿd al-Dīn, 51
bawwābs, 64, 74, 81, 191, 193, 199, 201

Baybars, al-Sayfī, 17, 102
Baybars al-Bunduqdārī, al-Ẓāhir, 51, 61, 98, 145, 174
Baybars al-Jashnakīr, al-Muẓaffar, 52–53, 56, 133
al-Bayhaqī, Aḥmad b. al-Ḥusayn, 186n
Bayn al-Qaṣrayn, 48, 54, 57, 61, 63, 70, 89, 94, 144, 145, 146, 188, 190, 191
Berchem, Max van, 164
al-Bījūrī, Burhān al-Dīn Ibrāhīm b. ʿAlī, 87, 107–8, 124
Bīlīk al-Khāzindār, 51
biographical dictionaries, as a source for the history of education, 14, 18, 23, 29, 32, 75–76, 88, 92, 99, 102, 103, 110, 147, 150, 170, 172, 172n, 179, 197, 204
al-Birmāwī, Majd al-Dīn Ismāʿīl, 87
al-Birmāwī, Shams al-Dīn Muḥammad, 107
books, 28, 29, 30, 31; attitudes toward, 26; copying of, 25; cost of, 25; publication of, 24
bribery, 97–98
al-Bukhārī, Muḥammad b. Ismāʿīl, 75, 150, 154, 155, 156, 157, 162, 170, 171, 178, 186n, 187, 211, 213–14
Būlāq, 53
Bulliet, Richard, 13
al-Bulqīnī, ʿAlam al-Dīn Ṣāliḥ, 23, 42, 105, 105n, 209
al-Bulqīnī, Jalāl al-Dīn ʿAbd al-Raḥmān, 121, 189n, 209
al-Bulqīnī, Shihāb al-Dīn Aḥmad, 54
al-Bulqīnī, Sirāj al-Dīn ʿUmar, 42, 121, 122, 142, 157, 163, 189n, 209, 210, 211
al-Bulqīnī family, 52n, 143, 164, 171
al-Busīrī, Sharaf al-Dīn, 175

caliphs, caliphate, 10, 183
Caucasus, 10
Central Asia, 7
charity, 191–92
Christians, 131–32, 183
Citadel (of Cairo), 45, 53, 67, 72, 130, 135, 144, 147, 154, 159, 192; recitation of *ḥadīth* in, 156, 212
classes: organization of, 78–85; in private homes, 87–89, 169, 171, 173; time of, 79–81, 115. *See also* individual subjects
clothing, and the ulama, 182–84
controllers. See *nāẓir*
Crusades, Crusaders, 8, 9, 130, 143
currencies, 77
curriculum: of *madrasas*, 7; choice of, 82–84

Damascus, 8, 9, 97, 113, 114, 120, 121, 145, 164, 170, 171, 177, 178, 196
dār al-ḥadīth al-Kāmiliyya, 87, 113, 121n, 156
dawādār, 65n, 66n, 152, 154
dhikr, 59
dirāya, 30

endowment deeds. See *waqfiyyas*
endowments. See *waqfs*
eunuchs, 51, 142, 145
Europe, 6, 27–28
exegesis, Quranic. See *tafsīr*

faqīh, 4, 170; as title given to Mamluks, 150–51
faqīhas, 175
farāʾid, 200
Faraj b. Barqūq, al-Nāṣir, 133, 146, 189
al-Fāraskūrī, Zayn al-Dīn ʿAbd al-Raḥmān, 111–12
farrāsh, 64, 74, 197, 199
Fāṭima bint ʿAbbās al-Baghdādiyya, 174
Fāṭima bint Khalīl ibn Aḥmad, 179
Fāṭima bint Qānibāy al-ʿUmarī al-Nāṣirī, 164
Fatimids, 8, 51, 130–32
fatwās, 98, 98n, 121, 148, 153, 202
fiqh, 4, 7, 8, 12–13, 17, 28, 30, 34–35, 64, 84, 200–201, 206; classes in (generally), 46, 58, 69, 82–83, 91, 132; Ḥanafī, classes in, 41, 45, 47–48, 49, 51–53, 57, 59, 61–62, 67, 71–72, 74, 79–80, 83, 84, 90, 93, 138, 139, 149, 163, 164, 185, 191; Ḥanbalī, classes in, 48, 52–53, 62, 67, 79, 90, 93; Mālikī, classes in, 48, 49, 52–53, 62, 67, 79, 90, 93, 138, 163; Mamluk students of, 147–52, 154; Shāfiʿi, classes in, 48, 49, 51, 52–54, 57, 61–62, 67, 71, 74, 79–81, 90, 93, 139, 148, 163, 164, 191; women students of, 166, 168, 169, 173–75, 180. *See also* professorships
foreign students, 91–92
furūsiyya, 149
al-Fusṭāṭ, 8, 46, 51, 61, 86, 108, 122, 131, 195, 202

Geniza, 5
al-Ghawrī. *See* Qānṣūh al-Ghawrī
al-Ghazālī, Abū Ḥāmid Muḥammad, 175, 205
al-Ghumārī, Muḥammad b. Muḥammad, 158, 158n
Gospels, 5
grammar. *See* linguistic sciences

Haarmann, Ulrich, 143, 147
ḥadīth, 3–5, 7, 12–13, 17, 34, 59, 64, 161, 201, 205–8, 210, 217–18; "canonical" collections of, 186n, 213, 213n; classes in, 46, 48, 52–53, 57–58, 61–62, 67–69, 72, 79n, 82, 86, 91, 93; collections of, 24; *ijāzas* for, 31, 157, 159, 170, 176–78; Mamluk students of, 148, 150, 151–52, 154, 155–60; recitation of, 63, 72, 150, 152, 169, 171; recitation of, during Ramaḍān, 74, 75, 156, 180, 213–14; standards for the transmission of, 176–81; transmission of, 29, 30–33, 39, 94, 120, 155–60, 167n, 170, 171, 175–81, 186–87, 200, 210–26; women as students of, 170–71, 175–81. See also *ijāzas*; professorships
ḥāfiẓ, *ḥuffāẓ*, 29, 74, 76, 186n
ḥājib, 66n, 149
ḥajj, 4, 91–92; substitutes during, 117
al-Ḥajjār, Abū 'l-ʿAbbās Aḥmad, 158, 177–78
Ḥājjī Khalīfa, 28
ḥalqa, 7, 86
Hama, 178
Ḥanafīs, Mamluks as, 47, 147, 149–50
ḥarīm, 161
al-Ḥarīrī, Abū Muḥammad Qāsim, 169
Harrān, 52
Ḥasan, al-Nāṣir, 51, 61, 67, 139
Hebron, 178
Ḥijāz, 10, 120
al-Ḥijāzī, Abū 'l-ʿAbbās, 94
ḥuḍūr, 59
Ḥujjāb bint ʿAbd Allāh, 175n
al-Ḥuṣnī, Taqī 'l-Dīn, 104n, 117

iʿāda. See *muʿīd*
Ibn ʿAbd al-Ḥaqq, Sharaf al-Dīn, 117
Ibn al-ʿAdīm, Kamāl al-Dīn ʿUmar, 112, 124
Ibn al-ʿAdīm, Nāṣir al-Dīn Muḥammad, 118n, 124
Ibn al-Amāna, Badr al-Dīn Muḥammad, 108n, 110
Ibn al-Amāna, Taqī 'l-Dīn ʿAbd al-Laṭīf, 108, 108n
Ibn al-Amīn al-Khaṭīb, 94n
Ibn Asad, Shihāb al-Dīn Aḥmad, 35, 110, 156, 212
Ibn ʿAsākir, al-Qāsim b. Muẓaffar, 179
Ibn al-Athīr, Majd al-Dīn, 187
Ibn Bint al-Aʿazz, Taqī 'l-Dīn, 112
Ibn Birdis, ʿAlā' al-Dīn ʿAlī, 159
Ibn al-Bukhārī, 215
Ibn al-Dīrī, Badr al-Dīn, 97
Ibn al-Dīrī, Saʿd al-Dīn, 104, 155
Ibn Duqmāq, Ibrāhīm, 45n
Ibn Ḥabīb, al-Ḥasan, 45n, 148, 215
Ibn Ḥajar al-ʿAsqalānī, Shihāb al-Dīn Aḥmad, 23n, 25, 32, 35, 87, 88, 95–96, 151, 155, 157, 159, 170–71, 176–79, 181, 195, 197, 200–201, 204, 209, 210, 213; professorships held by, 45, 97, 109n, 110–12, 115, 119
Ibn al-Ḥājj, Muḥammad, 35–37, 87–88, 95–97, 171–73, 182–84, 188, 202, 216
Ibn Ḥajjī, Najm al-Dīn ʿUmar, 107
Ibn Ḥanbal, Aḥmad, 159, 186n
Ibn Ḥannā, Bahā' al-Dīn ʿAlī, 122
Ibn Ḥannā, Fakhr al-Dīn Muḥammad, 122
Ibn Ḥannā, Tāj al-Dīn Muḥammad, 52, 53
Ibn Ḥarīz, Sirāj al-Dīn ʿUmar, 117
Ibn Hishām, 178
Ibn al-Hīshī, Abū Bakr, 176
Ibn al-Humām, Kamāl al-Dīn Muḥammad, 89–90, 100, 108
Ibn al-ʿImād, ʿAbd al-Ḥayy, 178
Ibn al-ʿIrāqī, Walī 'l-Dīn Aḥmad, 23, 89, 120–21, 123, 201
Ibn al-ʿIrāqī, Zayn al-Dīn ʿAbd al-Raḥīm, 120–21, 156
Ibn Ismāʿīl al-Ḥanafī, Aḥmad, 42
Ibn Iyās, 47, 56, 97
Ibn Jamāʿa, Badr al-Dīn, 22, 24, 25, 26, 36, 37, 38, 53, 54, 60, 79, 81, 93–94, 108, 166, 184–85, 190, 211
Ibn Jamāʿa, ʿIzz al-Dīn, 106, 108, 114–15, 120, 170, 211
Ibn Khaldūn, ʿAbd al-Raḥmān, 21, 26, 31, 35, 104n, 114, 132, 134, 143
Ibn Khiḍr, Burhān, al-Dīn, 195

Ibn al-Kuwayk, Abū Jaʿfar, 157
Ibn Māja, 186n
Ibn Mālik, 175
Ibn Marzūq, Ṣafī 'l-Dīn Ibrāhīm, 137, 137n
Ibn al-Muḥammira, Shihāb al-Dīn, 110
Ibn al-Mulaqqin, Jalāl al-Dīn ʿAbd al-Raḥmān, 209
Ibn al-Mulaqqin, Nūr al-Dīn ʿAlī, 209
Ibn al-Mulaqqin, Sirāj al-Dīn ʿUmar, 121n, 206n, 209
Ibn Muẓaffar, 28
Ibn al-Naḥḥāl, Badr al-Dīn Ḥusayn, 94
Ibn al-Naqīb, Shams al-Dīn Muḥammad, 215
Ibn Naṣr Allāh, Aḥmad b. Ibrāhīm, 123n
Ibn Nāẓir al-Ṣāḥiba, Shihāb al-Dīn Aḥmad, 159
Ibn Sābiq, Burhān al-Dīn Ibrāhīm, 196
Ibn al-Ṣalāḥ, ʿUthmān b. ʿAbd al-Raḥmān, 187
Ibn al-Sallār, 131
Ibn al-Shiḥna, ʿAbd al-Barr, 213
Ibn Sukkur, Shihāb al-Dīn Aḥmad, 200
Ibn Taghrī Birdī, Jamāl al-Dīn Yūsuf, 49, 148, 151, 155, 159
Ibn al-Ṭaḥḥān, Zayn al-Dīn ʿAbd al-Raḥmān, 159
Ibn Taqī, Muḥyī, 'l-Dīn ʿAbd al-Qādir, 116
Ibn Taqī, Shihāb al-Dīn Aḥmad, 110
Ibn Taymiyya, 59, 174
Ibn ʿUbayd Allāh, Badr al-Dīn, 154
Ibn Ukht Bahrām, 29
Ibn al-Walākhshī, Riḍwān, 131
Ibn Zāda. *See* al-ʿAjamī, Badr al-Dīn Maḥmūd ibn Zāda
ifāda. See *mufīd*
iḥtisāban, 87
ijāzas, 31–33, 39, 157, 159, 167, 170, 172, 176–78, 200–201, 201n, 211, 215; false or fictive, 31–32; for *iftā'*, 31, 152–53; issued to children, 32, 120, 170–71; for the *mīʿād*, 209; for *tadrīs*, 31, 152–53
ijāzat al-samāʿ, 33
ijmāʿ, 4
al-Ikhnā'ī, Tāj al-Dīn Muḥammad, 116
ʿilm, value of, 3–6, 95, 133–34, 168, 184
ʿilm al-mīqāt, 69
imāms, 17, 47, 54n, 63, 69, 72, 74, 78n, 90, 96, 110, 114, 122, 145, 191, 193–97
imlā', 24
Īnāl, al-Ashraf, 156
informal teaching, 85–94
iqṭāʿs, 138
Iran, 189
Iraq, 7, 8, 17, 89, 143
al-ʿIrāqī, Zayn al-Dīn, 35
al-Isfahānī, Abū Shajjāʿ Aḥmad, 169
Ismāʿīlīs, 8, 51, 131
ʿIsmat al-Dīn bint al-Malik al-ʿĀdil, 163
isnād, 31, 76, 157–58, 177, 187, 213–14
īwāns, 47, 67–69, 70, 72, 73, 78

jābī, 65
jadal, 30
jāmiʿ, 16, 47–49. *See also* mosques
al-Jammāʿīlī, Taqī 'l-Dīn ʿAbd al-Ghanī, 201n, 211
Jānibak al-Dawādār, 49
Jānibak al-Ẓāhirī (d. 1463), 101, 144n
Jānibak al-Ẓāhirī (husband of Zaynab), 153
Jaqmaq, al-Ẓāhir, 50, 152, 159
Jaqmaq al-Ashrafī, 153
Jawhar al-Khāzindār, 84
Jawhar al-Lālā, 72, 142n, 144, 192
Jāwul, 139
Jerusalem, 9, 92, 117, 120, 196
Jews, Judaism, 183; education, 5–6, 40, 40n, 86; emphasis on learning, 5–6; memorization in education, 28, 29
judges. See *qāḍīs*
jurisprudence. See *fiqh*

Kāfūr, al-Shiblī, 142n, 144
kaḥḥāl, 64
Kairouan, 22
kalām, 175
kannās, 64
kātib al-ghayba, 75
kātib al-sirr, 65n, 66, 66n
kātib ṭabaqāt al-muḥaddithīn, 215
Khadīja bint ʿAlī al-Anṣārī, 173
Khadīja bint Amīr Ḥajj al-Baysarī, 173
Khadīja bint al-Dirham wa Niṣf, 56, 164
Khadīja al-Dimashqiyya, 179
al-Khalīlī, Fakhr al-Dīn ʿUmar, 122–23
al-Khalīlī, Majd al-Dīn ʿAbd al-ʿAzīz al-Dārī, 122
khān, 7
Khān al-Khalīlī, 51
khānqāhs, 16, 17, 48–49, 84; as centers of education, 50–56. Individual *khānqāhs*: al-Baybarsiyya, 56, 133; al-Jamāliyya (of

Jamāl al-Dīn Yūsuf al-Ustādār), 50, 57, 62–63, 69n, 70, 78, 79, 79n, 80, 80n, 82n, 84, 89, 92, 93, 97, 100, 101, 109n, 111, 112, 114n, 127, 133, 141, 167, 191, 194, 195, 195n, 199n, 201, 213; of Mughulṭāy al-Jamālī, 49, 57, 59, 72, 77, 83–84, 124, 191, 206–7; al-Nāṣiriyya (at Siryāqūs), 56, 58, 133, 211; Saʿīd al-Suʿadāʾ, 56, 90; al-Shaykhūniyya, 25, 62, 90, 97, 104–5, 108, 109n, 110, 112–13, 118, 124, 155; of Zayn al-Dīn Ṣidqa, 74, 78, 78n, 81, 84, 199n
khāṣṣa, 184, 202
al-Khaṭīb al-Baghdādī, 166
khaṭībs, 17, 47, 54n, 55, 55n, 63, 69, 72, 74, 96, 183, 194–97
Khawand Tatar al-Ḥijāziyya, 145
al-Khawārizmī, Humām al-Dīn, 100, 101n
Khayr Bak, 151
khāzindār, 140
khilʿa, 100, 182
khirqa, 174
Khurasan, 8
Khushqadam, al-Ẓāhir, 126, 154
Khushqadam al-Zimām, 93, 125, 142n, 191, 194n
khuṭba, 49, 51, 144, 183, 205–6; in educational institutions, 19, 54–56, 63, 69, 123n, 163, 190
al-Kinānī, ʿIzz al-Dīn Aḥmad, 173
Kitbughā, al-ʿĀdil, 138
al-Kulustānī, Badr al-Dīn Maḥmūd, 111
al-Kūrānī, Jamāl al-Dīn, 118
kuttāb. *See* primary schools
kutub al-raqāʾiq, 205

Lājīn, al-Manṣūr Husām al-Dīn, 52, 62, 70, 138, 144, 191
Lapidus, Ira, 13
al-Laqānī, Burhān al-Dīn Ibrāhīm, 118
leaves of absence, 91–92
librarians, 64, 74, 75, 196–98, 198n
libraries, 18, 24, 53n, 64, 75, 123, 138, 196–97
linguistic sciences, 7, 18, 28, 53, 64, 69, 82, 84, 86, 88, 200, 206
logic, 13, 18
Louis IX, 9

madhhabs, 7, 16, 26, 45, 47, 63, 78, 78n. See also *fiqh*; professorships
mādih, 198
madrasas: in Aleppo, 131, 211, 215; in Alexandria, 8, 9, 131; cruciform shape of, 47, 78; in Damascus, 8, 9, 62n, 97, 121, 145, 164; definition of, 16–18, 47–50; first, in Cairo, 8, 46; in Iraq, 17; in Jerusalem, 99n; in Mecca, 152–53; origins of, 6–9; rural, 9; in Syria, 17, 47, 112; in Upper Egypt, 121–22. Individual *madrasas*: al-Aljāyhiyya, 139, 190n, 208; of Āl Malik, 148; al-Almāsiyya, 144n; al-Āqbughāwiyya, 49n, 57n, 62, 89, 113, 148, 155; of Arghūn al-Nāṣirī, in Mecca, 152–53; of al-Ashraf Shaʿbān, 45; al-Ashrafiyya (of al-Ashraf Barsbāy), 41n, 47–48, 55n, 56, 58, 62–63, 64–65, 69n, 70, 77–78, 80–81, 89, 90–92, 99, 104, 108, 113, 114n, 125, 155, 185, 194n, 195n, 197, 197n; al-Ashrafiyya (of al-Ashraf Qayt Bāy), 55n; al-ʿAshūriyya, 163; al-ʿAṣrūniyya, in Aleppo, 215; of Aydakīn al-Bunduqdārī, 137; al-Aytamishiyya, 111; of Badr al-Dīn al-ʿAynī, 45; al-Baqariyya, 208; al-Bāsiṭiyya, 99, 174, 196; al-Bulqīniyya, 122, 143, 164; al-Fāḍiliyya, 89; al-Fakhriyya, 49, 69n, 87, 90, 107, 124, 155; al-Ghawriyya, 17, 41n, 45, 55n, 64, 193, 197, 197n, 199, 204; al-Ḥasaniyya, 19–20, 49, 55, 62, 67–70, 77, 111–12, 119, 130, 137, 188, 190, 192, 193, 199, 200, 207–10; al-Ḥijāziyya, 54, 145, 163, 189, 208; of Ibn al-Sukrī; 46n; of Ibn Yaʿqūb, 46n; of Jānibak al-Ẓāhirī, 101, 144n; al-Jānibakiyya, 42, 49; al-Jawhariyya, 72–75, 78, 80, 84–85, 144, 192, 194n, 196, 204, 214n; al-Jāwuliyya, 49n, 57n, 123, 139, 156; al-Kahhāriyya, 46n, 113; of Khadīja bint al-Dirham wa Niṣf, 56, 164; al-Kharrūbiyya, 42; of Khayr Bak, 151; al-Maḥmūdiyya, 141, 197; al-Majdiyya, 122, 123; al-Mankūtimuriyya, 62, 87, 89, 137–38, 196; al-Manṣūriyya, 48, 55, 57, 70, 103, 105–6, 108, 110–14, 118, 146, 200; al-Marzūqiyya, 137, 137n; al-Mihmandāriyya, 49n, 57n; al-Muʿizziyya, 61; al-Nābulusiyya, 46n; al-Nāṣiriyya (of al-Nāṣir Muḥammad), 48, 57, 62, 69n, 70, 77–78, 87, 113, 115, 144, 155, 190, 197n; al-Nāṣiriyya al-Ṣalāḥiyya, 54, 103, 104n, 113, 115, 117; al-Nizāmiyya, in Baghdad, 8; of

madrasas (*cont.*)
Qalamṭāy, 74, 80, 127n, 191, 193, 194n, 197n; al-Qamḥiyya, 103, 104n; of Qānī Bāy Qarā, 55n, 193; al-Qarasunquriyya, 89, 156, 189; al-Quṭiyya, 90, 123, 163; al-Sābiqiyya, 87, 156, 208–9; al-Saʿdiyya, 123; al-Ṣāḥibiyya al-Bahāʾiyya, 122, 188; al-Ṣalāḥiyya, in Jerusalem, 99n; al-Ṣāliḥiyya, 48, 54–55, 113, 190, 191; al-Ṣarghitmishiyya, 41, 62–63, 72, 76–77, 79n, 80n, 82n, 90, 91, 92, 94n, 97, 109–10, 114, 115, 132, 137, 149, 194n, 195n; of al-Sayfī Baybars, 17, 41n, 55n, 75, 102, 127n, 193, 197n; al-Sayfiyya, 94, 113; al-Sharafiyya, in Aleppo, 211; al-Shirābshiyya, 46n; al-Sukriyya, 123; al-Sunquriyya, 174; of Taghrī Birdī, 149; al-Ṭaybarsiyya, 148; al-Ṭūghāniyya, 149; al-Ṭughjiyya, 144; of Umm al-Ashraf Shaʿbān, 163, 190n, 204; of Umm Khawand, 164; of Yashbak al-Ẓāhirī, 154; al-Ẓāhiriyya (of al-Ẓāhir Barqūq), 58, 62–63, 65, 69, 78, 79–80, 80n, 82, 89, 91–92, 94, 104, 111, 117, 126, 132, 144, 145–46, 156, 167, 196, 203, 207, 209, 212–15; al-Ẓāhiriyya (of al-Ẓāhir Baybars), 48, 57, 61, 145, 157; al-Ẓāhiriyya (of al-Ẓāhir Baybars), in Damascus, 145; al-Zimāmiyya, 188
Maghrib, 21
Maḥallat Rūḥ, 169
al-Maḥallī, ʿAlī b. Muḥammad al-Dīrūtī, 169
Maḥmūd b. ʿAlī al-Ustādār, Jamāl al-Dīn, 140–41
majlis, 7, 41
Makdisi, George, 6n, 7, 13, 15
al-Makhbazī, Shams al-Dīn Muḥammad, 201n
maktab. *See* primary schools
Mālik b. Anas, 151
al-Malik al-ʿAzīz ʿUthmān, 52
al-Malik al-Ṣāliḥ, 9–10, 48, 137
Malika al-Ṣāliḥiyya, 176
al-Mālikī, Abū ʾl-Jawād, 200
maʿlūm al-niyāba, 116
Mamluks: and education, 128–60; ethnic origins of, 10; given the title *faqīh*, 150–51; given the title *muftī*, 154; government and politics under, 9–12, 132–34; and the Ḥanafī rite, 47, 147, 149–50; interest in religion and education, 142–60; marriage into ulama families, 11, 153–54; as *nāẓirs*, 66; as patrons, 100–102; role in establishing schools, 12, 15, 61–62, 128–46; as students of *fiqh*, 147–52, 154; training of, 146–47; and transmission of ḥadīth, 155–60
al-Manāwī, Badr al-Dīn Muḥammad, 123
al-Manāwī, Bahāʾ al-Dīn Aḥmad, 123
al-Manāwī, ʿUthmān b. Muḥammad, 123
Mankūtimur al-Husāmī, 137–38
manuscripts, 14, 29
al-Maqdisī, Majd al-Dīn Sālim, 117
al-Maqrīzī, Taqī ʾl-Dīn Aḥmad, 29, 45–46, 49, 52, 54, 57–58, 86, 113, 122, 129n, 139, 141, 147, 148, 164, 189, 197, 200, 210n
maqṣūras, 51
market inspectors. See *muḥtasibs*
Maryam bint Aḥmad ibn Ibrāhīm, 179
mashhad al-Ḥusayn, 123
mashyakhas, 148, 157, 176, 179. See also *muʿjams*
masjids. *See* mosques
al-Matbūlī, Aḥmad b. Mūsā, 206
mathematics, 13
mawlid, 172
al-Maydāwī, Aḥmad b. ʿAlī, 206
medicine, 29, 52, 62
memory, memorization, 25, 28–30, 79–80, 180–81
merchant-scholars, 95–96
mīʿād, 206–10
midrāsh, 6
miḥrāb, 47
minarets, 47
Mongols, 8, 9, 10, 143
Morocco, 21
mosques, as centers of education, 7, 16, 50–56. Individual mosques: of Āl Malik, 55, 148, 157; of ʿAmir ibn al-ʿĀs, 51–52, 53, 86, 103, 108, 195, 202; of Āq Sunqur al-Salārī, 53, 55; of Aṣlam al-Nāṣirī, 49, 53; al-Azhar, 51, 86–87, 88, 93, 112, 131, 148, 192, 195, 201, 211; al-Ḥākimī, 51–55, 103, 200, 208, 212; of Ibn Ṭūlūn, 29, 42, 45, 51–55, 62–63, 69–70, 77n, 79n, 82, 103, 113, 114–15, 117, 156, 191, 195, 195n, 203, 208, 212, 214; al-Khaṭīrī, 53, 55; al-Maghribī, 53–54; al-Māridānī, 53, 55, 104; of al-Muʾayyad Shaykh, 41n, 62–

65, 69–70, 76, 78n, 79n, 80, 82n, 84, 97, 100, 104, 116, 117, 127n, 155, 156, 193, 198–200, 212; al-Ṣāliḥī, 80, 92; of al-Shiblī Kāfūr, 53–54, 74, 80, 93, 144, 194n; of Sūdūn min Zāda, 41, 53, 62, 70–73, 78, 126, 140, 194n, 195n, 207, 213; of Uzbak al-Ẓāhirī, 53n, 151, 204; of al-Ẓāhir Baybars, north of Cairo, 209; of Zayn al-Dīn al-Ustādār, 55n, 57, 72, 74, 84, 114n, 195n, 199n, 207
Mottahedeh, Roy, 13
mu'addib, 4, 35, 81, 198. *See also* primary schools
mubakhkhirs, 64, 74, 199
Mubārak, ʿAlī Pāshā, 122, 129n
mudhākara, 27
muezzins, 17, 55, 63, 72, 74, 81, 122, 191, 193, 196, 198, 200
mufīd, 40–41
muftī, 154, 209
Mughulṭāy al-Jamālī, 57
muḥaddiths, 35, 155, 158–59, 176–80, 186–87. See also *ḥadīth*
Muḥammad, al-Nāṣir, 11n, 61, 70, 106, 133, 139, 144, 146, 148, 163
muḥasibs, 97, 161
muʿīd, 20, 40–42, 122
mujaddid al-ʿaṣr, 185
muʿjams, 33–34. See also *mashyakhas*
al-Mukattib, Khaṭṭāb b. ʿUmar, 204
mukhtaṣar, 28
mulāzama. See *ṣuḥba*
munāẓara, 30, 180
al-Mundhirī, Zakī 'il-Dīn ʿAbd al-ʿAzīz, 205n
munshids, 153
al-Muqri', Ibrāhīm b. Aḥmad, 201n
Muslim ibn al-Ḥajjāj, 155, 170, 178, 186n, 213–14
musnid, 186n
mustamlī, 39–40
mutaraddidūn, 93
mutaṣaddir, 215
Muʿtazila, 186n
al-Muzammalātī, Shihāb al-Dīn Aḥmad, 201n
muzammalātī, 201

Nablus, 178
nā'ib al-salṭana, 138
nā'ibs, 105, 116–19, 123n, 125
al-Nasā'ī, 186n
al-Nāsikh, Shihāb al-Dīn Aḥmad, 212
al-Nawawī, Muhyī 'l-Dīn Abū Zakariyyā, 169, 187, 196n, 205
naẓar, 65–66. See also *nāẓir*
nāẓir, 19, 64–66, 98–99, 102, 106, 107–8, 114, 136, 136n, 165, 191; stipends of, 136–37. See also *naẓar*
nāẓir al-khāṣṣ, 141
al-Niʿmānī, Ibrāhīm b. ʿAlī, 123n
Niẓām al-Mulk, 8
Nūr al-Dīn ibn Zangī, 8, 131

older students, 39, 89
oral transmission, of texts and knowledge, 24–31, 59–60, 157–58, 217–18
Ottomans, 10, 129

patrons, patronage: within families, 119–27; Mamluks as patrons, 110–102; ulama and, 107–27
personal relationships, and education, 21–43, 179–81
Petry, Carl, 13, 189, 195n, 197n
philosophy, 13
plague, 211
prayer, 4
preachers. See *khaṭībs*
primary schools, 7, 28, 47, 71, 74–75, 81, 90, 198, 203. See also *mu'addib*
professorships, 7, 8, 17–18, 20, 45, 149, 196; appointments to, 96–127; inheritance of, 123–27; qualifications for, 76–77; resignation of, 109–12; sale of, 97–98; simultaneously, 112–16; as a source of wealth, 95–98. Subjects: *farā'id*, 200, 200n; *ḥadīth*, 48n, 62, 72, 76, 82, 82n, 89, 100, 105–6, 108, 109n, 110–11, 114, 115, 115n, 118, 156, 157, 209, 213; Ḥanafī jurisprudence, 41, 42, 47–49, 51–53, 58, 59, 62, 72, 74, 76, 77–78, 79n, 82, 82n, 89, 91n, 92, 97, 100, 104–5, 109–10, 113, 114, 115, 118, 124, 125, 127, 135, 137, 155, 194n; Ḥanibalī jurisprudence, 47, 48, 53, 62, 79n, 82, 82n, 91n, 113, 115n, 117, 206; Mālikī jurisprudence, 47, 48, 52, 53, 62, 79n, 82, 82n, 91n, 99, 110, 113, 117, 118, 189; medicine, 29, 62; *qirā'āt*, 82, 82n, 110; Shāfiʿī jurisprudence, 47, 48, 51–54, 57, 62, 82, 82n, 89, 91n, 107–8, 109n, 110–11, 113,

professorships (*cont.*)
114, 115, 117, 122, 127, 135, 137, 189, 194n, 195, 209; *tafsīr*, 48, 52, 62, 72, 76, 78, 78n, 79n, 82, 82n, 84, 87, 100, 111, 117, 118, 125, 127, 207, 209. See also *fiqh; ḥadīth; qirā'ā; tafsīr*

Qadariyya, 186n
Qāḍī Khān, Fakhr al-Dīn, 170
qāḍīs, 14, 55, 65, 89, 90, 96, 97, 132, 151, 156, 166, 182, 191; and administration of *waqfs*, 98–99, 102–5, 134–35, 165; Ḥanafī, 106, 135; Ḥanbalī, 113; as professors, 113; Shāfiʿī, 99, 105–6, 105n, 112–13
al-Qāhirī, ʿAbd al-Raḥmān b. ʿAlī, 209
Qalamṭāy, 135
Qalāwūn, al-Manṣūr, 11n, 48, 61, 69–70, 139, 146, 148
al-Qalqashandī, Aḥmad b. ʿAlī, 67, 103, 108, 116
al-Qalqashandī, ʿAlā' al-Dīn ʿAlī, 108, 108n, 197
al-Qalqashandī, Jamāl al-Dīn Ibrāhīm, 197
al-Qalqashandī, Taqī 'l-Dīn, 152, 159, 195, 196, 197, 213
al-Qanā'ī, Shihāb al-Dīn Aḥmad, 90
Qānṣūh al-Ghawrī, al-Ashraf, 12, 17, 61, 135, 148
qara'a ʿalā, 24, 177
Qarāfa, 74, 174
al-Qarāfī, Shams al-Dīn Muḥammad, 88
Qāri' al-Hidāya, Sirāj al-Dīn ʿUmar, 96, 104–5, 113, 118n, 155
qāri' al-ḥadīth, in the Citadel, 156
qāri' al-kursī, 205–6, 208
al-Qāyātī, Muḥammad b. ʿAlī, 80
al-Qaymarī, Badr al-Dīn Ḥasan, 200
Qayt Bāy, al-Ashraf, 97, 104, 104n, 134–35, 148, 152
al-Qazwīnī, Jalāl al-Dīn Muḥammad, 113
al-Qazwīnī, Najm al-Dīn ʿAbd al-Ghaffār, 169, 185
qirā'āt, 21, 89, 151, 154; classes in, 48, 53, 57, 61–62, 67–69, 82, 91, 93
qubbas, 63, 67, 71, 73, 113, 145, 163, 199. *See also* tombs; *turbas*
al-Qudsī, ʿIzz al-Dīn ʿAbd al-Salām, 99n
al-Qudūrī, 175
Quran, 3, 4, 5, 7, 59–60, 75, 94, 106, 132, 147, 148, 161, 166, 167, 169, 172–73, 196, 204, 207–8; instruction in, 203; memorization of, 28, 29, 150; recitation of, 19, 63–64, 144, 152–53, 192–93; variant readings of: see *qirā'āt*
Quran readers, 17, 47, 53n, 55, 63–64, 69, 72, 74, 75, 96, 145, 153, 164, 193, 198–201, 204
al-Qurṭubī, Shams al-Dīn Muḥammad, 206n
quṣṣāṣ, 204–5

raḥḥāla, 178
Ramaḍān, recitations of *ḥadīth* in, 74, 75, 156, 180
rashshāsh, 64
ra's nawbat al-umarā', 66n, 140
rational sciences, 7. See also *ʿulūm ʿaqliyya*
rawk, 138
ribāṭ al-Āthār, 53–54
ribāṭ al-Baghdādiyya, 174–75
ribāṭs, for women, 163, 173–75
Rifāʿiyya, 48
riwāya, 30
Rosenthal, Franz, 25
al-Rūmī, ʿAlā' al-Dīn ʿAlī, 100

sabīl-kuttāb, 47, 71, 74. See also *maktab*
al-Saftī, Badr al-Dīn Muḥammad, 102
al-Saftī, Shihāb al-Dīn Aḥmad, 102
al-Saghānī, al-Ḥasan b. Muḥammad, 187
ṣāḥib. See *ṣuḥba*
al-Sakhāwī, Shams al-Dīn Muḥammad, 23, 25, 42, 77, 88, 97, 110, 123, 150, 154, 155, 159, 161, 167, 169, 171, 172–73, 176, 177, 179, 196, 201, 201n, 204–5, 211
Saladin, 8, 9, 46, 56, 131, 163
salaries, 77–78, 82, 82n, 91n, 135, 194, 194n, 197, 209
samāʿ, 33, 158, 179, 215
Samaritans, 183
samiʿa min, 24, 177
sanad. See *isnād*
al-Sandabīsī, Zayn al-Dīn ʿAbd al-Raḥmān, 111
al-Ṣanhājī al-Azharī, Shihāb al-Dīn Aḥmad, 88
Sanjar al-Jāwulī, 106, 139, 148, 154, 156

sāqiya, 19
Sāra bint Taqī 'l-Dīn al-Subkī, 170
Ṣarghitmish, 53, 76, 149
schools: as centers of worship, 63–64; differing sizes of, 66–85; established by scholars, 121–23; and names of founders, 132–34, 164; nonacademic functions in, 188–93; number of, in Cairo, 46, 46n, 128–29; number of, in Damascus, 62n; public worship in, 189–93; terminology, 16, 45–50. See also *khānqāhs; madrasas;* mosques
Shaʿbān, al-Ashraf, 11n, 53, 139, 146, 164
shadd, 65
al-Shāfiʿī, ʿAbd al-Qādir b. Abī Bakr, 201n
al-Shāfiʿī, Karīm al-Dīn ʿAbd al-Karim, 205
al-Shāfiʿī, Muḥammad b. Idrīs, 3, 12, 52, 53, 148, 216
shāhids, 28, 65, 80, 90, 206, 212
Shāhīn al-ʿAlāʾī, 151
sharīʿa, 4, 5, 7, 60–61, 98, 168, 173
al-Shāṭibī, al-Qāsim, 175
Shaykh, al-Muʾayyad, 61, 70, 100, 133, 157, 165
shaykhs, authority over students, 34–39. *See also* personal relationships
Shiʿis, Shiʿism, 8, 51, 130–32
al-Shīrāzī, Ibrāhīm b. ʿAlī, 201n
al-Shumunnī, Kamāl al-Dīn Muḥammad, 109n, 110–11
Sibṭ Ibn al-ʿAjamī, Ibrāhīm, 35, 211
Ṣidqa, Zayn al-Dīn, 74
al-Sīrāmī family, 127; Jalāl al-Dīn ʿAbd al-Raḥmān, 127n; Nūr al-Dīn ʿAlī, 127; Sirāj al-Dīn ʿUmar, 127n
Siryāqūs, 56, 133, 211
Sitt al-Quḍāt bint Abī Bakr Ibn Zurayq, 171
student stipends, 7, 8, 17–18, 44, 47, 58, 62, 72, 90–91, 91n, 93, 210
al-Subkī, Bahāʾ al-Dīn Aḥmad, 113, 121n
al-Subtī, Tāj al-Dīn, 40–41, 59, 83, 114–15, 153, 176, 184–88, 205, 208
al-Subkī, Taqī 'l-Dīn ʿAlī, 98, 113, 121, 121n, 202–3
substitutes. See *nāʾibs*
Sūdūn min Zāda, 140
Sūdūn al-Ẓāhirī, Sayf al-Dīn, 151
Sufi convents. See *khānqāhs*
Sufis, Sufism, 15, 19, 26, 53n, 54n, 74, 79n, 90, 93, 100, 125, 138, 139, 144, 191, 194, 196, 204; and education, 47–50, 56–60, 79n, 84–85; shaykhs of, 17, 47, 49, 54n, 57–60, 64, 93, 100, 102, 104, 118, 125, 191, 195; women and, 174–75. See also *khānqāhs*
ṣuḥba, 26, 34–35, 179
sultans, 58, 61–62, 69–70, 76, 97, 129, 132–33, 143; and appointments to professorships, 99, 102–7. *See also individual names*
Sunni revival, 8, 130–32
Sunnis, Sunnism, 8, 10, 51, 130–32
Sunqur al-Saʿdī, Shams al-Dīn, 174
al-Suyūṭī, Jalāl al-Dīn ʿAbd al-Raḥmān, 21, 25, 32, 176, 181, 185, 188
Syria, 7, 8, 9, 10, 17, 65, 97, 112, 120, 128, 138, 140, 143, 147, 159, 164, 177, 189, 197

al-Tabarānī, Sulaymān b. Aḥmad, 186n
ṭabīb, 64
al-Tafahanī, Zayn al-Dīn ʿAbd al-Raḥmān, 104, 111, 114–15
tafsīr, 7, 17, 51, 60, 64, 86, 89, 185, 205–8; classes in, 46, 48, 52, 57–58, 62, 67–69, 79n, 82, 91, 132
Taghrī Birdī al-Bakalmishī, 149
Taghrī Birdī al-Ẓāhirī, 159
Taghrī Birmish al-Faqīh, 154–55, 159
Tamurlane, 140
tannāʾīm, 40n
tawqīʿ, 103–4, 108
Ṭaybars, ʿAlāʾ al-Dīn, 148
ṭaylasāns, 183
teaching assistants, 39–42. See also *mufīd; muʿīd*
Thousand and One Nights, The, 4
Tibawi, A. L., 6n, 17, 18
al-Tirmidhī, 159, 186n
tombs, 75, 143–46, 164, 193. See also *qubbas; turbas*
Torah, 5, 29
Ṭūghān al-Ḥasanī al-Ẓāhirī, 149
Ṭughjī, Sayf al-Dīn, 144
turbans, 182
turbas, 144. See also *qubbas*; tombs
Turkish language, and Mamluks, 11
Turks, animosity toward, 142–43
Ṭūsī, Naṣīr al-Dīn, 25

ulama: competence of, 183–88; defined, 13–14; as founders of schools, 121–23; low-ranking, 193–201; as patrons, 107–27; in society, 3–6; as a subject of study, 13–14
ʿulūm ʿaqliyya, 13
ʿulūm naqliyya, 13
Umm al-Ḥusayn bint ʿAbd al-Raḥmān, 169
ustādār, 140–41, 189
uṣūl al-dīn, 17, 64
uṣūl al-fiqh, 17, 64, 84, 175, 196, 206
ʿutaqāʾ, 66n, 136, 136n
Uzbak al-Ẓāhirī, 151–52, 159–60

versifications, of texts, 28

waqfiyyas, 60, 67, 83, 98n, 101, 102, 114–15, 117, 126, 145, 198, 199, 208; as source for history of education, 15–16
waqfs, 8, 12, 19, 65, 67, 83, 98–99, 134n; establishment of, 60–61; Islamic law of, 60–61; as means to protect wealth, 134–42; payments from, to heirs of founders, 134–42; value and total expenditures of, 69–70
waqqāds, 64, 74, 199
waʿz, 205
al-Wazīrī, al-Khaṭīb, 117
wazīrs, 122–23, 131, 141
wealth: importance to education, 119; Islamic attitudes toward, 95; and professorships, 95–98
women: as administrators of *waqfs*, 164–65; classes for, in private homes, 171, 173; education of, attitudes toward, 161–62, 168; education of, and family relationships, 169–71; exclusion from schools, 166–67; as founders of schools, 162–64; as students of *fiqh*, 166, 168, 169, 173–75, 180; and Sufism, 174–75; and transmission of *ḥadīth*, 175–81. See also *ribāts*
writing, instruction in, 203–4

al-Yahsūbī, ʿIyād b. Mūsā, 214n
Yalbughā al-ʿUmarī, 45, 52n, 139–40
Yalbughā al-Ẓāhirī, 157
Yashbak al-Faqīh, 154, 156
Yashbak al-Ẓāhirī al-Ṣaghīr, 154
al-Yūnīnī, ʿAbd al-Qādir, 176n
Yūsuf al-Ustādār, Jamāl al-Dīn, 70, 100–101, 101n, 133, 141, 189

Ẓāhirīs, 26
zakāt, 4, 168
al-Zamakhsharī, Maḥmūd b. ʿUmar, 185–86, 186n
al-Zarnūjī, Burhān al-Dīn, 38, 79, 119
zāwiyas, 52, 58; established by scholars, 123; of Ibn Ḥannā, 52; of al-Imām al-Shāfiʿī, 52, 103, 108; al-Khashshābiyya, 52n, 103; al-Majdiyya, 52; of Zayn al-Dīn Ṣidqa, 74–75, 78n, 80, 84, 208
Zayn al-Dīn al-Ustādār, 74
Zayn Khātūn bint Ibn Ḥajar, 170
Zaynab, wife of Sultan Īnāl, 173
Zaynab bint ʿAbd Allāh, Ibnat al-ʿAryānī, 170
Zaynab bint ʿAbd al-Raḥīm b. al-Ḥasan al-ʿIrāqī, 170
Zaynab bint al-Amīn al-Aqṣarāʾī, 153
Zaynab bint al-Kamāl, 177
Zaynab al-Ṭukhiyya, 169–70
ziyārāt, 145–46